JUST FOLKLORE

Also by Elliott Oring

*Israeli Humor: The Content and Structure
of the Chizbat of the Palmah*

*The Jokes of Sigmund Freud:
A Study in Humor and Jewish Identity*

Jokes and Their Relations

Engaging Humor

Edited by Elliott Oring

Humor and the Individual

Folk Groups and Folklore Genres: An Introduction

Folk Groups and Folklore Genres: A Reader

JUST FOLKLORE

Analysis
Interpretation
Critique

Elliott Oring

Cantilever Press
Los Angeles, California

Copyright © 2012 Cantilever Press
All rights reserved

ISBN 978-0-9855214-0-0 paperback edition
ISBN 978-0-9855214-1-7 hardback library edition

Library of Congress Control Number: 2012907047

Distributed by

LBD Publishers
4247 Whiteside Street
Los Angeles, CA 90063
www.legalbooksdistributing.com

and

Cantilever Press
P.O. Box 3557
Long Beach, CA 90803-0557
www.cantileverpress.com

This book is printed on acid-free paper.

For

Michael Owen Jones, Barre Toelken,
and William A. Wilson

just folklorists

Contents

Acknowledgments   ix
Introduction   xiii

1. The Arts, Artifacts, and Artifices of Identity   *3*
2. Whaling Songs and the Context of Fantasy   *26*
3. Totemism and the A.E.F. Revisited   *46*
4. The Structure of a Joke Repertoire   *55*
5. Forest Lawn and the Iconography of American Death   *70*
6. Dyadic Traditions   *80*
7. Legend, Truth, and News   *91*
8. Legendry and the Rhetoric of Truth   *104*
9. On the Tradition and Mathematics of Counting-Out   *153*
10. Definition and Devolution   *167*
11. Transmission and Degeneration   *181*
12. Thinking through Tradition   *220*
13. Generating Lives: The Life History of a Life History   *240*
14. Victor Turner, Sigmund Freud, and the Return of the Repressed   *265*
15. Missing Theory   *284*
16. Folk or Lore? The Stake in Dichotomies   *294*
17. Anti Anti-*Folklore*   *306*
18. Theorizing Trivia: A Thought Experiment   *317*

Notes   323
References   353

Acknowledgments

There are many people to thank for a book that is comprised of work produced over decades. I owe Kenny Goldstein (1927-1995) a great debt. His liner notes on albums of folk music first made me aware of and drew me to the field of folklore. I am also greatly indebted to Alan Dundes (1935-2005). His erudite, insightful, provocative, and accessible essays provided a model of what folklore analysis could and should be. Dan Ben-Amos, Gillian Bennett, Trevor Blank, Simon Bronner, Inta Carpenter, Frank de Caro, Tim Correll, Larry Danielson, Robert Georges, Bruce Giuliano, Henry Glassie, Robert Glenn Howard, Bill Ivey, Michael Owen Jones, Barbara Kirshenblatt-Gimblett, Norman Klein, Jay Mechling, Wolfgang Mieder, Dorothy Noyes, Melford Spiro, Tim Tangherlini, Barre Toelken, Peter Tokofsky, and Bert Wilson all read and commented on one or more of the essays in this volume. I have profited from their remarks, their criticisms, and their own publications. My thanks also to Hillel Barzel, Gerry Beer, Stanley Burstein, Alvin Hurd, Harold Martin, Pál Rózsa, and Robert L. Wheeler on matters of language, history, culture, and mathematics.

This volume would never have come to pass had Gloria Reinman not graciously offered to retype those essays that had been published before the advent of the computer age. Bruce Carpenter designed and composed the book, Tim Mayer designed the cover, and Tom Satorhelyi offered sage advice on publishing. Mahmoud Omidsalar and Teresa Omidsalar helpfully tracked down elusive bibliographic sources, and Paul Jordan-Smith was a godsend on website construction. Kathleen Stocks and Alejandro Omidsalar proofread the manuscript, as did Norman Klein whose keen eye always manages to latch on to errors and infelicities that I blithely overlook. The mistakes that remain in the text, however, are my own.

Other friends and acquaintances encouraged this work, and some, unbeknownst to them, provided examples of folklore that found their way into the essays in this volume: Mahadev Apte, Ben Benson, Jon

Coleman, Linda Coleman, Kerstin Danielson, Benjamin Fass, Mary Georges, Robert Georges, Bruce Giuliano, Genevieve Giuliano, Jess Hordes, Naomi Hordes, Judit Katona-Apte, Tadashi Nakamura, Jon Olson, Natalie Olson, Mark Oring, Katie Oring, Fred Reinman, Linda Samuels, Dianne Smith, Judith Terzi, Hrag Varjabedian, Jon Yoder, and Hilda Yoder.

Most of the essays in this volume have been previously published. They have been changed, however, to greater or lesser degrees. In some there are changes of phraseology or the addition of citations. In others, new paragraphs, sections, figures, and notes have been added. A few have been substantially reformulated. One essay is new.

Permission is gratefully acknowledged to reprint the following essays in this volume: "Dyadic Traditions," *Journal of Folklore Research* 21(1984):19–28 © Indiana University Press; "Generating Lives: On the Construction of an Autobiography," *Journal of Folklore Research* 24(1987):241–262 © Indiana University Press; "Theorizing Trivia: A Thought Experiment," *Journal of Folklore Research* 33(1996):241–244 © Indiana University Press; "Folk or Lore? The Stake in Dichotomies," *Journal of Folklore Research* 43(2006):205–218 © Indiana University Press; "Chizbat Humor and the Boundaries of Israeli Identity," *Journal of American Folklore* 86(1973):358–366 © American Folklore Society; "The Arts, Artifacts, and Artifices of Identity," *Journal of American Folklore* 107(1994):1–23 © American Folklore Society; "Anti Anti-'Folklore,'" *Journal of American Folklore* 111(1998):328–338 © American Folklore Society; "Legendry and the Rhetoric of Truth," *Journal of American Folklore* 121(2008):127–166 © Board of Trustees of the University of Illinois; "The Devolutionary Premise: A Definitional Delusion?" *Western Folklore* 34(1975):36–44 © Western States Folklore Society; "On the Tradition and Mathematics of Counting-Out," *Western Folklore* 56(1997):139–152 © Western States Folklore Society; "Missing Theory," *Western Folklore* 65(2006):455–465 © Western States Folklore Society; "Victor Turner, Sigmund Freud, and the Return of the Repressed," *Ethos: Journal of the Society for Psychological Anthropology* 21(1993):273–294 © Society for Psychological Anthropology; "Totemism and The A.E.F Revisited," *Southern Folklore Quarterly*

41(1977):73–80 © University Press of Kentucky; "Legend, Truth, and News," *Southern Folklore* 47(1990):163–177 © University Press of Kentucky; "Forest Lawn and the Iconography of American Death," *Southwest Folklore* 6(1985):62–72 © Elliott Oring; "Whalemen and Their Songs: A Study of Folklore and Culture," *New York Folklore Quarterly* 27(1971):130–152 © New York Folklore Society; Transmission and Degeneration," *Fabula: Journal of Folktale Research* 19(1978):193–210 © Walter de Gruyter.

Photographs of scrimshaw are courtesy of the New Bedford Whaling Museum; *Joy of the Waters* courtesy of Forest Lawn Memorial Parks and Mortuaries; WWI 42nd Rainbow Division patch courtesy of snydertreasures.com; Palmach photos courtesy of Palmach House, Tel Aviv. Other photos are by Elliott Oring with touchup by Nathan Power and Claire Oring. The photographer of Bruce is unknown.

Introduction

*It requires a very unusual mind to undertake
the analysis of the obvious.*
— Alfred North Whitehead

THE TITLE OF this book derives from the oft-repeated phrase: "That's just folklore." The phrase is usually employed to reject a contribution to a conversation or an argument. Along with other locutions—"You must be joking," "So what?" "Says who?"—it is meant to discount the truth of some proffered proposition or evidentiary statement and deem it inconsequential to the communicative exchange. Pragmatically, such phrases might be termed *dismissives* as they serve to dismiss the import of a fact or assertion.

The sense that folklore is somehow inconsequential has a number of sources. In the nineteenth century, when the term *folklore* was first coined, the prevailing paradigm for the analysis of folklore materials was the doctrine of survivals (Tylor 1874, 1:16).[1] Calendar customs, superstitions, legends, ballads, proverbs, children's games and so forth were understood to be, or to contain, survivals from earlier times. Survivals were ideas and behaviors that had been appropriate to more archaic and more primitive cultural stages which had persisted through force of habit into modern times. The doctrine of survivals was conjoined with theories of evolution.[2] Evolution proposed that society and culture continually develop and progress over time. Survivals were elements of thought and behavior that persisted despite this course of cultural advance. They were the intellectual artifacts that evidenced the evolution of culture, much as fossils found in old geological layers evidenced the evolution of life.

Because the ideas and modes of thought of primitive humans were held to be illogical (Levy-Bruhl 1966 [1923]:59–60) or mistaken (Frazer 1942:57; Tylor 1874, 1:23), survivals were equated with error, and subsequently *folklore* came to serve as a synonym for error in popular, and even scholarly, parlance. As culture was held to be moving towards an expansion of rationality, increased scientific and technical knowledge, greater morality, and the promotion of human happiness (Tylor 1874, 1:26–27), knowledge and practices rooted in error were to be identified and rooted out (2:453).

All theories decline and the theory of cultural evolution was no exception.[3] The doctrine of survivals eventually faded as new ideas about the materials of folklore developed. Survival, however, was not the only concept that served to link the materials of folklore to an historical project. Another even older concept was tradition. *Tradition* did not have the same connotations as *survival* although both referred to ideas and practices that persisted from the past. Traditions might be old, but survivals were ancient. Survivals were remnants, relics. They were like shards from a vessel that was no longer whole and whose use could not be observed but only inferred. Survivals signified a rupture in the continuity of culture. Traditions, on the other hand, were handed down. They implied continuity as well as an integration of thought and practice. If traditions characterized older forms of living, it was because those forms continued to serve those who practiced them. A tradition could prove valuable for social life. A survival, however, was valuable only for the purposes of scientific inquiry and historical reconstruction.

Those folklorists who held to the principles of the Enlightenment found survivals a powerful concept for understanding human development and for tracing the course of human history. Tradition, however, could serve those opposed to the Enlightenment. Romantic folklorists often saw more barbarism in the modern than in the ancient world. Traditions were valuable and beautiful and needed to be preserved in the face of soulless rationality and mechanized industry. Nevertheless, to the extent that tradition connoted practices characteristic of former times, folklore would again be discounted as antiquated, quaint, and passé.

At the turn of the twentieth century, a revolution occurred in the approach to understanding human behavior. The invention of the fields of sociology (Durkheim 1964 [1895]), psychoanalysis (Freud 1953 [1900]), and linguistics (de Saussure 1966 [1907–1911]) shifted the explanation of human behavior from historical to contemporary forces. De Saussure's linguistics explored language as a synchronic system. Sociology sought the explanation of social facts in other social facts. Psychoanalysis posited the existence of unconscious ideas that continually acted to motivate the behavior of individuals and groups. Psychoanalysis conceptualized folklore not as error but as fantasy—albeit fantasy grounded in a ruthless logic.[4] Although folklore studies never directly adopted either the theories of Durkheim or Freud, and only encountered de Saussure filtered through the structuralism of Claude Lévi-Strauss (1955), these perspectives proved enormously influential.[5] It was accepted that an understanding of folklore depended on a knowledge of the social world in which that folklore existed and of the minds of the individuals who created, transmitted, and responded to it.[6]

The effort to understand the materials of folklore as contemporary products required a new sense of how the materials of folklore were interrelated. Folklore, rather than being conceived as a survival or tradition, was reconceptualized as an expression, as *art* (Bascom 1955; Ben-Amos 1971:10). Art is not ordinarily considered a trivial subject, but since folklorists continued to document and analyze many of the same materials—tales, ballads, proverbs—that were studied under older conceptualizations of folklore, the sense of their insignificance continued to haunt the discipline. They were not, after all, "high" or "fine" art, and by most standards, they were not even "good" art. In fact, it was questionable whether they could be considered art at all. Certainly they were not discussed in the pages of art journals or studiously analyzed by critics in magazines and newspapers. So, folklore was conceived of as art by folklorists but by virtually no one else.[7] Consequently, even as art, folklore could yet again be dismissed.

Finally, the term *folk* has not been one that has inspired respect. Originally employed to designate the peasantry, it eventually came to refer to a range of marginal social groups in complex societies: rural farmers, urban poor, religious and ethnic minorities. The folk themselves were somehow holdovers from other times and places. They resisted the forces of social development. They did not represent where society was going but what was being—and properly should be—left behind. Indeed, the folk were those who perpetuated the errors embedded in their lore. The modern attempt to redefine *folk* to refer to "any group of people whatsoever" (Dundes 1965:2) served only folklorists. It did not resonate in the more popular understandings of the term.[8]

Everything that would seem to be wrong with *folklore*—its association with the past, error, the fantastical, vulgar aesthetics, and a world of marginal and powerless groups—is also what gives the field its peculiar strength. Folklorists are attuned to the ways that the past is a resource—deliberate and unwitting—in the construction of the present. The world is forever changing, although not as profoundly as is often thought. Commemorations for dead MySpace friends, for example, bear strong resemblances to those constructed before the invention of the Internet (Dégh 1994:153–193; Dobler 2009). The medium will affect and may radically transform such commemorations, but they are not constructed *de novo*, and they will continue to reflect the modes of expression on which they were based.

The contribution of folklore studies to the understanding of artistic expression is rarely noticed by art historians and critics who focus on a limited range of objects and a particular genealogy of creators and innovators. Their perspective is rooted in connoisseurship: the identification of aesthetic excellence within a particular cultural tradition (Stecker 2000:51). While folklorists have also recognized aesthetic excellence and reveled in the connoisseurship of esoteric performances, they are focused, first and foremost, on art as expression. What does the folklore explicitly and tacitly say? How does it comment on the situations and circumstances of its creators, purveyors, and consumers? The study of folklore as art is a contribution to the understanding of society. Furthermore, the study of local principles of aesthetics—what is called "folk aesthetics"—serves to document the differing standards by which excellence is judged. Folklore studies not only expands the range of objects that might be considered to be art, it enlarges the understanding of the codes that inform the production and underlie the appreciation of those same objects.

The tendency of folklorists to gravitate towards marginal or otherwise overlooked social groups is valuable precisely because sociological understanding cannot rest solely in a grasp of the mainstream. The world is composed of different groups, some closer to the centers of technology, wealth, and power than others.[9] There are two billion people in the world without electricity, let alone access to the Internet (Munasinghe 2008). How do they figure in the study of contemporary societies? The President of Columbia University characterized the situation succinctly: "At a time when economic, political, and cultural patterns that have originated in the West are celebrated, often uncritically, as universally applicable, the arts, humanities, and social sciences can provide detailed data and informed interpretations of particular traditions that continue to shape the attitudes and behavior of billions of people the world over" (Rupp 1999:4). Many folklorists could easily regard this as a mission statement for the entire field.

I was brought to the study of folklore because the materials were fascinating and the efforts to explain their existence and persistence stimulating. However, to claim that some things may be interesting does not speak for their importance. Nevertheless, it should not be hard to grasp that in folklore one can see how people conceptualize worlds—personal, familial, regional, occupational, ethnic, national—and imagine their places within them. These imagined worlds, however, are not necessarily transparent. The job of the folklorist is to document these worlds, understand something of the milieux in which they are propagated, and unravel their organization and meanings.

Folklore studies must remain focused on the study of the stuff of folklore. The description, analysis, and interpretation of these materials is time consuming and difficult enough. That is not to say that there should be mechanical analysis and interpretation of proverb after proverb, legend after legend, or tale after tale. The study of these materials needs to proceed in relation to knowledge acquired and with theoretical principles proposed by other fields of study. The operative word is *relation*; not conformity. The study of folklore should speak to larger questions in the understanding of human behavior, but folklore might be as likely to challenge these understandings as to confirm them. The study of folklore is a benefit to no one if it is only a happy application of abstract theory to locally acquired examples. Explanation and interpretation are more than matters of "if the shoe fits." A shoe that is too loose might accommodate almost any foot; if too snug, it can irritate. In the worst cases, as with Cinderella's step-sisters, the foot may be mutilated to fit the shoe. Folklorists should be attentive to theoretical formulations born in other fields, but they should also build up theory from the analysis of their own materials.[10]

The reflexive turn in the social sciences beginning in the 1980s affected a number of disciplines, including folklore. Reflexivity occurs when systems of analysis and interpretation turn back on themselves and make themselves the objects of study. In the production of knowledge, the role of the producer in the creation of that knowledge and the means by which that knowledge is produced are highlighted (Ruby and Myerhoff 1982:2). Understanding knowledge production can be of great value, but if such scrutiny becomes the overriding concern, the effort undermines itself. Knowing how a discipline produces knowledge remains important only to the extent that the discipline continues to produce knowledge. It is as though the definition "folklore is what folklorists study" (Brunvand 1998:7) were generally accepted and the task were simply to analyze why and how folklorists study the things they do rather than to study the things themselves.[11] If folklore is simply what folklorists study, then the entire field is no more than an investigation of the conceptualizations, analyses, and interpretations that have been offered by folklorists.[12] All of planetary astronomy cannot be reduced to an accounting of the conceptual and political underpinnings of the disagreements among astronomers as to whether Pluto is a small planet or a large object in the Kuiper belt. How objects get defined and redefined over time are not irrelevant matters in planetary science, yet they cannot be considered the whole of the subject. Likewise, folklore studies cannot and should not be reduced to the contemplation of folkloristic practices.

The essays in this volume address the stuff of folklore—their definition, analysis, and interpretation. Some essays focus on ballads, legends, beliefs, games, jokes, and material culture. Other essays engage basic concepts in the field—tradition, identity, symbol, theory, group, definition, experiment, fieldwork—with the aim of clarifying these concepts and making them productive in baseline folklore research. The chapters in this volume were written over a period of forty years. Even though certain of them utilize methods of analysis that may no longer be in vogue, they still bring to light matters that are both interesting and, I believe, important. Folklore can reveal the ideas and attitudes of those people who create and consume it. I trust these essays will serve to demonstrate that folklore should not be casually dismissed—it is never *just* folklore.

JUST FOLKLORE

1. The Arts, Artifacts, and Artifices of Identity

Over the course of more than a century and a half, different definitions of folklore have been entertained: survival, oral tradition, verbal art, artistic performance. Different theories have been employed over the same period: evolution, diffusion, psychoanalysis, functionalism, structuralism. Nevertheless, there has been no sense among folklorists of any discontinuity in the work that they do. Definitions and theoretical perspectives have changed, but the underlying enterprise carries on. What is it that creates a sense of unity in a field that has undergone so many changes in the conception of its subject and in the manner of its approach? Is there some unarticulated project in folklore studies that underlies the trajectory of folklore research? Identity would seem to be a concept that corrals the diversity of definitions and theories within a comprehensive program of research. Although an old word, identity catapulted into psychological discourse only in the 1950s and 60s; particularly with the introduction of the notion of "identity crisis" (Erikson 1959; 1963; 1968). Despite its emergence within psychological theory, however, the term can offer a conceptualization of what the field of folklore has been about since its inception.

> *I am large, I contain multitudes.*
> —Walt Whitman

BEFORE THE 1970s, the term identity was largely absent from the discourse of folklorists. It first appeared in the title of an essay in 1971—in Richard Bauman's "Differential Identity and the Social Base of Folklore" (1971a).[1] Since then, the term has become prominent in an ever-increasing number of essay, conference, and book titles. At the 1993 Annual Meeting of the American Folklore Society meeting in Eugene, Oregon, seven sessions employed the term in their titles. Twenty years before, at the 1973 Annual Meeting in Nashville, Tennessee, not a single paper title included the term. This increasing focus on identity in folkloristic discussion has not gone unnoticed (Sjöman 1992:13). As late as 1983, Alan Dundes felt justified in writing that "very few folklorists have paid much attention to the concept of identity," and in his own essay, "Defining Identity through Folklore," set out to correct the oversight (1983:236).

In truth, many of the recent references to identity often employ the term in the most transparent and self-evident way. Definitions of "identity" are vague if not absent entirely. This vagueness has been noted even by those who explicitly confront the concept (e.g., Erikson 1959:102; 1968: Kakar 1979:ix-xi; Royce 1982:17).[2] Vague and fuzzy concepts, however, are not always the result of laziness or sloppy thinking. Often vagueness and fuzziness mark the presence of a *primitive concept*, a concept that is so fundamental to thought and discussion, that is so protean and powerful, that it in large measure escapes—indeed, is defeated by—precise definition.[3]

Nevertheless, it may be worthwhile to sketch, if also only vaguely, some outline of this concept and locate the position of folklore studies in relation to it. The concept may, in fact, be broken down into three interrelated concepts—individual identity, personal identity, and collective identity.[4] By *individual identity*, I refer to that sense of space-time connection with states, thoughts, and actions from the past. It is the sense that allows me, for example, to recognize that the individual who wrote this essay is the same one who wrote the other essays in the volume and submitted them for publication.

Personal identity, while it depends upon a sense of individual continuity and contributes to it, refers to particular mental dispositions and contents, and not merely to the sense of continuity itself. It is composed of memories, identifications, and repudiations of individuals, ideas, and experiences that come to constitute a perhaps shifting, but nevertheless discernible, configuration. What underlies these configurations can be said to constitute and distinguish a person. The sense of personal identity may be experienced naïvely as "who one is," but it is analyzable only in relation to a set of objectified descriptions—that is, in terms of what one is and where one stands in the world (Lynd 1961:14–15; Montefiore 1993:213). It is related to the acceptance of certain "values, goals, or meanings" (Thorat 1979:66). Personal identity is not merely a sense of continuous being but a particular quality of that being (Erikson

1959:23; 1968:50). Personal identity is shaped from experiences that are unique to the individual as well from those common to a collection of individuals. In psychological parlance, it is "psychosocial" (Erikson 1959:101; 1968:22–23).

Collective identity refers to those aspects of identity that are derived from experiences and expressions common to a group. It is recognition of this collective aspect of identity that produces the deep sense of identification with others—the consciousness of kind (Thorat 1979:66). The term *collective identity* has meaning only as it refers to an intersection of personal identities and has no existence apart from the psyches of particular individuals. Nevertheless, it may be conceptually distinguished for the purposes of analysis and discussion, and it may be important to do so, as so much of personal identity is predicated upon the introjection of the common and collective.

Admittedly, this discussion is both crude and incomplete. I have outlined it here in order that there is some common, if vague, sense of what might be implied when the term *identity* is employed. There are a couple of points worth noting. First, there has been something of a complementary distribution of disciplinary interests with respect to identity. What I have called *individual identity* has been of interest predominantly to philosophers and some psychologists. *Personal identity* has largely been the territory of psychologists and some anthropologists and folklorists. *Collective identity* has been mainly the concern of folklorists and anthropologists and perhaps a few psychologists.[5]

Second, identity is not a kind of behavior, expression, or experience, nor is it any assemblage of behaviors, expressions, or experiences, although such is the stuff that may shape identity. Identity in some sense stands "behind" experience. As it is rooted in the psyche of individuals, it is not describable in behavioral or experiential terms. Thus, the collective identity labeled *cultural identity* is not congruent with a culture or any subset of it. It is of a different order and though it may only be apprehended and explained through an attention to cultural behaviors, it is distinct from them. In the Russellian sense, a cultural identity is of a different logical type and cannot be conflated with culture itself.[6]

I would argue that the seemingly recent awakening of folklorists to questions of identity is deceptive, and that despite the relative absence of the term in earlier discourse, the question of identity has long been at the heart of the folkloristic project. Indeed, the *very definition of the term* folklore *has been little more than an effort to privilege an array of cultural materials in relation to a concept of identity.* It would seem that over the past 250 years, folklorists have had something of a unified topic and a common set of purposes which become intelligible in terms of a concept of identity and its vicissitudes. If folklorists hope to understand what they are and have been doing, they need to put a concept of identity at the center of their discussions.

The involvement of folklorists with identity has proceeded under various guises: under what I am calling the arts, artifacts, and artifices of identity. Each of these terms represents a conceptualization of a relation between what we now call folklore and identity. I employ the term *artifact* in an archeological sense; not only as something man-made but as something out of time and place. By artifact, however, I do not mean to suggest only something material; the term is meant to refer to any material, verbal, or behavioral form that is held to exist apart from the times and conditions of life in which it was originally fashioned and employed. By *arts* I refer to organic, creative processes—largely unconscious—by means of which the world is transfigured. *Artifice* is used to suggest the idea of manufacture: a process that is deliberate, controlled, utterly replicable, and expedient. In what follows, I hope to suggest the ways in which the folklore enterprise has revolved around the notion of identity; how in the effort over the past two hundred years to define its subject, folklore has been imagined as an art, artifact, or artifice of identity.

Johann Gottfried von Herder was in some sense responsible for introducing the artifactual model of folklore. It was Herder who reconceptualized the notion of the "common interests" at the root of social organizations. These interests had been thought to be founded upon a set of contractual arrangements—arrangements which were at once voluntary, reciprocal, and fundamentally utilitarian. Herder disputed this rather mechanical conception of social and political life. He regarded nature in general and sociopolitical organizations in particular as operating organically rather than mechanically. Natural societies were not cobbled together—they grew (Barnard 1965:31). Although this growth was shaped by environmental and material conditions, the state of any organism was inevitably a consequence of its previous states much as the nature of an adult is a consequence of its childhood and youth. Phylogeny, in some sense, recapitulated ontogeny. Every society in every historical period was built upon its past (Clark 1955:190,194).

Thus, for Herder, the connections of a natural group were genetic (although not biological). Its members inherited a language, a literature, and a body of custom that linked them to the generations that preceded them and to one another (Barnard 1965:70). Such a group constituted a *Volk*—a nation, a people; not merely a state. What bound this group together were not arrangements of mutual convenience, but a consciousness, a common character, and distinctive set of purposes (Barnard 1965:57–61).

The character and consciousness of a *Volk* could be readily grasped in its *Volkslied*—the poetry which constituted its "entire treasury of life; doctrine and history, law and morals, ecstasy, joy, and comfort" (quoted in Clark 1955:253), and which was the expression of the "weaknesses and perfections of a nationality; a mirror of its sentiments, the expression of the highest to which it aspired" (Herder quoted in Wilson 1973:825). *Volkslied* was a poetry close to nature, spontaneous, created in living action, at once the quintessential expression as well as a molder of the nation's spiritual essence (Clark 1955:253). To be true to oneself and one's humanity, one had to be in tune with this spirit. Herder recognized that genuine folk poetry was possible at every stage of a nation's history. He considered, among others, Homer, Sophocles, Chaucer, and Shakespeare folk poets (Schütze 1921:120). Nevertheless, a nation could lose touch with itself. A nation that had submitted to foreign influence and reveled in the imitation of others, might rediscover its identity in its poetic artifacts, in those expressions of the nation when it was still whole and pure (1922:378). Such artifacts could be found in the mouths of those who lived close to nature and in accordance with the manners and customs of their ancestors.

Herder situated identity in artifacts from the past. Others would assume the responsibility for the painstaking reconstruction of those artifacts and the reclamation of that past. Jacob and Wilhelm Grimm set out to document and describe Germanic mythology, the source of all the "energies and inmost impulses" that lay at the root of German national development (Grimm 1966 [1835], 3:xxiv; Peppard 1971:49). Legends and fairy tales were regarded as the detritus of ancient myth, as festivals, games, and calendar customs were artifacts of olden heathen worship. The task of the Grimms was to recover this mythology, which had almost been obliterated by the Christian faith, and relate it to, and distinguish it from, the mythologies of neighboring peoples (Grimm 1966, 3:xxiv-xxxiv).[7] If the reconstruction of the ancient mythology itself was the major effort, the Grimms were not oblivious to the identity that lay behind this mythology. Jacob Grimm himself raised the question: "What is the true fundamental character of Teutonic mythology" (xlvii)? Although his answer to this question was tentative and sketchy—certainly in comparison to the volumes describing the reconstructed mythology itself—he nevertheless attempted it. The Teutonic mythos, he wrote, was "wild" rather than "tame" (xvi), crude yet simple, rough yet sincere. It emphasized "paternal authority," a "reverence for woman," and "modesty and virtue." It expressed a reluctance to "exhibit the immeasurable in visible images" and revealed an "earnest thoughtfulness" lacking in vanity and directed toward the sublime (xlvii–l). Yet, if ancient artifacts were the most direct route to the recovery of authentic German identity, that identity remained a powerful force shaping German culture and history through the centuries. Jacob Grimm even glimpsed in Teutonic mythology the "whole germ of German Protestantism" and the necessity of the Reformation first arising in Germany (l–li). If identity might best be grasped through the scrutiny of artifacts, the identity itself was no artifact but a vital force.

When in 1846, William Thoms was moved to offer the word "folklore" in place of "popular antiquities," his expressed wish was that someone might achieve for the British Isles the kind of synthesis that Jacob Grimm had achieved for the mythology of Germany (Thoms in Dorson 1968a, 1:52–54). Seventeenth-century English antiquarians believed in the legitimating value of the past (de Caro 1972:41). In their view, contemporary practices were legitimated by ancient precedent. In their efforts to discover ancient precedents for a variety of political and religious institutions and prerogatives (e.g., common law, Parliament, the antiquity of the English Bible, priestly marriage, and anti-popish laws), the aims of these antiquarians were essentially practical (42–49). Nevertheless, their approach presumed that authentic institutions reflected ancient practice and custom. By the end of the eighteenth century, the practical cast of antiquary interest began to give way to a more theoretical orientation that held that antiquities could reveal the "romantic and poetical simplicity of former ages," and were "the most faithful records of the GENERAL character of a people" (Thomas Burgess quoted in de Caro 1972:57). By the time Thoms coined his felicitous phrase, the antiquarian view had absorbed, and in some sense transcended, that of the Grimms; for it was held that in mythology and superstition could be traced "the earliest formation of nations, their identity or analogy, their changes, as well as the inner texture of the national character, more deeply than in any other circumstance, even in language itself" (Wright 1969 [1846], 1:237)[8]

While the Herder-Grimm conceptualization of folklore as ethnic artifact had been absorbed in Thoms's notion of folklore and folklore research, it was transmogrified by the evolutionary perspective of "Mr. Tylor's science." Edward Burnett Tylor argued, in his opus *Primitive Culture*, that civilization was the outgrowth of a panhuman savage past, and the development of civilization could be evidenced by a class of facts known as "survivals"—customs and ideas that made sense only in terms of the primitive circumstances in which they originated (Tylor 1874 [1871], 1:16), circumstances which corresponded in large measure with conditions of contemporary savage tribes (21). Although Tylor believed in the psychological unity of mankind and in the ineradicable debt of civilization to its savage forebears, for folklorists, savagery and civilization came to be viewed as categorically distinct states (Bronner 1986:29). And even though the division between savage and civilized could not be viewed as genetic or insuperable, "peasants and the uneducated" were relegated to the other side of civilization (Hartland in Dorson 1968a, 1:234,243).

Tylor had merely noted in passing that there was "scarcely a hand's breadth difference between an English ploughman and a negro of Central Africa" (Tylor 1874, 1:7). For British folklorists, however, this was no casual analogy but a fundamental axiom.

Tylor's evolutionary theory transformed the nature of the discourse about the past. First, the past of which folklore was an artifact was the *primitive* past of a savage humanity, not merely an *ancient* past of some ethnically defined folk. Second, folklore (i.e., survivals) was something to be escaped with the advancement of civilization and not something to be cherished or reclaimed (Tylor 1874, 2:453).[9] Finally, whereas for Herder and the Grimms the primary identifications and disjunctions of peoples were determined by lines of descent—i.e., along ethnic lines—for the British survivalist folklorists, they were along "class" lines. The peasant emerged as a figure with a way of life and mentality so distinct as to be almost beyond understanding. Folklorists attempted to grasp the mentality of this class who stood apart from civilization, whose life was rooted in the countryside, whose knowledge was communicated by word of mouth, whose customs were local and diverse and were not imposed from above (Alfred Nutt in Dorson 1968a, 1:260–261).

For the survivalists, as for Herder and the Grimms, folklore was an artifact. It was not creative but habitual (Mason 1891:98). The task of the folklorist was to grasp the mentality of that category of people who did not act "in accordance with the rules of science and culture" (97). Folklore was the portion of Anthropology which attempted to grasp the "mental and spiritual side of humanity" (Hartland in Dorson 1968a, 1:231). Folklore was fundamentally "psychological" (Burne 1914:1), and its materials could be fathomed by grasping the "qualities of the uncivilized imagination" (Andrew Lang in Dorson 1968a, 1:297). Folklore was the interior, emic aspect of culture—the body of native thought and opinion—not simply an accumulation of customary behaviors (Mason 1891:103). Folklore was an artifact of identity, because through folklore one could establish and ascertain the underlying common qualities of those who were fundamentally *unlike* oneself. If, today, the efforts of the Victorian folklorists do not strike us as concerned with identity, it is because the survivalists were attempting to delineate the identity of a category of people which shared no common history, were bound by no principles of social organization, and possessed no consciousness of kind. While a self-conscious civilization could define itself in terms of the savagery from which it believed itself to have emerged, savagery could not imagine, let alone define, itself. Savagery was a category that existed only in the minds of the members of a civilized society.[10]

The ideas of Herder and the Grimms were interpreted differently in England than in the emerging nations of Europe. For these nations, the ethnic principle remained central. In Finland, in fact, the ideas of Herder and the Grimms had been, to some extent, anticipated. Henrik Gabriel Porthan (1739–1803) believed that in Finnish folk poetry could be found a "clear and unspoiled spring" where one could "distinguish the real ancient spirit" of the Finnish people (Porthan in Wilson 1976a:20). His student, Christian Lencqvist, argued that "the heathen worship and superstition of the Finns" survived in the poetry that could still be collected among the common folk (Lencqvist quoted in Wilson 1976a:22). When it came, Finland was more than ripe for Herder's philosophy of nations and his disquisitions on the nature of folk poetry. In 1817, Carl Axel Gottlund called for the collection of Finnish folk poetry and its organization into "a new Homer, Ossian, or Nibelungenlied." "For what is folk poetry," he wrote, "except the crystal in which nationality mirrors itself, the spring from which the nation's original feelings rise to the surface" (Gottlund quoted in Wilson 1976a:33). In 1835, Elias Lönnrot answered Gottlund's call with the first edition of the *Kalevala*.[11]

There were those who believed that in editing and arranging the folk poetry he collected, Lönnrot had merely restored the *Kalevala* to its original form. Others doubted it had ever existed as a single, unified epic. Close studies of the poems themselves began to cast doubt upon their originality and distinctiveness. In 1885, Julius Krohn asserted that the elements from which the *Kalevala* had been constructed were not of Finnish origin at all, but drew, rather, upon a fund of lore common to many nations.

The premise that folklore was an artifact of identity, the relic of an ancient mythology in which the character, spirit, and feelings of a nation were embedded, had always depended upon another premise: that oral channels of transmission could faithfully *preserve* such artifacts. In sixteenth-century England, the argument over the credibility of oral traditions had already been engaged (de Caro 1972:62). While the Grimms never studied the problem, Jacob claimed amazement at the fidelity of tradition and how "exactly [the common people] seize and transmit to posterity the essential features of the fable" (Grimm 1966, 3:xiii). In the preface to *Kinder- und Hausmärchen* [*Children's and Household Tales*], they took pains to characterize the zealousness of Frau Viehmann in reproducing the same narration and her promptness in correcting any mistakes (Peppard 1971:61–62). Nevertheless, they recognized that change was inevitable in the oral process, and they were not loath in *Kinder- und Hausmärchen* to conflate texts, tighten plot structure, and alter phraseology in the effort to present something that was at once more accessible and in some sense closer to the completeness and integrity of the original (69–71).

If the *Kalevala* did not faithfully preserve the elements of an ancient and distinctly Finnish identity, in what sense could it be regarded as Finnish at all? Julius Krohn argued that although the original elements from which the epic was constructed were not distinctly Finnish, the attachment of the Finnish people to their national epic might remain unshaken. For from a common stream of tradition, the Finnish people had wrought something unique. Even though the substance of the *Kalevala* had been borrowed, Krohn claimed that it had been "so independently recast" that it reflected a "purely Finnish character and spirit" (Krohn 1971:15; Krohn quoted in Wilson 1976a:55).

The spirit and character of a people were thus to be grasped, in Krohn's terminology, in the process of "*artistic transformation*" (Krohn 1971:15, my emphasis). Folklore could reflect this spirit and character only to the extent that it was stamped by this process. Thus, improvisation, which had been viewed as a threat to the preservation of authentic identity, now could be viewed as the very expression of that identity. Oral tradition and oral transmission came to redefine folklore, as transformation came to be viewed as the means by which identity was invested in lore.[12]

The very same reconceptualization of folklore as an art—rather than an artifact—of identity was also carried out in the Anglo-American tradition of folklore scholarship. Frances B. Gummere's theory of ballad origins assumed that the ballad was an artifact of primitive poetizing. Gummere felt that such poetry could not be the product of individual poets but only of the group.[13] In effect, Gummere's communal theory of poetic composition attempted to rationalize the Grimms' notorious characterization of folk composition as "*das Volk dichtet*" ["the Folk compose"]. Communal creation, according to Gummere, stamped the ballad with its peculiar characteristics—impersonality, repetition, anonymity—but this kind of poetic composition occurred only under primitive conditions. Oral tradition was the enemy of such poetry. For Gummere, consequently, there were two kinds of improvisation: there was the "improvisation of verses in a singing, dancing throng" at the moment of ballad composition (1907:22), but there was also "the great factor of oral tradition which ... made over and over again the stuff of this communal song" (62). This remaking of the ballad was a threat to its original and authentic voice, so that in Gummere's view, if "the primitive way of life" still spoke in the ballad at all, it was only with "very faint and far away tones" (15, 63, 338, 344).

Gummere's effort to distinguish the folksong on the basis of its communal composition came to be opposed by a number of theorists working with different premises. George Lyman Kittredge, though supporting Gummere's views in a number of instances, nevertheless argued that the ballad might be composed in any number of ways. The folk had to accept it, however, for the "course of oral tradition ... [was] essential to the production of a genuine ballad" (Kittredge quoted in Wilgus 1959:34). Cecil Sharp, as a Darwinian evolutionist (as Tylor and his followers were *not*) viewed oral transmission, not as a process by which folksong is preserved, but as a "process by which it grows and by which it is created" (Sharp 1907:10). For Sharp, folksongs were not born but made. Individual variation, like biological mutation, made the development of folksong possible. But individual variations, like most mutations, are destined for extinction. As only mutations which confer some adaptive advantage ultimately survive, only song variations which appeal to the community are ultimately perpetuated (11–12). The community may play no role in the origin of a song, but it plays the essential role in the selection and shaping of a folksong. Wrote Sharp: "National peculiarities must ultimately determine the specific characteristics of the folksongs of different nations" (29).

Phillips Barry arrived at the same view without the Darwinian framework. The folksong was the result of "individual invention plus communal recreation" (Barry quoted in Wilgus 1959:69). It was "*tradition* that ... [made] the folksong a distinct genre" (Eckstorm and Barry 1930:2), and, for Barry, tradition was merely a summary term for creation and re-creation by individual ballad singers (Barry 1936:16). For Barry, folksong was a "psychological problem" (Barry 1933:5), reflecting the dispositions—conscious and unconscious—of the individuals and groups that sang them. Gordon Gerould, in large measure, confirmed Barry's view. Regardless of their origins, ballads were "submitted to the same processes of remaking" (Gerould 1923:22). The ballad was a product of the "*art of tradition*" (24, my emphasis), for "traditional impulses and traditional aptitudes ... acted upon it" (27). The publication of Gerould's book *The Ballad of Tradition* pretty well marked the end of any concern with ballad origins and the concern with folk poetry as an artifact of identity (Gerould 1957:3, 169). The ballads of tradition were not the poetry of some primitive folk, but "reflect ... the opinions and feelings" and "the emotional lives of ordinary people" (134–135). If they bore a relation to the thoughts and feelings of the past, it was only because their makers had not relinquished their "old ideas and old ways" even in the face of a new and changing world (161–162). If they reflected the past, it was because, among certain people, the past was still very much alive.

The transition from the study of origins to the study of tradition and transmission was not simply an awakening to the fact that tales and songs and other forms changed. That folklore changed was in no way a discovery of turn-of-the-century folklorists. But in the twentieth century, folklorists began to reconceptualize the relation of change to the delineation of identity. The facts of change could no longer justify the situating of identity in reconstructed aboriginal forms. If folklore reflected identity at all, that identity was invested in the lore by the processes of tradition itself.[14]

The historical-geographical or "Finnish" method of research as formulated by Julius Krohn and elaborated and codified by Kaarle Krohn has always been something of a Rube Goldberg operation in folklore studies. Despite its prominence in the first half of the twentieth century, it required all kinds of elaborate efforts and costly expenditures of energy in order to produce results of seemingly dubious consequence.[15] Certainly as a method that was concerned to trace the peregrinations of specific forms of folklore across national and continental boundaries, it would seem almost antithetical to issues of identity. Types of folklore rather than the characters of peoples would seem to have been its single focus of interest. Yet the method was developed to recover the original forms and sources of the poetry of the ancient Finnish nation in which Finnish identity was held to abide (Wilson 1976a:63–64). What Julius Krohn had hoped to demonstrate through the application of this method was the utter distinctiveness of the *Kalevala* materials. He failed in this demonstration (Krohn 1971:14), and he was forced to locate Finnish identity elsewhere—in the processes of tradition.[16] In other words, the development of the method was intimately tied to the project of identity.[17]

The attacks directed at the Finnish method are instructive because they precisely targeted its movement away from identity research. Carl von Sydow criticized the method for ignoring the place of folklore in the life process. Von Sydow introduced a number of concepts—such as *active* and *passive tradition bearer* and *oicotype*—that represented tradition as an organic process. It is significant that oicotype has been repeatedly identified as a potentially fruitful concept by contemporary folklorists (Dundes 1989:72–72), because it is oicotype that directs folklorists back to issues of identity. As von Sydow himself recognized, an oicotype is a tradition that is imprinted with a "distinct character" of a "national, provincial, [or] parochial" order (von Sydow 1948:16, 243). Roger Abrahams and Alan Dundes, who perhaps have made the most mention of the concept, emphasized its potential to illuminate a group's "attitude and approach toward life" (Abrahams 1979:399) and its "local ideological and world view tendencies" (Dundes 1989:73), thereby re-linking the historic-geographic method with the project of identity.[18]

If the term *oicotypification* was only rarely used by folklorists, the process that the term designated became central in folklore studies. For Richard M. Dorson, the materials drawn from the stock of international forms were colored by "national characteristics and historical conditions." If American folklore exhibited "distinctive qualities," it was because Americans marked their Old World lore with "the fresh materials of their experiences" (Dorson 1945:3).[19] The historic-geographic method was important for Dorson only to the extent that it was "comparative" and allowed for the delineation of distinctly national and regional patterns. Thus, despite the clear debt that the folktales of North America owed to England, changes wrought on the Old World tradition in the New World could be clearly discerned. American tales had more variants than their English counterparts. Motifs concerning fairies and elves were absent in the American variants, and the number of American variants containing humorous motifs—with particular emphasis on lying—far outnumbered those found in England. It was suggested that an exaggerative tendency already extant in Europe exploded when it confronted the New World wilderness, American migratory patterns, and the social conditions of the frontier (Baughman 1966:xii-xvi). It was upon such comparative research that Dorson's own claims for the distinctiveness of American humor—and indeed, that this humor constituted an American "comic mythology" (Dorson 1939:xv)—ultimately depended. Dorson was sympathetic to any effort to delineate an American *oicotype*, even if he never used the term. He particularly lauded Stanley Edgar Hyman for his essay "The Child Ballad in America" (Hyman 1957) and its attempt to describe the transformation of those English and Scottish songs by an "American ethos, with its denial of death, its resistance to the tragic experience, its deep repression of sexuality, its overriding pieties, and its frantic emphasis on the rationalistic, the inconsequential, and the optimistic" (Dorson 1978a:105).

The rooting of identity in the transformations wrought by tradition was a major change in the conceptualization of the relationship between folklore and identity. However, the idea that identity was still in some way tied to the past was not entirely eradicated. But the significance of that past was changed. The "past" did not specify some specific *moment* in time when a folk was whole and pure, but rather the *stretch* of time necessary for a group to imprint its lore with the distinctive aspects of its identity (Ben-Amos 1971:7). This was at first thought to require generations to achieve (von Sydow 1948:242). Furthermore, the transformation had to be achieved by the group as a whole. The process was democratic and participatory and could not be achieved by only a few individuals (Dorson 1952:7). Variation in the lore was not considered to be a mark of degeneration of some pristine original, but rather an indicator of the genuine article (Dorson 1945:215). Variation indicated that the lore was being subjected to transformation. Whatever its source, the folk were in the process of making the lore their own.[20]

Inevitably, the question would have to be confronted, whether explicitly or implicitly, as to who was specifically responsible for making folklore and how long it would take for a group to mark its lore with its own peculiarities and characteristics. With the disintegration of the image of the slow, plodding, independent, homogeneous, and basically integrated "traditional society" (Abrahams 1971:24–25; Bausinger 1986:27), and with the awareness of the rapid change in life wrought by industrial, market, and media forces on such societies, the question naturally arose as to how a group's identity could be tied to traditions shaped in other times, by other causes, and under a completely different set of conditions (Abrahams 1971:26). Even Dorson recognized that American folklore and the "dominant goals and aspirations" that it reflected were in constant flux. The "impulses" that directed the production of American folklore—religious, democratic, economic, and humane—changed precipitously with each shift in socio-historical circumstance (Dorson 1973:1).[21]

Consequently, folklorists set out to relieve folklore of the burden of tradition (Ben-Amos 1971:8–9). The method employed was the redefinition of folklore. Definitions of folklore as "verbal art" (Bascom 1955), "artistic communication in small groups" (Ben-Amos 1971:13), "performance" (Bauman 1975:290), "enactment" (Abrahams 1977:84–85) or "the aesthetics of everyday life" (Kirshenblatt-Gimblett 1983:234) all served to eradicate any necessary connection between folklore and the past.[22] Instead, folklore was art born in the aesthetic "event"; an event which had to be grasped in terms of the "unity of process, product, and context" in the here-and-now (Bauman 1971b:v; Bauman 1977a:123).[23] The production of folklore was not a matter of duration but was once again of the single moment—only a moment in the present rather than the past. In effect, every folklore event involved a "singing dancing throng" in the throes of its improvisatory and creative impulses.[24]

Performance approaches tended to emphasize "small group" settings defined primarily in terms of the roles of performer and audience, rather than in terms of regional, ethnic, or occupational characteristics. Yet this reorientation in folklore studies never lost touch with the project of identity. Art simply became the touchstone of that identity. For art was an essential, not an "accidental," quality of folklore (Ben-Amos 1971:13). Art embodied the "most vital expressions of culture" and was the "key to its value system, self-conceptions, and anxieties" (Abrahams 1977:79; 1971:28). This turn to art was, in truth, only a return, as Herder had rooted identity in art some two hundred years before. For Herder, only art that was spontaneous, natural, and unconscious could reflect the true identity of a people. Performance approaches, however, would emphasize responsibility (Bauman 1975:293), artifice (Abrahams 1971:18) and self-consciousness (Abrahams 1977:89) as intrinsic to displays of identity. Art, in its translation of the ordinary and everyday into the extraordinary and strange was conceived of as a kind of "commentary" (103) that individuals and groups made on who they were and what they were about. It is a "story ... [people tell] themselves about themselves" (Geertz 1973:448).[25] The "power of performance to create, store, and transmit identity" resided in its "reflexive nature." Art could "turn, bend, or reflect back" upon a group the "components which make up their public selves" (Victor Turner quoted in Fine and Speer 1992:8).

If performance emphasized the aesthetic character of folklore creation and signaled a turn toward poetics, it nevertheless accepted as "given" that artistic communications involved "distinctive symbolic patterns" that referred beyond the boundaries of the enactment itself and that were tied to the identities of their creators (Bauman 1977a:126–127).[26] The coon dog traders studied by Richard Bauman, in their effort to establish their trustworthiness, invariably engaged in forms of storytelling that undermined the very identity they were trying to project (Bauman 1986:31). Ed Bell embellished and expanded his tall tales to accommodate his emerging identity as a "public storyteller" (105). In the treasure tales told by older Mexicanos of Cordova, New Mexico, Charles Briggs found a "dialectical unfolding of moral principles" with respect to the values of "bygone days" and "nowadays" with tellers attempting to situate themselves in relation to the values of each sphere (Briggs 1985:309). At every turn, the storytelling was shown to be enmeshed in the effort to define and project a certain identity. In other words, poetics serves to enhance efforts to delineate personal and cultural identities—it does not supplant them.

Thus, performance "theory" in no way abandoned the concern with identity.[27] When the sense of identity could no longer be rooted in the ancient artifact, or the process of tradition, it was re-rooted in artistic production—in a species of expression that was presumed to hold a privileged relation to the deepest concerns of both individuals and groups.[28]

In 1950, Richard M. Dorson coined the term "fakelore" to characterize those "spurious and synthetic" commercial productions which were not creations shaped and tempered in the forge of tradition but were passed off as though they were (1971:9). Dorson suggested that folklorists examine such artifices, but more as a defensive tactic—as a study of the "relationship between mass culture and folklore patterns" (Dorson 1959:211). He did not intend to validate such productions as folklore. There are those who view the boundary between folklore and fakelore as real and important. There is a sense that authentic identity has to defend itself against the artifices of the culture industry (Fox 1980; Limón 1983). Yet there was also a sense that fakelore had to be considered as part of the folklore question (Bausinger 1968:126). After all, the artifices of popular culture can also embody the values and attitudes of the people (Dunlop 1975:375; Hobsbawm 1984:263,307; Abrahams and Kalčik 1978:224; Rihtman-Augustin 1978:167). Furthermore, popular culture is shared by a much larger segment of the population than any piece of folklore ever was (Dunlop 1975:375). If people responded to these artificial creations, thought of them as folklore, and employed them as folklore, were they not in some sense folklore (Dégh 1984:188)?[29] According to this view, identity did not depend on who one's ancestors were, or what had been inherited from them, so much as it depended upon an act of imagination (Abrahams and Kalčik 1978:228). The past plays a role in the sense of identity only as a construction of the present (Handler and Linnekin 1984). Paul Bunyan is or is not important to the extent that he does or does not hold a place in the American imagination of self. The fact that Bunyan may be a creation of a few popularizers, advertisers, and boosters is beside the point. In an advanced consumer age, people purchase everything, including their pasts (Carpenter and Vidutis 1984:183). Who they are is encoded in what car they drive, what cigarette they smoke, what club they join, and what celebrations they attend (Lewis 1961:80–81; Anderson 1990:114,126). Not tradition-directed, inner-directed, or even other-directed (Riesman 1950:11–26), postmodern man is product-directed; known by what he does and does not consume: "Single male seeks non-smoking female who appreciates fine wines, French cuisine, Woody Allen films, catamarans, and foreign travel—for meaningful relationship." And so folklorists turned to the study of rap music (Keyes 2000), standup comics (Fulton 2004), bumper stickers (Salamon 2001), sport (Gutowski 1972; Robidoux 2002), fairground contests (Kruckemeyer 2002), historical dramas (Ivey 1977), and ersatz rituals (Byrne 1997; Thompson 2003); that is, to the "artifices" of personal and group identity.

Folklore studies have not really been about antiquities, about oral tradition, or about art, although each of these concepts has stood at the core of a major definition of the subject matter. Far from being a new direction or concern in folklore studies, identity has always been a central concern—in fact, *the* central concern—of the field. The definition of folklore has been anchored to a concept of identity. That is to say, the definition and redefinition of folklore has been a process of conceptualizing and reconceptualizing a set of cultural materials and their privileged relation to the identities of individuals and groups. When identity was held to reside among some ancient *Volk*, folklore was conceived of as antiquities and relics, as artifacts of a past that could still reveal an authentic identity. The delineation of collective and personal identity demanded the reclamation of that ancient past. When identity was manifested in the processes of selection and recreation, folklore was defined as those materials shaped in oral tradition. When identity could no longer be situated in a durable past, it was invested in the creative act itself, and folklore was defined as an aesthetic communication. And when identity came to be regarded as a construction, folklorists began to turn to the full output of cultural production from which identities—if only transitory ones—might be fabricated.

Inevitably, the question arises, why hasn't folklore's concern with identity been obvious before? One answer is that, for the greater part of its history, folklore studies has been more concerned with the discovery, collection, and preservation of the artifacts of identity than with the question of identity per se. Another answer is that folklorists often do not recognize a concern with identity when the term itself is not employed. Furthermore, folklorists who have focused largely on collective identity have had to employ a mode of analysis that to some extent disguises this concern. The work of two "randomly selected" folklorists can serve to illustrate the point.

When Barbara Kirshenblatt-Gimblett analyzed large collections of painted and embroidered Ashkenazic Torah binders, she made the following observations: these binders were made from the cloth on which the infant boys lie during circumcision; they are embroidered with the child's name, birth date and zodiac sign, and a wish that he grow up to a life of Torah, marriage, and good deeds; they are presented to the synagogue on the occasion of a child's first visit and are used to bind the Torah on that occasion and on the occasion of the boy's bar mitzvah. Her close analysis of the decorated object itself focused upon letters that represent concepts, numerical representations of words, the floral and faunal elaboration of letters, the iconic value of letters, and so forth. All of this, Kirshenblatt-Gimblett argued, pointed to the centrality of the word, and not merely the word, but the creative word, that brings forth life, which binds that life into a coherent whole, and binds the life of the individual to that of the community. Life and Torah are one—each a commentary on and interpretation of the other (Kirshenblatt-Gimblett 1982:136–146). These binders, however, are more than the "stimuli" and "guides" to ritual activity that Kirshenblatt-Gimblett claimed. They reflect and condition the deepest affirmations of individual and community. They embody what being a religious Jew is all about. They are expressions of a Jewish identity.

Henry Glassie found that Turkish folk art crystallized into three "styles." Objects were *sade* or chaste if their useful form dominated the work—if their natural materials were displayed. Objects were *canlı*, or spirited, in the sense that they were spontaneous, highly colored, and welcomed the accidental effect. The third style, *ciddi*, was serious and disciplined. It was effected through patience and masterly control in which form was overlaid with patterns of symmetrical repetition. *Sade, canlı,* and *ciddi* are more than characterizations of form and technique. They are all manifestations of spirit—forms of devotion. They are deeply implicated in being an artisan, a Muslim, and possibly in just being a Turk. One would expect, that although they become particularly visible in artisanship, they are implicated in a range of everyday and not-so-everyday behaviors. They are "dynamic essences"—aspects of who and what these people are (Glassie 1993a:73).

Neither Glassie nor Kirshenblatt-Gimblett ever invoke the term *identity* in their accounts, yet it is something like identity to which their discussions of art and artistry relate.[30] Since folklorists necessarily approach identity as "semiotically constituted" (Ewing 1990:256), it is not entirely surprising if they grasp only vaguely what is, in fact, being talked about. So much of the discussion seems to take place at the level of signs that they tend to think it is a discussion *of* signs. They fail to take note of the understood pronouns that motivate the discussion. Yet when folklorists analyze the lore they have collected, they invariably refer to underlying "attitudes" (Stahl 1977:21), "ideas," "premises" (Dundes 1971:95), "values" (Kirshenblatt-Gimblett 1983:183), "value centers" (Wilson 1983:160), "emotional cores" (Kotkin and Zeitlin 1983:98), "purposes" (Benedict 1959:46), "conflicts" (Oring 1981:129), "themes," "affirmations" (Opler 1945:198; Spicer 1971:796), "desires" (Seitel 1980:22), "visions" (Dorson 1961:14), "prejudices" (Dorson 1969:229), "aspirations" (Dorson 1973:1), "anxieties" (Abrahams 1971:19), or "mentalities" (Bausinger 1990:3). The allusions to the deeper project are ever present.

Even when research and writing by folklorists do not directly or indirectly relate to identity, it seems that identity remains a potent force in folklore studies. Folklore has often been described as interdisciplinary. In one sense, this merely recognizes that the materials that folklorists study can be profitably approached using the concepts and methodologies of a number of disciplines. But folklore is also interdisciplinary in the sense that the central project of folklore studies has been said to lie in one or another discipline. Folklore studies have been alternately reckoned as studies in *art, society, history, communication,* and *mind.* There are any number of folklorists who might claim one of these as *the* central concern of the folkloristic enterprise.[31] Folklorists often move with some ease between such concerns but rarely ask whether these disparate concerns orbit around any kind of center—whether they all relate to a more pivotal inquiry. Identity may be the dark matter standing at the center of the folkloristic enterprise whose gravity is responsible for directing studies into orbits about these other concerns. Identity seems to be what integrates the diverse interests of folklorists into some sort of comprehensible configuration. *Identity is what binds an idea of folk to a notion of lore.*

Every new definition of folklore has naturally involved some effort to distinguish it from its predecessors; has involved some demonstration of the ways in which an older definition was misguided or mistaken.[32] I have tried to focus on something that all the disparate definitions share—to suggest a deeper and continuous concern in the folklore project of the past centuries. Herder is regularly recognized for his concept of *Volk* (a concept that has been regarded somewhat ambivalently by contemporary folklorists [Abrahams 1993:28–30; Smith 1989:1]). But he is less recognized as the founder of modern psychology (Schütze 1923:130). It was Herder who saw imagination, feeling, and reason as part of a single faculty, a faculty uniquely shaped by history and environment. For Herder, each individual and group has its own distinctive identity. Yet this identity could never be known directly—it could only be approached through its expressions. Art gave this identity expression—both reflecting and shaping its substance and contours (Taylor 1989:368–377). Art was authentic when it was the spontaneous expression of this inner identity. Herder bequeathed to folklorists more than the concept of folk; he set the terms in which the discussion and debate of folklore would proceed. Whenever folklorists speak of folklore as "expressive" or debate its "authenticity," they are speaking in Herder's terms.[33]

To suggest that identity is, and has always been, at the center of folklore studies—and that the definitions of folklore over the centuries have been efforts to privilege certain kinds of materials and processes in relation to identity—is merely to suggest that folklorists begin to rethink what folklore studies are about and how they might proceed with them. Certainly, folklorists need to examine the concept of identity in a more explicit and deliberate manner.[34] They need to determine whether the multifold and seemingly diverse interests of folklorists in aesthetics, history, society, communication, and mind might be made to fruitfully coalesce in a notion of identity. An explicit focus on identity might put a greater emphasis on long-term, in-depth explorations of particular groups rather than ever-shifting, surface engagements with many. Folklorists can begin to explore in what ways their studies augment, deepen, or contradict those depictions of identity delineated by other disciplines using other methods and materials. Folklorists might attend to the development of an idiom for identity description rather than relying on the disparate, commonsense categories that have long been employed. Personal identity and its articulation with folklore forms and processes should merit increasing attention. Situations in which identity is challenged or denied—that is, situations of identity conflict—may prove particularly promising for investigation, as they are arenas in which the contours of identity become prominent and visible. And it would seem, at some level, folklorists might make contact with the psychological literature in their pursuit of what has been at root a psychological project.

Of course, endlessly intoning the word *identity* will offer no solution to folklore's problems. In fact, scrutiny of the concept may only serve to widen and deepen them. Yet the observation that identity is old, under-theorized, and potentially problematic is not a petition for its dismissal. Although there are a number of disciplines that are currently interested in identity—anthropology and psychology especially—they have come to it rather late. Anthropology's concern has been culture—its operation and growth—while psychology's concern with mind, has been, until recently, a concern with a psychobiological rather than a psychosocial construct. But a concept of identity has always been central in folklore studies, and it would seem that folklorists should pay it more than a little attention.

2. Whaling Songs and the Context of Fantasy

The relationship between the real world and the narratives which depict that world has posed problems to thinkers for millennia. Herodotus (484–425 BCE?) in describing the youth of Cyrus the Great of Persia dismissed the tradition that he was suckled by a bitch by pointing out that he was raised by a cowherd's wife whose name was Cyno which means "bitch" (1947:69). Similarly, a story about the oracles of Dodona in Greece and Ammon in Libya related that two doves flew from Thebes in Egypt and alighted at these places. The doves spoke in a human voice and directed the establishment of an oracle to Zeus. Herodotus suggested that the oracles were introduced by women who were carried off by the Phoenicians and sold as slaves. They were called "doves" because their language was foreign like the chattering of a bird. "For how can it be conceived possible that a dove should really speak?" (144–145).

Reconciling the world described in narrative with the world as it is held to operate proved a task for folklorists of the nineteenth and twentieth centuries as well. Max Müller argued that myths describing the extraordinary exploits of the gods were in fact descriptions of natural phenomena recounted in language whose meaning had been forgotten (Dorson 1955). Evolutionary folklorists attributed the barbaric acts of the gods to more primitive beliefs and practices which survived in the accounts of more civilized peoples (Lang 1910:45–63). Sigmund Freud would suggest that the distortions found in myths and tales were not to be understood historically but symbolically—in unconscious wishes that are expressed most commonly in ordinary dreams (Freud 1953, 4:122–133).

Whales have been hunted from earliest times both in the Old World and the New. Basques turned whaling into an industry; an industry adopted by the English and Dutch. By the nineteenth century, however, Americans were the dominant power. Whaling produced the oil that lit the lamps and lubricated the machines of a growing urbanizing and industrializing society. The development of large-scale petroleum production eventually destroyed the whaling industry. Whaling had its own distinct lore including a body of songs peculiar to that occupation.

Pigs dream of acorns, and geese dream of maize.
—Hungarian proverb

How is the culture of a particular folk group reflected in its lore? How does this lore function psychologically and socially? The relationship between folklore and other aspects of culture has been a subject of study since the beginning of the twentieth century. In a rejoinder to those who saw the content of folklore as inspired by the observation of and reaction to natural phenomena, Franz Boas stated that in Tsimshian myth, "The formulas of myths and folktales ... are almost exclusively events that reflect the occurrences of human life, particularly those that stir the emotions of the people" (1916:880).[1] Boas went further, however, than merely pointing to a social inspiration for folklore. He felt that the life of the people who created the lore was accurately reflected in their creation, and in *Tsimshian Mythology* and in *Kwakiutl Culture as Reflected in Mythology*, he attempted to provide something akin to ethnography on the basis of the scrutiny of their folklore. Boas realized, however, that there were incidents in myth and tale contrary to everyday experience. Boas felt that such incidents were merely the realization of everyday wishes: "Is it not one of the characteristics of the imagination that it gives reality to wishes?" (1916:880).[2]

Ruth Benedict also viewed folklore as a reflection of culture: "A living folklore ... reflects the contemporary interest and judgments of its tellers, and adapts incidents to its own cultural usages" (1935: 1:xiv). Benedict paid more attention to the discrepancies between culture and the lore than Boas did, but like Boas, she regarded folklore as wish fulfillment. "Folklore therefore in those cases where it does not mirror contemporary custom owes its distortions to various fanciful exaggerations and compensatory mechanisms" (xx, xxi). For example, polygamous motifs in Zuni mythology could only be the result of "grandiose folkloristic convention" because there was no evidence that the Zuni—or any Pueblo society—ever practiced polygamy. In lore, polygamy was a "mythological exaggeration" and a "compensatory daydream" (xvi). Thus, the distortions of cultural life and institutions in folklore have purpose. They serve to fulfill unconscious wishes and compensate for deficiencies that are otherwise unfulfilled in the context of ordinary social life.[3]

The relationship between the fictions of folklore and the realities of social life are explored in a very different cultural context below. The songs of the nineteenth-century American—and to some extent, British—whaling men are examined in relation to the realities of whaling life and the whaling enterprise. To what extent do the songs reflect the culture of the whalers? How do the songs deviate from the realities of occupational life? What wishes were fulfilled and what compensations, if any, were offered by folkloristic exaggerations?

The songs about whaling originated among men engaged in the profession, and evidence indicates that these songs were perpetuated almost exclusively by men who had gone whaling. A large portion of a whaler's total song repertoire was shared by other occupational groups—especially sailors, but also lumberjacks—but the songs that deal with the pursuit of whales were peculiar to whalers.

The whaling life was likely to appeal only to three classes of men: those who were fugitives from society; those determined to work their way up until they owned a ship of their own; and those who thought they were going to see the world and gain adventure (Chatterton 1930:106). Merchant seamen were rarely recruited for whaling voyages as they made poor whalers (Ashley 1938:100).[4] Thus, except for the officers and the harpooners (or boatsmen) for each whaleboat—about four per ship—the crew was usually comprised of men who had never been to sea before (80).

Green crews were attracted by the mention of adventure and a promise of a short successful voyage (115). Shipping agents posted circulars advertising for five hundred or a thousand "stout young men" promising that full outfits would be provided (Hohman 1928:90). These agents were also outfitters, or worked together with outfitters, to corral the crews and provide them with the necessary gear for the voyage (90). Outfitters took great advantage of the "greenie's" ignorance of sea life, and the outfits they provided were often of substandard quality and credited at inflated prices. Ship owners paid the agents for the recruits they delivered and for the cost of their outfits, but a recruit's bill for his outfit was deducted from his share of the profits at the end of the voyage. Substantial interest was charged for this "loan," and by the time a whaler returned home from his voyage, he could owe a considerable sum of money. Outfitters were called "landsharks" because of their rapacity (Ashely 1938:134).[5] This situation is accurately described in song:

> 'Tis advertised in Boston
> New York and Albany
> Five hundred young Americans
> Are wanted for the sea
>
> They take you down to Bedford
> That famous whaling port
> And give you to some landsharks
> To board and fit you out
>
> It's then that they will show you
> Their fine clipper ships
> They say you'll have five hundred sperm
> Before you're six months out (Huntington 1964:42–43).

The last of the above verses refers to the fact that the shipping agents and outfitters used deceptive tactics to promote whaling as an adventurous, comfortable, and speedy enterprise. Whaling ships, of course, were not "fine clipper ships" that moved cargo across the oceans at great speed. Whaling ships were barks built for stability and endurance, not speed. They were small, cramped, and—by a sailor's standard—ugly. The average length of a sperm whale voyage in the heyday of American whaling was about forty months, not six. No ship was likely to take five hundred sperm whales in the whole of its voyage. Five hundred sperm would have resulted in more oil than a normal whaling ship could carry. Thus, the song reflects the division between what the agents and outfitters advertised and the reality the whalers came to know once they had set out on their voyage.

Between the debt to the outfitter, debts to the ship owners for supplies drawn from the "slop chest" during the voyage, and the expenditures in riotous living after returning to port—a style of living often encouraged and facilitated by these same outfitters—it was possible for a whaler to return home after a three- or four-year voyage in debt. Agents could then use these debts to force a man into yet another whaling voyage (Chatterton 1930:101).

> As I went walking down the street I met big Dixie Brown,
> He looked me in the face, sure, and eyed me with a frown,
> Saying, "the last time you were paid off, with me ran up a score,
> Now take my advice, give you a chance to go to sea once more"
> (MacKenzie 1928:255).

That there was a majority of green hands among whaling crews might explain the existence of a song that specifically focuses on what should be packed in one's sea chest. What was truly needed for the voyage, as well as the quality of those supplies, however, was likely to be learned only after the ship had sailed:

> A chest that is neither too large nor too small
> Is the first thing to which your attention I'll call
> The things to put in it are next to be named
> And if I omit some I'm not to be blamed
>
> Stow first in the bottom a blanket or quilt
> To be used on the voyage whenever you wilt
> Thick trousers and shirts woolen stockings and shoes
> Next your papers and book to tell you the news
>
> Good substantial tarpaulins to cover your head
> Just to say keep it furled N.C. nuff said
> Carry paper and ink pen wafers and wax
> A shoemaker's last awls and some small tacks (Huntington 1964:7–8).

There is nothing inappropriate in the list of items mentioned in this song. In fact, when compared with actual items contained in a whaler's outfit (Hohman 1928:99), the song mentions some important items that were unlikely to be provided by an outfitter: e.g., tobacco, writing and reading materials, and medicines.[6] On the other hand, it neglects other basic items such as a spoon, plate, cup, and knife. The song ends, "Some things I've omitted, but never mind that; eat salt junk and hard bread and laugh and grow fat" (Huntington 1964:8). Salted meat and hard bread were indeed staples of the whaler's monotonous diet (Hohman 1928:131–134). The final line is, of course, ironic, as one would never grow fat given the quality and quantity of the food provided and the amount of work there was to do.

Once a green crew was put aboard a ship, the ship sailed.[7] Watches were assigned, and the first weeks at sea were spent getting one's sea legs and learning the skills necessary for maintaining and sailing an ocean-going vessel. Some skills had to be mastered very quickly. Clifford Ashley kept a journal of his voyage aboard an American whaler in 1904. In his account, he recorded the captain's first instructions to the crew, especially to the green hands:

Just remember, I'm boss on this ship. When you get an order, jump. If I catch any one of you wasting grub, I'll put him on bread and water for a month and dock the rations of the whole watch. You greenies have got just a week to box the compass and learn the ropes; after that, no watch below til you do (1938:5).

The song known as "Blow Ye Winds" reflects the difficulties of some of the tasks that the green hands had to master:

It's now we're out to sea my boys
The wind comes on to blow
One half the watch is sick on deck
The other half sick below

Next comes that damned old compass
It will grieve your heart full sore
For there is two and thirty points
And we have forty-four

Next comes the running rigging
That all of you must know
And if you don't know it in fifteen days out
You'll lose your watch below (Huntington 1964:43)

Gale Huntington feels that the reference to the forty-four point compass is to a compass that actually existed, although he is at a loss to explain how one fits eleven points into ninety degrees (1964:46). The reference, however, is more likely a literary exaggeration ludicrously expressing the difficulty the green hand had in mastering the use of the unfamiliar instrument.

Every crew member had to stand a two hour watch at the masthead on the lookout for whales (Ashley 1938:7–8). The rolling of the ship was felt more keenly at the top of the hundred-foot masthead than it was on the deck of the ship:

But that is not all to his sorrow he will find
Two hours to the masthead he must go.

He descends to the deck with head dizzy and sick
And for his life he would not give a damn (Huntington 1964:41).

In the earliest days of American whaling, crews were made up mostly of Yankees with a few local Indians. Native Americans had hunted whales in the pre-contact period, and they had knowledge and skills that were absorbed by the developing American whaling industry (Hohman 1928:50). As the industry grew, whaling crews consisted of a mixture of nationalities, and white Americans were often in the minority. Crews included blacks, Indians, Polynesians, Maoris, and Portuguese picked up in the Cape Verde Islands and Azores on the outbound voyage. Relations between the different ethnic components of the crew were not always harmonious. For example, Portuguese were often despised because they were willing to work for a smaller percentage of the profits, were perceived as dirty, and accepted payment to perform menial tasks for other crew members (Hohman 1928:54; Chatterton 1930:105). A whaling song registers a complaint about the equality enforced on a ship's crew.

> The captains of the whalers are abolitionists
> They go in for amalgamation
> A nigger or a Portuguese is treated like a man
> But Americans are dogs on Desolation
>
> These cowards and villains for they are such a race
> They are a disgrace to all civilization
> Are our worthy friends who call themselves men
> And command these prison hulks on Desolation
>   (Huntington 1964:39).

One does not have to believe that ship captains were actually abolitionists—although Quakers were prominent in the American whaling industry—to understand the importance of creating a sense of comradeship and cooperation among the members of a small whaling crew.

Once the whaling ship has set out for the whaling grounds all the gear is prepared and made ready for use. Lines are stretched and coiled in their tubs, harpoons and lances are sharpened and things are made ship-shape. Each hand is assigned to a whale boat and boat drills are conducted. Although lookouts are maintained at all times, they become more vigilant as the ship nears the whaling ground. Whales "sound" or dive to feed, and when they surface to breathe, they spout, frequently blowing a jet of vapor into the air that is visible for miles. When the lookout spies the spout, he cries, "Bloows, there she blows." The captain will then spring into the rigging and fix his field glasses in the direction indicated by the lookout. Gear will be placed in the boats, and the captain will give the order to lower away (Church 1960:29–30).

> Next morning at daybreak
> About five o'clock
> The man at the masthead
> Cried yonder she spouts
> Where away does she lay
> And the answer from aloft
> Two points on our lee bow
> And about three miles off
>
> Then it's call up all hands
> And it's be of good cheer
> Put your tubs in your boats
> Have your bow lines all clear
> Away up your boats now
> Jump in you boat's crew
> Lower away now lower away
> My brave fellows do (Huntington 1964:2–3).

The boats spread out to cover a large area and wait for the whale to rise. When the whale appears, the boats make toward the most favorable point of attack. The harpooner at the bow of the boat hurls the harpoon into the whale, and the boat immediately backs off to keep clear of the whale's flukes. The officer in the stern and the harpooner in the bow change places in the boat. When the whale is struck, it may sound immediately or it may swim along the surface at a very fast pace. In either case, the line attached to the harpoon is played out, though it is turned around a post set in the stern of the boat—the loggerhead—to retard the whale's progress. When the whale slackens its speed, the line is drawn in and the boat is hauled alongside the whale. The officer of the boat then plunges a six foot lance into the whale's lungs several times in order to kill it. The boat will then back away from the whale in its death struggle or "flurry." The water becomes extremely bloody during this struggle. When the whale is dead, it rolls over on its side with its fin projecting above the water. Whalers call it "fin out" (Church 1960:30–32).

> There she blows there she blows
> Man the boats for nothing stay
> Such a prize we must not lose
> Lay to your oars away away
> Give way careful steer
> Launch the harpoon laugh at fear
> Plunge it deep the barbed spear
> Strike the lance in swift career
>
> Give her line give her line
> Down she goes through foaming brine
> Sponge the side where the flying coil
> Marks the monster's speed and toil
> But though she dives to the deepest ground
> Where the lead line fails to sound
> Where the coral gardens hide
> 'Tis all in vain 'tis all in vain
> She hath that within her side
> That will bring her up again
>
> Spout spout spout
> The waves are purling all about
> Every billow on its head
> Strangely wears a crest of red
> See her lash the foaming main
> In her flurry and her pain
> Take good heed my hearts of oak
> Lest her flukes as she lies
> Swiftly hurl you to the skies
> But lo her giant strength is broke
> Now she turns a mass of lead
> The mighty mountain whale is dead (Huntington 1964:19–20).[8]

The description in the above text is quite accurate, even in its details, except for the mention in the first stanza of the striking of the lance following closely after the strike of the harpoon. In reality, the lance strike might follow many hours after a whaleboat first "fastens on" to a whale with the harpoon.

Often there was a rivalry between the different whaleboat crews from the same ship in hunting the whale. Boat officers encouraged this rivalry. Ships' logs often contained drawings or stamps of whales taken and the initials of the successful whale boat (Hohman 1928:178). The rivalry was not always a friendly one, however. Ashley noted the captain's instruction to his crew from his 1904 voyage: "Let every man work for the ship; I don't mind a little healthy competition between the boats, but if any dirty work goes on, I'll break the rascal who does it" (1938:5) In the songs, what appears to be a healthy competition is often depicted:

> Now our boats being lowered there arose a contest
> Among the boat crews to see which should do best
> Spring on says the headsman don't let them pass by
> When up starts a whale and lay on is the cry (Huntington 1964:14)

> Now see each boat advance
> Eager to gain first chance (Colcord 1938:189).

One song, "The Bark Gay Head," is devoted entirely to the praise of the different boat crews:

> We'll cheer my noble hearties
> For the larboard boat and crew
> Mr. Hazzard's their boat leader
> He's a gentleman good and true
> There's Hussy John and Taylor Dick
> And a boatsteerer named Couch
> And when they lower in their boat
> They know what they're about (Huntington 1964:35).

It is unnecessary to analyze every song which involves an attack on a whale. In the songs in which such a scene appears, it is depicted realistically with little exaggeration or idealization. The literary expression accurately, if concisely, represents whaling custom.

Many details in the songs allude to practices that would only be understood by those engaged in the whaling industry. There is a difference between hunting the sperm whale in tropical and subtropical regions, and hunting the right whale and bowhead whale in temperate, sub-arctic, and arctic waters (Chatterton 1930:15). A song called "The Coast of Peru" might be expected to concern sperm whales:

> Our captain has told us
> And we hope it will come true
> There's plenty of sperm whales
> On the coast of Peru (Huntington 1964:2).

There was also an economic difference between the two fisheries. The right whale was hunted in the early eighteenth century off the coast of Long Island and Nantucket. The bowhead whale was hunted only in arctic waters. In the heyday of the whaling industry, both species were hunted for their whalebone (baleen) as much as for their oil. Only the right and bowhead whales produced bone of commercial length and quality. "Right whale's oil ain't worth beans" (Ashley 1938:9, 66). Sperm whale oil made the best candles for illumination and proved a superior lubricant, and it brought two- to three-times the price of right whale oil (Hohman 1928:292). Nantucket devoted itself almost exclusively to the sperm whale even when the pursuit of right whales made more economic sense (284, 306).[9] Sperm whalers however would capture right whales when they happened upon them.

> New Bedford folks are fond of whales
> The largest are the best sir
> And when the sperm whale cannot be had
> Then right whales they will do sir (Huntington 1964:38).

The sperm whale was a much more dangerous prey than the right whale. The sperm whale could attack with its flukes or jaw. The right whale was dangerous mainly for the great sweep of its flukes (Hohman 1928:147). The bowhead was sluggish and non-combative. The main danger to the whalers in the arctic fisheries was the ice, fog, and bitter weather. The arctic environment was responsible for the loss of numerous ships and men engaged in whaling on the northern grounds (Chatterton 1930:38, 39, 146). In 1871, thirty-three vessels in the Arctic Sea, nearly the whole of the fleet, were destroyed by ice. It is not surprising, therefore, that the songs of the arctic fisheries make many references to the bitter arctic weather:

> And when we came to that cold countrie,
> Where the frost and snow and the wind doth blow
> And the daylight never away.

> Where the icebergs float and the stormy winds blow
> Where the land and the ocean is covered with snow (Grieg 1963:lxxxv).

> Through many a blow of frost and snow
> And bitter squalls of hail
> Our spars were bent and our canvas rent
> As we braved the northern gale

> The horried isles of ice cut tiles
> That deck the Arctic sea (Huntington 1964:38).

The sperm whale, unlike the right and bowhead whales, was well armed and pugnacious and had teeth so that he could attack with either tail or jaw. A whaling proverb states it concisely, "Beware of a sperm's jaw and a right whale's flukes" (Ashley 1938:65; Chatterton 1930:15, 80). Thus, in the following song it is possible to identify the type of whale being hunted by the allusion to the whale's jaw:

> Now this advice 'tis well to take
> To place your iron firm sir
> And look out sharp and keep quite clear
> From fins and flukes and jaws sir (Huntington 1964:21–22).

This identification is supported by the first stanza of this song which describes the whales as swimming in shoals. "Sperm whales are found in pods or schools, except for an occasional 'lone bull'... but the Bowhead whales are not gregarious. Generally they swim singly or in twos or threes" (Ashley 1938:75).

> A whaling scene I'll now relate
> On ocean's bosom wide
> In boats away far from their ship
> In chase of shoals of whales sir (Huntington 1964:21).

In the song "The Cruise of the Dove," it is also mentioned that the whale pursued is the sperm, and there is a reference to their swimming in schools in the phrase "logs around us:"

> With courage undaunted by oars and by sail
> So nimble we chased the spermaceti whale....
>
> Right ahead and abeam on each hand them we spy
> Like logs around us so sweetly they lie (Huntington 1964:13–14).

In some cases, it is difficult to definitely identify the type of whale that was being hunted merely by referring to words or phrases in the song texts. Such allusions are quite capable of disappearing in the process of oral transmission, even in close variants of the same song. In one version of "The Coast of Peru," there is nothing to indicate the type of whale captured, although at the outset of the song it is clearly stated that their intended prey is sperm whale (Huntington 1964:2). In another version of the same song, though the intended prey is sperm whale, the attack described is one on the right whale because of the reference to the "long dart." Right whales were harpooned from a greater distance than sperm whales because of the greater sweep of its flukes (Ashley 1938:78–79). The "long dart" was used exclusively for an attack on the right whale (Lloyd and MacColl 1956).

> Lay on said the harpooner
> For I'm hell to long dart (side 1, band 7).

In Huntington's version of the song, it merely says:

> Lay on Captain Bunker
> I'm hell for to dart (Huntington 1964:3)

Arctic whalers did not carry tryworks aboard ship for boiling down the blubber to extract the oil. They brought the blubber home in casks since the cold northern temperatures helped preserve it, and their voyages rarely lasted longer than six months. For the longer sperm whale voyages in tropical regions, it was necessary to have a works aboard to "try out" the oil. British Greenland whalers did not carry tryworks aboard before 1875 (Ashley 1938:96), and by that time whaling was a dying industry. It is not to be expected therefore, that trying out the whale would be mentioned in the songs of the Greenland fishery, and it is not.[10] But tryworks are often mentioned in the songs about the sperm whale fishery:

> We towed him along side
> And with many a shout
> We soon cut him in
> And began to try out
> Now our whale she is tried
> And likewise stowed down (Huntington 1964:4).

Trying out the oil was arduous work. Once whales were captured, the crew would work long watches until the last barrel of oil was stowed below. Razor-sharp cutting implements were employed, the decks of the ship were slippery with blood and oil, the sails were begrimed with soot, and there was the ever-present danger of fire. Numerous songs refer to the process even if they never describe its dirty and dangerous character.

Now our whales are turned up and we prepare for our toil
We will soon get on board with the blubber to boil
When it's boiled out and stowed down in the hold
We'll drink greasy luck to the whalers so bold (Huntington 1964:15)

Row row row
In our vessel she must go
Changed into a liquid stream
O'er the broad Pacific's swell (20).

Whaling songs would seem to support Boas's view of folklore as a mirror of culture. The culture and the environment of the whalers are realistically depicted, often in great detail. The songs are clearly a product of the occupational life. If Boas and Benedict are right however, there is little room for wish fulfillment or compensation. The songs adhere too closely to reality. There are no obvious fantasy elements, exaggerations, or idealizations that might serve to fulfill wishes.[11]

Melville Jacobs criticized Boas's approach to oral literature. Jacobs saw the study of the content of oral literature as a check on the overt, expressed, institutionalized elements of culture, and as a clue to those elements of which the society's members were totally unconscious (Jacobs 1959a:130). According to Jacobs, neither Boas nor other folklorists had "perceived or demonstrated that the contents of myths and tales included projections of *points of stress* in the society: that is, events and social relationships portrayed in an oral literature connected with relationships unsatisfactorily resolved by social structure and custom" (Jacobs 1959b:130, my emphasis). Thus, the correspondences between folklore and culture might be regarded as indicators of stress rather than as wish fulfillments. In other words, the folklore was more symptom than consolation.

Certain tension-ridden relationships portrayed in the songs—those between the boat crews of the same ship and between crew members of different nationalities—have already been discussed. Many of the songs also explicitly express resentment against the captain and the mates. A great number of ships' officers treated their crews with brutality and contempt. Strict discipline on board a whaler was required because the work was not only hazardous and demanding, but there were some rough, untrustworthy, and downright dangerous people among the whaling crews. Nevertheless, accounts suggest that physical brutality and verbal abuse were standard procedure (Hohman 1928:120–125).

> Here's to all skippers and all mates
> I wish you may do well
> And when you die may the devil
> Kick you all into hell (Huntington 1964:46)
>
> They'll flog you for the least offense
> And that is frequent too
> And the best that you will get from them
> Is plenty more work to do
> So do it now and damn your eyes
> I will flog you till you're (blue)
> My boys I wouldn't say it all
> But it is all too true (16–17).
>
> The captain's name was Jenny
> From Mattapoisett town
> He walks upon the quarterdeck
> And there you'll see him frown
> He is the meanest captain
> That ever you did see (35).
>
> For toward the end of the voyage they treat you mighty rough
> They cause you trials and tribulations
> For if you have any pay they would have you run away
> And pocket all your earnings on Desolation (39).

The last verse refers specifically to a practice not uncommon in the whaling industry. Towards the beginning of a voyage, when a lot of money had been invested in acquiring and equipping each individual whaleman, captains and mates were very concerned about desertion of crew in foreign ports. They did everything in their power to prevent it. But as a ship neared its capacity of cargo and the return to home port was anticipated, some unscrupulous officers tried to create conditions that would promote desertion. A greater portion of the cargo would then fall to ship masters and owners (Hohman 1928:66–67).

There were some captains, however, who managed to maintain discipline on their ships without the constant employ of physical abuse, and who earned the respect of their crews (Hohman

1928:125). Songs record such characters as well, although less often:

> Our captain's name was Butler
> A man fine and bold (Huntington 1964:14).
>
> The captain walked the quarterdeck
> And a jolly little fellow was he (12).
>
> When this news to our captain came
> It grieved his heart full sore
> And for the loss of a 'prentice boy
> It was half mast colors all brave boys (12).

This last verse, in some versions is altered to make the captain appear as a villain with no feelings whatsoever for his crews:

> The whale gave a flurry with his tail
> He upset the boat lost a half a dozen men. . . .
> Bad news bad news the captain said
> It grieved his heart full sore
> But the losing of the hundred barrel whale
> It grieved him ten times more (Lloyd and MacColl 1956: side 1, band 1).

If a boat was overturned or destroyed in the pursuit of a whale, the killed whale would be attended to before the crew clinging to the wreckage of their craft in mid-ocean was rescued (Bullen 1899:42).

Even if a captain were not abusive, feelings toward him would have been ambivalent. The crew had to depend on the captain to navigate the ship, find the whales, and see them safely through the voyage. Consequently, crews would have wished to regard him as dependable and concerned with their welfare; someone worthy of trust and admiration. The captain, however, was also responsible for making rules and meting out punishment, so he was resented as well.

The outstanding relationship that was unresolved in the whaling enterprise was that between the whalers and the whale, since the whale was outside social structure. A whale's behavior is not governed by social rules and cultural practices. As the outcome of an encounter with a whale was uncertain, this relationship was obviously a point of stress. This uncertainty is clearly reflected in the popular whaling proverb, "A dead whale or a stove boat" (Chatterton 1930:73). In Jacobs's view, therefore, it is no surprise that the encounter with a whale would be projected upon the screen of folklore. Indeed, an attack upon a whale is a major motif in most whaling songs. Generally, the whalers are successful in their attack on the whale, although there are songs in which the whale gets the best of the situation (Huntington 1964:11–12).[12] Because of the uncertainty in the relationship, the whaler's attitude toward the whale is also ambivalent. The whale is often nobly referred to as "mighty whale (19), "mighty mountain (20), and as the mighty mythological sea-beast of the Bible, "Leviathan" (Huntington 1964:20). The whale is also "our friend the enemy" (Bullen 1899:38), and in "The Wounded Whale," the whale is actually mocked while in its death throes:

> While so loud and so shrill the cry from our seamen
> Mocking the whale in her terrible hour
> Now looking at her die see the blue signal fly
> Here she goes fin out and the contest is o'er (79).

Boat crews did in fact cheer when a whale ceased its struggle and turned fin out (Hohman 1928:165).

All the points of tension reflected in whaling songs, however, are about conscious tensions. The whalers were hardly unaware of the racial animosities among the crew, their abuse by ship's officers, or the potentially disastrous outcomes of their encounters with whales. Jacobs has argued that what is overtly denied and repressed is projected on the screen of folklore (Jacobs 1959a:130). The stresses depicted in whaling songs, however, were not matters of unconscious repression. The points of stress were entirely conscious, although the occupational culture may have offered few methods or opportunities for airing or alleviating them. If the tensions were conscious, the emotions they engendered would still require suppression and control. This might explain why even conscious points of stress are projected onto the screen of folklore.

The songs seem to have been oblivious to the *system* which exploited the whalers. This exploitation was rooted not merely in capitalistic labor but in a particular form of economic enterprise in which the whalers assumed much of the entrepreneurial risk yet garnered few of the rewards. Whaling proceeded according to a system of "lays" or shares. Whalers' compensation was a percentage of the cargo. Between 1836 and 1885, an American whaling captain might receive somewhere between six to nine percent of the value of the cargo. A green hand during this period might receive about a half a percent. Whalers were not paid a time or piece wage. While on board the vessel, they paid for everything except sleeping accommodations and food (both were often horrific). Replacement clothing, tobacco, medicine, and other needs had to be purchased out of ship's stores at extortionate rates. Thus whalers assumed the same business risks as the owners and agents but received no additional compensation for the assumption of those risks. If a venture were unsuccessful or only modestly successful, years of labor could result in debilitating debt. Unskilled forms of shore labor had clear advantages over whaling. The most menial shore laborers earned two to three times what whalers might earn in the course of a voyage (Hohman 1928:217–243). The songs never confront or criticize this economic system. The songs always direct opposition to individuals or statuses: masters, mates, and owners. The system of lays itself was never challenged in reality or in the folklore. The exploitive nature of the economic system went unrecognized and unchallenged.

Boas and Benedict would have undoubtedly felt that whaling songs fully confirmed the hypothesis that social life determined folklore content. Yet even they might have wondered why there was so little fantasy in the songs. Why did whalers sing about an environment that was utterly familiar and that described their occupation so faithfully? There were so many whaling adventure themes, exotic stories, and narrow-escape incidents that they could have drawn upon for the creation of song (Chatterton 1930:124), that a question remains as to the purposes of singing about such commonplace experience.[13]

Whaling songs overwhelmingly deal with the hunt and capture of a whale and the trying out of its oil. These images are quite realistic. Yet it is in these realistic images that the basic wishes of the whalers are embedded: the wish for a full ship and the wish to return home. The capture of the whale is a symbol of the return home because whaling ships only returned to their home ports when they were filled with oil:

With our ship bumper-full we'll homeward repair (Grieg 1963:lxxxv)

Our ship she is full and home we are bound (Huntington 1964:15).

That a strong wish to return home existed among the whalers is unquestionable. Whaling voyages could last three or four years. The ship *George* had been away from her homeport for forty-seven months and had succeeded only in taking 1200 barrels of oil (Chatterton 1930:77). The longest voyage on record lasted *eleven years*. The desertion rate from whalers was understandably high (Hohman 1928:64–69; Ashley 1938:103–105).

That the whaling scene was a symbol of the wish to return home is confirmed by the differences found between songs of the sperm whale and the Greenland fisheries. The capture of the whale served as a wish fulfillment only in the sperm whale fishery. Greenland voyages lasted only six months, the six summer months, and the ships then left the whaling grounds before winter set in–regardless of how many whales had been caught. Consequently, descriptions of the capture of whales are absent in the songs of the Greenland fishery. The one description of an attack on a whale in the songs of the Greenland fishery has the whale escape (Huntington 1964:11–12). In the songs of the sperm whale fishery, however, descriptions of the capture of whales appear. The devotion to the procedure of capturing the whale, boiling down the oil and stowing it below was an expression of the wish for a "full ship"—the prerequisite for the return home.

In the sperm whale fishery there often would be periods of weeks or months when no whales would be sighted, let alone taken (Chatterton 1930:74). If these whaling songs were sung during these periods when the wish to return home was undoubtedly at its peak, it would support the hypothesis that they functioned as a wish fulfillment. There is no definite evidence that the songs were sung during these periods, as the context in which folksongs were sung was rarely recorded. Ashley, however, in describing these long periods of ill luck, offered some indication:

> In the duration of a long whaling voyage there came inevitably a time when no whales were taken or sighted for weeks, or even months, when apparently there was none left in the ocean, when one day, no different from all the rest, succeeded another that seemed interminable; *a time when home and the end of the voyage were still so far away that it was futile to look forward to them.* The same food, the same faces, the same sea, and the same routine, day after day without end, *and not one barrel of oil nearer "full ship"*.... Nerves began to fray; friends began to look askance at one another, *to interrupt familiar songs and yarns* (1938:102, my emphasis).

Songs were sung during these long periods of idleness, when the prospects of return home were at their lowest. Those songs that described the whaling scene might have served as a fulfillment of the wish; a wish if uttered explicitly might lead to frustration, anger, and conflict.

The association of the whaling scene with the wish of return is also supported by the whalers' art of scrimshaw. Scrimshaw was a process of carving or etching whale tooth and bone. The products were sometimes useful but mostly ornamental. Most scrimshaw was made "as keepsakes for the folks at home" (Stackpole 1958:1). The images etched into the tooth and bone were mainly those of women, ships, and the whaling scene—the whaling scene being the dominant image in scrimshaw art (51). Images of women in scrimshaw demonstrate that it was an art practiced when thoughts of wives and sweethearts at home were paramount. Whalers lavished their greatest effort and care in making a busk—a long flat vertical stay in the front of a corset—because a busk would be worn close to a woman's heart. This piece of whalebone was regularly illustrated with images of the whaling scene (114).

The time for scrimshaw and the time for songs were the same; the long periods of idleness when no whales were sighted and no whaling could be done (Ashley 1938:102–103). Thoughts of home would have been paramount in the minds of whalers at those times, and that is when images of men killing whales and boiling down their oil were inscribed in both their oral and material arts.

If folklore is compensatory and fulfills wishes, it does not necessarily demand the imagining of exotic landscapes, the performance of impossible or unusual tasks, or the reaping of stupendous rewards. The young child may identify with the unpromising hero who outwits giants, slays dragons, and wins kingdoms because the child is weak, inexperienced, and impoverished. The folktale hero fulfills the child's wishes for position and mastery in a world dominated by powerful adults. Fantasies, however, are contextual. The whalers' wishes were to do what they were paid to do, to do it safely and well, and to complete the enterprise in as short a period as possible. They had no need for extravagant fantasies. The whalers' wishes were to scale, and their fantasies were constructed out of the stuff of their everyday lives.

3. Totemism and the A.E.F. Revisited

Totemism was a word coined in the nineteenth century to label a special relationship that was believed to exist between the members of a social group and a species of animal, plant, or material object. Often the members of the group believed themselves to be descended from their totem species. Although the term totemism derived from an Ojibway word, it was believed that the "classic" cases of totemism were to be found in Australia (Spencer and Gillan 1899). Totemistic beliefs regulated a range of social, political, economic, and religious behaviors in these hunting and foraging societies. Early folklorists attempted to understand both the origins of totemism and its impact on human affairs (Frazer 1934[1910]; Lang 1970 [1905]).

The theories that folklorists and anthropologists use to explain behavior, belief, and social structure develop, for the most part, in attempts to understand societies unlike our own; societies often characterized as "primitive" or "folk." The extent to which a theoretical perspective has value, however, depends upon its application to situations beyond those in which it is first developed and to which it is first applied. A theory that is applicable only to a single case is not much of a theory (although a theory that purports to explain everything is not likely to be much of a theory either.) But anthropologists have pointed to behaviors in modern Western societies that appear in some basic respects to mirror what takes place in the totemic complexes reported for technologically simple societies. To what extent can a theory developed to understand totemism among hunters and foragers be applied to the analysis and understanding of practices in complex societies?

> *I am become death, destroyer of worlds.*
> —Bhagavad-Gita

IN 1924, RALPH LINTON called attention to the curious development of a "pseudo-totemic complex" among the members of the 42nd division of the American Expeditionary Force stationed in France during the First World War (Linton 1924). The 42nd division, it was said, had been named the Rainbow Division by higher officials because it comprised units from an assortment of states whose regimental colors were as variegated as a rainbow. After the division arrived in France, non-division personnel persisted in referring to division members as "Rainbow" and individual division members would identify themselves as such as well. Several months after the use of this name became prevalent, a feeling of sympathy developed between the divisional organization and its namesake. At first, the appearance of a rainbow was considered a good omen for the division. Later a belief became entrenched that a rainbow always appeared when the division went into battle. An appearance of a rainbow over the lines in the evening was considered especially lucky, and after a victory, soldiers attested to the appearance of such rainbows even when meteorological conditions made such appearances very unlikely (297).

Because of contact with other divisions who had emblems, the rainbow later developed as a divisional emblem, and was surreptitiously painted upon various kinds of divisional equipment. After the armistice, a standardized design was officially permitted. A similar development took place with individual shoulder insignias. Linton postulated that the complex of behavior and belief that developed in the A.E.F. was fully as rich as those designated "totemic" in many primitive societies.

Claude Lévi-Strauss cites Linton's article as a contribution to the American anthropological indifference to the totemic problem; for what had been made eminently clear since the writings of Franz Boas and Alexander Goldenweiser in the early decades of the twentieth century was that there was no stable complex of traits that could be delimited by the term *totemism*. In reality, the use of plants, animals and other natural phenomena as names or emblems; the belief in a relationship (often of descent) between clan and species; killing and eating taboos; and exogamous clan organization only rarely coincide in a single ethnographic situation, although each of these traits is often encountered in the absence of the others (Goldenweiser 1910:264–268). Lévi-Strauss, consequently, denies the reality of any institution that might properly be labeled *totemism* and characterizes most of the anthropological scholarship on totemism as the investigation of an "illusion" (1963a:15). But where Lévi-Strauss was unwilling to grant totemism institutional existence, he was willing to recognize it as a process of the human mind; as a "classificatory device whereby discrete elements of the external world are associated with discrete elements of the social world" (1963b:7).

Under this radically reformulated definition, the catalogue of contemporary totemic occurrences may be extended. The two cases presented below derive from the more recent experiences of American "expeditionary forces" in Vietnam. These cases permit an appreciation of the diversity of forms generated by the totemic process, as well as an evaluation of Lévi-Strauss's theory in accounting for the behavior and belief of "civilized," and not merely "savage," social groups.

The first case developed in 1967 and 1968 among the members of an Air Force Para-Rescue Squadron who were operating as military police securing the perimeters of American air bases in Vietnam. Generally, the men of this squadron would undertake night and day patrols in teams of twelve to intercept North Vietnamese regulars and Viet Cong that were active in the area. On one occasion, while on patrol, the team was involved in a major firefight that developed between the 101st Airborne Brigade and some North Vietnamese regulars. There was extensive small arms and mortar fire and the team was pinned down in trenches awaiting the arrival of support gunships and rescue. During the heaviest part of the fight, however, the men noticed that some distance off to one side of the trench, a mongoose was attacking a large snake (not a cobra). Despite all that was taking place, the men became fascinated with the progress of this mini-battle in the world of nature. As it turned out, the mongoose was victorious, and after the firefight ended, the team returned to base bringing the mongoose with them. When one of the men suggested that the mongoose had been instrumental in turning the tide of battle, the notion was generally disputed. But once the idea had been planted, it was not so easily dismissed: "A lot of guys scoffed at it. I myself kind of thought about it, laughed about it, and forgot about it until the next time around. When we were pulling security, and when you are alone and when you are worried about being wounded or killed, you know, you begin to think about things like that" (Interview with A. Herald [pseud.], 3 March 1972).

Shortly, though not immediately, after the firefight, security teams began to take the mongoose with them on patrol. It was on one of these patrols—led by the mongoose tethered to a little leash—that another transformation in the group's attitude toward the mongoose occurred. A Viet Cong had planted grenades and dug himself in alongside the trail awaiting the passage of American troops. It would have been possible for the lead men to have overlooked the ambush, but the hairs on the mongoose's back went up and it started jumping up and down. Because of the antics of the mongoose, this Viet Cong "zapper," as he was called, was spotted.

Because of these incidents, the mongoose began to assume a more important place in the thinking and behavior of the group: "We really came to rely on the mongoose to come through. It's like we turned off our own senses and relied on the mongoose's alone. A lot of guys really dropped their guard. They figured that depending [upon] how the mongoose would react while we were on patrol was how we would fare" (Herald, 3 March 1972). Subsequently, the mongoose's senses were extended not only to the presence of the enemy and the imminence of a firefight, but to the prediction of the outcome of the fight as well. The mongoose would remain comparatively passive in what would turn out to be small skirmishes; but in fights where it became necessary to call in army units or air support, the animal's behavior would appear much more frenetic.

This relationship between the group and the mongoose had reached a level that might be characterized as "mystical." It was a relationship that my informant found difficult to express: "I feel that we established a closeness with the mongoose. I mean closer than you can get with a typical domestic pet. I don't really know how to put it into words—I mean it seems kind of ridiculous to say a oneness—but I really thought that the mongoose was looking out for us and we were looking out for the mongoose" (Herald, 3 March 1972).[1]

Members of this squadron eventually came to be known by other groups as "Mongoose." Trucks were painted with mongoose figures and some squadron members even had themselves tattooed. By the time my informant left Vietnam, this complex of behavior closely resembled that described by Linton for the 42nd Division in France.

The second case involving the totemic process varies considerably from the first. It developed among a platoon of approximately twenty infantrymen in 1969 and 1970. The skull of a Vietnamese was dug up by platoon members while routinely exploring a fresh gravesite for possible caches of enemy arms and ammunition. Skulls were in demand in the infantry. Infantrymen would keep them while they were in Vietnam and then would try to smuggle them out of the country. They were usually unsuccessful because skulls, I was informed, never seemed to get through the mail. This particular skull, however, was not claimed by any individual and became a group possession. It was named "Bruce," given a hat, sunglasses, a combat infantry badge and even a pair of pants, and was mounted on the top of a stake. Whenever the platoon moved from one encampment to another, Bruce moved with them. The stake would be planted in the ground to serve as an identification marker for the platoon. Within the platoon encampment, whenever there were parties or guys would get together drinking, or if group pictures were being taken, someone always would make sure Bruce was involved. When on the move through Vietnamese villages, Bruce would often be brandished in order to intimidate the local population. The members of the platoon implied that the skull on the pole was a fate that uncooperative Vietnamese could expect. The more contemptuous the reaction elicited from the Vietnamese, the greater the hilarity of the men.

The platoon in general was committed to the aggravation of all but other combat infantry. In fact, anyone who was not combat infantry was considered a "Rimp." Rimp is a phonetically pronounceable shift from *r-e-m-f* which is the acronym for *rear-echelon motherfucker*. Combat infantry were known as *Grunts*.[2] Rear-echelon people had a very easy tour of duty from the point of view of combat infantry. They accumulated more money, had less rigorous assignments, received quicker promotions, and they didn't have to do any dirty work (since they had the South Vietnamese population to do everything for them). They were the object of a great deal of hostility and antagonism (to the extent that occasional shots were fired at them). Whenever the platoon would enter or leave a base, they would yell and curse and throw things at the rear-echelon people. Those who tried to be friendly towards them would meet with rejection. If someone gave them the peace sign they would give him the "finger." If anyone shouted "peace" they would yell "war" and suggest they "shouldn't knock something until they tried it." All peace slogans and hymns were revised with "war" and "aggression" substitutes. With all of this, they would brandish Bruce about at the end of his pole (Interview with S. Barton [pseud.], 14 May 1975).

According to Lévi-Strauss's definition of the totemic process cited above, both of the behavior-belief complexes described should qualify as instances of totemism. Each involves a classificatory act in which elements of the natural world are associated with elements of the social world. Admittedly, the principles of association differ. The mongoose stood in some sort of mystical relationship to the Air Force Para-Rescue Squadron. Bruce, however, was considered a member of the infantry platoon. Nevertheless, both could serve as emblems to represent the entire social group.[3]

Structuralists have viewed totemic representations as a code. The choice of representations is not arbitrary but, rather, is designed to convey messages about social realities utilizing symbols drawn from the world of nature organized in a series of contrasts and oppositions (Lévi-Strauss 1963b:2). The natural species are often chosen as symbols not because they are "good to eat" (as Radcliffe-Brown proposed in his first theory of totemism [1952:129–130]), but because they are "good to think" (Lévi-Strauss 1963a:89). This general perspective is not without value in the analysis of the contemporary data, although modifications in some of its specific corollaries are necessary.

The elevation of the mongoose to significance for the para-rescue squadron is based upon a "thinkability" that is emotionally charged and contextually derived. It is only in the context of a particular life and death struggle with the enemy that the opposition between mongoose and snake becomes a "significant thinkable." Given all the possibilities of stimuli received by the security team during the firefight, it is only the stimulus of the mongoose fighting the snake that is accorded significance because of its structural similarity to the social reality of the moment. It must have been viewed by the team members in terms of a homology: *we are to the enemy as the mongoose is to the snake.* It is only the temporal coincidence of conflict in the social and natural worlds that accords the mongoose its special status. It is important to note that a lasting identification develops between only one set of terms in the homology: the security team and the mongoose. No permanent association develops between the enemy and the snake, for the enemy is never faunally characterized. The structure as a whole does not persist. Furthermore, the identification with the mongoose required additional reinforcement for its stabilization. That reinforcement came when the mongoose proved instrumental in saving the team from ambush. After that incident, the identification with mongoose was firmly established.

When the mongoose began to be employed as an emblem and members of the squadron were referred to as "Mongoose," this identification achieved autonomy. It was no longer dependent upon the original homology for its significance. Nor can it be understood at the level of the social system. There is no way to contrast "Mongoose" with the "Wolf Hounds" (an army unit that was operating at the same time) and understand the mongoose as a symbol of the group. The process by which the mongoose achieved symbolic significance is not relevant to the differentiation of military units from one another. When they are viewed from the perspective of social differentiation, these totems may be regarded as arbitrary.

Unlike the case with the mongoose, skulls already possessed what Radcliffe-Brown has called "ritual value" prior to the elevation of Bruce to a group emblem (1939:18–19). The value of skulls at the individual level, however, is directly related to the significance of Bruce as a group symbol. The combat infantry saw themselves as markedly distinct from all other American groups. They were the only ones that were actively engaged on a day-to-day basis in a deadly shooting war. Members of the platoon anticipated being killed or maimed in combat. Rimps, on the other hand, though nominally a part of the Vietnam War, were ensconced in relative safety and comfort. They were the very antithesis of what the real war was all about. They represented all the values, attitudes and behaviors alien to a theater of war. The combat infantryman inverted all of these values, and these inversions were most clearly reflected in platoon songs. For example, "Red roses for a blue lady" became "Red tracers for my M-16"; "All we are saying is give peace a chance" became "All we are saying is give war a chance"; and "And we'll all feel gay when Johnny comes marching home" became "We'll all be dead by Christmas of this year." If we wished to phrase the relationship between combat infantry and rear-echelon personnel formally it might read: *rimps are to grunts as living men are to dead men*. The realization of this abstract formula is the recruitment of a dead man into the platoon. Bruce was a platoon *member*. He possessed elements of infantry uniform, he appeared in platoon pictures, and he was listed in unofficial platoon rosters.

Despite the differences between the behavior-belief complexes described in our two examples above, both are classifiable as totemism. They are classifications of aspects of a social world in terms of a natural one. Moreover, it would appear that elements of current theory are useful in illuminating the dynamics of both totemic processes. Each may be expressed in terms of a homology that provides an insight into the nature of the relationship between species and social group.[4] Nevertheless, questions arise regarding the applicability of other aspects of Lévi-Strauss's analysis; most notably, his contention that totemism involves a homology "not between social groups and natural species but between the differences which manifest themselves on the level of groups on the one hand and that of species on the other. They are thus based on the postulate of a homology between *two systems of differences*, one of which occurs in nature and the other in culture.... This structure would be fundamentally impaired if ... the entire system of homologies were transferred from relations to terms" (1966:115).

In the examples from Vietnam, however, it is the analogy of terms that is fundamental. The para-rescue squadron is like the mongoose; the combat infantry platoon is like Bruce. Systems of difference play no part here. The system resolves itself into a relationship between individual terms.

The 42nd Division's sojourn in France during World War I gave rise to a case of totemism that was motivated in part by its "Rainbow" name. That was not the case for the two groups in the Vietnam conflict. Nevertheless, all these contemporary cases of totemism proceed from acts of social classification shaped, in part, by feelings of fear and foreboding with two of the cases rationalized by quasi-supernatural belief. Linton's hypothesis that contemporary and "primitive totemism are results of the same social and supernatural tendencies" expressed under different conditions seems on the mark (1924:299). The value of any anthropological or folkloric method of analysis and interpretation applied to social groups around the world can only be reckoned in terms of what it ultimately can teach us about behavior and belief in our own culture.

4. The Structure of a Joke Repertoire

Structure is a relationship of parts; to one another and to the whole which they comprise. Folklore genres and sub-genres are often defined and distinguished in terms of their structures (Propp 1968; Georges and Dundes 1963), and certain structures may be characteristic of particular cultural traditions (Dundes 1963). Although jokes have long been defined in structural terms (Koestler 1964:35; Raskin 1985:99; Oring 1992:1–6), joke structure has not been utilized to unravel joke meaning. Yet, the quest for the meaning of folklore may depend exactly upon the ways contents are arranged within specific genres. Beyond the structure of the jokes themselves, there is the question of the structure of a repertoire as a whole. The repertoires of individuals and groups—whether of jokes, tales, or songs—are unlikely to be random collections of texts. Texts can relate to one another and reveal an order that bears on their meaning and points to the reasons they are valued and performed.

Jokes are well-known in American culture. There can be, however, a danger in the analysis of familiar and even prized joke materials. The sense of appreciation may short-circuit understanding—not of the humor itself—but of how the jokes do their humorous work. There are advantages in analyzing exotic materials even—perhaps especially—if that humor fails to amuse and entertain the analyst. Undistracted by the qualities of particular jokes, insights may be obtained that can be brought back to the analysis and understanding of our own humorous expressions allowing them to be seen in a new light.

> *A joke is not anything that resides in its thought,*
> *we must look for it in the form.*
>
> —Sigmund Freud

ALL SOCIETIES categorize the elements of their physical, social, and cultural reality. Folklore, as one aspect of that reality, presents no exception to this rule and is classified in accordance with various schemes, simple or complex, depending on the extent to which a society attributes importance to its oral literature. There have always been a large number of terms in Hebrew employed in the classification of Jewish verbal culture. Since biblical times, many literary categories have been distinguished: *mashal* (exemplum, proverb), *agadah* (legend), *midrash* (homiletic interpretation), *sippur* (story), *ma'aseh* (tale), *ḥidah* (riddle), *ḥokhma* (wisdom), *bediḥah* (joke). Each of these categories bears a Hebrew name and a venerable genealogy in the Hebrew lexicon. However, with the Jewish resettlement of Palestine, a new category came into being—*chizbat* [tʃizbæt]. It is immediately evident that this category sports a non-Hebrew title as [tʃ] is not a Hebrew phoneme. Indeed, *chizbat* is the sound feminine plural of the Palestinian Arabic *chizba* and means "lies." This term came into Hebrew usage in the 1940s with the formation of the Palmach and came to designate their particular repertoire of humorous jokes and anecdotes.

The Palmach

The Palmach was an underground commando organization formed by the Haganah High Command in 1941 in response to the threat of a Nazi invasion of Palestine. After the German defeat at El Alamein, the Palmach was maintained to provide the *yishuv* [the Jewish community in Palestine] with a trained, fully-mobilized strike force. Because the Palmach was an illegal organization in the eyes of the British authorities that governed Palestine, and because the funds to support such a force were lacking in the yishuv, Palmach platoons were stationed on kibbutzim [collective farms] throughout the country. The kibbutz offered a cover for Palmach members and their activities. Palmach recruits worked a half of every month to earn their bed and board and were thus able to engage in military training for the other half. Until the termination of the British Mandate over Palestine, the Palmach worked, trained, promoted illegal immigration, protected yishuv settlements and transportation, and occasionally engaged British police and army units. With the United Nations' partition of Palestine in 1947, the withdrawal of British forces, and the declaration of the State of Israel in 1948, Palmach battalions absorbed the brunt of the Arab attacks while the remainder of the country mobilized for war. During the War of Independence, although its battalions remained intact, the Palmach was officially disbanded and absorbed into Zeva Haganah Le-Israel, the Israeli Defense Forces (Alon 1970, 1971).

Militarily, the Palmach was in some sense a parody of a modern army. Its underground status required that it conduct acquisitions, recruitment, training, and operations while avoiding detection by a British police and military garrison that exceeded 100,000 men. Its arsenal was obsolete or homemade and always insufficient. Membership in the Palmach was voluntary, and those who volunteered resisted strong temptations to serve in the British Army in the war against Germany or in the more extreme underground organizations in their struggle against the British. They served in order to provide the yishuv with a capable and dependable strike force at the command of its elected leaders. The Palmach consisted of dedicated youth, male and female, who were on a first name basis with their officers, devoted more than half their time to agricultural labor, were immersed in the ideals, values, and lifestyles of the kibbutzim on which they worked, and whose concept of punishment was exclusion from some military operation or exercise. The Palmach represented the coming of age of the first significant generation of *sabra* [native born] youth. Their unique situation was not lost upon them, as they said: "The Jews of Israel are the elite of the Jewish people, and the Palmach is the elite of the yishuv" (Guri 1968:147).[1] It was within such a group that the chizbat first crystallized.

The Chizbat

The chizbat is a body of jokes, anecdotes, and tall tales. Many concern Palmach figures engaged in characteristic Palmach activities: stealing chickens from the kibbutz, using and misusing the Hebrew language, operating against or avoiding the British, in conflict with Arabs, training, illegal immigration, playing practical jokes on members of the general population. Certain select characters that had no special association with the Palmach, such as Old Elyovich of Kfar Giladi, Avraham Shapira of Petah Tikvah, Suramello of Jerusalem, and Dr. Mahmoud of Beit-Jann, also appear prominently in the chizbat repertoire.

But if the chizbat is an anecdote or joke that concerns characters or situations in the yishuv, it cannot be said to include all anecdotes concerning such characters and situations. The word for "joke" in Hebrew is *bediḥah*, and there were many stories about situations in the yishuv that were regarded by the Palmach as *bediḥot* rather than as chizbat. Informants regularly made the point that although the chizbat literally meant "lies," it expressed some kind of truth: "It doesn't have to be all right, but it's not all wrong" (Interview with Hayyim Guri, 22 February 1970); "A story that happened but a little bit imagination" (Interview with Didi Menusi, 2 November 1970); "A chizbat is always a little bit true" (Interview with Shaul Beber, 11 November 1969). At first, one suspects that by truth, informants mean that the characters named in the chizbat were real people or the events depicted bore some relation to actual occurrences. But when the same informants attested to the historical veracity of one chizbat and denied with surety any basis for another, this view is not sustainable. What is meant by "truth" would seem to relate not to any historical reality but to some ahistorical, metaphorical realm. It is this quality of truth that distinguishes the chizbat from the *bediḥah*—the joke: "There were many attempts to make jokes into chizbat so that they would be more acceptable, and they breathed their last. You felt by the smell that it was essentially a joke. . . . It is possible that occasional jokes sneaked into the corpus of chizbat, that were worked into chizbat, but for us it didn't matter because it acquired a new value" (Interview with Dan Ben-Amotz, 4 February 1970). What then made an anecdote about a character, situation, or event a chizbat rather than an ordinary joke? What kind of transformation would be necessary to change a joke into a chizbat?

Humor

Humor involves the linking of disparate conceptual categories and their associated ideas. Humor is based upon incongruity, but not any incongruity but *appropriate incongruity*. A joke is a form of humor in which an appropriate incongruity is only revealed in the final utterance (Oring 1992:81–93). For example: Q: When is a door not a door? A: When it's ajar [a jar]. This riddle is a type of joke common among older children. The basic incongruity is formulated in the riddle question; there is something that is both a door and not-a-door at the same time. The answer suggests a means by which such an incongruity can be made appropriate. A door that is "a jar" is clearly not a door but, at the same time, it is virtually indistinguishable phonologically from a door that is "ajar," a state that is appropriate to a door. The incongruity—indeed, contradiction—proffered in the riddle question is overcome by recontextualizing the problem in terms of the homophonies of the English language. Humor depends upon apprehending the two incongruous domains that are conjoined, if only by a trick, in the punchline.

Not all jokes are linguistic jokes. Many are conceptual jokes and their appropriateness lies in a conceptual relation rather than a linguistic one. For example,

> A bald-headed man and his friend are standing outside a restaurant after eating dinner. Just then a seagull flies over and defecates on the bald man's head. The friend is very upset and says, "Oh, that's awful. Can I do something? Let me get some toilet paper."
>
> The bald man rumbles, "Don't bother. He's probably a quarter of a mile away by now."

Toilet paper, while it is normally used for wiping behinds—and human behinds at that—is also used on occasion for wiping up small amounts of dirty and defiling substances. This latter use is what a joke listener should presume when he hears the friend's offer to get some toilet paper. It is incongruous when the bald man assumes the toilet paper is for the behind of the bird, but it is also appropriate because the chief function of toilet paper is for wiping bottoms, not heads.

Chizbat are, for the most part, jokes, but they are by no means transparent texts. They often depend upon personal, local, or other esoteric cultural knowledge.

> On Sabbath afternoons, the mayor of Tiberias goes out, generally in the accompaniment of his wife, and strolls pleasantly in the streets. Once, he passed the house of Ofer and saw Mr. and Mrs. Beber sitting on the porch. "Shalom, Mr. Beber," said the mayor. "Shalom, honorable mayor," said Ofer's father. "Can we come in for a bit?" asked the mayor. "Please, please," said Ofer's parents. They brought chairs out onto the porch and put on the table a bowl of fruit: peaches, grapes, melon, watermelon, and also a few apples. The mayor took two grapes and his wife took a peach.

> They ate slowly, and according to their faces did not appear satisfied. Finally, the mayor could not restrain himself and asked, "Tell me Mr. Beber. Do you have any fruit in the house?" "All the fruit is in front of you," said Ofer's father. "Isn't there even a small cucumber?" asked the mayor (Oring 1981:47–48, 150–151).

Although the style of a joke is discernible, the joke itself is not. The punchline does not seem to be a punchline. There is no revelation or insight; there is only puzzlement. Why does the mayor ask if there is any fruit in the house when a whole bowl sits before him? Why would the mayor consider a small cucumber to be a fruit when he fails to acknowledge the apples, grapes, melons, and peaches that have been placed before him? In order to understand this chizbat, it is necessary to understand something about the structure of humor and how ideas are utilized to create humor.

All jokes depend on the perception of appropriate incongruities. But recognizing appropriate incongruities in turn depends upon knowing the ideas that are connoted by the objects, actions, and words within the joke. Often these connotations are known only to cultural insiders. In order to grasp the appropriate incongruity in the chizbat about Ofer's parents and the mayor of Tiberias, esoteric knowledge is required. Tiberias is a town on the shore of the Sea of Galilee. Ofer, a Palmachnik [a Palmach member], comes from a family of European, socialist Jews. While they speak Hebrew and are familiar with Jewish culture, they are not religious. When the mayor and his wife join the Bebers on their porch, the Bebers offer them a bowl of fruit in accordance with the dictates of European hospitality. But the mayor of Tiberias and his wife are not European Jews but Eastern Jews. They were raised in traditional, religious families and come from Arab countries in the Middle East. Whereas the offering of a bowl of fruit is an appropriate gesture of hospitality among Europeans, the offering of a small cucumber or pickle is the customary gesture of hospitality among Jews from Arab lands. Thus the incongruity of the mayor's question in the punchline is appropriate. The cucumber is the functional equivalent of fruit for the purposes of hospitality in Eastern cultures. The fruit that the Bebers offer the mayor and his wife does not serve as a hospitality food for them and is thus not "fruit" from their perspective.

Only a pickle can serve that function. Consequently, although a cucumber is not a fruit from a Western point of view, it is a fruit from the Eastern point of view because it fulfills the function that is intended by the offering of peaches, grapes, and so on. The puzzlement evoked by this joke evaporates once the perspective that informs the mayor's question is recognized as appropriate. Ultimately, an outsider can recognize the existence of a joke, even if it is not particularly enjoyed.[2]

The delineation of the appropriate incongruity in the chizbat about Ofer's parents and the mayor of Tiberias not only shows the text to be a joke. It also reveals what the joke is about. At root, this chizbat is not about mayors and citizens or fruit and vegetables. The joke is about the opposition between European and Levantine world views.[3] While hearing the joke, the listener first assumes a European perspective towards its content. The listener—like the Bebers—must regard the placing of a bowl of fruit before the mayor and his wife as an entirely proper gesture of hospitality. The listener must likewise be initially baffled by the mayor's request for a cucumber. But this bafflement should immediately be replaced by humor when the listener suddenly recognizes the Levantine perspective that motivates the mayor's seemingly strange request.

The Repertoire

A significant number of other jokes in the chizbat repertoire are also structured around the opposition between European and Levantine.

> After dinner the gang went as usual to the culture shack to listen to some good concert. One night, they found Abu Layish by the radio turning the knob this way and that, and finally he stopped on Cairo and listened to the reading of the Koran. "Let's hear music," they said to him. "There is no music," he said. "I already looked. There's nothing. Only concerts, and they give me a headache" (Oring 1981:90, 232).

Abu Layish, although Jewish and a dedicated member of the Palmach, must be marked as Levantine. His thinking and behavior are closer to that of an Arab peasant than to a European Jew. When Abu Layish says that there is no music on the radio, he means that there is no Arab music. For him, Western classical music is not a subcategory of music at all; it is merely noise that brings on headaches. Abu Layish's musical classification is incongruous given a European or Western perspective; a perspective that holds the symphonic concert to be the highest form of musical expression. The perplexity aroused by Abu Layish's comment, "No music ... only concerts" is resolved once this Levantine perspective is understood.

In the chizbat, it is not always the Levantine perspective that incongruously emerges to challenge an assumed European one. The movement may also take place in the opposite direction:

> One ideological instructor is hiking. In addition, he is a *Jecke*, the most naïve person ever to be with a group, and they are hiking and they go to an Arab village, and they see an Arab beating his wife. A very natural occurrence. It's his wife and he wants to beat her. And then he says, "I don't understand why he hits her. Couldn't he try explaining to her" (Oring 1981:246)?

The stereotype of European propriety in Israeli folklore is the *Jecke*, or German Jew. The term derives from the German *die Jacke* ["jacket"], an item of clothing that served to characterize the formality of the German-Jewish immigrants to Palestine. The German Jew is held to be a person who retains the refined and polite forms of his homeland in an unsuitable environment. *Jecke*s believe that their ways of behavior are right and civilized. They are clueless about alternative ways of behaving and are baffled by other cultures and other customs. In the chizbat, this *Jecke* figure is superimposed on yet another stereotype, the kibbutz ideological instructor; a social revolutionary dedicated to principles and theories of socialism, even when they are in conflict with the realities of everyday life. The *Jecke*'s remark in the chizbat is incongruous; it displays a complete lack of understanding of patriarchal authority among Arab peasants. He imposes his European perspective of gender relations onto a Levantine society, and it is this perspective that emerges as appropriately incongruous.

European/Levantine is not the only opposition at work in the chizbat. A number of other oppositions underlie significant portions of the repertoire.

> There was never a doctor or veterinarian in Yavne'el. When a mule would break its leg, they would ride to Mesha and bring a farmer from there who called himself a veterinarian. Once the donkey of the Abramsons got hurt, and Amos rode to Mesha to bring the veterinarian. When they reached the yard, the veterinarian tied his horse and took down his sack. In the sack he always had a rope, a scythe, a whip, disinfectant, and a pocketknife. When he came to examine the donkey, the children of Yavne'el gathered around and one opened the sack to see what was in it. "*Kinderlakh*" [Yiddish: "children"], he yelled, "don't touch the *instrumentim* ["instruments"]" (Oring 1981:98, 197).

Mesha and Yavne'el are two neighboring agricultural villages in the Lower Galilee. Both were founded in the first decade of the twentieth century. Even in the 1940s, the Galilee was still considered the backwoods, the boondocks. Donkeys, mules, and horses were major sources of power for agricultural work and transportation. Trained veterinarians were not available, and some local farmer usually fulfilled their functions.

The geographical setting, the two villages, the veterinarian, and especially his implements are characterized as crude and unrefined. But when the veterinarian tells the children of Yavne'el not to touch his *instrumentim*—a Hebraized Latin word—he characterizes them as technologically sophisticated, thus suggesting that his medical enterprise falls within the domain of scientific culture. This claim, of course, is incongruous given his background, his training, and the crude tools he actually employs. Yet it is also appropriate since, technically speaking, the rope, scythe, and pocketknife are his instruments.

The chizbat above depends upon the fundamental opposition between primitive and civilized. An expectation of primitiveness is established only to be shattered by an incongruous expression of culture and refinement that is, in some sense, appropriate. This primitive/civilized opposition informs a number of other chizbat as well. In some texts, such as the one above, it is the claim to civilization that shatters expectations conditioned by an otherwise primitively marked scene. In others, it is the primitive that erupts within the framework of civilization.

When the war broke out in the country, they assembled all the Haganah officers in Tel Aviv and evaluated new methods of warfare against the Arabs, and they especially dwelt upon psychological warfare. Everyone made suggestions and everyone argued about them. Only Yeruḥam sat on the side and kept quiet. Finally, they turned to him as an expert on Arab questions and asked what suggestions he had. "First of all," said Yeruḥam, "we must know how many regiments the Arabs have."

"All right," they said. "Let's say that we know."

"Afterwards we have to prepare cages appropriate to the number of regiments."

"What cages?" they asked. "What are the cages for?"

"Regular cages with doors that one can open by pulling a rope. Afterwards you have to prepare smoke bombs."

"*Nu?*" [Yiddish: "Well?"]

"When an Arab regiment mounts an attack, we build a smoke screen behind which are one or two cages. When the smoke disperses, you open the cage doors and let the *dab'a* [Arabic: hyena] loose that was inside. For every regiment one or two *dab'a*s, and we will win the war (Oring 1891:64–65, 178–179).

During the War of Independence, the yishuv military command gathers to discuss strategy—particularly, abstruse concepts of psychological warfare. Yeruḥam, a Yemenite Jew recognized for his knowledge of Arab personalities, culture, and affairs, is asked for his assessment. He proposes some cockamamie plan to release caged hyenas at charging regiments of Arab soldiers. At one level this plan is completely ludicrous and incongruous. It would seem to have absolutely nothing to do with serious military strategy, let alone scientific notions of psychological warfare. But the plan is in some measure appropriate because of the position that the *dab'a* holds in traditional Arab belief.

The *dab'a* was believed to have powers to bewitch solitary travelers in the night—either through its laugh, by rubbing up against them, or by staring into their eyes. It would then lead bewitched victims to its lair and devour them. The *dab'a* was greatly feared by Arab Bedouin and fellahin and figured significantly in their folk narrative (Hanauer 1935:202–203; Boneh 1987).

Within the context of a discussion of psychological issues, Yeruḥam proposes a crudely crafted scheme whose rationale is a primitive belief. There is no abstract theory upon which his strategy is based nor are there any psychological subtleties in his approach. His suggestion is nevertheless appropriate since the hyena was, in fact, greatly feared in rural Arab communities. In this chizbat, therefore, it is the crude and the primitive that incongruously disrupts scientific, "civilized" discourse.

A corollary of the primitive/civilized opposition is the opposition between dirty and clean. Expectations of normal standards of cleanliness and hygiene are regularly violated in the chizbat by some Palmachnik's behavior or comment.

> Say what you will about Avivi, but one thing you have to admit. In the entire Palmach, it was hard to find a better rifle instructor than he. That is, not that he was something special, but he simply knew how to find a suitable example for every lesson. And when the guys heard an example, they immediately knew what Avivi was talking about.
>
> For example, he would say, "Fellows. A rifle is not an ear. The rifle you have to clean daily" (Oring 1981:103, 183).

The expectation is that one's body is cleaned regularly if not daily. But Avivi, the rifle instructor, incongruously assumes that personal hygiene cannot serve as a suitable model for the care of ordnance. Avivi's assumption in the case of the Palmach is appropriate, however, because the Palmach deliberately cultivated an unwashed image.

If excessive dirt is incongruous within an assumed sphere of cleanliness, excessive cleanliness becomes incongruous within the sphere of Palmach slovenliness and grubbiness.

> Yonah was the most spoiled person in the entire Palmach. They saw him at eight in the morning by a kiosk in the bus station in Haifa asking for a glass of seltzer. When the proprietor gave him the seltzer, he tasted it and asked him to add a little raspberry syrup. When the proprietor added the raspberry, Yonah took a toothbrush from his pocket, put on paste, brushed his teeth, and rinsed with soda (Oring 1981: 104, 199).

Yonah's excessive attention to personal hygiene is clearly incongruous by ordinary, let alone Palmach, standards.

66   *Just Folklore*

The chizbat conditions a set of expectations which are incongruously—though appropriately—violated. These expectations constitute what may be called the *stance* of the chizbat. As we have seen in the three oppositions of European/Levantine, primitive/civilized, and dirty/clean, either of the elements in the oppositional pair may be the basis for the stance *or* for an appropriately incongruous violation of the stance. For example, when a European perspective is assumed, a Levantine perspective may be discovered to be operating, and vice versa. Thus the chizbat, indeed all jokes, depend on a tension between incongruous categories or scripts.[4]

But the significance of the chizbat categories emerges only when the full range of oppositional pairs that inform the repertoire have been identified:

A	B
Levantine	European
primitive	civilized
dirty	clean
secular	sacred
boorish	cultured
unemotional	emotional
self-assured	shy
slovenly, unregimented	disciplined, regimented
practical	theoretical
improvisational	ideological
terse	rhetorical
strong, violent	weak, non-violent
linguistic competence	linguistic incompetence
slang	poetry
age group	kinship
sabra image	*galut* image

The oppositions in the above table recur throughout the chizbat repertoire. What is surprising is that they are not an arbitrary set of oppositions but are systematically related to one another. Each column forms a coherent configuration. Column A represents a complex of values and traits basic to the *sabra* image—to the image of the native born Israeli. Column B, however, represents a complex of values and traits associated with the *galut* image: the image of the Diaspora Jew, the ghettoized European, the exile personality.

The elements of the contrasting images represented by the traits in the two columns have long been recognized by commentators on Israeli national character:

> [The sabra] is a buoyant, extrovert type with a heightened sense of living and purpose, centered around the new nation and the New State, and in complete antithesis to the model of the Ghetto Jew. . . . A Jew transformed into an Israeli is a sturdy, robust, and lusty fellow, non-emotional with rough edges and no complexes. . . . He styles himself on a peasant mentality. . . . He rejects complexity and intellectuality, and he likes to think of himself as a simple straight-forward man without far-fetched ideas and claims. He rejects emotionality, softness, familism, possessiveness and the bourgeois mentality. . . . He hates verbosity and long winded phrases, he has little time for big talk, for juggling with words and abstractions (Zweig 1969:3–12).

> [Being a sabra is] knowing what to say at the right moment. Not showing any weakness. Being in the "in." Acting out the tough guy. Behaving like an Arab so as to appear like a native Israeli. Laughing at aliens (newcomers and those not born in Israel). Disrespecting one's elders ("old" commanders who had passed the age of 30). Doing everything for a friend. Dressing simply and modestly, but according to clear and well-defined rules. Not nominating oneself for an important job (D. Shḥori quoted in Katriel 1986:85).

The chizbat repertoire clearly revolves around two images of central concern to the Palmach: the *sabra* image which they created and after which they modeled themselves, and the *galut* image that they abhorred and consciously and actively rejected. But what does the chizbat have to say about these images? Does the chizbat's utilization of the elements of these images contribute in any way to an understanding of the Palmach?

Depending upon the particular chizbat being told, the stance moves between columns A and B. Each time a chizbat conditions the expectation of values belonging to one image (e.g., the expectation that offering guests a bowl of fruit is a legitimate gesture of hospitality from a European perspective), it is disrupted by the awareness that values of the opposing image are in some sense appropriate as well (e.g., offering a bowl of fruit is not a legitimate gesture of hospitality from a Levantine perspective). The definition of a situation solely in terms of a single set of values is not possible. Neither set is totally relevant or irrelevant. In essence, the chizbat explores the images of *sabra* and *galut* Jew and demonstrates that each must lead to a recognition of the other. The chizbat shows that the Palmach's dissociation from the image of the European Jew and their adherence to new characterological and cultural models is not genuine. The transformation is not complete and cannot be completed. Incongruously, the attempt of the Palmach to divorce themselves from their European-Jewish heritage only emphasizes the strength of their connections to it. It was this message, articulated again and again throughout the repertoire, that gave the chizbat its particular truth and made the chizbat a special order of joke; an order of joke that merited a distinct name and a distinct place in the minds and hearts of the Palmach.

Incongruity Theory as an Interpretive Methodology

Approaching a joke repertoire in terms of appropriate incongruities leads to an analysis in some ways reminiscent of the structural analysis proposed for myth and folktales by Claude Lévi-Strauss.[5] The syntagmatic (plot) structure of a narrative is ignored in the pursuit of paradigmatic (thematic) structures framed in the form of binary oppositions. Both approaches emphasize the conceptual relations of narrative elements, but paradigmatic structures ignore their place or function in the plot. Thus in the story of Oedipus, Lévi-Strauss does not regard Oedipus's marriage to his mother as a *consequence* of killing his father but as an *inversion* of it. The marriage conveys the idea of extending blood relationships much too far, whereas the killing suggests that such relationships have not been extended nearly far enough (Lévi-Strauss 1955:433). In the joke about the mayor and the bowl of fruit, the fruit, in some sense, is an inversion of the pickle. While they are both hospitality foods, they operate as such only in inverse cultural realms.

Despite these similarities, differences exist between Lévi-Strauss's structural analysis of myth and the incongruity analysis of jokes. The binary structure of humor is intuitively recognized by all but the most unreflective of joke tellers and listeners. When tellers try to explain a joke that listeners have failed to apprehend, they regularly resort to highlighting the elements that reflect the underlying oppositions: "The mayor is an Eastern Jew where a pickle is offered in hospitality—get it?" Furthermore, certain details of jokes are absolutely crucial, not only to the comprehension of the jokes, but to their very conceptualization as jokes. The change or eradication of such a detail can destroy the possibility of regarding the text as a humorous one. One could not, for example, substitute a raisin for a pickle in the story of the mayor and still reasonably expect that a humorous communication would result.

This is hardly the case with myth. The oppositional structure of myth is a theoretical assertion. It is not clear whether this structure is grasped by myth tellers and their audiences. Nor has it been established that changes in narrative detail can serve to vitiate the mythic structure of a narrative. Consequently, it is impossible to say which elements are central and crucial to the symbolic interpretation of a myth and which are truly superfluous details. The appropriate incongruities of jokes, however, are more than armchair formulations about the underlying structures of humorous texts. Such structures are genuinely verifiable with respect to real groups of tellers and listeners. The same cannot be said of myth. Perhaps the analysis of the paradigmatic structures of myth might have benefited from a grounding in the more explicit and verifiable structuring of humor. Perhaps Lévi-Strauss should have begun with jokes.

The central point, however, is that incongruity theory can lead beyond definition—beyond the statement of conditions that are necessary and sufficient for the identification of a humorous text. Incongruity theory can serve as the basis for an interpretive methodology that can enhance the understanding of humorous repertoires. Through a close analysis of the categories or scripts incongruously united in humorous expressions, a potential exists for apprehending a society's deepest conflicts and concerns.

5. Forest Lawn and the Iconography of American Death

Forest Lawn Memorial Park in Glendale, California, cannot be considered folklore in any usual meaning of the term. Its plan and architecture are the products of professional designers and engineers with considerable economic resources at their disposal. Forest Lawn was established to meet the needs of a rapidly growing, urban population at the very moment when the United States emerged as a world power. Created at the beginning of the twentieth century, it continues to operate vigorously in the twenty-first.

Forest Lawn is an assemblage of material objects organized within a contrived space intended to fulfill specific functions. Nevertheless, it can be regarded as a text and can be read. Text *originally referred to an object; a thing woven rather than a thing composed of words. A cemetery is a text in that it has content, style, and motifs. It displays structure and pattern that in some measure resemble the structures and themes of folklore genres. It has meaning. In fact, a reading of Forest Lawn belies the story of its origins. It is not at its root the invention of an individual inspired by nature and a sense of the divine. It is rather the outgrowth of something more prosaic: American history and tradition.*

> *Flesh suffers; marble is forever.*
> —Richard Lacayo

IN 1916, HUBERT EATON became the manager of a fifty-five acre, rural cemetery in Tropico, California called Forest Lawn. It was on New Year's Day of the following year that Eaton received the vision that led him to transform a little, failing cemetery into one of America's most famous, second only perhaps to the National Cemetery in Arlington, Virginia (St. Johns 1959:1–12).

Today over 300,000 "loved ones" are entombed, interred, and inurned within the sacred grounds of Forest Lawn Memorial Park, Glendale. Fifty thousand weddings have been performed in its three churches, and more than a million tourists visit it annually.[1]

Prior to the development of Disneyland, Forest Lawn was southern California's most popular tourist attraction. However, Eaton's success with Forest Lawn was not without struggle, and in many quarters, Forest Lawn's fame and reputation might be more properly described as notoriety.[2]

A good deal of this notoriety was inspired by Evelyn Waugh's 1948 satire *The Loved One* (1965) and the even more excessive film based upon the novel. Waugh viewed Forest Lawn as tainted by the artificiality, superficiality, and sentimentality of Hollywood. He saw Forest Lawn as banishing death and selling eternal life for those who could afford its cosmetic treatments for the deceased, its quilted caskets, and earthquake proof ventilated crypts. Stated Waugh: "The body does not decay; it lives on more chic in death than ever before, in its undestructable Class A steel and concrete shelf; the soul goes straight from the Slumber Room to Paradise where it enjoys endless infancy" (1947:84).

Waugh's view has certainly conditioned subsequent responses to Forest Lawn, particularly in the national media. *Saturday Review* referred to Forest Lawn as "Ever-Ever Land" (Sutton 1958), and *Time* sardonically dubbed it the "Disneyland of Death" (1959:107). Even singer John Denver was not to miss out on the fun and recorded Tom Paxton's satirical song "Forest Lawn" on one of his early albums (1970). The satire continues even today on YouTube ("History of Forest Lawn").

But there is something wrong with uncritically accepting a satirical portrait as the basis for understanding. And Waugh's portrait, though excellent and amusing as literature, leaves something to be desired as interpretation. It is appropriate, therefore, that a reconsideration of Forest Lawn begins, not with Waugh's interpretation, but with the set of questions that he posed: "What will the professors of the future make of Forest Lawn? What do we make of it ourselves? Here is the thing, under our very noses, a first-class anthropological puzzle of our own period and neighborhood. What does it mean" (1947:77)?

Waugh's questions are substantial enough to merit a serious response even if they were somewhat facetiously propounded. Although it will not be possible to render a complete and detailed portrait of Forest Lawn here, it should be possible to delineate the character of the place sufficiently to offer a response to Waugh's query.

Inscribed on the 25′ x 28′ tablet known as "The Builder's Creed," which stands in the forecourt to the Memorial Terrace of the Great Mausoleum, is the substance of Hubert Eaton's vision for Forest Lawn:

> I believe in a happy Eternal Life.
> I believe those of us who are left behind should be glad in the certain belief that those gone before who believed in Him have entered into that happier life.
> I believe, most of all, in a Christ that smiles and loves you and me.
> I, therefore, know the cemeteries of today are wrong because they depict an end, not a beginning.
> I therefore prayerfully resolve ... that I shall endeavor to build Forest Lawn as different, as unlike other cemeteries as sunshine is unlike darkness, as Eternal Life is unlike Death.

In fulfillment of these propositions, Eaton set out to create not only a safe repository and garden of memory for the dead, but also a place for the "sacred enjoyment of the living" (*Art Guide* 1941:1). To this end he established a great park with green rolling lawns—unbroken by tombstones or other raised markers—with tens of thousands of shrubs, flowers, and trees (non-deciduous and forever green); replicas of Old World country churches; singing birds and splashing fountains; a great Mausoleum-Colombarium; as well as one of the largest collections of marble statuary and stained glass ever assembled in America.

The presence of all this beauty was to "dissolve man's fear of oblivion and bolster his faith in immortality" (1941:1). The "immortal" works of art in marble and glass, as well as the scientifically constructed mausoleums and colombaria, reinforce this belief. "We build Forever," reads the inscription in the Great Mausoleum. The proposition, though Ozymandian in its claim, nevertheless seems sincere.

The message of immortality is communicated at Forest Lawn at different levels. At the level of formal mythology, it is represented in the Sacred Trilogy—three works of art that depict the dramatic and theological foci in the life story of Jesus: The Last Supper, the

Crucifixion, and the Resurrection. *The Last Supper* is a recreation of Leonardo da Vinci's famous fresco in a brilliant stained-glass window set in the Court of Honor in the Great Mausoleum. *The Crucifixion* is a massive oil painting by the Polish artist Jan Styka. Its size (if stood on its side it is approximately the height of a twenty-story building) required the construction of a special hall to house and display it. Also housed in the same hall is *The Resurrection*, a somewhat less massive painting that was commissioned by Forest Lawn to complete the trilogy. *The Crucifixion* itself is somewhat unusual, not merely for its size, but for its subject, which is not a crucified Christ, but Christ at the moment before his crucifixion in a posture of serene faith and confidence in the eternal life that awaits him.

It may seem surprising, given the basic Christian orientation of Forest Lawn as represented in the Sacred Trilogy, that a minority of the hundreds of marble statues that grace the gardens, courts, terraces, and sanctuaries are explicitly Christian in theme.[3] And very, very few of them depict the figure of Jesus. Most prominent are the reproduction of Michelangelo Buonarotti's *La Pieta*, Bertel Thorvaldsen's *The Christus*,[4] and an original sculpture by Vincenzo Jerace *For of Such Is the Kingdom of Heaven*. It was Hubert Eaton's vision of the Christ that limited its appearance at Forest Lawn. The greatest part of extant statuary depicts Christ on the cross, a joyless suffering Christ. What Eaton wanted was a smiling Christ, a Christ that "loved you and me"; what Eaton called an "American Christ." Despite contests and competitions, Forest Lawn never found its American Christ, but it acquired Jerace's *For of Such Is the of Heaven*. Eaton was reputedly to have said to Jerace, "It is not my smiling Christ, but it is a kindly Christ, a Christ to whom the little children came" (*Art Guide* 1941:81).

The centrality of the Sacred Trilogy substantially establishes the Christian context of Forest Lawn, despite the quantitative meagerness of explicitly Christian themes in its otherwise large inventory of sculpture. Explicit Christian themes are reiterated, however, in the mosaics, reliefs, stained glass, and inscriptions that appear throughout Forest Lawn's courts, churches, and mausoleums.

If Forest Lawn could not present the American Christ who smiled and loved you and me, it could present the love. The inscriptions proclaim it, the weddings celebrate it, and the statuary depicts or evokes it. In the garden adjacent to the Court of David in the Triumphant Faith section of the park stands Ernesto Gazzeri's *The Mystery of Life*, a large group containing eighteen life-sized human figures. Through the center of the work flows "the mystic stream of life" (of real water), and each figure represents a person of different character, station, and circumstance in their moment of response to this great mystery. The work was created specifically for Forest Lawn, and Forest Lawn (with the approval of the Royal Superintendent of Fine Arts of Italy and Victor Herbert) offers its solution to this mystery: "Love is the end and all of living." The theology of Forest Lawn is a theology of love. "Love lives forever and is reborn," says Forest Lawn (*Pictorial Forest Lawn* 1953:7). It is not only the basis of life in this world, but it is the key to life in the next.

At Forest Lawn, one representation of love is romance. The Wee Kirk O' the Heather is a replica of Annie Laurie's church in Dumfriesshire, Scotland. The eight stained-glass windows tell the story of Annie and Douglas of Fingland and their tragic love affair. The Ring of Aldyth, through which bridal couples clasp and pledge their devotion, is reputedly based on a romantic Saxon legend with a happier climax. Over the chancel of the Church of the Recessional is inscribed "Now abideth faith, hope, love, these three: and the greatest of these is love" (1 Cor. 13:13).

The representations of love that are focal in the iconography of Forest Lawn, however, are those of domestic love. Death is not an end, it is a "going home," and Forest Lawn is virtually littered with images of idealized domesticity. The child—asleep, at play, mischievous, curious, content—is a primary image for sentimental reflection; as is the family group, invincible in its love and devotion; and the mother and child, the essence of love pure and uncomplicated. In this theology, man is not depraved, nor is he judged. He is an innocent, as loving and as loved as a child, and it would seem that it is primarily within this structure of family sentiment that man is redeemed and reborn.

In a cemetery context, it is difficult to ignore the abundance of statuary that glorifies the human body. Scores of marble and bronze men, women, and children all emphasize the beauties of the flesh.

The statues seem to impute a physical referent to the immortality that Forest Lawn proclaims, and not merely a spiritual one. Indeed, all the contemporary embalming and cosmetic practices strive to present a physically pleasing last portrait of the deceased to family and friends. Scientifically designed crypts that promote "desiccation but not decay" (*Art Guide* 1941:40) contribute to the message that the life beyond involves not merely the immortality of the spirit but, in some unexplicated manner, the endurance of the flesh as well.

There is a brief and perceptive moment in the film *The Loved One* (1965) when the protagonist finds himself wandering about a hall filled with marble figures of nude and semi-nude women. Suddenly, when he is sure no one is watching, he plants a hasty kiss on the breast of one of the statues. Although Forest Lawn acknowledges the physical beauty of its statuary, it does not entertain the notion of its sensuality. Beautiful, yes; erotic, no. The following description of Harriet Whitney Frishmuth's statue *Joy of the Waters* appears in one of the editions of Forest Lawn's *Art Guide*:

> With upflung hands and windblown hair, this gay young girl eagerly greets the onrushing waves. Well known for her lyrical figures, Miss Frishmuth has displayed here a sound knowledge of human anatomy and a sincere desire to attain the ideal of beauty in her work. The basic theme is spiritual. The girl, by her action and by the evident keen enjoyment on her face, expresses the happiness that comes to a receptive and believing heart which accepts and receives the blessings of God's all-embracing love (*Art Guide* 1941:54–55).

The description is typical. While recognizing the beauty of the female anatomy, the statue is unambiguously assigned a spiritual context. Physical beauty should not evoke a physical response but a spiritual one. Sensuality is subordinated. The possibility of the erotic is denied. The surreptitious kiss bestowed by the film hero was a denial of this denial.

Forest Lawn is dedicated to the stirring of national as well as domestic sentiments. Representations of relics, personages, and ideals that evoke the spirit of American freedom and democracy permeate the park. Statues of George Washington, Abraham Lincoln, Henry Clay, Daniel Webster, Theodore Roosevelt, as well as personifications such as *Pro Patria* and *The Republic* can all be found. In the Court of Freedom stands a recreation of John Trumbull's painting *The Signing of the Declaration of Independence* that has been constructed of more than 700,000 mosaic tiles. At the base of the statue of Washington stretches a section of the Liberty Chain that was used to bar British access to the Hudson River during the Revolutionary War.

Besides love, patriotism, and beauty, there are a series of other virtues to which Forest Lawn is clearly committed—those that constitute or contribute to the formation of what might be called "good character." In the forecourt of The Church of the Recessional, a replica of the Parish Church of St. Margaret's in Rottingdean, England, where Rudyard Kipling worshipped for several years, are inscribed three of Kipling's famous poems: "Recessional" (after which the church is named), "If," and "When Earth's Last Picture Is Painted." Tolerance, faith, humility, reverence, trust, truth, courage, vision, and determination—these are the virtues that are evoked throughout Forest Lawn again and again.

Forest Lawn also evokes a sense of efficient organization and commercial success. Forest Lawn was one of the first cemeteries to utilize media advertising stressing the economic and organizational benefits of its services. Furthermore, the economic significance of the distinctions between the different plots, crypts, niches, caskets, urns, and memorials that are available at Forest Lawn serve as markers of individual success in life. With few exceptions, anyone is entitled to the memorial that they can afford.[5] You may be buried simply or grandly. You may not be able to take it with you, but at Forest Lawn it is certainly possible to indicate you once had it.

What then is one to make of Forest Lawn? What is the solution to the "first-class anthropological puzzle" that Waugh propounded? Is Forest Lawn some Hollywood fantasy, locally bred and born? In the first place, it must be recognized that the fundamental concept that shapes Forest Lawn is not new. In the early nineteenth century, in reaction to the grim, gloomy, and neglected cemeteries of Puritan tradition, as well as the offensive, overcrowded, and health-hazardous cemeteries of the city, the rural cemetery movement was born. The members of this movement advocated the acquisition of large, attractive acreage outside the city limits that would serve

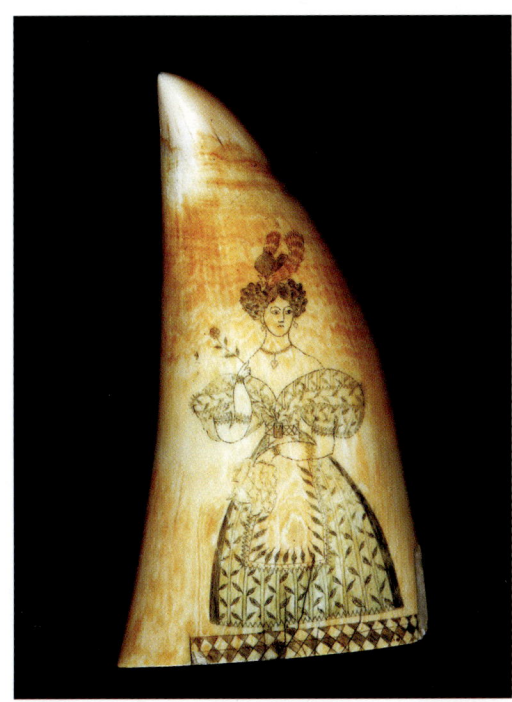

Obverse and reverse of scrimshaw whale tooth.
COURTESY OF THE NEW BEDFORD WHALING MUSEUM

Obverse and reverse of scrimshaw busk.
Courtesy of the New Bedford Whaling Museum

WWI 42nd Rainbow Division patch. Courtesy of snydertreasures.com

Bruce, Cu Chi, Vietnam 1969.

Palmachniks in hand-to-hand combat training.
COURTESY OF PALMACH HOUSE, TEL AVIV

Palmach campfire: the prototypical venue for the telling of chizbat.
COURTESY OF PALMACH HOUSE, TEL AVIV

Tombstone, 1769, churchyard, Boston, Massachusetts.
Copyright © Elliott Oring

Mt. Auburn Cemetery, founded 1831, Cambridge, Massachusetts.
Copyright © Elliott Oring

Joy of the Waters (1919) by Harriet Whitney Frishmuth.
Courtesy of Forest Lawn Memorial Parks and Mortuaries, Glendale

Love's Treasure by Leone Tomassi is but one of Forest Lawn's many representations of the family and the love that binds it together.
Copyright © Elliott Oring

Nude with Apple by Elie Jean Vezien, Forest Lawn Memorial Park, Glendale.
Copyright © Elliott Oring

as a sacred and inviolable resting place for the dead. The graves and memorials were to be set in beautiful foliage and landscaped surroundings. Fences that were constructed around family plots had to be made of durable metal or stone (not wood and not slate, the standard materials of the Puritan graveyard). The memorials themselves were to be artistically controlled by the cemetery trustees to insure their aesthetic effect. It was hoped that such cemeteries might become schools "of instruction in architecture, sculpture, landscape gardening, and arboriculture"(French 1975:69–71).[6] Furthermore, these cemeteries were regarded as schools of religion and philosophy where the memorials to the dead were to serve as inspirations to the living. The symbolism on the memorials was not grim, and Christian symbolism was only infrequently used. It was expected that the amalgam of the beauty of nature and art would teach that death is not an end and time not a destroyer. It was also hoped that the art would make the lessons of history tangible and thus give people a sense of historical continuity and instill feelings of patriotism and national pride.

Beginning with Mount Auburn Cemetery in Cambridge, Massachusetts in 1831, the rural cemetery movement rapidly spread: Laurel Hill Cemetery, Philadelphia (1836); Greenwood Cemetery, Brooklyn (1838); Allegheny Cemetery, Pittsburgh (1844); Spring Grove Cemetery, Cincinnati (1845). By the middle of the century, there were few major cities or towns without a rural cemetery.

These cemeteries were exceedingly popular. No visitor from abroad could visit Boston without being taken on a tour of Mount Auburn. Laurel Hill Cemetery boasted 30,000 tourists a year. In the latter part of the century, the internal fencing that had delineated the boundaries of family plots began to be removed, an innovation that resulted in an aesthetically integrated park which gave rise to the "lawn cemeteries" popular after the Civil War.

Thus, Hubert Eaton's Creed to the contrary, the Forest Lawn concept was not essentially new, but well within the tradition of the nineteenth-century rural cemetery. Like Forest Lawn, the rural cemeteries of the nineteenth century were not merely places for the disposal of the dead but cultural institutions that served to instruct, inspire, and ennoble the living. But if Forest Lawn is within the rural cemetery tradition, it is not simply another rural cemetery. To answer Waugh's question, it might be best not to view Forest Lawn as a cemetery at all, but as a twentieth-century memorial to the tastes and values of nineteenth-century American Victorianism.

Victorian culture was essentially an Anglo-Saxon Protestant culture, and Anglo-Saxon Protestantism is amply reflected in Forest Lawn's rural English and Scottish churches, Saxon legends, Tudor architecture, and in the overwhelming majority of its client population (until 1959, only Caucasians were permitted to be interred at Forest Lawn).[7] The artistic tastes manifested in the art and architecture of Forest Lawn are those commensurate with the popular tastes of Victorian America. The idealized subject matter, sentimentality, the use of literary and classical associations, didacticism, and extraneous symbolism were all characteristic of the artistic expectations of Victorian culture. It is no accident that there is virtually no modern or abstract sculpture in Forest Lawn. The patriotic strains, the encouragement of what would later be called "the inner-directed personality" (i.e., the building of "good character") and the repression of sensuality are well-known Victorian traits. The focus upon the family, the child, and the mother-child relationship reflect the Victorian sanctification of the family unit, the importance of childhood, and the exaltation of motherhood.

What might appear to be a naïve theology which seems to stress a rather simplistic immortality of flesh and spirit, reuniting innocent loved ones in some kind of domestic heaven, is entirely in keeping with conceptualizations of the after-life that were propagated in the huge consolation literature of nineteenth-century America.[8] Forest Lawn's vision is, in fact, more subtle and less extreme.

Love, Death, and Success are the three great themes that Carl Bode sees running through much of the American culture of the mid-nineteenth century—a "trio for Columbia" as he called it (1959:269–276).[9] And these, indeed, are the great themes of Forest Lawn as well. In contemplating Forest Lawn it is necessary to see Death as simply one of Forest Lawn's major themes. What emerges from this perspective, then, is not a view of a cemetery, nor even a Victorian cemetery, but a twentieth-century exhibition of and memorial to the culture of Victorian America.[10]

Since the 1970s, the clientele of Forest Lawn has changed dramatically. Hispanics, Armenians, Koreans, Chinese, and Japanese have become major consumers of Forest Lawn services and properties. The change in the population in part reflects the change in the population of southern California generally and the Glendale area specifically. But considering that Forest Lawn was restricted to Caucasians until 1959, the change is dramatic. Yet, it would be wrong to say that the park has changed in its style or spirit. Chinese characters may appear on bronze grave markers, and neo-classic statues may bear Korean or Hispanic names on their pedestals. However, the park, the structures, the art, and the thematic emphases have not changed. These remain as before. It seems that the Victorian values and tastes represented by Forest Lawn are precisely those that these populations respect. Despite the fact that Victorianism had declined before many of these people had come to this country, they appreciate the beautiful landscapes; the representational art; the spiritual tone; and the respect for family, nation, and character. Perhaps they are misreading the park, but I suspect not. It is rather that Victorianism never succumbed to modernism. If Victorian values were consciously repudiated by the cultural elite, they never lost their hold in the largest segments of American society. These values continue to be inculcated and absorbed, even in immigrant and minority communities that have never identified with the cultural vanguard and whose values are closer to those that Forest Lawn would conserve.

Of course, it becomes no less easy to satirize Forest Lawn. For those who do not share the tastes, virtues, or confident faith that it represents, Forest Lawn will remain curious, comical, or pathetic. Born of another region and some other century, Forest Lawn will seem out of time and place. But Forest Lawn is not some Hollywood fantasy or whole-cloth fabrication for mass consumption. It displays a deep and powerful current in America which has not disappeared and which should not be ignored.[11]

6. Dyadic Traditions

Tradition is often encountered by folklorists as a mass of inherited behaviors and beliefs (Ben-Amos 1984:117–119). How the components of this mass originate are often obscure, and when they can be recovered, it is often only by means of speculative reconstruction. Traditionalization is the process of turning expressions into traditions by linking them to the past or by creating the need, desire, and conditions for their future reproduction (Hymes 1975:353–354). Traditionalization creates traditions on a daily basis.

Folklorists have not shown much interest in two-person groups. Dyads have largely been the province of sociologists and psychologists (Becker and Useem 1942; Indvik and Fitzpatrick 1982). The study of dyads, however, offers perhaps the best glimpse into the creation of traditions and an understanding of the reasons for both their preservation and extinction. Dyadic traditions parallel traditions in more complex sociological groupings, but also present characteristics peculiar to themselves.

> *Two's company, three's a crowd.*
> —Anonymous

IN THE EARLY nineteenth century, with the inception of the scientific study of folklore, folk traditions were held to be reflective of social organizations of considerable breadth. Thus, peasant stories, saws, and customs scrutinized by the Brothers Grimm were believed to reflect the past beliefs of Teutonic nations (Grimm 1966, 1:10) just as the popular antiquities reconceptualized by W. J. Thoms under the rubric *folklore* were held to illuminate the past of Anglo-Saxon and Celtic societies (Thoms in Dorson 1968a, 1:52–54). As the idea took hold that folklore was essentially an expression of the present rather than a survival from the past, the attention of folklorists progressively turned toward smaller and more intimate groups as the loci of tradition: occupational groupings, ethnic minorities, and religious organizations.[1] This shift in the sociological bases of folkloric expression eventually culminated in Alan Dundes's dictum that the folk were "any group of people whatsoever that shared at least one common factor" (Dundes 1965:2), and that the term *folk* should not be restricted to any age group, class, or ethnicity. "Who are the folk? Among others, we are" (Dundes 1980:19).[2] Although Dundes imagined the possibility of a two-person group, he concluded that "probably the smallest group would be the individual family," and indeed, significant attention has been paid by folklorists to expressions of family folklore (Boatright 1958; Zeitlin et al. 1982; Greenwood 2004).

However, the family is not the absolute minimum organization of enduring relations in society. A simpler form exists called the *dyad*. A dyad is a more or less enduring interaction between two individuals who primarily relate to one another as persons rather than as occupants of social statuses. Thus, dyads are characterized by low degrees of formality and embeddedness. That is to say, there is a lack of dependence on formal role relations, and the relationship is embedded to a very low degree within a larger social organization (McCall et al. 1970). Friendships and conjugal relationships are the kinds that might be immediately recognized as conforming to these criteria.[3]

Dyadic traditions refer to behavioral and linguistic routines that are generated, endowed with significance, and maintained within the dyadic relationship. The behavioral and linguistic patterns are traditional to the extent that both individuals are aware that these patterns are to some degree recurring or are related to previous patterns of behavior. In other words, traditionality is based on the recognition by the members of the dyad that the patterns have a history—if only a brief one—in their relationship and a sense that they may continue to operate in the future. Dyadic traditions are primarily private presentations. Although these traditions may occasionally be performed in the presence of others, their major arena of expression is within the dyad itself. While traditional expressions by the dyad to others are not without interest, I restrict the term *dyadic traditions* to those that occur within this minimum unit of social organization.[4]

Perhaps the first question should be: Do dyadic traditions exist? The answer is an unqualified "yes." A second question follows naturally: What is to be gained from the study of such traditions?

The answer to this question is more qualified, but as the simplest form of social organization, dyads may provide the clearest and most uncluttered arenas for the study of the formation and communication of traditional expression (Simmel 1950:122).

Most of the traditions I have collected can be superficially categorized as names, metaphors, gestures, interactive routines, and rituals. The documentation of such traditions was usually accomplished by interviewing people who knew me well and who trusted me to respect their relationship and guard their privacy. Such a situation obtains primarily with friends, and even friends remain in fairly complete control of what they choose to reveal. Therefore, I can make no claim to representativeness and would be greatly surprised if I had encountered more than a small percentage of the types of traditions that exist in two-person groups. Nevertheless, a complete recounting even of the traditions I have collected remains beyond the scope of this essay. Instead I will review those traditions that exemplify major characteristics of the corpus.

Dyadic traditions illustrate, as no others, that the sources of tradition are *unpredictable*. That is, it would be impossible to predict what aspects of experience are endowed with significance and elevated to the status of tradition by the dyad.[5] For example, one Los Angeles couple in their early forties was given to exclaiming "Cuernavaca!" whenever they encountered a dead dog, dog wastes, or heavy bus exhausts. The expression derived from their experience on one particular street in this Mexican city, which they had visited on one of their vacations, and which was filled with dogs, dog waste, a dead dog, and which opened onto an avenue filled with buses and their polluting diesel exhausts.

This same couple also developed the habit while brushing their teeth of spitting out the toothpaste with the exclamation, "Ptui! Huey, Dewey, Louie" (a traditional Jewish expression for spitting followed by the names of Donald Duck's nephews). They customarily referred to body odor as "Chef Boyardee" (a food smell and taste they particularly disliked and pronounced by accenting the second rather than the third syllable), and toasted one another, not with the Scandinavian *skoal*, but with "Skolnik" after the name of a former landlord. The unpredictability and seeming triviality of such traditions cannot be ascribed to the peculiarity of this dyad alone. Many other cases could be cited. Another dyad, for example, derived a set of pseudonyms, regularly used over the course of several years, from the label of a button of an elevator in which they happened to once ride. The names eventually came to be inscribed in calligraphy, executed on vellum, and surrounded by an elaborate graphic design.

What is to be made of such traditions? What do they accomplish? In the example of the couple who exclaimed "Cuernavaca!" to express their reactions to certain aspects of urban living (dead dogs, dog wastes, air pollution), they simultaneously realize several things:

(1) They test whether the members of the dyad are sensitive to the same aspects of immediate experience and whether they share a common orientation towards that experience.
(2) They symbolize the intimacy of their relationship through the use of a highly encrypted code which signals that they know one another in ways unknown and unknowable to others.
(3) They are made to recall a past experience in which they both participated. Consequently, such traditions activate a sense of the past and the shared history of the relationship.

It is noteworthy that such a seemingly trivial stimulus should carry so much import. But objects and experiences are not in themselves significant or insignificant. Significance is something bestowed, and it may be hypothesized that in their effort to symbolize intimacy, the dyad tends to deliberately choose the seemingly trivial and fortuitous as the foundation for their traditions.

If it is characteristic of conjugal and friendship dyads to rename the various aspects of ordinary experience using highly esoteric expressions, they are not content to merely rename. Often, the traditions they create comment in direct ways upon the relationship itself by characterizing elements of its structure, function, and ethos. For example, Sigmund Freud was accustomed to writing "*corragio Casimiro,*" or merely the abbreviation "*C. C.*" in his letters to his friend and colleague Karl Abraham. This expression derived from an experience of Abraham's during a vacation in the Italian Alps. He climbed a mountain in the company of two Italian guides who had brought some raw meat with them for their lunch. When they reached the summit and set to cooking it, the guides discovered that the meat had spoiled, but one encouraged the other to eat it saying, "*corragio Casimiro.*" Freud used this expression to encourage Abraham in the formidable task of organizing the psychoanalytic movement and in keeping it pure, while Abraham referred to himself as "Casimiro" in his responses (Abraham and Freud 1965:146, 157, 158).

Another pair of friends described a tradition that arose quite spontaneously between them. Both were males who had known each other for many years. One had been born in Israel but had come to the United States while fairly young. He had forgotten much of his Hebrew, and English had become his native language. Both individuals had for many years been educated in the Hebrew language and Jewish tradition at religious schools, and although they could converse in Hebrew, they considered their knowledge of both the language and the tradition far less than warranted by their long years of study. They reported that their particular tradition arose while dining at a restaurant. When the drinks came, one toasted the other with the Hebrew toast "*le-Ḥayyim!*" ("to Life!"). The other promptly responded, "*be-yad ha-lashon*" ("in the power of the tongue"). The response was based on the biblical aphorism "*Mavet ve-ḥayyim be-yad lashon*" ("Death and life are within the power of the tongue" [Prov. 18:21]).[6] Of course, there is no substantive connection between the toast and the aphorism other than the sharing of the word *ḥayyim.* The response was consequently perceived as incongruous and humorous. Both members of the dyad agreed that the malapropism came to serve as a concise and appropriate comment on the level of their knowledge of the Hebrew language and Jewish tradition and thus they maintained the expression in their active repertoire of routines.

One last example of this type of tradition derives from Martha Weinman Lear's book *Heartsounds.* The book is about Mrs. Lear's husband, Harold, and their relationship following his heart attack. Harold, it seems, had a more developed sense of responsibility and work ethic than his wife, and he had a tendency towards occasional expressions of self-righteousness and sanctimoniousness. As Mrs. Lear reported:

> I had joked about it, or tried to. Once, just a year married, he had frozen into some righteous stance about something-or-other, and I had made my face go sour and dour, quite like the faces of American Gothic, and held up a table fork as though it was a farmer's pitchfork and said, "Quick! What painting am I?" He had broken into laughter. . . . And after that, anytime he started getting righteous, I would hold up the fork or three fingers, and yell, "Pitchfork! Pitchfork!" and he would laugh (Lear 1980:91).

In this last example, one can see how a particular dyadic tradition depended upon a more pervasive cultural symbolism. Dyads regularly utilize ideas and behaviors common to the larger society, but endow these with unique characteristics or meanings.

One couple regularly celebrated their anniversary with a bottle of champagne. This rather commonplace ritual would seem to be a simple enactment of a more widespread tradition of anniversary celebration, and indeed, it had begun as such. On their first anniversary, this couple decided to open a bottle of champagne in keeping with a traditional cultural model. As they were not accustomed to drinking much champagne, and as their experience with opening champagne bottles was minimal, the husband took elaborate measures to insure that nothing untoward occurred. He wrapped the bottle in a towel, pointed the cork in a relatively safe direction, and stood near the kitchen sink in case the bottle should overflow. The bottle was opened without incident, but before the champagne could be poured, the bottle slipped out of his hand, rolled across the floor, and emptied its contents under the refrigerator. It took more than an hour to clean it up. Since that time this couple has celebrated their anniversary with champagne. Observation alone would lead one to believe that this couple was following a cultural tradition. What they have traditionalized, however, is the *difference* between their own first anniversary celebration and the one they imagine to be common and appropriate in the larger society. Theirs was a dyadic tradition. The forms of the two celebrations were identical; their meanings were significantly different.

Another couple actually incorporated an object from popular culture into their interaction. The couple had been married for thirty years, and both husband and wife were workaholics. They

86   *Just Folklore*

worked long, hard hours at demanding jobs and never took vacations. Weekends were rarely spent in leisure activities. One day the wife came across an advertisement in a newspaper by the Colorado Tourism Board which depicted an adult and small child skiing. The adult was supporting the child between its legs as they skied. The caption read: "Nobody ever looked back and wished they'd spent more time at work." The wife cut out the ad and taped it to her husband's toothbrush in the medicine cabinet. When he found it that night, it led to their reminiscing about the times they had had together when their kids were still small. Several days later the wife found the ad in the potato bin. The ad continued to be placed in surprising locations over the next several years, but usually in some context that communicated more time should be taken for the things that each of them enjoyed. When their twenty-five year-old son was married, they passed on a copy of the advertisement to him (Fletcher 1990:61–69).

Many dyadic traditions are *ephemeral*. They can spring into existence and disappear in relatively short periods of time. Many names, metaphors, and linguistic routines are not only dropped but forgotten as well. Several informants indicated they had a host of expressions and routines but could only remember a few. Undoubtedly some of these are only seemingly forgotten and constitute a repertoire that may be activated at any moment, but the informants are probably also correct that many of their traditions are irretrievably lost.

Dyadic traditions also seem capable of extraordinary and rapid *evolution*, as can be demonstrated with the instance of a pet name. The woman's name was "Judith," but because the couple was Jewish, a development took place from Judith to its Hebrew equivalent "Yehudit" and to its Yiddish diminutive "Hudl." From "Hudl" it was transformed to "Hud" and "Huds." From "Hud" it became "Huk" and "Hukus" (through the affixture of the deliberately mispronounced last syllable of the Yiddish word *tukhus* meaning buttocks), finally stabilizing for a brief period of time between "Hud," "Hukus," and "Tukhus."

Another conjugal pair reported that the male on occasion referred to the female as "penis breath," a phrase borrowed from one of the characters in Steven Spielberg's blockbuster film *E. T.*

This sobriquet eventually evolved to "*tepuli* breath" after the male finished reading Gary Jennings' novel *Aztec* in which this Nahuatl word for penis repeatedly appeared (1980:80, passim).

Folklorists are not unfamiliar with the extinction and transformation of traditions, but what is startling here is the excessive rate of change. Yet as a numerically minimal social unit, the dyad is prone to such change because the decision of only a single member is required for a tradition to disappear. If one ceases to participate, the tradition cannot be maintained in the unit. Furthermore, in large organizations, there is the moral and political force of a majority. Dissenters are often asked or made to conform. In dyads there is no majority. The traditions established result from implicit and explicit negotiations between the two persons and consequently are subject to any changes initiated by either one (Simmel 1950:137).

There may be another reason why dyadic traditions change so rapidly. The dyad, by definition, is an organization that cannot grow by adding or replacing members or expanding structurally. Instead, dyads may grow with the sense of exclusive knowledge that each member feels he or she has about the other—that is with the growth of intimacy (126–128). The deliberate creation, transformation, and extinction of traditions may serve to reflect and participate in this growing sense of intimacy.

Some dyadic traditions are thematically traditional rather than comprised of traditional content. Thus one couple greeted one another according to predetermined linguistic rules:

> He: Hi toots!
> She: Hi boots!
> He: Hi shmoots!
> She: Hi doots!

The exchange by no means needed to utilize the same phrases each time. It could begin with an entirely different opening yet progress along similar lines by altering consonants and maintaining the end rhyme:

> He: Hi babes!
> She: Hi shmabes!
> He: Hi grabes! etc.

It has already been observed that dyadic traditions test whether members of the dyad share a common orientation toward both the past and the present. The above exchanges suggest that these routines serve to communicate about the mood-states of the dyad members and ascertain whether a unity or harmony of mood exists. A member who refuses to participate in the routine sends an important message to the other person. Such communications are especially important in dyads where moods may have a disproportionate effect on the processes of interaction (Simmel 1950:135–136). Formal role relations involve culturally defined and relatively predictable expectations of behavior. Mechanisms that serve to evaluate mood-states of members of the dyad may increase the predictability of behavior and reduce the potential for conflict in interaction.

The members of another friendship pair were accustomed to trading insults that assailed the intellectual capacities of the other. No particular utterances were repeated, but each understood that when the opportunity arose, one could attack his compatriot along traditional thematic lines.

> A: I think I'll blow my brains out.
> B: I suggest you use a small caliber bullet.
>
> A: I've been getting these severe headaches. I'll bet I have a brain tumor.
> B: I'm sure it's not a *brain* tumor.
>
> A: I've been doing some hard thinking.
> B: Any thinking you do is hard.

Intellectual capacity was not the only traditional theme for such exchanges. Sexual capacity, physical appearance, and the quality of the relationship itself were also noted as themes for creative exchanges in this and other dyads.

Dyadic communication often seems to involve *insult* or *threat*. This has already been encountered in connection with the pet names "Hukus" and "Tukhus" as well as "*tepuli* breath." Some would dismiss this as an instance of ambivalence or the result of temporary resentments and regard it as sufficiently explained.[7]

Rarely, however, is the ambivalence or resentment demonstrated let alone correlated with the language or frequency of insult, so the hypothesis remains more truism than clarifying concept. Others would suggest that certain relationships provide the *license* to insult. To the extent that this is true, it also tends to mask the processes underlying the exchange of insults among intimates and tends to dismiss such behavior as merely another instance of license or permitted disrespect (Gluckman 1963:118, 168–169; Masheter and Harris 1986:17).

The examination of insults in dyadic relations is instructive. Traditionally exchanged insults are not perceived as insults. Rather they are regarded as their opposites: expressions of intimacy. The principle seems to be that the better two people know one another as persons, the less they depend on the literal meanings of received messages. The knowledge of their relationship frames the messages in an interaction, particularly those dealing with the relationship itself. The frame transforms—inverts—the messages so that literal insults emerge instead as signs of affection (Bateson 1972:177–193).

A particularly illuminating example of the operation of this transforming principle derives from my own experience. I have a close friend, a physician by occupation, with whom I frequently exchange traditional insults not unlike those already described. I am also in the habit of asking his medical opinion about occasional physical symptoms I experience. One time, after he questioned me closely about a symptom I had brought to his attention, I asked him what it all meant. Quite soberly he assured me that it didn't really mean anything at all, and that there was nothing to worry about. He must have seen the look of consternation that crossed my face because he immediately started laughing. What he realized was that if he truly wanted to reassure me, he should have said something like, "You'll be dead by morning." For a moment he had forgotten the transforming frame of our relationship and had employed a mode of reassurance appropriate only outside the dyad. I, on the other hand, had employed the frame in interpreting the message: if he were literally reassuring me, something must be desperately wrong.

In this case, the *failure* to threaten or insult caused the communicative problem. This situation cannot be adequately explained in terms of emotional ambivalence or notions of license. The principle called to attention is precisely the one that explains the preponderance of traditional insult and threat in dyadic units: the more intimate the people communicating, the more their relationship transforms the literal meaning of a message than the literal meaning of a message transforms their relationship.

The preceding discussion leads to a more general principle concerning the nature of dyadic traditions. The intimacy and sincerity of dyadic relationship is established and maintained through the regular violation of normal propriety. That is, it depends to a great extent on the violation of the rules that regulate encounters between strangers (Suttles 1970). Traditionalizing the response to dog wastes or body odors, ritualizing spitting in the bathroom sink, reveling in the exchange of insulting epithets or childish rhyming names are all, to some degree, violations of the behaviors thought to constitute normal social proprieties. In dyads, improprieties are created, traditionalized, and celebrated in the effort to engender and symbolize the intimacy of the relationship.

The overwhelming number of dyadic traditions I encountered in my research were *humorous*. Certainly it is possible that these were the only kinds of traditions my informants cared to reveal. Nevertheless, humor and play are prominent modes of traditionalized dyadic expression. Georg Simmel has argued that the dyad is an endangered and irreplaceable social unit. The death or secession of either member destroys the whole. Consequently dyadic relations engender ever-present feelings of melancholy and tendencies towards the sentimentalization of the relationship (1950:124). If such feelings are present, however, they do not directly express themselves in those dyadic traditions that are visible to the outsider.[8] Rather, it is the spirit of play that strongly imprints the culture of this relationship, so that one must be prepared to acknowledge that play and humor are important languages for the expression of intimacy and affection.[9]

7. Legend, Truth, and News

Nineteenth-century English folklorists focused their attention on survivals of savagery in the rural and urban lower classes to evidence the evolution of civilization from lower to higher stages, and to delineate the mentality of that geographically proximate class that nevertheless remained so remote intellectually from civilized society. The peasants persisted in their belief in spirits, sprites, and goblins and in the practice of their charms, spells, and rituals in the face of scientific discovery and industrial technology. The divide between savagery and civilization was nothing less than a divide between stages of thought and ultimately reducible to the difference between truth and error. What is the relation between modern truths and traditional errors? For example, wherein lay the truth of Christianity? Was it revealed religion or yet another system of belief that evolved from primitive animism? On this question the Victorian folklorists were largely silent. Similarly, what is the relation between the legends that are entertained as true, but which folklorists largely discount, and those accounts that contemporary folklorists consider to be true, but whose truth depends on the acceptance of the judgment of strangers? What, in other words, is the relation between legend and news?

> *Heaven have mercy on us all—Presbyterians and Pagans alike—for we are all somehow dreadfully cracked about the head, and sadly need mending.*
> —Herman Melville

THE STUDY OF FOLKLORE can be characterized by two complementary yet competing perspectives—the delineation of ideology and the discernment of art. From the crystallization of folklore studies in the late eighteenth and early nineteenth centuries, both of these strains were clearly evident. Nationalism motivated the perusal of legends, beliefs, and customs in an effort to reconstruct the ancient ideology that had defined and inspired the nation, while Romanticism motivated the collection of peasant poetry to catalyze a literary renaissance.

These perspectives continue to inform folklore studies, and each has assumed dominance at particular times and in particular places. Nineteenth-century British evolutionary perspectives focused almost exclusively upon the ideological foundations of contemporary custom (Lang 1910) while contemporary American perspectives have pushed folklore study towards the documentation and analysis of the aesthetic in everyday life (Ben-Amos 1971; Bauman 1986; Jones 1987). Neither perspective has as yet succeeded in obliterating the other. While aesthetic perspectives have tended to highlight tales, songs, and hand-made objects, contemporary ideological perspectives hover around the legend and related categories: belief (Honko 1964), memorate (Pentikäinen 1973), rumor (Mullen 1972), folk history (McWilliams 1978), and folk ideas (Dundes 1971).[1]

Legends have no form (Dégh and Vázsonyi 1976:93). The category of the legend is a function of the credible. The participants in legend communication must *entertain* the truth of the account. This is not to say that all must believe the account to be true, but only to admit that the issue of belief is central to the communication between the parties. In other words, the account must be communicated as though credible to someone, even if not to one of the participants in the communication (119). Appropriate responses to legend might include, "Incredible!" "Nonsense!" "Let me tell you what happened to a friend of mine," or "Only he could believe such a story." However, such responses would prove inappropriate to Märchen, songs, and jokes.

Yet the category of legend is doubly a function of the credible.[2] For there to be legend, there must be someone who fundamentally doubts the truth of the legend account. This someone is usually the folklorist who bestows the *legend* label. In other words, the legend is a category defined by credibility within a larger frame of incredibility.[3] Despite claims that legends can be true, or contain "factual elements" (Mullen 1972:98) or "kernels of truth" (Fine 1979:478),[4] it is the fundamental skepticism of the folklorist that generally finalizes the category of legend.

The kinds of accounts conceptualized as legend are those which, from the folklorist's point of view, depend upon information that is unnatural, unknowable, or unlikely. Since they are unnatural, accounts of ghosts and spirits are regularly placed into the legend category (Brunvand 1986a:161–165). The unknowable—information that is beyond the reasonable knowledge of ordinary men—such as accounts of the origins of geological formations (Dégh 1972:76), the contents of ancient undisturbed barrows (Ranke 1973:129–132), or the location of lost objects (de Caro 1968:25–26)—also are subsumed under this category. Accounts that are internally inconsistent, stretch the definition of normal coincidence, or are too artful, also tend to fall into the legend class.[5] But perhaps the ultimate arbiter of legend status is the existence of multiple versions. The greater the number, distribution, and variation of the versions of the account—i.e., the more "traditional" it is—the more likely that legend status will be conferred. This status is granted not so much because the account qualifies as genuinely "oral," but because it characterizes the account as genuinely incredible, for the curious events reported could not have happened to so many different people in so many different places (Brunvand 1981:xii).[6] Thus, the legend is a function of the ideology of the folklorist. It concerns what some folk are capable of entertaining as true that folklorists, for the most part, are not. "Tradition," consequently, emerges as an ambiguous term in the folklorist's lexicon. While it can privilege artistic expression—"traditional embroidery," "traditional architecture," or "traditional music"; it delegitimizes knowledge—"traditional beliefs," "traditional ideas," and "traditional history." It is no wonder that folklorists have not been able to woo the general public away from using the term *folklore* to label untruth or mistaken belief; it is a usage to which folklorists themselves are still mightily committed.

In the nineteenth century, false knowledge and mistaken belief were interpreted historically. They were the survivals of a primitive world view. Logical within their own original philosophical and religious framework, they were nevertheless wrong. They were historical residues of often rational, though mistaken, beliefs and practices. In the twentieth century, these same beliefs were viewed as the products of contemporary forces. Though fundamentally irrational, their raison d'etre was sought in their symbolic meanings and in their social and psychological functions.

At one time, the study of legend was confined almost exclusively to its oral formulations. Orality had been the touchstone of the legend as it was of all folklore.[7] In recent decades, however, folklorists have been more willing to approach written, printed, and electronic media sources. We can even speak of "media legends" largely purveyed and perhaps known only through mass media communication (Phipps 1980). Yet the willingness on the part of some folklorists to acknowledge the "interpenetration" of mass and folk culture (Bausinger 1968:131; Dorson 1972:41; 1978c:37–42) has not lead to a genuine encounter with the media as such.[8] More importantly, it has not led folklorists to an encounter with their own ideological program.

What is the relationship between the content of legend and the remainder of media content? At one level, there is a simple answer to this question. At the boundary of legend is not the myth or Märchen with which it is forever being compared (Bascom 1965; Dégh 1972:72; Oring 1986a:124–126). At the boundary of the legend is *news* (Hobbs 1978; Brunvand 1981:11, 13; Ward 1981, 2:373–374).[9] Were folklorists to suspend their disbelief, contemporary legendry would immediately resolve itself into the category of news. This observation poses a distinct challenge to folklorists. A genuine encounter with this basic category of folklore requires a simultaneous encounter with those reports, accounts, and stories that we ourselves have come to regard as fundamentally credible— that is, the reports, accounts, and stories that we read daily in the newspaper (Stephens 1988).[10]

If "news" is merely defined as any "new or unfamiliar information," news is as old as language itself—older, in fact. However, if we regard "news" as a type of information published in a "newspaper" (Warren 1959:13), then we are dealing with a considerably more recent phenomenon.[11] Of course, not everything published in a contemporary newspaper is necessarily thought of as news. Advertisements, puzzles, comic strips, editorials, gossip columns, reviews, recipes, letters to the editor are usually conceptualized as something other than news even though they may communicate much that is new. The definition of "news"—like the definition of *folklore*—is exceedingly problematic. To define news as "published accounts of actual, recent events or situations" may serve to eliminate puzzles, comic strips, and recipes from consideration, but many advertisements would still qualify, and much that appears in gossip columns and letters to the editor might qualify as well. An editorial that would not be news in the newspaper in which it was published, would be news in the newspaper which reported its appearance (e.g., "*Midvale Tribune* Opposes Mandatory Bussing"). It would seem that what is thought of as news in a newspaper is that which is framed in a newspaper as news.[12]

Newspapers—miscellanies of news published periodically, and connected by uniformity of title, ownership, and style of make-up—begin only in the sixteenth century, and appear in English only in the seventeenth.[13] Nevertheless, poetic and prosaic accounts of events were regularly published in book and broadside form before the appearance of periodical news publication. In certain respects the contents of these early publications were not unlike those of today.[14] Once separated from the extraneous matter with which they were often published, these early publications reported the affairs of state; battles; the affairs of the monarch, the court, and other personalities of the age; murder and mayhem; miracles and prodigies; fires, floods, earthquakes, and other calamities (Shaaber 1966).

There was no set process for ascertaining the accuracy of these accounts, and, except perhaps in the case of private intelligence, whether governmental or commercial, no organizations in place for collecting them. Only rarely were reports eyewitness accounts and many were often copies or translations from other publications (Shaaber 1966:168–188).[15] Moreover, these accounts tended to be occasions for moralizing, and the rhapsodies on the significance of the event could overwhelm the description of the event itself. Thus, a tract titled *Fire from Heauen. Burning of the body of one Iohn Hitchell of Holne-hurst... the 26. of Iune last 1613* devotes barely more than one of its twenty pages to the description of the burning of the body over a period of three days and the inability of anyone to extinguish it, while the remainder is a homily on the spiritual significance of the event (204). The murder of Sir Thomas Overbury occasioned no less than fifteen book and broadside accounts which were, however, mainly given to lamenting, counseling repentance, and admonishing evil (142–143). *The King of Denmarkes welcome:*

Containing his ariuall, abode, entertainment, both in the Cities and other places is also filled with verses celebrating the arrival of King Christian IV in England (26–27).

Today, we might have cause to doubt the accuracy of the information contained in many of these books, ballads, and "relations."[16] Yet, there is no reason to assume that such accounts were doubted in the seventeenth century—at least no more than our own newspaper accounts are doubted today. The difference between the two kinds of accounts is perhaps less a question of their truth as of their rhetoric of truth. The moralizing frames of the sixteenth-century accounts were a part of that rhetoric. No matter how bizarre, an account of an event was likely to be considered true if it evidenced the accepted moral order. What was contrary to this order was deemed "falsehood" and "lies" (Weisberger 1961:2). Thus, moralizing and pious commentary, rather than detracting from the credibility of an account, aided and abetted it.

In the twenty-first century, "factuality" and "objectivity" are the standards by which the credibility of news is measured. They are its rhetoric of truth. The "press" is not a reference to a machine, but to a powerful organization dedicated to seeking out facts and reporting them objectively. Objective reporting demands a separation of facts from values; a separation of assertions about the world that are true and verifiable from those that are distorted by personal preference and bias (Schudson 1978:4–6). Values or interpretations, when they are expressed, are attributed to a source and thus become facts of the account (Sigal 1986:16). Should values or interpretation be voiced by the press itself, they are framed as editorial or opinion and distinguished from news.[17] Reports of events that are explicitly shaped by allegiance to a particular social or moral order are suspect accounts. Factuality and objectivity are in themselves distorting, however.[18]

Factuality and objectivity foster the illusion that the news is a transparent representation of events and enjoys a privileged relationship with reality. This is an illusion because (1) the selection of what is to serve as news can be neither factual nor objective; (2) the news is organized and communicated as "stories"; and (3) news can never be independent of the process of collecting it.[19] There is no factual or objective basis to the news because values govern the conception, collection, and selection of news. As these are shared rather than personal values, they are often effectively disguised. News must be more than recent; it must be newsworthy, and within the notion of *worthiness* is subsumed the ideology of news.

Why, for example, are the following stories news? On May 17, 1988 the *Press Democrat* reported that a California Black Bear had wandered out of the countryside through certain residential sections of Santa Rosa, California and back into the countryside ("Town Awakens" 1988). Two days earlier, an Associated Press report appeared in the same paper concerning a 450-pound tiger in the Houston Zoo that had ripped through an inch-thick, reinforced window to kill its 59 year-old keeper ("Zoo Tiger" 1988) In June, the paper carried an Associated-Press-captioned photo of a bee-keeper trying to remove a swarm of bees from the car of a woman in Maastricht, the Netherlands that had infested her car while she was on an outing in the country ("Bee Careful" 1988). And *Time* noted ("Stalking" 1988) that near Sarasota, Florida, a four-year-old girl was dragged off by a ten-foot bull alligator and later found dead in the animal's jaws. Because of public reaction to this occurrence, the state of Florida was going to permit a controlled hunt to reduce the alligator population that had been protected since 1962. The notice was accompanied by a photo of a man pulling an alligator from the water into what appears to be his back yard. The alligator is half in and half out of the water and neighbors seem to be observing the activity from their own yard.

Each of these reports was of a recent event. Each of the reports seemed entirely credible, and emanated from an authoritative news organization. The richness of detail—the age of the zookeeper, the weight of the tiger, the thickness of the glass window, the length of the alligator, the name of the beekeeper, the species of the bear—enhanced the credibility of the account. Accompanying the bee report was a captioned photo that showed a person in protective garb scraping what was said to be a swarm of bees into a basket. The license number of the car and its Netherlands sticker were clearly visible, as was a small group of spectators, one of whom was identified in the caption as the owner of the car. The report about the bear in Santa Rosa was accompanied by a detailed map that traced the route of the bear's perambulations through the city as well as a schedule of sightings.

What constitutes the newsworthiness of such accounts? A number of "qualities" that characterize news have been identified: immediacy, proximity, prominence, oddity, conflict, suspense, emotions, consequence (Warren 1959:15–27). One or more of these qualities will be identifiable in every news story. While proximity and consequence would characterize the account of the bear for Santa Rosans, the stories of the zookeeper, the alligator, and the swarm of bees would neither be proximate nor consequential. These stories are news primarily by virtue of their oddity and/or emotion. What characterizes all these accounts as a class, however, is a common focus on the violation of a boundary between wild and civilized domains. The boundary between the wild and the domestic is likewise a concern of folklore. In *Deutsche Sagen* [German Legends], the Brothers Grimm included an account of St. Florentius who marked a boundary around his cultivated fields that miraculously prevented wild animals from entering them and eating his vegetables and grains (Ward 1981, 2:62). Richard Poulsen has described a practice by farmers in the American West of hanging dead hawks, coyotes, and other predators from their fences (1982). Among other intrusions of the wild into the city, Jan Brunvand reviewed the accounts of alligators in the New York sewers. In the fullest forms of the legend, baby alligators brought back from Florida as pets were flushed down the toilet. Many survived and grew in the sewers and occasionally attacked sewer workers (1981:91–98).

Of course, this boundary is also a topic of casual everyday conversation. When I mentioned to a friend that I had finally verified the dates of the "bear story" in the *Press Democrat*, a guest—a physician from San Francisco—asked, "What bear story?" When I told her that a bear had walked through parts of Santa Rosa, her response was, "No kidding!" This launched a conversation among the three people present—me, my friend who had also read the bear story, and the physician from San Francisco—about why the bear found its way into town. My friend offered the explanation that some residential parts of the city were hilly and fairly wild, whereas I recalled something in the newspaper account suggesting that drought had stimulated the bear to leave the hills in search of food. Perhaps a half hour later, the physician, who had just moved into a new apartment, talked about getting a pet bird and inquired whether parakeets were particularly noisy. I pointed out that mynah birds and parrots were raucous, at which point my friend reported that there were flocks of wild parrots in Alhambra, California (a city adjacent to Los Angeles) that were a real problem because of the noise they made. When the physician inquired further, my friend explained that these parrots were once pets that had escaped and bred in the wild. The physician once again expressed astonishment. Thus the boundary between the wild and the domestic, and reports of the violation of this boundary—wild animals that enter the city, pets that become wild—constitute an interest that is not restricted to any single medium of communication. They constitute an ideological field.

No good folklorist would likely regard the above news reports or conversations as deriving from or contributing to the alligators-in-the-sewer legend. They share not a single motif. (Presumably accounts of bears found in the sewers of Santa Rosa would evoke more interest.) The point is that there has been a tendency to view the relations between oral, printed and electronic media syntagmatically—that is, in terms of their contiguous connections. Legend scholars have been interested in the folklore motifs that newspapers and novels pick up from the oral stream and the ways in which news and literature feed into that stream. Thus, Brunvand can entertain a credible 1935 report in the *New York Times* about the sighting and slaying of a seven-and-a-half foot alligator in an East 123rd Street sewer as a potential *source* of the urban legend. He likewise comments on Thomas Pynchon's novel *V* as a particularly creative *use* of the legend theme (1981:92–93, 96–97). Similarly, Gary Alan Fine, noting a large number of legal suits concerning the presence of decomposed mice in soft-drink bottles, suggested that folklore forms may not be a function of the imagination alone, and that the urban legends centered on this motif may have multiple origins in oral accounts of these cases (Fine 1979b:478, 481–482). What has yet to occur, however, is the conceptualization of a single ideological domain to which folklore, news, literature, and court cases belong—that is, the recognition that our everyday news and court cases are as much symbolic constructions as our legends and novels (Berger and Luckman 1967; Gans 1980:297–299).[20]

Of course, news is usually more than just information about boundary problems. The news is most often communicated as "stories," and stories are coherent conceptual structures. Events make stories but stories conceptualize events. The following story again concerns the violation of boundaries between wild and domestic:

> LEOPARD KILLS TOT. Nashville, Tenn.—A leopard fatally mauled a toddler whose father used the animal in his rock n' roll nightclub act and had fought a bill to restrict ownership of dangerous exotic animals, authorities said.
>
> Five leopards owned by Joe Savage escaped from their cages Wednesday at the singer's home on 200 acres near Ashland City, said police Lt. Jim Blackmore.
>
> An orange spotted leopard attacked 2-year old Nikka Savage in the family's yard, where the child was playing, police said.
>
> The leopards were captured soon after the attack ("Leopard" 1988).

On the surface, newspaper accounts look quite different from the narratives to which folklorists are accustomed. News reports usually employ an inverted pyramid construction. They begin with the climax, move on to matters of secondary interest, and conclude with particular details (Warren 1959:85–87).[21] In the above account, we learn of a child's death before we learn of the father keeping the leopard at home. The upright pyramid, with the climax toward the end, is particularly characteristic of fictional folk narratives. It also is the form of construction frequently employed for human-interest stories in the press.[22] We have come to associate the inverted construction with the communication of "fact" while the upright construction is associated with "fiction."[23] However, the upright pyramid and inverted pyramid are merely distinctions in report construction—they are not differences in narrative structure—and they can readily be transformed into one another: "A father kept leopards at his home. He used the leopards in his rock n' roll act and had actively opposed legal restriction on the keeping of wild animals. One day the leopards escaped from their cages and killed his child who was playing in the yard." Conceptually, this is the same narrative, so the upright and inverted constructions are primarily rhetorical, not narrative distinctions.[24]

Like some legends, factual, objective news reports imply a moral as well. In "Leopard Kills Tot," a father *behaves foolishly* (ignores warnings restricting the ownership of dangerous animals) and *selfishly* (to serve his rock-n'-roll nightclub act), and is grievously *punished* (his child is killed). In some ways, the moral structure of "Leopard Kills Tot" is analogous to that of "Alligators in the Sewer." The alligators from Florida enter homes as pets. When an attempt is made to get rid of them by flushing them down the toilet, they remain under the city, and attack its human inhabitants (sewer workers). Like the news report, the legend implies that if someone thoughtlessly invites something wild into domestic space, they may not be able to control or get rid of it. The wild will always remain a threat. In fact, the only element that is necessary to fully realize the full potential of this moral structure is the eruption of the alligators out of the sewers to threaten the population of New York that put them there (rather than just a few sewer workers). If this structure has yet to be realized in oral legends, it has been realized in the cinema (*Alligator* 1980).

"Leopard Kills Tot" is but one in a stream of stories with which we are inundated each news day; some imply a clear moral, most do not: a driver is ejected from his car and killed in a Los Angeles freeway accident while the teddy bear next to him remained buckled up and secure ("Teddy Buckled" 1988); a school bus driver overturns her bus with 29 passengers on the way to receive a safety award ("Safety Record" 1988); a cat greets its owner and accidentally severs a vein in the 80 year-old woman's leg causing her death ("Cat Greeting" 1988); a guest drowns at a party for 100 lifeguards who are celebrating the first year without a drowning at a city pool (Romano 1986:44); teen-agers walking hand-in-hand are struck by lightning—the girl survives because she is wearing rubber-soled shoes ("Lightning" 1988); a mother and daughter, living miles away from one another, die on the same day from unrelated causes ("Mother, Daughter" 1987).

In the sixteenth and seventeenth centuries, such stories would have evidenced a divine order. They would have been passed on orally, featured in sermons, and published in tracts as testimonies to the hand of Providence in human affairs (Dorson 1973:17–19).[25] Today such stories, for the most part, are indecipherable. Their ironies challenge our notions of causality and our comprehension of a natural order (Barthes 1972). Such stories stand in marked contrast to those that address political and economic matters and which are explicitly conceived within a web of motives, forces, consequences, and significations (Carey 1986:172). The fundamental indecipherability of the ironic stories may, in fact, serve to persuade us that causality and order indeed reign in the domain of political and economic affairs (171). Whatever their significance, these stories are the providences and prodigies of our age, and it seems that folklorists should be bound to study them.[26]

To date, the newspaper has proven problematic for the folklorist. In fact, the newspaper would seem to be the very antithesis of folklore for it (1) highlights the new over the old; (2) replaces the fabulous with the factual; (3) emphasizes the objective over the subjective; (4) makes the private public; (5) produces uniform and authoritative texts; (6) is based in the spectatorship of strangers (a "public") rather than the interaction of familiars (a "community"); (7) is managed and scheduled rather than a spontaneous communication; (8) is produced by an organization with technological, social, political, and economic power; (9) is a commercial venture and deeply involved in the standardization and commodification of culture. One would be hard put to identify any institution that stands so unmitigatingly opposed to folklore which—correspondingly—is concerned with the traditional, fabulous, subjective, intimate, variable, communal, spontaneous, powerless, and non-mercenary. The newspaper stands as a distinct challenge to folklorists to examine their own ideology and address their own program—for while folklorists have chosen to describe and study expressions that reflect this latter set of values, their own descriptions, analyses, and interpretations do not proceed from these values. Folklore studies are not supposed to be traditional, subjective, or fabulous. Folklorists are located in powerful, bureaucratically-organized institutions, write for anonymous audiences, and are paid for their work. In other words, the values of folkloristics and the newspaper are one.

This divergence between the values we study and the values by which we study might not be so problematic were it not for two factors. First, folkloristics remains true to its romantic origins. Folklorists acknowledge the values of folklore expression as legitimate and important, while being unable to make use of them in their work.[27] Second, folklorists have claimed that the folk are not some particular group but everybody. "Who are the folk? Among others, *we* are" (Dundes 1977:34). But how are folklorists to study themselves if, at the center of the work that defines them, they must avoid the values that characterize folklore expression. The folkloristic study of folklorists could only be left to deal with the margins of folkloristic activity (e.g., Reuss 1974).

The concept of folklore was born as part of a program of cultural criticism so powerful that it reshaped the boundaries and literatures of nations. Today, folklorists tend toward marginal groups and marginal processes in the world. Indeed, there may be both merit and safety in such a program. But if folkloristics ever expects to regain its position as a critical force, it will have to discover a way to look at the center of things without losing a distinctive folkloristic perspective. It will have to gaze at Medusa without being turned into stone.

8. Legendry and the Rhetoric of Truth

Correspondence is the basis of one theory of truth. A statement is true if it corresponds to actual conditions in the world. "It is snowing outside" is true if it is, in fact, snowing outside. However, many—perhaps most—statements cannot be verified in this fashion. Statements about the future must await the passing of future events. Even statements about past or current conditions may not be verifiable through direct observation. Legends are narratives generally told by and to people who did not witness the events reported. Verifying their occurrence against observations of the world is not possible. In fact, legends are accounts of extraordinary events. As such, many of the events reported in legends do not even correspond to everyday understandings about how the world is supposed to work.

Unlike a folktale or joke, legend is a kind of narration that depends on the notion of truth. Folktales and jokes need not be believed and are generally not believed. Folktales and jokes are received only as "stories"—not as faithful reports. Such is not the case for legend. Legends do not begin, "This never happened." The truth of a legend must be entertained, even if that truth is ultimately rejected. The truth of a legend is entertained as a result of its rhetoric. Numerous tropes—linguistic and paralinguistic turns—serve to recommend the account as potentially, even plausibly, true. The truth of legend, in other words, is constructed in the course of its presentation. It is to be understood as a performance of truth.

> *I never set eyes on her in my life; but he that told me the story said this was so true, that I might vouch it for a real truth, and even swear I had seen it all myself.*
> —Miguel de Cervantes Saavedra

LEGEND IS PERHAPS one of the most exciting genres of folklore research today. The stuff of legends—the supernatural, the horrific, the disastrous, the uncanny, the improbable, and the comical—is the stuff of our everyday attention and conversation.[1] Furthermore, there is wide interest in these sorts of expressions. The general public evinces this interest in its consumption of books, television shows, and films about legends; and there is an interest on the part of public institutions—government, industry, the press—to gauge the extent and understand the willingness of people to believe a host of unlikely events.[2]

The downside of legend, from the point of view of the folklorist, is that no one seems to be able to pin down precisely what it is. Is it a narrative that proposes as true an account of events in the world that is objectively false (F. Ranke 1925:14)? Is it a narrative whose truth is the object of negotiation and debate (Dégh and Vázsonyi 1976:119)? Is it a narrative composed of traditional motifs (G. Bennett 1999:4; Ellis 1994:68; P. Smith 1989:98)? Is it to be distinguished from the anecdote or the personal experience story (Dégh 1991:15)? Is it restricted to a particular type of communicative channel or conduit (Dégh and Vázsonyi 1976:96)? Is it a process to test and define the boundaries of the real world and gain control over "ambiguous situations" (Dégh 1991:32; Ellis 1987:34, 68)? Is it a narrative that, unlike the folktale, is without form (Dégh and Vázsonyi 1976:93)? Is a legend told as true in one situation still a legend when told merely for entertainment in another (Ellis 1994:70–1)? Is legend a narrative at all (G. Bennett 1989a; Dégh 1996:34; Georges 1971:11; Nicolaisen 1987)? An exchange on these issues has been going on for the past thirty years, and although much of the discussion has been quite engaging, it would be premature to say that there is anything like complete agreement. As one prominent legend scholar concluded, "At best, then, the term 'legend' is probably a term of convenience which should not be taken too literally; at worst, it may be a misleading simplification" (G. Bennett 1991:189).

Most legend scholars hold that legend has some relation to belief; more specifically, that legends involve a debate about a belief (Dégh 2001:97). While this may be so, the problem is that almost everything entails belief. My shopping list entails the belief that the items written on it are available at the supermarket. Should a debate as to whether the local market actually stocks the items on my list make this discussion a legend? Folktales also entail belief, the belief that the events they describe do not really happen: giant beanstalks do not grow from magic beans, and wolves do not swallow humans whole. Furthermore, the discussion of belief has relied too heavily on accounts of the supernatural (e.g., Dégh 2001:216). The recounting of a supernatural occurrence invites belief in a separate domain of agents and forces.³ A comic tale about a series of accidents, however, entails no generalized belief other than that a concatenation of unlikely events could occur (Shuman 2005:89–119). To merge both of these instances into the same category of "belief" would obscure a distinction that might be worth preserving.

I prefer the notion that legend is concerned with matters of truth.⁴ First and foremost, a legend makes a claim about the truth of an event. It is or approximates a narrative. Much of the commentary and debate about the *event* that the narrative recounts is likely to be non-narrative in nature. Belief, rumor, and ritual (Dégh 2001:83–6, 403–404) may be related to legend but can be distinguished from it. For the whole, I would employ the word "legendry," an imprecise term to suggest a range of expressions that gravitate around such narratives. Legends may lead to the discussion of belief beyond a belief in the narrative incidents themselves. They may evoke discussion about the constitution of the world and the principles by which it operates. On many occasions, however, they do not.

It has long been noted that legendry possesses what has been called its own "belief language." This is the language of tradition—a common fund of knowledge that forms the "belief vocabulary" with which communications are constructed and which are cemented together by "the appropriate linguistic bonding agents" (Hóppal quoted in Dégh and Vázsonyi 1974:279). Without recourse to this belief language of agents, objects, forces, and signs, a proposition or narrative may be misinterpreted or totally misunderstood. Even when communities share beliefs, as in a belief in the devil, their belief languages may create very different understandings of what constitute the signs of his presence. A European, for example, would likely recognize a person with a horse's hoof as the devil. A North American might miss this identification, however (Dégh and Vázsonyi 1974:279–80). Belief languages often have specific histories situated in the life of particular communities. They are only sometimes shared. But what frequently seems to be shared in the enactment of legendry are the means of making claims for the truth, plausibility, or untruth of an account.⁵ Not a few students of legendry have commented on strategies for making narratives appear true (e.g., Blehr 1967:259–60; Ballard 1980; G. Bennett 1984, 1999; Boyes 1984; Correll 2005; Dégh and Vázsonyi 1976:11–2; Ellis 1987; G. Smith 1979; M. Wilson 1997). But these strategies—these "authenticating devices" (G. Bennett 1989a:2)—have generally been identified piecemeal in the process of discussing particular legends, legend clusters, and performance situations. These devices, however, would seem to coalesce in what might legitimately be described as a rhetoric—a *rhetoric of truth*. My concern here is to outline and illustrate this rhetoric. I am not interested in the rhetoric of the genre per se (Abrahams 1968). I am only interested in how legends are made to seem true (or untrue).

Legendry seems particularly apt for a study of the rhetoric of truth. Statements that are accepted as obviously true generate little commentary. "We comment on something we regard as false, something whose truth is open to debate, and on the occurrence of a 'true' statement when we had some reason to expect a false one" (Hobbs 1987:139). H. Paul Grice's cooperative principle for bona fide communication is based on four maxims, one of which is the Maxim of Quality: say only what you believe to be true (1975:45–7). Truth, in other words, is to be assumed unless something serves to signal otherwise. Legends, however, make claims that are perceived to be extraordinary. Because legendary narratives tend, regardless of their subject matter, to make such claims, they require the deployment of a rhetoric to allay doubts and foil challenges.

There are two claims that a legend can make regarding its truth. The first is for the truth of the account as it is given. If the narrative is about a surprise party in which a person embarrasses himself before a group of hidden guests, as in "The Surpriser Surprised" (Jansen 1979), then a claim is made that the party took place and the embarrassing behavior occurred in front of the guests as described. If the narrative is about a babysitter high on drugs who puts the baby she is caring for in the oven thinking that it is a turkey (Brunvand 1981:65–9), then the claim is that the account accurately reports what she did. But there is a second claim that some—but not all—legends make. Some legends make claims that go beyond the facts. The facts themselves call for further interpretation. A narrator told of a wealthy man who had a telephone installed in the mausoleum where he planned to be entombed, because he felt that he would come back to life. He promised to call his wife when he did. Several years later they found that his wife died of a sudden heart attack after she picked up the phone. When they checked the mausoleum, they found the receiver off the hook (Baker 1982:204). This legend presents a set of facts but asks the listeners to make the following inferences as well: that the man came back to life and called his wife and that she was so shocked to hear his voice that she died. A persuasive claim for this interpretation might require the narrator to present evidence to discount alternative hypotheses: that the phone in the mausoleum had not accidentally been left or deliberately taken off the hook; that the wife had a heart attack when she was on the phone with someone other than her husband. In other words, even if the facts of the case are accepted as true, the possibilities of coincidence or deception need to be eliminated. An interpretation of the events is called for: supernatural, happenstance, or ruse.[6]

Rhetoric is the art of persuasion. But if the legend's rhetoric of truth is learned, it is not explicitly taught. There are no manuals for its instruction or schools dedicated to its practice. It is a "folk" or "vernacular" rhetoric (Howard 2005) acquired by native speakers conjointly with the grammatical rules of their language, their sociolinguistic sensibilities, and their socialization for storytelling.[7] Here, I present this rhetoric, with some modifications, in terms of Aristotle's categories of ethos, logos, and pathos. Ethos is concerned with the character of the speaker, or in the case of legends, the speaker and the purported legend source. By ethos, I refer to matters concerning the narrator that bear upon the credibility of the account. Logos is concerned with the argument of the narratives and their attendant commentaries. Pathos focuses on the dispositions of the audience. Aristotle stresses the emotional aspects of audience response, but I would include cognitive and moral aspects as well (Aristotle 1991:38–39).[8]

Although the number of techniques or tropes in legendry's rhetoric of truth is undoubtedly finite, it should not be presumed that the catalogue below is complete. Nor do I make claims for it beyond Western

European and American legend repertoires in modern times. Nevertheless, comprehensiveness is a worthwhile goal. The hope here is to name, characterize, and illustrate as many tropes as possible based largely, although not exclusively, on a perusal of transcribed oral texts. Examples are drawn from a number of narratives to show that the tropes in question are not peculiar to a particular social group or performance situation. Some of the tropes outlined below have been previously identified by legend scholars. Others, however, have not.

Outline of Tropes

ETHOS

- The Authority of the Source
- Risk to the Narrator
- Distancing
- Judgment
    - Reflexivity
    - Alternative Explanations
    - Reluctance
    - Ignorance
    - Testing
- Expressions of Concern

LOGOS

- Intonation, Countenance, and Demeanor
- Laughter and Humor
- Framing
- Narrative Positioning
- Assertions and Affirmations
- Witnesses and Experts
- Corroborative Invitations and Challenges
- Discounting Alternative Explanations
- Narrative
- Narrative Strategy
- Narrative Detail
- Story Logic
- Paralogism
    - Behavioral Consequence
    - Emotional Reaction
    - Evaluation
    - Physical Evidence

- Instance of a Class
- Theory
- Secondary Legends
- Aesthetic Effects
  - Dramatization
  - Humor
  - Foreshadowing
  - Concealed Plot Functions
  - Synecdoche

PATHOS

- Cognitive Expectations
- Emotional Expectations
- Moral Expectations

ETHOS

The Authority of the Source

The authority of a source depends, to some extent, upon the social position of the narrator and/or the reputed source of the narrative. A narrator may be the source of the narrative (as in a memorate), or a narrator may attribute the narrative to some other source: a relative, a friend, or the friend of a friend. The status of the narrator and/or source in a rhetoric of truth can be entechnic or atechnic. That is to say, how the narrator and source are presented can be embodied in the discourse itself (entechnic), or it may stand outside the discourse (atechnic) (Aristotle 1991:37). The authority of the narrator and sources may be a matter of established knowledge. For example, in a legend I collected that I call "Messages from the Dead," the narrator was a physician. I knew this individual to be a licensed and competent physician, and his status lent authority to the narrative he related. However, the narrative itself—which concerns one of his patients whose daughter has died and who sends a message to her mother from the other world—also establishes his status as a practicing and concerned physician. Consequently, his status as a physician and any authority that might attend that status are presented in speech for anyone who might happen to hear it, even if they had not independently recognized him to be a doctor.

The status that bears upon the truth of an account is not simply a matter of professional or high-prestige positions. Doctors, flight attendants, paramedics, soccer players, or garbage collectors may bring authority to their narrations depending on the speech situation and the nature of the matter conveyed. Often, one of the most important status distinctions that bears on such authority is that of insider versus outsider with respect to some particular social group.

Not infrequently, the source for a narrative is a written account, the printed word, or some other communicative medium. The status of these sources may be previously known or established through speech: "Once in this magazine, like, I read . . ." (G. Bennett 1989b:308), "I think it were in the *Weekend* magazine" (G. Bennett 1989b:309), or "When I read about it, I've believed it" (G. Bennett 1999:37). Newspapers, radio, and television often have a degree of credibility, because they are public and produced by organizations that are supposed to check information and have the resources for doing so.[9] A Mexican girl disobeys her mother and goes to a nightclub and dances with a handsome young man who, in actuality, is the devil. In some versions, the woman is found dead. In another, she is impregnated by the devil's tail. One narrator claimed, "It came out in the newspapers and everything; it even came out on the radio" (Sobek 1988:152). However, another narrator, discussing a similar story, stated, "This was documented in a very famous Mexican newspaper called *Alarma*." This statement is ironic since *Alarma* in that person's opinion was a "rag," so the attribution is actually meant to undercut the credibility of the account (149–150).

The authority of the source may rest less on social status than on attributes of character. The character of the source and the physiological and psychological state of the source often become critical in producing a credible account. Thus, the physician who related "Messages from the Dead" identified the mother of the dead child as the source of his account. In characterizing the mother, the physician said that he had seen the patient many times before and that "she's an educated woman, she's very verbal, and she's always been there for legitimate complaints and nothing hypochondriacal" (Interview with Steven Barr [pseudo.], 13 November 1975).

Such attestations of character and sobriety are frequent: "I tell you that an aunt of mine seen a fairy. Now she believes that, and I believe her because I know her and she wouldn't tell a lie" (Ballard 1980:38); "The poor man, they do say they are mostly in his head now, but sure he was a fine fresh man twenty years ago, the night he saw them [the fairies]" (Correll 2005:14); "It wasn't drink; look at John Arch that never tasted a drop in his life" (6).

The character of a source may be discussed explicitly, as in the examples above, or alluded to indirectly. In a Mormon variant of the "Vanishing Hitchhiker" legend, the hitchhiker disappears from the backseat of a vehicle after proclaiming that the end of the world was approaching and that the occupants of the car should immediately start storing food as the church had advised. In these stories, the drivers of the vehicle are often Mormons on their way to do temple work or leaders on their way to a church meeting. Although these persons are not explicitly identified as the source of the story, people engaged in such activities are regarded by Mormons to be the most worthy and upright. Given the implication that the story could only have originated with the account of such worthies, an attestation of character is present, if only implicitly (W. Wilson 1975:87).

Risk to the Narrator

Some rhetorical force would seem to inhere in the risk that a narrator takes in telling his or her story. The more risk a narrator takes in telling a tale, the more likely the story would be perceived as true. In "Messages from the Dead," for example, a physician tells of a patient's deceased daughter who seems to write symbols on a chalkboard in her mother's garage. The physician had shown no previous interest in or disposition toward supernatural encounters or interpretations. Yet his recounting of the event suggests that he entertains their possibility. But the physician also tells of his attempt to dissuade his distraught patient from visiting a psychic in order to deal with her experience. The physician places himself in a difficult situation: he seems to entertain the patient's account, yet he admits he could not support her in seeking help from an expert in such matters. He also indicates that he repeated the account to a number of his colleagues—doctors and nurses—potentially exposing himself to challenge and perhaps ridicule. A narrator who tells a story that casts himself in a negative light or risks his reputation—professional or otherwise—makes an argument for the plausibility of his account.

In his famous book, *Liber Facetiarum* (ca. 1450 C.E. ; Hurwood 1968), Giovanni Francesco Poggio Bracciolini includes a great number of the jokes and anecdotes—mostly dirty—of his day. But it also includes an infusion of legendary materials. In a series of stories about monstrous animals, Poggio tells of a cow that gave birth to an enormous serpent that proceeded to suck out all of the cow's milk before departing. The cow later gave birth to a normal calf. Poggio states that "this was communicated [to the Pope] in a letter from Ferrara" (Hurwood 1968:47; see also Ellis 2001a:81). Taking the risk of reporting the account to a superior speaks to the faith of the reporter in the event and enhances the credibility of the account.

Distancing

"Distancing" refers to the degrees of separation between a narrator and the presumed source of the narrative. Georgina Smith (1981:169) classifies narrative in terms of such distances. They are either (1) "incorporated" (that is, memorates), (2) "semi-incorporated" (accounts of events attached "to a relative, named friend, or local character"), or (3) "detached" (narratives told without attribution of sources and the person or persons to whom the events purportedly happened).[10] Because distancing relates to the position of the narrator with respect to the events recounted, distancing is included in the category of ethos. Distancing directly relates to the authority of the narrator.

The more unambiguous the source of a narrative, the more believable the narrative is likely to be. Likewise, the closer the connection of a narrator to his or her source, the more credible the account is likely to be. Thus, it is often in the interest of the narrator in establishing the credibility of a narrative to identify a source and to specify his or her relationship to that source.

114   *Just Folklore*

The first-person memorate is likely to be the most suasive type of account, for the narrator claims to report something he or she has experienced. The narrator takes full responsibility for the account.[11] There is no basis for suggesting that story elements have been misapprehended or corrupted in a chain of transmission. To question such a narrative would be to challenge the narrator's judgment, truthfulness, memory, and perhaps even sanity (Slotkin 1988:107).

More distanced accounts are generally less credible (Bennett 1988:16; G. Smith 1981:168). Distances, however, are relative. Accounts from family members and close friends are more distant than a first-person narrative, but they are not so distant as an account from a person with whom the narrator has no social connection: a friend of a friend, or some otherwise unnamed or unspecified source.

The following attributions in legends display differing—and I would argue, increasing—distances between the narrator and the source of the events reported: "My mother was a Blackfoot Indian. I was ten years old when I had my first experience" (Pisarski 1980:131); "Well, and it's one that happened in my life when my father died. We went to the funeral and . . ." (G. Bennett 1984:86); "Oh, my father-in-law saw that. . . . Ooh yes! No doubt about that! When he was quite young! In Manchester!" (G. Bennett 1989a:2); "Last week, this twenty-four-year-old woman came in to see me specifically because she was having trouble sleeping. . . . Now talking with her, she started to describe . . ." (Steven Barr, 13 November 1975); "And Diane Dugan knew these two boys personally" (Ellis 2001b:123); "The girl's family lives in the town where my brother teaches, in North Jersey" (Jansen 1979:65); "This story was told to me by my roommate last summer [i.e., 1970]. He heard it from a person he had known when he lived in the dorm during the previous semester at . . . [the university]. The incident happened to some friends of this person in northern Kentucky, where he was from" (Jansen 1979:85); "Devil's Hollow, as I heard and recall it . . . (Gutowski 1980:79); "Well the way I heard it . . . " (Lecocq 1980:273); "It is reported . . . " (W. Wilson 1975:84); "This was a small college at Christmas and Thanksgiving vacation" (Grider 1980:154).

Distancing is, to some extent, a matter of choice. Undoubtedly, many narrators would be reluctant to personalize an occurrence that they had only heard about third hand. If all narratives were personalized in order to enhance their credibility, there would be no third-person narratives. Nevertheless, Edgar Slotkin (1988) has shown a narrator switching from a third-person to a first-person presentation of the legend "Swinging Chains." The legend describes a short engineer named Bert who always reached up and hit a series of eight chains hanging before the power plant boilers to set them swinging as he passed. After Bert died on the factory premises, the chains would suddenly start swinging of their own accord, as though he were passing under them and hitting them as he did when alive. The narrator's reason for the change in distance was not necessarily to enhance the truth of the account but to play to a particular audience member (103–105). Nevertheless, the switch from a distanced account to a first-person account would have considerable rhetorical force for someone who had never heard it told as a third-person account.[12]

Similarly, a letter writer to a British newspaper claimed that her sister worked in the social security office and "signed the bill for a colour television set for someone on supplementary benefit." A newspaperman checked with the letter writer, who admitted that it was not really her sister but one of her friends who signed the bill. "I just put that in my letter because it looked better" (G. Smith 1981:170).[13]

It is not surprising that legend distance often settles on the familiar "friend of a friend" (sometimes acronymized by folklorists as "FOAF"; [Brunvand 1984:51; Dale 1978:13]). It is a convenient rhetorical average. On the one hand, one source of the narrative is someone known to the narrator, someone whose character and judgment are presumably trustworthy. The friend's friend (or cousin's friend, or friend's cousin, or neighbor's aunt), however, is a stranger to the narrator. The narrator cannot vouch for the person at two removes, although presumably the narrator's friend might. The friend-of-a-friend attribution therefore establishes a close connection to a source with one known and supposedly trustworthy link and one unknown and potentially untrustworthy one. The formulation is a brilliant compromise in that the narrator can establish a relation to a potentially credible source without being held accountable for it.

Sometimes a narrator will establish a connection to one of the characters in the narrative who may or may not be the source of the story itself. That the character is the source may only be implied. In an account of "The Wife Left at the Roadside" (or "The Nude in the RV" [Brunvand 1981:132–6]), the narrator frames the narrative with "It was my aunty's neighbor who we knew very well. . . . Hayes, their name was" (G. Bennett 1988:14). In some cases, it is clear that the character could not be the source of the story. "I talked with him many, many times," said the narrator of the "Swinging Chains" protagonist. But the narrator left the plant where they both were working and returned only after the man was dead, when the legend about him had already begun (Slotkin 1988:93). Nevertheless, the connection to the individual increases the account's credibility.

There are circumstances in which the failure to specify a source might actually add to a narrative's credibility. This occurs when a source is purportedly known, but the names and relations are suppressed to protect the persons involved. "This really happened in. . . . The names are withheld because they are very well-known people in the community" (Glazer 1988:140). "Did you read about the poltergeists? You should talk to the lady who moved to seven homes, was haunted for fourteen years. Course I can't give her address, I don't think she would be in the mood to talk to you" (Dégh 1995:87). Or, "He claimed he was 'too well known' in the community to be attached to something as misunderstood as ghostdom" (Ellis 2001a:93). The rhetorical move is clear, for there would be no point in attempting to protect the identity of people in a story if the story itself were not true.

Judgment

Of all the character traits that narrators must display in their narration, discernment and judgment are the most central to establishing the truth of the account. Narrators endeavor to establish themselves as sober, perceptive, and critical individuals—not given to fantasy or gullibility. They attempt to register that the events they recount, though often extraordinary, are nevertheless real. Legends are often filled with effects to register the good judgment of the narrator. There are several basic ones: reflexivity, the consideration of alternative explanations, reluctance, the admission of ignorance, and testing.

Reflexivity: Often, narrators narrate reflexively so that, in the course of their relation, they evaluate the account from the perspective of their listeners. Who has not begun an account of an unusual or incredible experience with, "You are going to think I'm crazy, but . . ."? Narrators introduce their account by highlighting its incredibility, only to trump it with the evidence of their own experience. So begins an encounter with a spirit that haunts an old family homestead: "I am not an atheist, but rather a non-believer. I believe only what I can see. If I had not experienced the following story myself, I would have laughed at it" (Valk 2006:41). Or, "I might not believe myself there are such things but for what happened to me not long after I was married" (Correll 2005:6). Or, "Shall I tell you why I have this belief as well, which sounds really—I mean anyone would think, did she see it or didn't she. . . ." (G. Bennett 1984:86). Or, "I am the type of person who doesn't believe in anything I can't see and only half of what I hear" (Dégh 2001:350). Narrators also anticipate questions that their listeners might ask in order to demonstrate that they have critically examined the problems raised by their accounts (Correll 2005:3–4).

Alternative Explanations: Frequently, narrators will proffer an alternative explanation for what they have seen, usually, however, to eliminate the likelihood of that alternative explanation. A woman claims that she saw three puffs of smoke in her father's bedroom after his funeral. Her father had been a smoker. She admits to being a smoker but says, "I wasn't smoking then." She continues, "Somebody else could have looked in the bedroom and had a cigarette before I went in, but I honestly did [see] about three [smoke] rings like that. Now the only thing that I've sort of satisfied myself was, 'Oh, yes! Somebody else has been upstairs, and they've gone in there you see for something or had a cigarette.' But they were there!" (G. Bennett 1984:86).

The offering of alternative explanations of events has been portrayed as a defensive strategy on the part of narrators. Narrators wish to protect themselves from charges of superstition and credulity (Correll 2005:8). This may often be the case. But the proffering of rationalistic explanations for seemingly supernormal events also serves to display the discernment that suggests that the narrator possesses a sound mind and good judgment—someone worthy of trust and belief.

Reluctance: In an account of a legend called "The Fast Food Ghost," the narrator goes to great lengths to suggest alternative explanations for his experiences, even as these explanations seem to evaporate one by one. The narrator claims to have seen a figure one night. He knew he had locked the store, but he thought he saw someone standing by the freezer area wearing a flat-brimmed hat and buckskin jacket. The image moved out of view down the hall. The narrator assumes a critical approach to his vision. He checks all the doors to see that they are locked and the restrooms to see that no one is there. Another sighting of the phantom took place at a later date, when the same narrator was walking past the pizzeria. He reported that he waved his arms to ascertain whether the image he saw might be his own reflection. The figure moved towards him, and he wondered whether it could be the headlights of a car. Then the image vanished (Ellis 2001a:127–128, 136).

The narrator claimed that he looked into local history to see whether any incident had occurred in the vicinity of the pizzeria. He didn't find that anyone had been killed there, but he was open to the possibility. He then stated, "I don't believe there's such a thing as a ghost, but I damn well want to find out what there was. . . . That's why I have to find out if there is something there. Am I just seeing things or is there something there? I think there is something there because of everybody having these spooky things happening" (131–132).

The narrator resists identifying the figure he saw as a ghost—even at his interviewer's urging—although he seems more open to the possibilities of a "spirit," some "physical force," or "magnetic energy" (132–133). Nevertheless, he has done some research to find out whether anyone had been killed in the vicinity, he has established that the figure is not likely to be material, and he is afraid of the manifestation. He has offered no real suggestion to explain what concept might account for what he saw other than his own misperception, which he suggests but does not seem to believe.

Bill Ellis feels that the narrator's sense of dissonance is the result of being forced to cast his encounters in an experientially ungrammatical way. Ghosts do not appear in pizzerias, shopping malls, or other venues of modernity. Because the narrator could not fit his experience into the traditional cast of ghostly sightings, he rejected the ghostly interpretation for fear of being thought deviant. He was caught between his experience and the language to express that experience (Ellis 2001a:138–141).

Ellis may be right, but the narrator's formulations also persuade that he is a trustworthy observer, one who questions and tests his perceptions, a rationalist unwilling to grasp at supernatural explanations even when no others offer themselves.[14] He presents himself as a reluctant witness or at least as a reluctant interpreter of what he has witnessed, and within his persistent self-questioning and his reluctance is much of his rhetoric of truth.

Ignorance: Sometimes narrators confess to an ignorance of the facts. In doing so, they present themselves as prudent chroniclers, resisting claims to complete knowledge. However, the overall account and its interpretation generally remain unaffected. Thus, in recounting the difficult relations between Bell Gunness—a woman who later proved to be a serial murderess and the topic of many narratives in La Porte, Indiana—and her neighbor, the narrator corrects herself about whose cows may have trespassed first: "It may have been that his [cows] went in there first and then he had to pay to get them back" (Langlois 1978:153). The narrator's obvious care in recounting the facts suggests that facts are not matters to be trifled with. The narrator is making an explicit effort to get things right, which enhances the credibility of the whole.

Testing: A narrator may indicate what tests were performed to authenticate evidence or to favor a particular interpretation. The narrator of "The Fast-Food Ghost" mentions how he checks his perception by waving his arms to eliminate the possibility that it was his own reflection that he was seeing. Teenagers describing a visit to a haunted cemetery site guarded by Indian ghosts often mention their unexplainable car trouble. The car would stall repeatedly "although there was nothing wrong with the engine 'cause we checked" (Meley 1991:8). Another teenager recounted how his brother and his friends called up on a ouija board the spirit of a Mrs. Brown, who told them how she died: "And [they] went to check up the house, and they asked them this and it were all true. And they went to her grave as well" (G. Bennett 1989b:306) in an effort to confirm the information that they had received.

In an isolated location in northern Indiana, a man was supposed to have killed himself after he killed his wife. He didn't leave a suicide note, but before he died, he built a strange fence around his house in which no section replicates the design of any other section. It was believed that the man had encrypted a suicide message in his fence. A light was always supposed to be on in his house on the hill. "Several of us did one time more or less concentrate on the fence and did conclude that part was true. . . . The light itself always burns. . . . I been down there every time of the day or night . . . and the same light was always burning" (Gutowski 1980:75–76).

In some respects, legend trips as a whole serve as tests of legends about haunted locations. If uncanny or frightening experiences occur, then they serve to confirm the truth of the original account. Most legend-trip narratives are legends in their own right and often displace or suppress the narratives that charter the legend trip in the first place (Meley 1991:12).[15]

Expressions of Concern

Many legends are reports of dangerous, tragic, or horrific events that have befallen certain individuals. Narrators often express their concern for members of their audience and urge them to avoid becoming victims themselves. Narrators issue warnings and exhort others to avoid certain locales and situations or to take certain precautions before engaging in specific behaviors. Narratives about strangers who cause people to be stuck with HIV-infected needles are one example. Friends are instructed not to go to particular movie theaters or night clubs. They are urged to be careful in reaching into coin-telephone change returns or instructed to closely examine pump handles at gas stations. In fact, the legend narrative may be invoked to justify such exhortations and warnings:

> "Hell no! Don't go there!"
> "Why not?"
> "Didn't you hear?"
> "Hear what?"
> "AAAHHH DAAAMM! You didn't hear the story about the girl?"(Correll 2008:65–67).

Expressions of concern establish narrators as caring individuals interested in the well-being of their interlocutors. Such individuals are more likely to be believed because their narratives are not related merely as matters of curiosity but for the benefit of others. To doubt the truth of the narrative is in some sense to doubt the good intentions that motivate it.[16]

LOGOS

Intonation, Countenance, and Demeanor

There are, perhaps, no more important factors in the rhetoric of truth than intonation, countenance, and demeanor. Those folklorists that have worked with transcriptions of legends have often noted their intonation in discussing legend credibility. Countenance and demeanor have been mentioned, if at all, only in passing (Brunvand 1981:5).

"Vera's voice . . . is low, her tempo slow, her intonation almost monotonous, even her bit of dialogue is hardly differentiated from the surrounding discourse. There is a sad, reflective quality in both the narrative and non-narrative parts of her utterance. She is plainly thinking out loud" (G. Bennett 1984:82). "She is notably tense at key moments of the narrative and her voice is full of a gasping nervousness throughout the whole performance. There are also marked 'no go' areas in the story, where her voice trails away in a prolonged low-falling intonational contour which seems specifically to deter challenge" (G. Bennett 1989b:296). "This interruption is signaled also by a shift from Mary Beth's narrative tone, in which pitch levels are flattened almost to a sing-song quality, back to the conversational tone that prevailed when the participants were freely exchanging comments" (Ellis 1987:50). "The result is a different kind of irony, as the statement is made in Bruce's 'amazed' intonation, and the careful description that follows in 'rational' tone leads only to more exact observation of the impossible and therefore to greater certainty that something supernatural is empirically there" (Ellis 2001a:136). The point here is not to generate a list of examples where intonation is central in the projection of story truth, but to suggest that the intonations of truth need study. Intonation can communicate seriousness, wonder, joy, excitement, fear, sadness, anguish, nervousness, irony, and doubt. Most people successfully understand the import of such intonations when they are deployed, although there is as yet no complete index of the means by which they serve to create a plausible account.

Laughter and Humor

Laughter and humor are often a part of legend performance. It would be natural to assume that the laughter of a narrator accompanying the relation of extraordinary events serves to discount the reality of the account in question or the interpretation that might be offered of them (Oring 2003:ix). Similarly, a humorous gloss would likewise suggest that an account is not to be taken seriously. A perfectly good illustration of these precepts can be found in Bill Ellis's transcription of a performance of "The Hook" legend (1987). Three women in their early twenties who had been friends through high school got together for an evening of socializing. One of them recorded the event for possible use in her university folklore class. The performance is punctuated by laughter; broad, humorous descriptions of events; and sarcastic commentary. The legend is clearly being told as entertainment. It is not intended to be believed. Ellis uses the laughter and humorous commentary to suggest a meaning for "The Hook" that had been overlooked by folklorists who had not analyzed tape-recorded and closely transcribed narrative performances (1987:54–57).

It is not possible to represent all the ways that laughter or humor adhere to legend performance. Some caveats may be offered, however, concerning their significance. There are different kinds of laughter, and not all are responses to humor or signify the discounting of the events related. Gillian Bennett remarks on the chuckles that accompany a legend told "for fun" (1984:80) and discusses the performance of "group sagas" that are "invariably told by two or more narrators, the audience chipping in, laughing, barracking, and accusing the narrator of 'rewriting history'" (G. Bennett 1989c:201). But Bennett also notes the "breathy giggles" and "tense, breathy laughter" that suggest the events related were not discounted but were regarded as true (G. Bennett 1989b:296).

Forms of laughter may also be associated with joy, wonder, triumph, and surprise. Even humorous laughter does not necessarily discount the truth of the message that it punctuates. A narrator related how he had briefly been a premedical student in Iran. His brother-in-law, a surgeon, would regularly invite him to observe operations that he performed. In one instance, an old woman came to the surgeon with an abdominal complaint. The brother-in-law had a saying: "Never let a thin membrane stand between you and an accurate diagnosis." He operated on her and found cancer throughout her abdominal cavity. He closed her up again and sent her on her way, expecting that she would shortly be dead. Sometime later, to the surprise of the surgeon, the woman returned with another complaint. He opened her up yet again. This time there was no sign of any cancer in the abdomen (Interview with M. Omidsalar, 24 November 2005).

The story was told in a light tone, and at the point of revealing that no cancer was found in the second operation, the narrator laughed. When asked whether this story was true, the narrator claimed that he was there and had witnessed both operations. His laughter was probably meant to emphasize the surprise and dismay associated with the observation of the second operation and possibly to comment on the arrogance of medical science and its presumption to know the workings and outcomes of disease processes.[17]

When a humorous legend is presented as true, a special guarantee may be needed: "This is very funny, but this is absolutely true" (G. Bennett 1988:14). Sometimes laughter may be of the discounting kind, without entirely negating the truth-value of the account. The laughter may be reflexive and serve to display that the narrator is aware of the unlikelihood of the events reported and the enormous leap that may be required to make sense of them. It may also be an attempt at face-saving: an expression of the ambivalence of a narrator who holds the facts of the account to be true, coupled with a reservation of judgment on their interpretation.

Framing

Framing concerns the degree to which a narrative is foregrounded in respect to the speech in which it is embedded. Certain folklore genres may open and close with formulaic frames, "Once upon a time" and "they lived happily ever after" perhaps being the best-known examples in the English language. In legend, the degree to which the narrative is foregrounded generally reduces its claim to truth. The narrative is characterized as a story rather than as a transparent representation of events. The difference is one between "words as words" and "words as world" (Ellis 2001a:100).

Words-as-words emphasizes the storied nature of the account: "In a small town in Utah, the story goes" (Jansen 1979:86); "There's this story back in Gary" (Barnes 1986:75); "There's this story of the birthday man who suffers gastric distress" (Jansen 1979:81); "Well, another story they tell about the fairies . . . " (Ballard 1980:35); "This is told as actually having happened" (Jansen 1979:84). Sometimes the introduction of the story uses the framing language of fictional genres: "I heard this story as a joke" (Jansen 1979:72); "Well, there's this businessman, see . . . " (75); "Do you know the one about the pregnant lady who was going to the doctor's . . . " (Barnes 1986:74); "I have heard other teachers mention it. I don't necessarily think it is a teacher's joke, but it's more the classic if you want to tell something that is going to flip people out" (Ellis 1987:42). Even the "Once upon a time" formula is sometimes employed (Jansen 1979:87). Some narrators may adopt the terminology of folkloristics itself in framing their accounts: "Well, let me see. I guess the place where the legend started was with this doctor" (Lecocq 1980:268), or "I know other versions" (Sobek 1988:151).

In words-as-world, pointing to the account as something told or passed on is avoided. The listener is thrust into the experience itself: "I was out riding with a bunch of guys and we finally ended up at the Tunnel" (Hall 1980:229). "What happened is they had gone to the grocery store" (Barnes 1986:76). "Wow. You're really getting into a heavy thing. Where do you begin? Yeah, this is the way it began" (Lecocq 1980:266). "Now I'll tell you one thing! When I was younger I used to look into teacups. Now mother had a friend . . ." (G. Bennett 1999:68). "[Did] I ever tell you about the Pizza Hut ghost? Um, people would not close alone at the Pizza Hut because of him" (Ellis 2001a:119).

In discussing Zuni narrative, Dennis Tedlock suggests that framing may be proportional to the extent that a narrative departs from audience expectations of reality— true stories are less likely to be framed (1983:165). That correlation would seem to apply in this culture as well. Certainly, those stories with formulaic openings are most likely to be regarded as fiction. But even narratives that are purportedly about real people and events, when framed as "stories," have considerably more work to do if they are to persuade an audience of their truth.

Matters of framing and distancing underlie the characterization of a narrative as "old" or "traditional." Old or traditional narratives are necessarily distanced from their sources and framed as words-as-words rather than words-as-world. Such characterizations necessarily raise questions about the truth of an account. The extent to which the mantle of tradition is likely to enhance believability would depend on the extent to which tradition is revered in a particular society. There are societies in which the invocation of tradition would in itself prove suasive. In contemporary Western society, for the most part, it does not.

Narrative Positioning

There is another kind of framing that can take place in legend performance. It is the framing of narratives with respect to other narratives. The narratives may be those performed in the same venue. A narrative may be embedded in the midst of narratives whose truth-value is higher or contrasted with narratives whose truth-value is lower. Narratives may also be positioned in relation to narratives explicitly invoked by narrators as a contrast to their own accounts. "There was no lie [in it]—whatever lies there are about fairies—[it was] neither a remarkable story nor lies" (Correll

2005:7). At present, there are not enough good transcriptions of complex, legend-telling events to adequately document instances of this move, but it seems likely that truth would be enhanced by the judicious positioning of an account in relation to others.

Assertions and Affirmations

Because of their extraordinary content, legends often are accompanied by explicit commentary on their truth (Ballard 1980:37). Assertions are those remarks that comment on the truth of the narrative: "And that's the God's truth" (Jansen 1979:76); "That's the truth. That happened" (Ballard 1980:38); "This incident is known to be a true story" (Glazer 1988:141); "That was as true as the sun shining in the sky" (Correll 2005:7); "That's true you know. There's no doubt about that" (G. Bennett:14); "This is absolutely legit" (Slotkin 1988:99). Affirmations are claims about the reality of the narrator's experience or world view. Affirmations interpose the evaluation of the narrator between the event and its truth-value: "There was something there. I know there was something there" (G. Bennett 1989b:308); "Isn't it extraordinary, that?" (G. Bennett 1984:84); "Some people think you've imagined these things, but no! I've heard my husband's voice, and there's not been a soul in that flat" (G. Bennett 1999:53); "I was very impressed by one of the stories told by one of my friends" (W. Wilson 1975:85). Bennett published a list of affirmations that she encountered in her study of women's supernatural narratives, ranging from "I firmly believe" through "I don't believe in that" (G. Bennett 1999:193). It is not clear if there is a difference in the suasive force of assertions and affirmations.

Witnesses and Experts

The authority of an account need not rest solely on the narrator or the source. Witnesses may be invoked to corroborate the account. Witnesses may be included as participants in the narrative action. In "Messages from the Dead," the doctor describes the mother finding her child's chalkboard with a skull and bones and the child's name written on it in the child's own hand. She asked her other children whether they had written on the board, but they denied it. When a neighbor stopped by the following day with her small daughter, she took her to see the chalkboard, but the neighbor's daughter had been playing with the board and had erased all the writing. The girl said she had been trying to write on it, but the chalk wouldn't write. "Now at this point the mother swears that this is what happened, with the neighbor standing by her side and the children standing there, that the skull and bones reappeared. . . . Now, there were two adults there and three children" (Steven Barr, 13 November 1975). In telling of a ghost that appeared one night in his bedroom chair, the narrator says, "And . . . my brother got right scared and . . . tell me to try and, tell me to turn [the] light on and I didn't. I were like paralyzed. I just couldn't turn it on!" (G. Bennett 1989b:308).

Shortly after the death of her sister's daughter, the narrator and some family members were in the kitchen preparing food for guests. They heard the crying voice of the sister. This sister was at the funeral home making arrangements. "We ran to this door. There were four of us. We ran to that door, nobody there, nobody. . . . If it would be only for me, they could call me a fool, or that I am raving, but all four of us ran" (Dégh 1995:291).

A variant of the "Vanishing Hitchhiker" legend tells of a couple that picks up a bearded, long-haired youth along the highway. After a time, the youth asks his drivers, "Do you know Jesus?" When they answer, a little uneasily, "Yes," he says, "That's good, because Jesus, that's me." When they turn to look at him, the back seat is empty. Greatly agitated, they relate their experience at the next gas station they come to. The station attendant says, "You are the tenth family today to come and tell me the same thing" (Klintberg 1989:88). The attendant serves as a witness to independent reports if not to the event itself.[18]

Often, witnesses are not characters in the narrative but attest to it in the commentary on the account. "But some of the neighbors say that her leg was as cold as ice. It is her own father who told me the story from beginning to end, and Denis O'Brien from Ballyline Bridge told it the self same way. But in truth he is afraid that it is a bit make-believe and that she merely pretended to be dumb and lame. He admits, however, that respectable people told him that her leg was cold as I have already said" (Correll 2005:13).

Experts are not necessarily witnesses to the events reported but authorities in the subject matter of the narrated event. Experts are appealed to in the justification of a narrative: "Listen, scientists are looking into this, isn't that so? You hear me? They directly look after such things to find out" (Dégh 1995:304). The truth of stories about lake monsters is enhanced, for example, when it can be reported that cryptozoologists are investigating the matter with scientific equipment (Gabbert 2000:121). There is the legend about gang initiations in which gang members drive with their headlights off. If an oncoming motorist should courteously flash his headlights to alert them to the fact, they then shoot into his car. This legend often circulated on the Internet, through e-mail messages, in faxes and photocopies, and orally. The hard-copy versions often begin with an authenticating introduction: "A police officer working with the DARE program has issued this warning" (Brunvand 2001:241). Of course, appeal to the experts can likewise be used to discredit an account. In telling a version of the "The Hairy-Handed Hitchhiker," the narrator states, "Andrew works for the Police Department and said, 'Oh that's nonsense!'" (G. Bennett 1988:15).

On occasion, an expert may be a witness as well. In 1856, the *Deseret News* in Utah gave an account of a bearded man in strange garb carrying a little Hebrew book. He read from the book to the crowd around him and represented himself as the Wandering Jew. "A learned Jewish Rabbi was sent to converse with him, which they did in the Hebrew language. . . . The Rabbi tested him in the Arabic, the Phenician [sic], and in the Sanscrit, but soon found that the aged stranger by far surpassed him in intimacy with them all" (Glanz 1986:108). So the rabbi serves as both witness to his appearance and expert on his linguistic abilities.

Corroborative Invitations and Challenges

Legend narration often involves the participation of listeners who ask questions, support or challenge events, and offer their own interpretations (Dégh and Vázsonyi 1976:104–107). Narrators may encourage the support of certain members of the audience, particularly those who have been witnesses to the events in question, know characters described in the story, or have had similar experiences.

By recruiting the support of others in the course of the narration, a narrator can reduce the dependence of the narrative on his own personal experience and judgment.

In telling about an old man who came out of a white house on a hill near a graveyard and started rolling down the hill, the narrator invites and receives corroboration (in square brackets) from someone else who claims to have seen him: "You know what I'm talkin' about don't you?"—["Yeah"]—"That little white house up on that hill?" (Peters 1988:228).[19] In telling a story of how a priest raised the soul of a dead man from Hell and restored him to a room in his son's house, the narrator concludes: "Now this story was told to me by an uncle of mine, and you remember, he used to sell milk round the town?"—["Uhuh, Joe"] (Ballard 1988:171). The invitation may be explicitly formulated as above or registered in the rising intonations of a question: "I know about a few week ago like I just start like getting a song in my head and I'm singing it and then I hear it on't radio next day?" ["Yeah, I've done that."] "Sometimes I like hum this song and my mum thinks you know she's singing same thing." ["I've done that."] (G. Bennett 1989b:294).

A corroborative challenge invites the listener to test some fact proposed in the narrator's account. Unlike the invitation, no response is called for at the time of the narration. Generally, the challenge cannot be met because the means of testing it are not immediately available. Slotkin cites an example of a hog butcher who maintained that he would not butcher his own steer or hog in a waning moon because the meat shrinks. After several assertions, he invites the listener to corroborate his experience: "And I said it was proven, that I done it, and seen it done. I say that anybody that wants to try it can try it and find out for their own satisfaction" (Slotkin 1988:89).

Discounting Alternative Interpretations

Proposing alternative interpretations can increase the credibility of narrators by showing them to be reasonable and discerning people. But if a narrator wishes to advance the truth claims of a particular narrative interpretation, that narrator must eliminate alternative interpretations of the events.

In the course of suggesting that some other smoker might have been in her dead father's bedroom before she entered, the narrator, in a legend discussed above, largely eliminates that possibility. Considering that she saw no one entering or leaving her father's bedroom, the rationalist explanation is belied by the perception of "three whiffs" or "three rings" of smoke that would have likely dissipated before she got into the room. She does not claim merely to have smelled smoke—something that might naturally linger in a room—but reports seeing the smoke as if the result of some kind of exhalation. It is important to note that once the alternative explanation is offered, interpretation becomes the focus of attention. What does the smoke signify? The narrator conclusively decides the matter with a secondary legend about the experience of her own daughter (discussed below).

Sometimes narrators suggest, either explicitly or implicitly, that it is up to the audience to draw their own conclusions about the account. The narrator only has the unvarnished facts to offer. In speaking of a man whose cart was overturned immediately after cutting a fairy tree, the narrator concluded, "I don't mean to say or imply anything, but this is the truth" (Correll 2005:8–9). In speaking of his own possible sighting of a lake monster, a narrator says, "It's possible it could have been a fish, I'm not going to stand on that. I'm not going to say it was Nellie or whatever. . . . Could have been a fish. It was big enough to be something. If it was a log, why would it have sank again? Why wouldn't it just float along in the water?" (Gabbert 2000:117).

Timothy Correll cites an example from the Irish Folklore Commission archives in which a man in Ballyshannon lay in bed for thirty years without getting up. They said he used to go with the fairies. "Whether it was true or not, I don't know. . . . He was able to tell them everything that was happening on the land, and he not out at all.... Don't you know well he must have been 'going with them'; what other way was he able to tell all that?" (Correll 2005:8).

Inviting the listener to make his or her own decision about the events described is deceptive. Listeners do not need to be invited to make sense of what they hear, so the offer is something of a ploy. Further, a listener's evaluation or interpretation is constrained by what the narrator has presented. One is expected to work with the facts as they are given. By the end of the description of the possibility of someone having smoked in the narrator's father's bedroom, attention is focused upon the source of the smoke, not its reality. In interpreting the ability of a bedridden old man to see what was going on in his community, the hearer is distracted from more basic questions: Was the old man truly bedridden? What communications did he receive from the outside, and what, if anything, was he able to see? Nevertheless, the invitation to interpret does make the narrator seem open to alternative suggestions and sound sincere in the quest for truth.

Narrative

Humans are a narrating species. There are no cultures in which narrative is not an important communicative resource. Narrative is itself a meta-message about the reality that humans share (White 1980:5–6). If narrative is universal, it may be local in its grammar, style, formulae, and performance venues. Narratives are formidable rhetorical tools capable of engendering a deeper commitment to ideas and organizations than other forms of information (W. Bennett 1978). There is experimental evidence that shows that information conveyed in a narrative is better remembered, more persuasive, and engenders greater belief than statistical information communicated on the same topic. This is true even for people trained to use and understand statistics (Martin and Powers 1983:100–101). Yet narrative presents only a single case, whereas statistical information can summarize a great number of cases. The proverb "'For instance' is not proof" is belied by the power of narrative to persuade on the basis of a single example (98).

Narrative Strategy

Gillian Bennett has argued that the presentation of a legend narrative has much to do with its claims to truth. She noted that in her work with supernatural stories in Manchester, England, her female informants employed two kinds of presentational strategies. One involved the straightforward telling of a personal experience that closely paralleled the structure outlined by William Labov and Joshua Waletzky for personal experience narratives: orientation, complication, evaluation, resolution, coda (Labov and Waletsky 1967:32–41). She also noted stories that were structured in "non-final, non-linear forms" (G. Bennett 1984:82–3). These latter stories were much looser in terms of the temporal unfolding of events and revolved around some central point to which the narrative repeatedly returned. Such narratives may return to an earlier time, introduce some new elements, and return to that previous time yet again. Elements of the story with central significance are repeatedly reformulated. Sometimes these loose patterns end with an invitation to clarification and discussion of what has been told (84–86).

Of forty stories told to Bennett in a linear fashion, only seven were told by women who seemed open to the idea of the supernatural. Most of the women open to supernatural belief preferred the looser, more circular patterns that focused less on story than on description, detail, and evaluation. "They revolve around the question of the truth and actuality of the experience, in order to classify and interpret it" (87).

In later work, Bennett compared the narration of a person who clearly represented his narrative as true with someone who obviously regarded his narrative as false—told "for true" versus told "for fun."[20] Neither of the narratives depended upon supernatural belief and, to folklorists, both were well-documented urban legends (1988:14–15). Bennett draws a number of contrasts between the presentations (many of which are addressed above and below), but in regard to the question of narrative presentation, the narrative purported to be true is executed in a straightforward linear fashion that corresponds to Labov and Waletsky's personal-experience structure (1967:19). Bennett notes that this narrative makes use of a "riffle and pool" (analogous to Frances B. Gummere's "leaping and lingering" [1907:91]?) effect, in which narrative movement is temporarily "dammed up" by explanation and dialogue. "It takes a long time for a simple tale to get told," states Bennett (1988:20), but the explanation and dialogue are necessary to create understanding and plausibility for the story. They are what make the tale interesting and convincing.[21]

Bennett sees the "riffle and pool" technique as characteristic of tales told as true (25), but this seems to contrast with her evaluation of the supernatural narratives she collected from women in Manchester that employed the more circular and less linear style.[22] Perhaps, the discrepancy depends on the Manchester narratives being of first-person experiences, whereas the story told "for true" was a more distanced account. Perhaps the circular narrative is a defensive, rather than a persuasive, strategy.[23] Bennett's Manchester materials emerged in interviews with women whom she had not previously known and whom she interviewed for only twenty minutes at a time (1999:176–177).[24]

Bennett also suggests that the circular strategies are more open and invite discussion, whereas the linear strategies close off discussion. Bennett's informants, however, were mostly older women. The openness of the circular strategy might relate more to the networking and consensus-building that characterize women's discourse (Tannen 1990). Linear presentations that might impede discussion and networking among women could prove stimulating for men, with their greater tolerance for "reason," interruption, and debate.

The question of which strategies create the most compelling and credible narratives remains open. Compelling narrative strategies may be distributed by age and gender. Certainly, there are very compelling legend narratives that have distinctly linear organizations.

Narrative Detail

If dates are the buttons on the fly of history, as a history professor once informed me, then details are the anchors of narrative veracity. A narrative without specificity as to character, locale, or time is of diminished plausibility. I received a memorate by e-mail from a man who was certain he had picked up a vanishing hitchhiker (he did not use the term), although the hitchhiker only disappeared after he let him out of the car at his destination. Unlike traditional hitchhiker legends, the hitchhiker makes no prophecy nor does he later prove to be a ghost, although the narrator suggested in his cover letter that he was "a ghost or guardian angel."

> In 1983, I was working as a local freight engineer for the Southern Pacific R.R., between McAllen and Brownsville TX.

> Prior to departing on the outbound leg to Brownsville, I called the Crewcaller in Victoria TX and requested to be relieved from my assignment by an extraboard engineer.
> The outbound trip took all of 12 hours and then we were off duty for 8 hours. At the most, all I really slept was about four-and-a-half hours. We are called 1½ hrs before our 8 hours are up to report for duty. By the time we got back to McAllen twelve hours later, the agent at the depot had gone for the day. I assumed that a relief engineer would cover my assignment at 6AM the following morning.
> The 4–5 hour trip to San Antonio was uneventful, and I arrived home at about 3PM. My family wanted to go to the mall shopping, maybe a movie, and out to eat. To say the least, by the time we arrived home, I was ready for bed (Personal communication from A. Terrell, 2 May 2003).

The account begins with elaborate detail about the narrator's occupation, his employer, some occupational terminology (crewcaller, extraboard engineer), his routes, the year, and the time involved in all his travels. In terms of the narrative, the point of this introduction is to establish how little sleep he got, how tired he was, and how upset he was to find that the railroad could not find a replacement, which required him to drive to McAllen to run the train back to Brownsville. It was on his drive to McAllen that he picked up the hitchhiker. He gives the precise intersection where he picked up the hitchhiker on the highway he was taking back to McAllen. It could be found on a map. (I found it on a map.) By the time he finished recounting his trip, he had mentioned passing Pleasanton, Alice, and Edinburg along the route.

Granted, he was writing a stranger who knows nothing about railroad operations and procedures or Texas geography (see G. Bennett 1988:22–23). Nevertheless, the exposition is unusually detailed. These details establish the narrator as someone who holds a responsible position and who knows exactly where he was, when, why, and where he was going. He comes across as a meticulous observer and a credible reporter.

Persons, places, and processes that are familiar to listeners might make the account more believable still (Tangherlini 1990:375–376; Tedlock 1983:163, 168, 173). Such details anchor the stories to the seasons, spaces, and activities of their own world. Thus, listeners who know the intersection of S. W. Military Drive and Roosevelt Street, where the hitchhiker was picked up, or who are acquainted with the foul-ups that can occur with work shifts may have invested substantially in the truth of the story even before its central events unfold.

Accounts that lack detail and specificity are likely to suffer from diminished credibility: "A man and a woman, and they had one baby, and this baby never slept. . . . But anyway, the father. . . . She went down to the . . . down to the town, or down to the village, or something, for something" (Ballard 1980:36); "It happened over a vacation, Thanksgiving, I think. Two girls stayed in the dorm by theirselves" (Grider 1980:147); "There was this lady who lived near this school. She lived up the road, and there's this pub that had been boarded up and things like that and she told me this story" (M. Wilson 1997:221).

Nevertheless, it is important for narrators to omit details that a narrator should not know (M. Wilson 1998:95 n. 6). "What the priest did or said, he didn't tell her. I wasn't told" (Ballard 1988:169). In a legend about a car being smashed into in a parking lot (discussed in the next section), the owners come out of the grocery store to find a note on their windshield. As the narrator gets into some detail about what was written in the note, moving beyond reporting to virtually quoting its contents, the narrator injects, "Oh, I don't know what it said" (Barnes 1986:76).

Story Logic

Even fictional tales have their own logical conventions. A poor peasant may come into the possession of a magic wallet that can never be emptied of gold, but he is, nevertheless, induced to sell it to a rich peasant, for without the sale, there is no story to tell (K. Ranke 1966:104–106). Popular television and film are filled with ludicrous premises and details. (For example, a hero pursued by killers knocks out one of his pursuers but does not bother to take his weapon.) In fiction, we often suspend our disbelief when we encounter premises or behaviors that are out of keeping with how the real world works. Although legends deal with extraordinary and even supernatural occurrences, their logic must adhere to the logic of everyday life, even if the central episode is unusual, extraordinary, and beggars commonsense explanation.

In the following legend there are some gaps in the logic of the narrative.

> What happened is they went to the grocery store and when they came out with all their groceries, they noticed that their car had been backed into . . . and I mean the side of it! I mean not just a nice little ding, a severe crash. And as they're looking around surveying all the damage . . . that had been done to their car and it was a station wagon of course . . . their family car. They noticed that on the windshield was an envelope with the words "We Apologize" written on it. So they opened the envelope and there is this nice letter saying we apologize for hitting your car and we don't have any insurance and therefore, we won't be able to reimburse you for the damage. But please accept these two tickets as . . . our . . . (Oh, I don't know what it said!) as our apology, you know, enjoy the basketball game this Saturday night. And it was this big basketball game that everyone was trying to get tickets to . . . like the nationals or something like that . . . something important. So that Saturday they all went to the basketball game and when they came home their house had been robbed . . . and it was robbed by these people who hit their car. (Barnes 1986:76)

The account was followed by a question asked by the interviewer as to how the people whose car was smashed knew that the people who damaged their car were the same ones that robbed their house. The answer was that there had been a string of burglaries that happened in the same way.

To many, this might prove an account of a perfectly logical, perhaps even elegant, crime. But certain details raise questions. Among them: (1) If the burglars wanted to get the couple to go to the game—and I presume that it was a couple that was in the store—why damage their car so badly? Why inflict damage so severe that it might be unusable for the Saturday night game, when a simple and less noticeable ding would do as well? (2) If the point of the escapade was to be able to burglarize a house without being observed, why commit a crime in the store parking lot that might so easily have been witnessed and reported? (3) How could the burglars be sure that the couple had no previous obligations—guests, for example—that might keep them at home the night of the game? Could they even be sure they were basketball fans? (4) And finally, and perhaps most telling, if the car was a station wagon—a family car—how would two tickets to a basketball game succeed in making the house unoccupied? It would seem that there would be children who might remain at home, with or without a babysitter.

Listeners often overlook such gaps in story logic. Nevertheless, such gaps serve as openings for questioning the credibility of an account (Fine and Turner 2001:10). Indeed, some of the logical problems would disappear with only a few minor alterations in the narrative details: the car was only slightly damaged, as might be effected by a surreptitious blow with a hammer or a well-placed kick; the car was a two-door coupe rather than a "family car."

Human psychological functioning must remain comprehensible even in the face of extraordinary events. A boy relates hearing from neighbors that some previous inhabitant of his house had killed himself in a chair and that the spot was haunted. He goes on to describe how he and his brother were awakened one night and "saw the imprint of a shadow" in the chair. At first the narrator thought he was looking at a coat, but then he realized that there was no coat there when he went to bed. His brother was also afraid and urged him to turn on the light, but he claims he was paralyzed with fear. The shadow looked something like their father, and though they were scared, they began to ignore it. "And . . . finally, we went to sleep." Someone in the assembled group in which the story was told asked, "You went to sleep with a ghost in the room?" (G. Bennett 1989b:308).

Whatever one believes about the reality of ghosts, the presence of a ghost that the narrator claims is scaring him to death should not lead to lapsed attention and sleep. The audience member challenges this implausible consequent of the events described and, in effect, questions the narrator's good faith in his representation that he believed there was a ghost at all.

In the vanishing hitchhiker narrative quoted above, the narrator goes into great detail to describe how long he had been on the job, how long it took him to get home, how he had gone out with his family, and how he had returned home and dropped off to sleep, only to be awakened by the railroad asking him to return to work for a shift up in McAllen, some five hours away. Although the narrator states that he took a cold shower, got a full thermos of coffee, and stopped along the way for more coffee, he asks the listener to trust his report that the hitchhiker completely disappeared after he let him out in McAllen. But the narrator has to some extent undermined his credibility as a witness by cataloguing how little sleep he had had in the previous forty or so hours (A. Terrell, 2 May 2003).

Paralogism

Paralogism—false inference—is discussed by Aristotle in *Poetics* rather than in *Rhetoric*, where it is only mentioned in passing. If A has as its consequent B, then people will think that whenever B occurs, A must be its antecedent (1982:74). The thinking is logically fallacious, but it nevertheless plays an important part in promoting the truth of certain events.[25] Contemporary legends make considerable use of paralogism. I would expand slightly on Aristotle's conception of the paralogism to include: *behavioral consequence*, as Aristotle characterized it, *emotional reaction, evaluation*, and *physical evidence*. All of these can serve as consequents that affirm an antecedent as true.

Behavioral Consequence: A narrative tells about a mother's ghost that returns and tells her daughter that she should cease crying because the mother's shroud "is wet with your tears. Cry no more for me." After listing the number of her own relatives from whom the narrator heard the story, the narrator concludes: "And she said that father . . . her father and brothers, and all, died, and she never shed a tear after, for one of them" (Ballard 1980:38). The daughter not crying at the death of her other relatives implies that the visitation from the dead mother must be true. Why else would she fail to grieve for her close kin?

A woman told the story of an unusual crime in which a woman answered her front door while holding a red-hot poker. She is confronted with a masked assailant. Seeing the poker, the assailant, thinking it is a gun, tries to grasp it. He runs away. Later, he turns out to be a neighbor living in the building who is identified by his burned hand. When challenged about the authenticity of the account, the narrator replied with indignation, "It's perfectly true, and the man was arrested and is in jail now" (Simpson 1981:203).

Emotional Reaction: Often narrators will register their emotional reaction to the story or to elements of the story or recount the reactions of others who were part of the event. The fact that emotions were aroused implies that there was something to arouse them. "I went about two years ago, me, R. J., and Mike. We weren't scared or nothing. You know, we just wanted to go over there and see if it was scary or whatever. So we went over and as soon as we got to the road that it was on, this big gush of wind pushed the car back—it was scary. We were really scared and we weren't even there yet" (Meley 1991:8). In the next example, the narrator conveys not only the idea that he was horrified by the ghost he saw, but that he is still horrified: "I was scared. She turned around and started smilin' at me, still winding up the clock, God!" (Peters 1988:230). Why be scared unless there is something to be scared of?

Evaluation: Many legends include commentary on the significance of the action described. Such evaluation suggests that the events on which narrators are commenting must themselves be true. In a 1935 version of "The Surpriser Surprised," a girl, on her birthday, goes up to her bedroom and takes off all her clothes with the intention of surprising her long-suffering fiancé waiting in the living room below. After describing this scene, the narrator comments, "I don't think she was desperate or anything like that—it was just she was so much in love and he was so patient." When she comes downstairs naked to her fiancé, everyone from her office is waiting in the living room to yell "Surprise!" She faints dead away and winds up in the state asylum. The narrator adds, "Isn't that something? Isn't that awful? Can you just imagine?"—leaving little doubt about the narrator's commitment to the truth of the account (Jansen 1979:66).

Similarly, in the story about the masked robber who grabs the hot poker held by the woman answering her door, the narrator concludes, "So you see, even in good flats you never know—even your own neighbours can be criminals" (Simpson 1981:203). If a commentary is offered on the significance of events, it strongly suggests that such events occurred.

Physical Evidence: Physical evidence can be material objects or objects created in discourse. In the area of Leksvik in Northern

Trøndelag, Norway, a soldier named Anders Solli was killed by wolves on his way to church on Christmas Eve in 1612. He killed many of the wolves with his sword, but they kept coming back. When his sword became frozen in its sheath, he was torn to pieces (Johnsen 1989:150). There is a cross and a stone to mark the place of his death, and the monument serves both as a stimulus to tell the Anders Solli story and as a fact with which to verify it (155). His sword is displayed in the Leksvik church.[26] There is also a song about the event that describes Solli meeting his death on a moonlit night. An astronomer had computed that there was no moon on Christmas Eve of 1612, and people tended to dismiss that element as a fabrication of the song's composer. In 1979, however, the astronomical data were recomputed and showed that in fact there was a moon. The first astronomer had overlooked the fact that the calendar used in 1612 was the Julian calendar and not the Gregorian calendar. Following the recalculation, people no longer apologized for describing the moonlit night in telling the legend (152–153). Thus the truth of the legend is buttressed by physical markers and artifacts. The physical position of the moon in relation to the earth and sun, which first operated to throw into doubt a motif in the legend, later served to confirm it.

A man whose leg swelled when he kicked at a bird sitting on his prize turnip found a large and painful boil rising on his leg. When the boil was lanced, a long white string came out of it and piled up on the floor. "The string was kept for years as proof for unbelievers, but the man always had a crippled leg to his dying day" (Rieti 1991:291).

Physical evidence can also be employed to delegitimize a claim. A group of people engaged in research on Bigfoot debunked the evidence of one of their own members. The woman claimed to have Bigfoot scat that she collected around the feeding stations that she put out in her back yard. When one member asked whether the scat had been analyzed, another member said, "Yes, well, I didn't have to analyze it. I know what it is. I've seen it before because I was raised in the country. It's raccoon 'ka ka'" (Milligan 1990:94). The woman's claim that Bigfoot visited her property is rejected, even though the existence of Bigfoot is not.[27]

Instance of a Class

Legends generally recount unique experiences. In fact, the proliferation of versions of a story about the same or a similar experience tends to undermine the truth of a legend account. Folklore, after all, has been defined as materials that exist in multiple versions (Dundes and Pagter 1975:xvii). But there are kinds of legends that escape this fate because they make a claim not only about a unique experience but also about some aspect of the world and its operation. The truth of legends about crime, for example, can be enhanced by citing multiple occurrences, because criminals often repeat crimes employing the same modus operandi. In the legend about the damaged car and the basketball tickets cited above, the narrator refers to the repeated occurrence of the crime in his area: "It was a string of thefts that happened this way" (Barnes 1986:76). In an e-mail message that I received about a credit card scam, the document asserted: "The police said they are taking several of these reports daily."

A supernatural legend may report a unique experience, but it also makes claims for the existence of certain supernatural entities and processes. Consequently, a legend told about an encounter with fairies may serve to uphold the truth of another and completely different fairy account. Even a mention of other instances, without the recounting of a narrative, serves to make the point that the narrative is just one instance of a class of common occurrences and therefore should be regarded as true. The gas station attendant in the Swedish legend about the hitchhiking Jesus reports that he had heard a similar account from ten other families that same day. The extraordinary becomes somewhat ordinary.

Theory

Occasionally narrators may produce a theoretical explanation for the phenomenon or event they have recounted. While this does not seem to be a frequent strategy, it does exist. In collecting stories and conversations about happy and unhappy houses—houses that have a good feeling to them or a malignant atmosphere—one of Bennett's informants offered the following theory:

> If it is possible you can get the voices of people who are living, you can get their voices in the air, that people can speak to you from a

> telephone from Australia, New Zealand, as if they were in the same room; and I've read or heard that every single word that's ever been spoken, every sound that's ever been made since the world came into being, is still here. Well, I think that your vibrations are all around you, and if there's evil, Hitler, or any of the dreadful atrocities, burnings at the stake, there's been heaps and heaps through history. You couldn't have terror and horror and violent physical pain and hatred and evil and it just disappears, just because the people have died. It's still there! And the same with very good people. (G. Bennett 1999:48–49)

A theory need not be framed in scientific or quasi-scientific terms. A theory appeals to a general principle by which the world is presumed to work—even a religious one. In speaking of the contacts between the living and the dead, one woman stated: "It was Saint Paul, wasn't it, said we're encompassed with a great cloud of witnesses" (G. Bennett 1999:115; see Heb. 12:1). Another woman, in explaining why the board that fell out of the bed with a loud noise indicated that her niece had died, theorized: "Wasn't it that her spirit came back and sat on the spring?" (Dégh 1995:303). Theories may be idiosyncratic and ersatz or communal and traditional. They may also be elements of comprehensive—religious, psychic, spiritualist, scientific—ideologies (Dégh 2001:281–282).

Secondary Legends

Secondary legends are legends told to buttress the claim of some other legend. A secondary legend follows the telling of or refers to the primary legend (although the secondary legend may prove more compelling and important than the legend it is marshaled to support). There is a legend about a tombstone in a southern Indiana cemetery that has the imprint of a chain along its side. It is believed that the tombstone is for Sarah Pruett, who was killed by her husband with a logging chain.[28] It is also held that if someone touches the chain during a full moon, that person will go insane. There are stories about people touching the chain and being chased by a big, bright light. "We didn't believe it, you know. We touched it during full moon and got out into the car and started to leave, and the driver looked in the rear view mirror; and that was all you know. 'Look, there's a white light!' Whoom! We were gone" (Clements 1980:259).

A narrator recapitulates some of this material and then tells,

> And there was one person who totally believed in this, the spirit coming back, and another one said this is just the doing of another prankster. And as they were leaving Prospect, as the road winds down backwards, and as they were driving, this car came out of nowhere behind them, and it was speeding up, and came closer, and closer, and run them off the road. And this person who did not believe, this one was driving the car. And when they found the car, the person who did believe the story was totally uninjured, and the person who did not, was dead. And there was a logging chain wrapped around his neck (Dégh 1996:39–40).

The memorate about a woman entering her dead father's bedroom following his funeral and seeing three rings of smoke (described above) is immediately followed by another account: "When my husband died, my daughter teaches ballet, or she did do, in Manchester. She does television work now. And-er-it was a very high building you know, and there was this stained glass window and she saw her father looking through this window! You see what I mean? And she's not like that! She's quite, you know, having a good time in life and—. You see what I mean? I suppose there's something in some things" (G. Bennett 1984:86). Her sensible and healthy daughter sees a manifestation of her dead father as her mother, the narrator, had seen of her own dead father.

When preparing to receive guests at the house after the death of her sister's daughter, the narrator and three others heard the sound of her sister crying, even though the sister was at the funeral home at the time. The narrator adds: "Now wait a minute. And before Betty died, some two weeks before, she was still at home, there was a sudden clattering sound in the house at night. My sister believed that the pastry board fell off the wall. But the next morning the board was still on the wall. . . . All this . . . then . . . was related" (Dégh 1995:291).

Aesthetic Effects

Aesthetic qualities have often been denied to the legend. It has been said that the legend is formless (Dégh and Vázsonyi 1976:93) and that its only artistry is "the skillful formulation of convincing statements" (Dégh 1972:74; 1995:230). In fact, the lack of artistry noted for legends may be part of its rhetoric of truth. Art and factuality are often at odds. The patina of authenticity generally does not easily adhere to highly structured forms, graceful metaphors, and poetically crafted language. The word "artifice" denotes both decoration and deception. The manufacture of an artistic narrative would suggest, all too often, the contrivance of its truth as well (Mackin 1969:206). Nevertheless, the legend does employ aesthetic effects, and a few of these are described below.

Dramatization: The techniques used to create the appearance of reality in a narrative may be different from those to convey truth. Tedlock wrote of Zuni *telapnaawe*—narratives told only at night during winter about a world that is somewhat like the world of today—and described the narrator's skill in making the story exciting, with lots of action, action that you can almost see right before your eyes. The narrators also quoted the story characters at great length. These techniques—dramatization and quotation—"contribute to the appearance of reality through their immediacy" (1983:167). *Telapnaawe* are fictions, and in fiction the appearance of reality enhances the story. However, the appearance of reality is just that, an appearance—an aesthetic surrogate. It is effective within the fictional frame. It may establish a sense of reality emotionally but not cognitively. Dramatization and extended quotation may undermine the credibility of legends. They look too much like art. A fiction needs to be made to seem real, whereas a truthful account does not. The legend account, consequently, tends to conciseness and passivity—it has more the nature of a report than a reenactment. Dramatic reenactment may be a signal that a legend is being told "for fun" rather than "for true."

Humor: Humor might also be considered an aesthetic attribute. A story that is humorous might be suspect from its outset, since a genuinely funny story has a raison d'être independent of the actual occurrence of the events recounted. The legend introduction "This is very funny, but this is absolutely true" (G. Bennett 1988:14) has already been cited above. A story, circulated on the Internet, deals with an extra-credit question posed by a professor on his chemistry midterm at the University of Washington: "Is hell endothermic or exothermic?" One student's answer was so "profound" that the professor supposedly shared it over the Web. The answer is, in fact, so cleverly formulated that it strains belief that a student could produce it under the pressures and constraints of a major examination. I had occasion to read the account to a friend over the phone, who stated that she did not believe it because it was really "too good to be true."

Foreshadowing: Other aesthetic effects may influence believability. Foreshadowing refers to the arrangement of events and ideas in narrative so that later events are anticipated and prepared for. It is generally considered a literary device and is regularly listed in dictionaries of literary terms (e.g., Cuddon 1976). In the vanishing hitchhiker narrative discussed above, events that unfold prepare the listener for the unexplainable disappearance of the traveler. As he begins his trip back up to McAllen, the narrator thinks to himself, "Man, I wish I had someone to go with me to McAllen tonight. No sooner than I turned onto Roosevelt, that there standing on the side of the road was a college-aged student with a paperback, holding a sign that said 'McAllen.'" The narrator stops and tells him, "Man, you are the answer to my prayers. Hop in. I'm going to McAllen and I was dreading going there alone." Twenty miles later, as fatigue sets in, the narrator stops at a greasy spoon for some pie and coffee. He asks the hitchhiker whether he wants anything to eat or drink. The hitchhiker asks only for a glass of water, and he doesn't even drink that. During the trip he tries to coax the hitchhiker into conversation, but "he didn't say anything much and did not go to sleep either." When the narrator finally lets the hitchhiker out in McAllen, he says to him that you were "an answer to my prayers" (A. Terrell, 2 May 2003).

The uttered wish for company on the trip, which is immediately fulfilled, the unwillingness of a college student to eat or drink or say much of anything during the four-and-a-half-hour trip, and the reiteration that the hitchhiker was "an answer to my prayers" all suggest that the traveler might be someone special—not just an ordinary college student.[29] Little bits of information, which in themselves are in no way extraordinary, prepare the listener for the hitchhiker's disappearance and the idea that the hitchhiker was no ordinary person. As a result, his eventual disappearance is not a complete surprise (A. Terrell, 2 May 2003).

Foreshadowing also takes place in "Messages from the Dead." The doctor relates, "Now the day the child died, that morning, when the girl woke up, she went to her sister's bedroom, sat down with her, and suddenly told her that she felt that she was going to die that day, and that she was going to be in heaven, and there she would be able to see her sisters. Now two hours later the child had the hemorrhage and twelve hours later the child died" (Steven Barr, 13 November 1975). Three days after the death, the child's writing appeared on the blackboard.

When questioned about the child's premonition of her own death, the physician regarded it as not that unusual, suggesting that it happens with children in a hospital setting who have terminal diseases, even if they have not been told of it. "As far as that is concerned, I was not as shocked as I was by the other things" (Steven Barr, 13 November 1975). By accepting the child's prophecy of her own death—indeed, in playing it down—the narrator prepares the listener to entertain the more extraordinary claim that the child could communicate from beyond the grave. There is also a sense of balance in the narrative as a whole. If the child has seen across the Great Divide in one direction, might she not be able to communicate in the other direction as well?

Hamish Henderson recorded the collaborative telling by the members of the Stewart family about the haunting of their house in Fife. The tale begins with an account of how relatives who were staying in the house one night heard noise on the stairs. The family dog was brought into the house and became very frightened, although no one was there. The tale is picked up with a relation of how one day the hand-pump pumped water of its own accord. It continues with an incident in which an attic door slammed shut when no wind was blowing. The whole concludes with the parents telling how they were paralyzed with fear one night while lying in bed and their observation of the specter of an old woman that disappeared before their eyes (Dégh 2001:142–148).

Concealed Plot Functions: Daniel Barnes has noted that many contemporary legends conceal their narrative functions (1986:70).

The significance of a particular action or narrative detail is not revealed until the end of the story. The girl who sits up all night in a car in a Lover's Lane and waits for her boyfriend to come back with a tow truck does not know that the scraping she hears on the car roof is her dead boyfriend swinging from the tree above the vehicle (71). Similarly, the owner of a Doberman does not realize that there is a burglar hiding in her closet whose fingers have been bitten off by the choking dog she has just taken to the veterinarian (Brunvand 1984:13–15). Barnes notes the similarity of this narrative strategy to the late nineteenth- and twentieth-century short story (1986:72).[30] Legend also shares this strategy with the joke, a genre in which the significance of an element in the narrative cannot be fixed until the punchline is delivered.[31]

Does the concealed-function form of contemporary legend detract from or enhance believability? Memorates rarely conceal their functions. News stories in newspapers do not conceal their functions either. The gist of a news story is generally presented in the opening paragraph. There is no suspense and no sudden, final revelation (Oring 1990:170–171). Concealed-function narratives invite their listeners to encounter the world in the same way as legend protagonists. Audience members replicate their misapprehensions and enlightenments. Does this experiential quality enhance believability? I have believed legends presented to me in this concealed-function form, and I have observed people strongly affirm belief in others. But given that many people today have been exposed to the concept of "urban legend" in books, films, newspapers, and television with its concealed-function form, might not the form itself signal the presence of "legend"—a traditional story that many people believe but that more discerning people should suspect?

Synecdoche: There are other instances in which an artistic effect would seem to affect believability. The legend "Swinging Chains" (discussed above) was performed and recorded as both a third-person and first-person account by the same narrator. In the first-person formulation, the narrator added an interesting detail. Bert was the short engineer who used to set the chains swinging as he passed by and who died in the plant, after which the chains would often swing of their own accord. In the first-person account the narrator adds, "He was an engineer there when they first built the plant" (Slotkin 1988:101). As Slotkin points out, this detail makes Bert "coeval with, and hence a sort of synecdoche for, the plant itself" (104). This small effect serves to explain why Bert's ghost would haunt the plant. After all, people die on the job every day without becoming ghostly presences at their places of work. But if Bert is, in some sense, bound to the plant in some special way by virtue of his lifelong association with it, it might make some sense that his presence would continue.

PATHOS

A legend is more likely to be regarded as true if it conforms to the *cognitive, emotional,* and *moral* expectations of its audience. These expectations are interrelated, although they are conceptually distinguishable. What does it mean to say that a legend is more persuasive if it meets cognitive expectations? It means that it is more persuasive if it conforms to the ideology and belief language of the listeners (Dégh and Vázsonyi 1974:279). A legend about a ghost, for example, is more likely to be believed if ghosts are an accepted conceptual category and if the ghost behaves as ghosts are expected to behave. In her essay "Shakespeare in the Bush," Laura Bohannan (1966) recounted her attempt to tell the story of Hamlet to Tiv elders in a Nigerian village. From the outset, the Tiv elders rejected the possibility of Hamlet's father being a ghost, since in Tiv culture the dead did not return. In their view, the phantom that Hamlet encountered could only have been a delusion caused by a witch. Consequently, the tale for these elders was about witchcraft. What had been presented by Bohannan did not conform to the ideology and belief language of her audience. Accounts that conform to the ideology and traditional language of a particular group are far more likely to persuade than those that don't.

Legends about the vanishing hitchhiker are a case in point. In one type of the legend, a hitchhiker in the back seat of a car warns the couple driving not to attend the Chicago World's Fair because a terrible calamity will occur. The hitchhiker then disappears. When the couple checks the address the hitchhiker had given them, they discover the hitchhiker had been dead for some years.

When this legend, which dates back at least to 1933 in the Chicago area, reached the Intermountain West, the hitchhiker became a Nephite. Nephites in the Book of Mormon are disciples who remain on earth to perform wondrous deeds. There are numerous stories about strangers giving succor and instruction to church members before disappearing. The vanishing hitchhiker warns the couple of their need to store food for an impending catastrophe as the church leadership had directed. What might have been a dubious account of a ghost reappearing at the scene of its death and its futile effort to return home is fitted into the conceptual framework of Mormon theology.[32] Nephites come back to instruct and aid good Mormons, so the hitchhiker is a Nephite, not a traveling ghost or other unspecified individual. Widely distributed legends are accepted and retold when they are integrated into the cognitive framework of the Mormon community (W. Wilson 1975). Even if a Nephite is not explicitly mentioned in the narrative, the hitchhiker will still be understood by many Mormons to be a Nephite. It is as a Nephite account that an otherwise widely circulating story is likely to be understood, entertained, and believed.[33]

Compelling legends should have an emotional resonance for their audiences. They should present language, images, and messages that stir preexisting emotional dispositions (e.g., see Fine and Turner 2001; Turner 1993). They are more apt to persuade if they can capitalize on resident fears and connect with deep-seated wishes. "I remember a child with a slice of bread with mayonnaise who was sitting next to a child who had a slice of pizza, grabbed the pizza out of the child's hand and stuffed it in her mouth. And I mean, what can you say to a child? I mean she was starving you know" (McIntyre et al. 2001:117). This is just one of the narratives that was said to have inspired the school- and community-based children's feeding programs that developed in Atlantic Canada in the 1980s. Each of these kinds of stories played upon the plight of a deprived child and was often accompanied by some salient image indicating the depth of the child's hunger—a child stealing food from other children, a child eating chalk, a child going through school garbage cans looking for food, a child stuffing himself with food at a school party until he is sick (115–117). These stories arouse the fears that adults have for children, as well as their desire to protect and alleviate misery. With such stories, there is a risk to the listener in *not* believing. Failing to believe potentially makes the listener complicit in perpetuating the suffering of little children. Tales that tell of child abduction, molestation, and murder arouse the emotions even more and increase the risk to the listener of failing to believe (G. Bennett 2005:247–303; Best 1987; Best and Horiuchi 1985; Victor 1990).

A legend is also likely to be more suasive if it reflects the morality of the listener. Stories told by Mormon missionaries tell of wayward missionaries who attempt to pray to the devil, confer priesthood on an animal or inanimate object, or violate rules governing missionary conduct. Such behaviors result in death or some other catastrophe. Saintly behavior brings reward. Saints avoid peril, and those who would assault or assail them are themselves punished (W. Wilson 1982:18–22). A Jewish narrative tells of a family that abandons secularism and keeps the Sabbath, and thereby checks the advance of their daughter's deadly disease (Yassif 1999:434–436). Wickedness punished, righteousness rewarded is the formula that underlies the religious legend, and stories that attest to this moral equilibrium are most likely to be accepted as true in their respective religious communities.

The women Gillian Bennett worked with in Manchester were more likely to accept accounts about omens, telepathy, and visitations from dead family members, because they were elderly, churchgoing individuals socialized to be intuitive, gentle, unassertive, caring, and selfless. Accounts that were acceptable to them reflected these values. Consequently, these women were open to an account of a dead mother returning to aid or comfort her daughter, because such accounts were in keeping with their values of affection and caring—affection and caring that could reach from beyond the grave. They were reluctant, however, to entertain stories about "ghosts," because ghosts were strangers, were selfish, and were thought dangerous (G. Bennett 1999:17–25). Stories about them did not resonate with these women's moral vision of the world.

Conclusions

The above outline of legendry's rhetoric of truth has much to teach us about how the legend does its work. It may have even more to teach us when it is compared with truth-making practices in various social and cultural groups and in other areas of discourse. Is there a single rhetoric of truth, or are there many? If many, how do they differ, how are they deployed, and what happens when the rhetoric of one speech situation is enacted in another?

There are other questions as well. How are strategies marshaled in particular performances? What strategies are most persuasive, and in what kinds of combinations? It is not hard to imagine a situation in which so many tropes are deployed that they call attention to themselves and decrease, rather than increase, the believability of the account. The legend's rhetoric of truth is not formally taught or studied. Its practitioners, in fact, often do not conceive it to be rhetoric at all. For them, it is simply as transparent a presentation of truth as language will allow.

Let us extend a little further the implications of the legend's rhetoric of truth. What if legend were defined as narration that invokes this rhetoric? What would be the effect of this characterization on the way legend was identified and studied? Folklorists have acknowledged that a narrative does not have to be false to qualify as legend (Brunvand 1986b:122–125; Dégh 2001:200; Dégh and Vázsonyi 1976:95–97; Wyckoff 2000:170–171). Nevertheless, folklorists gravitate to narratives that they almost invariably believe to be false (e.g., Campion-Vincent 2005:ix–xii; Fine and Turner 2001:3–12, 56). In other words, the acknowledgment really does not reflect practice. Were legend defined as a narrative performance that invokes a rhetoric of truth, all kinds of performances would immediately become eligible for legend status, from the truest of the true to the falsest of the false. In fact, truth and falsity would simply evaporate as relevant criteria. The advantage would be to remove the ideology of folklorists—explicit or implicit—from the consideration of what constitutes the object of study (G. Bennett 1989a:10; Oring 1990:163–164). Suddenly, all kinds of stories would be included in the legend category that had hitherto been ignored, including those that folklorists tell each and every day about the worlds of science, politics, or even folklore. There would be no basis for trying to distinguish between "heart-wrenching tales of unimaginable woe" and contemporary legend narratives (McIntyre et al. 2001:119).[34]

Within this greatly expanded category, scholars would be left to determine the problem that they chose to study. They still might be interested in told-as-true narratives that employed traditional motifs. There would be, however, a basis for an instructive comparison with those told-as-true narratives that do not employ traditional motifs.[35] (As it stands now, folklorists tend to regard narratives that employ traditional motifs as untrue, so there is really nothing with which to compare them. They are studied in isolation.) If they were interested in the relation of narrative to belief, folklorists would again be able to examine a range of narratives in which, for whatever reason, truth was thought to be sufficiently doubtful so that a special rhetoric was required.

The contrary situation is also suggestive. Narratives that meshed seamlessly with the ideology, sentiments, and morality of a group, such that they needed no rhetorical support, would not be considered legends, no matter how fabulous or absurd an outsider might find their contents to be. Stories of UFOs, Bigfoot, or ghosts might not qualify as legends in a group that did not invoke or demand a rhetoric of truth in their communication. Among Mormons, for example, Nephite stories might just be Nephite *stories,* were no special rhetoric invoked to persuade of their truth (see G. Bennett 1993:20). Nephites would just be part of the cognitive landscape, demanding no more in the way of justification than automobiles or temple work.[36] Legends would consist of only those stories that marshaled a rhetoric because they were felt to benefit from its trappings.

A definition of legend in terms of its rhetoric would shift the assessment of legend from matters of belief to the performance of truth. The landscape of the legend, consequently, would be altered in significant and interesting ways. And while such a definition would probably create as many problems as it might solve, at the very least, the beliefs of the folklorist would be removed from the constitution of the legend, and that narrative category would be relieved of some of the ideological baggage with which it has long been encumbered.[37]

9. On the Tradition and Mathematics of Counting-Out

Folklore research—all research—is driven by questions. Often these questions are theoretical. They emerge from a particular conceptual framework and seek to extend that framework to the understanding of new materials. Other questions are naïve. They are not driven by a theory but emerge from observation. They are basic "what," "why," and "how" kinds of questions. Naïve questions are as necessary as theoretical ones. An attempt to answer a naïve question may point research in totally new directions or turn previous theory on its head.

Folklore studies has not been much influenced by mathematics; not even statistics. There are a number of mathematical ideas—graph theory, probability, game theory—that might prove relevant to the analysis of folk narrative, music, dance, game, and ritual. It might not even require advanced abilities in the subject to identify some illuminating applications. The mathematics in the essay below is elementary, but it is possible to grasp the ideas presented without actually following the computations in any detail.

> His boyhood lasted 1/6 of his life;
> his beard grew after 1/12 more;
> he married after a 1/7 more;
> and his son was born 5 years later;
> the son lived to half his father's age;
> and the father died four years after his son.
> —the age of Diophantus

CHILDREN WERE PERHAPS the first non-peasant group to be seriously studied by folklorists. In 1846, in a note in *The Athenaeum*, William J. Thoms proposed the "good Saxon compound, Folklore" to designate those "manners, customs, observances, ballads, proverbs, etc., of the olden time." Thoms urged the collection and study of these disparate and seemingly "trifling and insignificant" materials because of the light that they, in aggregate, might throw on the ancient past. To illustrate his point, Thoms cited a Yorkshire children's divinatory custom. Children gather around a cherry tree and sing, "Cuckoo, Cherry Tree; Come down and tell me; How many years I have to live." Each child then shakes the tree, and the number of cherries that fall are held to indicate the life-years remaining. Thoms points to the relation between this Yorkshire custom and the prophetic qualities of the cuckoo's song described in Jacob Grimm's *Deutsche Mythologie* and to the belief that the cuckoo will not sing its prophetic song until it has eaten its fill of cherries thrice over (Thoms in Dorson 1968a, 1:54–55).

That children's custom stemmed from ancient practice became something of a rule of thumb in the nineteenth century, and folklorists set out to establish the specific relations between a host of contemporary children's expressions and the observances of the past.[1] Certainly, there are any number of children's games and pastimes that are ancient. Thus, games such as "I Spy" and "Blind Man's Buff" collected by W. W. Newell in New York at the close of the nineteenth century, are depicted in ancient paintings and are described in second century documents (Newell 1963 [1883]:160, 162–163). But many of the attempts to establish connections between children's custom and ancient practice were decidedly more tenuous.

In 1888, in *The Counting-Out Rhymes of Children*, Henry Carrington Bolton attempted to trace the origins and demonstrate the antiquity of the practice. Bolton regarded counting-out as having two dimensions. Counting-out was a form of divination by which the unknown was reckoned through casting lots. Yet counting-out also consisted of rhymes and doggerels that established the pattern of this procedure (26). Bolton was determined to show connections to ancient belief for both the practice and the verses.

Citing the Bible and the *Iliad*, Bolton had little difficulty in demonstrating the antiquity of casting lots to identify criminals, sacrificial victims, and military champions (26–34).[2] The rhymes themselves Bolton believed to derive from magical incantations that accompanied the casting of lots, although he acknowledged that the rhymes were probably "of more recent date than the custom itself" (35). Bolton cited numerous examples of incantations, many of which seem to contain nonsense words as do the children's rhymes. Bolton, however, was unable to cite any ancient examples of genuine counting-out, nor was he able to directly link a single magical incantation to a contemporary children's rhyme.[3] Consequently, Bolton was forced to establish his linkages between children's game and ancient divinatory practice in a more roundabout fashion.[4] Bolton approvingly cited T. W. Sandrey's attempt to link counting-out with the selection of sacrificial victims by ancient Britons, and his interpretation of the Cornish rhyme "Ena, mena, bora mi; Kisca, lara, mora di; Eggs, butter, cheese, bread; Stick, stock, stone dead" as a phrase of "great antiquity" which first lays a ban on a victim's chief articles of food, and foreshadows his death by beating (Bolton 1888:43). The difficulty in establishing connections between counting-out and ancient Celtic practices of human sacrifice are most tellingly revealed when folklorists fell back on scenes from nineteenth-century romantic novels to illustrate their arguments.[5] Thus Bolton cited R. D. Blackmore's *Lorna Doone* (1869) for a magical charm that seemed reminiscent of a counting-out rhyme (Bolton 1888:50), and the Reverend Sabine Baring-Gould quoted extensively from his own novel *Perpetua* (1897) to illustrate how, in Gaul, a maiden was counted out to be sacrificed to the spirit of the spring. As Baring-Gould confidently stated, "I have ventured to reproduce this, which although fiction, undoubtedly represents what actually took place" (Baring-Gould 1913:107–111). Of course, not all nineteenth-century British folklorists were enamored with the hypothesis that counting-out rhymes derived from ancient Druidic sacrificial practices. Some thought that evidence was lacking and that such interpretations were hopelessly uncritical (Northall 1892:341–342).

The survivalist approach to counting-out assumed that it was a form of lottery; a mechanism of divination whose outcome was unknown and subject to the vagaries of chance. This perspective on counting-out is supported in more recent works on children's lore, where counting-out is regarded as "similar to roulette" which consequently explains why it is considered "a fair, impartial way of choosing" among children (Knapp & Knapp 1976:27).[6] However, Kenneth Goldstein showed that counting-out was less random than previously supposed. Goldstein discovered that children strategically manipulate counting-out in order to exert control over outcomes. He described how children might add phrases to the counting-out rhymes if they ended on a child that the counter did not want eliminated; how a repertory of rhymes with different numbers of stresses were employed by the counter to deal with different numbers of children to be counted in order to produce favorable outcomes; or how the counter might skip himself in the count if his elimination seemed likely (1971:173–177). Goldstein even reported that one player had memorized the first position to be eliminated in any group of children of ten or less. After each count, this counter would reposition himself within the remaining circle in order to eliminate whomever he wished. As Goldstein notes, "This 'changing position' strategy was used by one extremely precocious nine-year-old boy who was considered something of a mathematical genius at school" (1971:177). A child in the play group who suspected that this "genius" was somehow manipulating the count—although he didn't know how—voiced his concern and found himself among the first to be counted out from then on (177).

Although the children who employed counting-out overwhelmingly agreed, on the one hand, that counting-out was "democratic" and that everyone had the "same chance" (1971:169), Goldstein documented that for some children counting-out was not entirely a matter of chance but a process that could be approached strategically with knowable, or at least partially knowable, outcomes. Of course, counting-out is not random. One would expect that repeating counting-out with a group of the same size and by the same count would produce an identical result, although the outcome for a large enough group of people might be unpredictable.

In his discovery of the use of strategy in counting-out, Goldstein was unaware that there existed a long-standing concern with such strategies; a tradition dating back to the late Middle Ages. The formulation of counting-out as a mathematical problem seems to appear first in Europe. A problem is included in the early 10th century Codex Einsidelensis (Smith 1917:64; Smith and Mikami 1914:84).[7] The 12th century Jewish scholar Abraham ibn Ezra mentions a problem of this type in his work *Tachbula*. Ibn Ezra's description of the problem involves being aboard ship with 15 students (S) and 15 good-for-nothings (G) during a storm. As the ship needed to reduce its load, it was agreed that every ninth person would be counted out and thrown overboard until only half of the original thirty would be left. Ibn Ezra arranged them so that every ninth person would be a good-for-nothing. The arrangement was 4S, 5G, 2S, 1G, 3S, 1G, 1S, 2G, 2S, 3G, 1S, 2G, 2S, 1G (Steinschneider 1880:123–124). This formulation of the counting-out problem appears in a number of the arithmetic and algebraic treatises and problem books of the Renaissance. It appears in a manuscript of the Parisian Nicolas Chuquet which was completed in 1484.[8] The problem is formulated with the same parameters as that of ibn Ezra, except the voyagers are Christians and Jews. The count is also by nines and the problem is to order the thirty passengers so that the Jews are thrown overboard and only the Christians remain. The solution is the same as that provided by ibn Ezra, although Chuquet provides a mnemonic verse by which the order of the ship's passengers might be remembered: "Populeam virgam matre regina tenebat" ("The queen held the mother's poplar rod" [?]; "The queen mother used to hold the poplar rod" [?]). Each vowel in the verse is accorded a numerical value ($a = 1$; $e = 2$; $i = 3$; $o = 4$; $u = 5$) and the thirty passengers are ordered according to the numerical value of the vowels of the verse beginning first with 4 Christians. Chuquet also suggests that the problem might be formulated with different numbers of Christians and Jews and with throwing out every 10th or 11th person, instead of the ninth person (Flegg, Hay, and Moss 1985:230).[9]

Variations of this problem appear in the sixteenth century in the works of mathematicians Niccolo Fontana Tartaglia (1499–1557), Gerolamo Cardano [Cardan] (1501–1576), and Petrus Ramus (1515–1572), among others (Ball 1960:220–221; Smith and Mikami 1914:84 n2). In 1612, Claude-Gaspard Bachet (1581–1638) published his first edition of *Problemes plaisants et delectables*. Problem XXIII is identical to that propounded by Chuquet, except that Christians and Turks are counted out rather than Christians and Jews. Bachet also offered a French mnemonic verse in place of the Latin for remembering the order of arrangement—"Mort, tu me falliras pas, En me livrant le trepas" ("Death, you will not fail to deliver my demise")—although it operated according to the same vowel cipher (Bachet 1874:119).[10]

Cardan seems to have been the first to relate this type of counting-out problem to the story of Josephus in *The Jewish War*. He called it *ludus Joseph*—the Josephus game (Ahrens 1901:288).[11] Josephus (Joseph ben Matthias) was a Jewish commander who was assigned the defense of the Galilee during the Jewish Revolt against Rome. He garrisoned Galilean towns, and in 67 A.D. he directed the defense of the town of Jotapata against the Romans under the command of Vespesian. When these Roman forces breached the walls of the town and began a massacre of the inhabitants and defenders, Josephus claims he sought refuge in a cavern under the city where he encountered forty other defenders also in hiding. These defenders had decided to take their own lives, and after Josephus failed to dissuade them, he suggested:

> Since we are resolved to die, come let us leave the lot to decide the order in which we are to kill ourselves; let him who draws the first lot fall by the hand who comes next; fortune will thus take her course through the whole number and we shall be spared from taking our lives with our own hands. For it would be unjust that, when the rest were gone, any should repent and escape. This proposal inspired confidence; his advice was taken, and he drew lots with the rest. Each man thus selected presented his throat to his neighbor, in the assurance that his general was forthwith to share his fate. . . . He, however (should one say by fortune or by the providence of God?) was left alone with one other; and anxious neither to be condemned by the lot nor, should he be left to the last, to stain his hand with the blood of a fellow-countryman, he persuaded this man also, under a pledge, to remain alive (Josephus 1927:685–687).

Josephus makes no mention of the type of lot employed, and there is no indication that counting-out was used. Nor is there any suggestion that Josephus manipulated the outcome in order to remain among the survivors. In fact, Josephus attributes his survival only to "fortune" or the "providence of God" (687).

Josephus's Greek text of *The Jewish War* was not the original draft of the work. There was an earlier Aramaic edition, now lost (Josephus 1927:ix). There are scholars who have held, however, that the Slavonic version of *The Jewish War* may derive from the lost

Aramaic draft (ix). It seems that the Slavonic version originated in Lithuania somewhere around 1250 A.D. and was later copied in a number of manuscripts in the fifteenth century. There are some who believe that the Slavonic version was translated from a lost Greek text which may have been based on the lost Aramaic version (Josephus 1927:xi; Josephus 1970:470).

The Slavonic version of *The Jewish War* abbreviates a number of events in the standard Greek text, but it also includes a number of passages not found there.[12] One of these passages pertains to the selection of the victims in the cave at Jotapata:

> And he, commending his salvation to God the Protector, said, "Since it is well pleasing to God that we should die, let us be killed in turn. Let him whose turn comes last be killed by the second." And when he had thus spoken, *he counted the numbers with cunning, and thereby misled them all.* And they were all killed, one by another, except one; and, anxious not to stain his right hand with the blood of a fellow-countryman, he besought this one, and they both went out alive (Josephus 1928:654, my emphasis).

This passage suggests that the method employed to establish the order of victims was a form of counting-out, and that Josephus somehow could foresee and manipulate the order of selection so that he would be the last to remain. But it is not clear how well-known the Slavonic version was in Western Europe and whether it had any influence on European mathematical tradition.

It was Bachet who explicitly formulated the story of Josephus in mathematical terms. Bachet, like the Slavonic version of *The Jewish War*, attributed Josephus's salvation to careful reckoning, rather than providence or fate (Bachet 1874:9). Bachet speculated that with a total of 41 men in the cave, and if they had counted out by threes, Josephus would have had to place himself in the 31st position to be the last remaining. And if he had wanted to save two companions, they would have to be in the 16th and 35th positions, as these would be the second- and third-to-last respectively (Bachet 1874:120–121). Thus, it would seem that Cardan and Bachet are responsible for formulating what has come to be known in contemporary mathematics as the "Josephus Problem," the Slavonic version of *The Jewish War* notwithstanding.

Counting-out was also of concern to Japanese mathematicians of the seventeenth century. The classical formulation of the question in Japan was the *Mameko-date* or "stepchildren problem." It appears in the *Jinko-ki* of Yoshida (Yoshida Shichibei Koyu, or Mitsuyoshi) in 1627, and in the *Mantoku Jinko-ri* of Muramatsu Kudayu Mosei in 1665. Seki Shinsuke Kowa, the successor to Yoshida, included it in his *Sandatsu Kempu* where he characterizes it as an "old tradition" (Smith and Mikami 1914:80–84). The problem is more elaborate than its formulations in the West. The problem, following the version in Seki, concerns a wealthy farmer who had thirty sons, fifteen by his first wife and fifteen by his second. The second wife wanted one of her sons to inherit all of the father's wealth so she proposed that all the sons be arranged in a circle and be counted out by tens until only one remained. That one would be the father's sole heir. The husband agreed, and the second wife arranged the sons in such a way that fourteen of fifteen of her stepchildren were immediately counted out. Feeling confident of her success, she suggested that the direction of the count be reversed beginning with a child of her choosing. This was also agreed to, but all her fifteen children were thus counted out leaving the sole remaining son of the first wife to inherit his father's fortune (Smith and Mikami 1914:82–83).[13]

It is not clear whether the problem originated in the East and made its way west, whether it originated in the West and made its way east, or whether it originated somewhere in between and made its way both east and west. Since problems in both the East and the West often describe two competing groups of fifteen members, with one set to be completely eliminated, it suggests that some relationship exists between the traditions. Curiously, the problem does not seem to appear in the Chinese mathematical literature (Needham with Ling 1979:61–62).

For centuries, counting-out problems continued to appear in the mathematical treatises and puzzle books of both East and West, yet no advancement took place in the solution of the problem. The problems, it would seem, were solved by brute force—physically drawing a diagram and counting out the requisite number until a result was obtained—and then, as in the case in the West, the solution was recalled through some mnemonic device. It was not until the very end of the nineteenth century that a generalization of the problem was proposed by mathematician Peter Guthrie Tait. Tait focused on the problem outlined by Bachet involving the predicament of Josephus in the cave (Tait 1898–1900, 2:432–435). Bachet had shown that with 41 men, and counting by threes, the last remaining would stand in the 31st position. The question is: what would be the last position in a group of *any* size counting by *any* number? While Tait could not provide a formula by which this last position could be computed, he outlined a method that could serve to compute such a position for a variety of cases, even if the number of persons to be counted were very large.

Tait began with a simple observation.[14] If there is a group of seven people and we count by three (that is, let n equal the number of people in the group, and let m equal the number by which people are counted out; so that $n = 7$ and $m = 3$), the order of elimination is indicated in the first circle below. (Inside numbers are the order of people in the circle. Outside numbers represent the order in which they are eliminated. The arrow points to the last person remaining after all others have been eliminated.) A group of eight people ($n = 8$ and $m = 3$) is represented by the second circle, and a group of nine by the third.

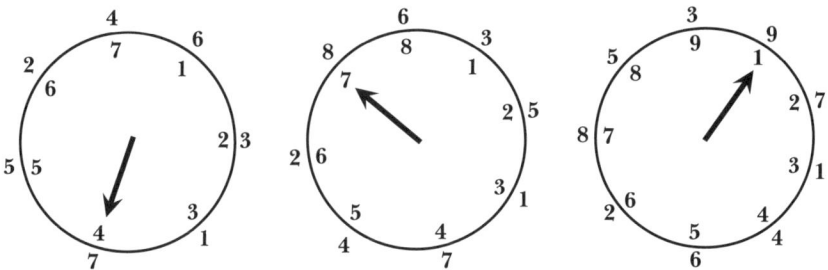

Figure 1

Thus, when $n = 7$, the position of the last person remaining when all the others have been counted out (a position we will call p) is the fourth. When $n = 8$ then $p = 7$. When $n = 9$, $p = 1$.

It can be seen that each time we add one more person to the group, the position of the last person will increase by 3 (since we count by threes; if we counted by some other m, p would increase by whatever that m is). So if $p = 4$ when $n = 7$, $p = (4 + 3) = 7$ when the group equals $n+1$ or 8. P should increase to 10 when $n = 9$, but since there are only nine people in the group, there is no person number 10. The tenth person in a circle of nine is, in actuality, number 1. (This is called *cycling* and will be addressed below.)

It is easy to show that if p is the last position in a circle of any group of n people, that the last position in a group of $n + 1$ people is $p + 3$. (It is not just true for the examples of $n = 7$, 8, or 9 in the diagrams.) To see this, we must work backwards. Start with a circle of $n + 1$ people (as numbered inside the circle). As soon as we start to count out by 3, the third person is eliminated. If we stop counting at this point, we now have a circle of only n people. Let us renumber the remaining circle of n people so that the person who was 4 is numbered 1', the person who was 5 is numbered 2', and so on until all the members of this new circle are renumbered.

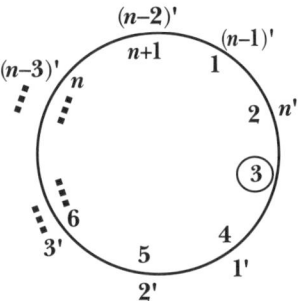

Figure 2

Each position in the circle of n members is 3 less than in the circle of $n + 1$ members. *Reversing* this relation, if we know p for group n, we know that for group $n + 1$ the last position will be $p + 3$. The exceptions will be when $p = (n - 1)'$ and $p = n'$. For in a group of size n, if $p = (n - 1)$, then in a group of $(n + 1)$ members p will be 1. And if $p = n$ in a group size n, then in group size $(n + 1)$ p will be 2 (cycling again!).

To summarize, if n is the number of people in a circle, and if p is the last person counted out in that group, and if m is the number we count by; then the last counted out in a circle of size $n + 1$ is $p + m$, or in the Josephus problem, $p + 3$. If we use subscripts to simplify our notation (such that $p_{(n)}$ refers to the p in a group of n persons, and $p_{(n+1)}$ is p in a group of $n + 1$ persons) then $p_{(n+1)} = p_{(n)} + 3$.

If we increase group n by some number other than 1, x let us say, then $p_{(n+x)} = p_{(n)} + mx$ or $p_{(n)} + 3x$ in the Josephus example where $m = 3$. Thus we can add $3x$ to any $p_{(n)}$ to compute the new $p_{(n+x)}$, *but this is only true so long as cycling does not take place.* For example, when $n = 9$, $p = 1$. If we increase n by 4 [let $x = 4$], then $p_{(9+4)} = p_{(9)} + 3(4) = 1 + 12 = 13$. And this is in fact correct. The last person remaining when $n = 13$ is the 13th. But if we try to increase $n = 9$ by $x = 5$ (so $n = 14$ altogether), the same computation does not work: $p_{(14)} \neq p_{(9)} + 3(5)$. That is because $1 + 15 = 16$, and the new p cannot be 16 in a group with only 14 members. Cycling has occurred.

Thus $3x$ can be added to $p_{(n)}$ to compute $p_{(n+x)}$ only so long as cycling does not occur between n and $n + x$. If cycling does occur between n and $n + x$, then one needs to know the n at which cycling has last occurred and compute $p_{(n+x)}$ from that point. Since we know that cycling has occurred when $n = 14$, and that $p_{(14)}$ cannot equal 16 (since the first computation of $p_{(14)}$ is greater than the number of people in the circle), we can easily compute what p should be for $n = 14$. All we need do is subtract 14 [i.e., $n + x$] from 16 [$p_{(9)} + 3(5)$] and we get $p_{(14)} = 2$ [since $16 - 14 = 2$]. Thus when $n = 14$, then $p_{(14)} = 2$. Note that when cycling occurs, we need to subtract $(n + x)$ from $(p + 3x)$ to compute $p_{(n+x)}$. Since we now know what p is when n is 14, we can compute the next time that cycling takes place. We know that when cycling occurs, the new p must either equal 1 or 2. To compute the next cycling, simply solve the following equation for x:

$(p + 3x) - (n + x) = 1$ or 2
We know that $p = 2$ when $n = 14$, so the computation is simple.
$(2 + 3x) - 14 - x = 1$ or 2
$2x - 12 = 1$ or 2

Since the answer must be a whole number, the expression cannot equal 1. So we set it equal to 2:

$2x - 12 = 2$; then $2x = 14$; and $x = 7$. Then $(n + x) = 21$.

What this shows is that starting with $n = 14$ and $p = 2$, the next time that cycling occurs is when $n = 21$ and $p = 2$.

If we wish to solve the Josephus problem as posed by Bachet, where there are 41 men, we must compute $p_{(41)}$ or who p is when $n = 41$. We must first determine whether cycling occurs again between $n = 21$ and $n = 41$. We repeat the computation: $p_{(21)} + 3x - (n + x) =$ 1 or 2. Substituting and simplifying we find: $2 + 3x - 21 - x = 1$ or 2. $2x = 20$ and $x = 10$. So the next time cycling takes place is when $n = 31$ (i.e., $21 + 10$) and $p = 1$. If we compute the next time cycling takes place we find it is at an n greater than the 41 men in our problem. So knowing that when $n = 31$, $p = 1$, and knowing that if we increase the size of group $n = 31$ by 10 to get $n = 41$, all we have to do is solve the following equation $p_{(41)} = p_{(31)} + 3x$, where $x = 10$ and $p_{(31)} = 1$. The solution $p_{(41)} = 1 + 3(10) = 31$. The last person remaining when counting out by threes in a group of 41 people is the 31st. This is exactly the solution that Bachet arrived at by brute force.

Someone might suppose that it would be easier to do the actual counting-out than engage in the computation, but this would be true only when n was very small. When $n = 2,000,000$, then the last remaining person is the 685,043rd. If one were able to count out on average one person per second (and assuming no errors), it would take over twenty-three days and nights of continuous counting to arrive at the same conclusion. (It would actually take much longer since one would first have to write out two million numbers in order to count them.) Tait's method has value.

Where does this all lead? What is its significance? This inquiry was first conceived after I asked several mathematicians whether it would be possible to write a formula that would determine the last counted out for any group n counting by any m. No theoretical concern prompted my question; only curiosity. When one mathematician recognized my question as a variant of the "Josephus Problem," the literature—including Tait's generalization—became accessible.[15]

Nevertheless, naïve inquiries may lead to more significant ones. One might note that mathematicians were drawn to the question of counting-out before folklorists; in fact, long before the existence of folklore as a field. This mathematical tradition is also a literary one as the problems are formulated in terms of stories that, at least in the West, involve counting-out people for death. I do not know what influence this tradition has had outside mathematical circles, but it seems possible that the mathematical tradition may have predisposed nineteenth-century folklore scholars to regard counting-out as related to the selection of sacrificial victims. In other words, a medieval and renaissance mathematical recreation might have influenced ethnological perspectives in the nineteenth century.[16]

A more theoretical concern emerges when one considers the depth of the mathematical tradition itself. It is remarkable that almost a millennium was required to move from the early formulations of the problem to Tait's generalization. The mathematics employed by Tait was available to the mathematicians of the Renaissance. He utilized no new mathematical discoveries. This serves to challenge the assertion that "where an invention or discovery becomes possible, that invention or discovery becomes inevitable" (White 1949:208). If this proposition is not mere tautology, it must confront the question of why Bachet's formulation and Tait's generalization of the Josephus Problem were separated by almost three hundred years. Starting with the Josephus problem, one might begin to assemble an inventory of discoveries and inventions that arise much, much later than what might be reckoned as their appointed times. From such simple questions, serious challenges to high-level theorizing may develop (Oring 1996).

Folklore and mathematics have yet to meet in any fruitful collaboration, despite the fact that mathematics is relevant to analyzing the structures of certain folklore forms; most obviously—but not exclusively—children's games. It has been suggested that folk games that are unfair or have optimal strategies (saddle points) might drop out of children's repertoires earlier than games that are fair or lack such strategies (Oring 1968:23). Certainly the counting-out ritual described by Goldstein began to be abandoned about the time that the children sensed there could be some degree of control over the outcome.[17] In many cases, the degree of unfairness of a game may only be reckoned mathematically. In other words, such a folkloristic hypothesis could only be tested with the aid of mathematical analysis. There are many instances in which folklore might benefit from a mathematical perspective. Although folklorists are unlikely to master the kinds of mathematics that might inform their own inquiries, they could develop a sense of when a mathematical perspective might prove relevant and contribute something to their understanding. Folklorists might start taking mathematicians to lunch.

10. Definition and Devolution

Definitions are characterizations of sets within a domain that can be distinguished from other sets in that domain (e.g., a pine tree is a tree that is evergreen, resinous, and has needles.) There are several ways sets may be distinguished. One can point to their members (ostensive definition), list their members (enumerative definition), or identify the traits that distinguish the members of the set (conceptual definition). There are situations in which each of these types is useful, but the theoretical terms of a discipline generally require a conceptual definition. The elements that are said to belong to the subset should be identifiable in terms of traits that distinguish them from other subsets in the domain. The definition is adequate when those traits are both necessary and sufficient for the identification. It is important as well to insure that the traits employed are not ambiguous or contradictory such that it is impossible to decide what is or is not to be included in the subset. Finally, if the definition is to prove useful, it should correlate with other disciplinary knowledge. Definitions are not explanations or theories, but the power of both depends on adequate definition (Alexander 1967:254–260; Kaplan 1964:51).

> *What is a ghost? Define one. Deduce for me the conditions of the possibility of a ghost. In what reasonable connection does such an apparition coincide with reason itself?*
> —Heinrich Heine

Alan Dundes first presented "The Devolutionary Premise in Folklore Theory" at the American Folklore Society Meeting in Toronto in 1967. In that paper—and in the published version that appeared two years later—he argued that folklore theories were inherently biased against progress. Folklorists were overly concerned with a "golden age of folklore" which had occurred in the far distant past and which they had set themselves the task of reconstructing. The folklore of the day was viewed as the result of degeneration and decay over time (1969:5). Dundes then showed the strains of this bias in the works of various folklorists including Max Müller, Hans Naumann, Walter Anderson, Stith Thompson, Gyula Ortutay, Gordon Gerould, Edward B. Tylor, Richard Dorson, Sigmund Freud, Rudolf Steiner,

168   *Just Folklore*

and Carl Gustav Jung (Dundes 1969).[1] Dundes felt that folklorists were unnecessarily wedded to this devolutionary premise and that they could and should assume an alternative presupposition in which folklore actually "improved" or "evolved" over time (19).

Following his oral presentation, a rather animated debate erupted as to whether folklore was actually devolving. Alan Lomax testified to the reality of devolution and bemoaned the extinction of folksongs, while Dundes simply accused Lomax of being immersed in the devolutionary Weltanschauung that had just been outlined in his paper. Lomax and others might quickly recognize their devolutionary bias, Dundes asserted, if they would only "look at the jokes" and register their vitality, popularity, and the aesthetics of their performance.

The notion of a devolutionary premise has established itself rather comfortably in the language and imagination of folklorists (e.g., Myers-Moro 1989:191; Toelken 1998:85; Bronner 2005:144; Golovakha-Hicks 2006:222; Walker 2008:237), but is it as fundamental to folklore theory as has been claimed? Two questions need to be addressed. (1) Does folklore actually devolve? If so, the devolution of folklore is not a bias of folklorists but an objective description of the world. (2) How was the argument for a devolutionary premise constructed? What does it presume, and on what evidence does it rest? This second question is actually primary since whether folklore is actually regarded as devolving depends on what devolution means and how it is assessed. Consequently, what needs to be established are: the definition of devolution; the specification of criteria for recognizing devolution; and the identification of the unit of devolution—what it is that actually does the devolving.

"Devolve" derives from the Latin roots *de* + *volvere*, literally to "roll down." In English, it has a range of meanings: to fall, or descend, or flow to. It can also characterize a property or responsibility that passes on to someone else, usually through forfeiture.[2] Although the meaning "to degenerate" is regarded as obsolete, it is still retained in biology, and it is this usage that is central for Dundes's devolutionary thesis (*OED* s.v. "devolve," "devolution").

It is a more complicated matter to identify the means by which devolution is to be reckoned since Dundes employs no single measure. When he identifies devolution in the work of the historic-geographic methodologists, he employs an *aesthetic* criterion. They are devolutionists because they regarded the original form of a folktale as its most noble, complete, and logical form which then degenerated in the course of time and transmission (1969:8). A *sociological* criterion crops up in establishing devolution in the work of Naumann, Anderson, and Thompson. Folklore devolves because they see it as moving from higher to lower social groups (6). In identifying devolution in the works of the depth psychologists C. G. Jung and Rudolf Steiner, Dundes employs a *functional* criterion since they hold that the spiritual truths of myths and tales no longer serve modern society. Their power and utility has weakened or been lost (16–17). *Systemic* and *semantic* criteria are used in the evaluation of Tylor and Müller. Folklore is a fragment that has survived from an old mythological system which has lost its integrity and meaning. *Vitality* is the basis for characterizing ballad scholar Gordon Gerould as a devolutionist because he saw folksong as dying under the influence of print and broadcast media (15). *Truth* serves to label Richard Dorson as devolutionary because he uses the word *folklore* to connote error. This criterion is the basis for categorizing as devolutionary all those who regard folklore as the antithesis of "education" (14).

What Dundes defines by extension fails to be defined by intension. That is to say, Dundes extends the term *devolution* over a range of theories—those of Naumann, Tylor, Jung, and others—but there are no traits that these theories have in common that serve to characterize the essential nature of the class (Alexander 1967:76–82). With such an array of means for identifying devolution, it is no wonder that devolution is found to be rife in folklore research.

Identifying devolution on the basis of such a variety of criteria can lead to some curious anomalies and contradictions. (1) Ballad scholars are devolutionary because they hold that such songs are dying out. Death and extinction, however, are an inherent part of any evolutionary theory. It cannot be considered a symptom of devolution. Paleontologists and archeologists focus on extinct biological and cultural forms but that hardly commits them to a devolutionary perspective. Extinction is not the opposite of evolution.³ (2) The decline in the faithfulness, truth, and wholeness of any particular historical narrative might be indexed as devolutionary, but this decline may be necessary for its aesthetic evolution. Art may be wrought from observations of the world, but it is not commensurate with an accurate rendering of those observations. Art demands elaboration and refinement. What is lost in completeness and truth may be a gain in art. (3) Although historic-geographic scholars may be devolutionary in their view of the aesthetic aspects of the folktale, they must be regarded as evolutionary when a vitality criterion is invoked since a single original form gives rise to a myriad of tale variants. (4) If some tradition evolves too radically in its structural or aesthetic features, it may no longer be recognized as traditional—i.e., as folklore. In a sense, it has evolved *out of folklore* and consequently has devolved.⁴

More confusions arise when identifying the unit of devolution—what it is that is supposed to be devolving. Edward Burnett Tylor was a champion of cultural evolution who, in Dundes's view, "forcefully argued the devolution of folklore" (1969:12). Tylor is a devolutionist according to Dundes because he regarded folklore—that is, survivals—as the "transformed, shifted, or *mutilated* fragments of culture" (1969:12). This last quotation, it should be noted, was not Tylor commenting on *folklore* per se—a term that he only occasionally employed—but on "art" objects that one was likely to find in a middle-class parlor: the fleur-de-lis of Anjou, the cornice with a Greek border, the style of Louis XIV (Tylor 1874, 1:17). Tylor had no great commitment to the term *folklore*, and it held no theoretical significance in his work.⁵ Tylor undoubtedly thought the stuff of folklore—primarily superstitious belief, children's games and rhymes, riddles, proverbs, legends—to be survivals, but he did not think of all survivals as folklore.

Survivals according to Tylor were those "processes, customs, opinions, and so forth which have been carried on by force of habit into a new state of society different from that in which they had their original home" (1874, 1:16). By definition, these elements of culture did not decay but merely *survived*. What had decayed was the philosophy and world view that once made these beliefs and practices meaningful and whole. Folklore itself did not devolve.

The problem arises again in Dundes's consideration of the devolutionary premise in the works of comparative mythologist Max Müller. Müller's theory of myth, according to Dundes, was devolutionary because it was rooted in a notion of "the disease of language." According to Müller, the fantastical and barbarous stories of the ancient Greeks resulted from the forgetting of the meanings of ancient metaphors—usually those describing heavenly phenomena. The metaphorical language survived while their original denotations did not. The rays of the sun, for example, might originally have been called "fingers" or lightning called "arrows" and "serpents." However, once these metaphors had lost their reference to heavenly phenomena, stories crystallized around them to make sense of them. They were taken as characteristics of animate beings—gods—rather than references to natural bodies and their actions. Thus, the Greek myth that told of Cronus swallowing and regurgitating his children was originally a metaphorical description of the heavens devouring and releasing the clouds (Dorson 1955:398–399).

While Müller's theory is predicated on a notion of language decay, the myths themselves—what Dundes would consider the folklore—depend upon the creation of a narrative that might be said to have evolved from dead metaphors: "These expressions remained long after their meanings had ceased to be understood; and as the human mind is generally as anxious for a reason as ready to invent one, a story *arose* by common consent, and without any personal effort" (Müller in Dorson 1968a, 1:86; my emphasis). To simply suggest that Müller's theory of myth is devolutionary is to belie the status of devolution in his theory. It is metaphor that has semantically devolved, not myth or folklore. Imprecision in identifying the unit of devolution—what does the devolving—allows for the identification of devolution when no devolution of folklore occurs. A distinction needs to be recognized between the devolution of folklore and folklore that is created as a result of the devolution of something else.

Hans Naumann's notion of *gesunkenes Kulturgut* [sunken cultural goods] is also devolutionary, according to Dundes, because he holds that folklore consists of those elements of culture that moved from higher to lower social strata. Similarly, Walter Anderson's and Stith Thompson's views of folktales are devolutionary because the tales move from "culturally higher" to "culturally lower" peoples (Dundes 1969:6). In these formulations, something isn't folklore until it moves from a higher to a lower social status. Again, it is not folklore that degenerates or decays. Rather culture becomes folklore when it moves into a sociological category of a lower rank. It is also not clear how Dundes's view of Naumann, Anderson, and Thompson as devolutionists can be reconciled with his appraisal of Tylor. Tylor, after all, regarded as folklore those cultural traits that carried over from lower stages of civilization to higher ones.

In establishing the existence of a devolutionary premise in folklore theory, Dundes was reluctant to identify situations of evolution. He did, however, point to the work of E. Sydney Hartland who suggested that folktales follow an evolutionary law. As incidents and motifs that have been shaped by a savage way of life move into higher stages of civilization, they change to accommodate their new cultural milieu. They evolve artistically (Dundes 1969:11). But Dundes uses Hartland as a foil. Hartland's evolution is the exception that proves the rule of the devolutionary premise in folklore.

But if Hartland could imagine the evolution of folklore, he might well have been following Tylor's lead. Tylor actually identified three kinds of survival and each appears capable of evolution. There are what might be called "primary survivals." These are basic mental processes that arose in the early stages of human development—such as the association of ideas or the doctrine of analogy—that persist in more advanced stages of civilization. In the savage stage of civilization, these processes were responsible for the belief in magic, the philosophy of Animism, and the formation of myth (1874, 1:116, 285, 296–297). But in the present, these same thought processes are the foundation of poetic imagination: "Poetry has so far kept alive in our minds the old animative theory of nature. . . . Both share in that sense of the reality of ideas, which fortunately or unfortunately modern education has proved so powerful to destroy" (1:292, 315). The mental processes are the same, distinguished only by the degree of reality accorded to the analogies adduced (1:296–297). In other words, Tylor saw evolution from mythopoesis to poesis.

"Secondary survivals" are those fragments of savage philosophy which persist into more advanced stages of civilization. "The German peasant, during his child's birth and baptism, objects to lend anything out of his house, lest witchcraft would be worked through it on the yet unconsecrated baby" (1:116). Secondary survivals involve an old form and its associated meaning persisting into later ages, although it is only a fragment of a formerly widespread religious-philosophical doctrine. Such survivals were also capable of evolution, as they could regain their former importance and systemic meanings. Tylor refers to this process as *revival*. Tylor saw medieval witchcraft and modern spiritualism as a direct "revival from the regions of savage philosophy and peasant folk-lore. . . . A great philosophic-religious doctrine, flourishing in the lower culture but dwindling in the higher has re-established itself with full vigor" (1:142). Since Dundes regards survivals which have lost their former meaning and importance as devolutionary, he should regard revivals, where such meaning and importance have been restored, as evolutionary. Tylor, it should be noted, saw such revivals as indications of intellectual and moral degeneration (1:139).

"Tertiary survivals" involve the persistence of an old form without its associated meaning. Sneezing formulas ("God bless you!"), drinking healths ("Wassail!"), and the taboo against saving a drowning man seem arbitrary and meaningless until the folklorists reestablishes their connection with some savage theological principle (1:97–104, 108–109). Yet these types of survival are also capable of evolution into what Tylor calls *partial survivals*: "the mass of cases where enough of the old habit is kept up for its original to be recognizable, though in taking a new form it has so adapted to new circumstances as still to hold its place on its own merits" (1:72).

There is ample evidence in Tylor's theory for the evolution of folklore. His concern, however, was to demonstrate the evolution of *culture* over time. Survivals could evidence this development because beliefs and practices that made little sense and held no import in later stages of civilization did make sense and have significance in previous stages. That could only mean that modern civilization evolved from savagery, and that savage cultures were not constructed from degenerated and fragmented pieces of civilization (1:32). The problem with survivals was not their shape but their context. Survivals were not mutilated and disintegrating in themselves, but the savage and barbaric stages of civilization which had given rise to these beliefs and practices were disintegrating and falling away. What had once characterized the state of all human societies now only existed in small and fast-vanishing groups dispersed throughout the remote landscapes of the globe (1:21).

It is worth an aside to register that although Tylor was an evolutionist, he was not a *Darwinian* evolutionist. In the Preface to the second edition of *Primitive Culture*, Tylor attempted to explain the omission of any references to Charles Darwin or Herbert Spencer. His work, he explained, was "arranged on its own lines, coming scarcely into contact with the previous works of these eminent philosophers" (1874, 1:vii-viii). Although Tylor could not fail to be affected by the enormous boost of attention to evolutionary thinking that Darwin's and Spencer's works excited, Tylor was correct in his claim that his work on culture owed little to them. Darwin never used the word *evolution* in the 1859 edition of *On the Origin of Species*. He spoke in terms of "descent" and "development." Tylor did not trace lines of descent or development in his work beyond identifying the great cultural stages that succeeded one another in history: savagery, barbarism, and civilization. He did not consider individual societies to be akin to species.[6] He made no attempt to show that the evolution of culture was the result of competition and natural selection. Had he done so, the Darwinian roots of his theory would have been incontrovertible. But culture evolved for Tylor along progressive lines: towards higher organization, greater power, greater reason, greater goodness, and increased happiness (1:27). These were not Darwinian ideas. If anything, they more closely reflect the ideas of the Marquis de Condorcet, Auguste Comte, and the milieu of pre-Darwinian social theorizing.[7]

William A. Wilson also challenged Dundes' neglect of evolutionary directions in earlier folklore theories. Wilson demonstrated that historic-geographic scholars Julius Krohn and Kaarle Krohn saw the *Kalevala* poems as beginning in Western Finland as small poetic units which evolved in complexity and beauty as they migrated eastward to Russo-Karelia. Only later did Kaarle Krohn reverse his position and argue that the poems were originally full accounts of actual historical events that fragmented as they moved, spawning "deficiencies, aberrations, and deformities" along the way (Wilson 1976b:242–247). Dundes, however, recognized only the devolutionary aspects of the Krohns' work and not the evolutionary.

Cecil Sharp outlined a theory of folksong in which songs evolved in a Darwinian fashion. The transmission of folksong was a process of creation and growth. Song variation was akin to biological mutation. Only those songs which were appreciated by the community were selected and survived. Variants which found no acceptance in the community were destined for extinction (Sharp 1907:11–12). Folksongs may not have begun their lives in the community, but they grew and were shaped in the process of oral transmission into communal songs (29). Phillips Barry echoed Sharp's views without the Darwinian terminology. The original source of the song was irrelevant. Many folksongs undoubtedly began in the versifying efforts of literate and published authors (Barry 1961:69–71). The folksong is made in a series of "re-creative acts" by singers with individual personalities. This is not a process of deterioration or disintegration but of "communal re-creation" (Barry 1933:4–6).[8]

Dundes noted that Gordon Gerould criticized fellow ballad scholars who "take it for granted that earlier ballads are likely to be better than later ones," but then registers the devolutionary tendencies in Gerould's presumption that: "Degeneration of noble themes and captivating tunes must have been going on ever since ballads became current" (Dundes 1969:10; Gerould 1957:185). But this line scarcely characterizes Gerould's overall view, for only a few lines earlier Gerould notes that, "folk-songs have been shaped by tradition into various forms, which not infrequently possess undeniable beauty of structure, of rhythm, of phrase" (1957:185). Although Gerould did not believe that just any singer could produce an aesthetic song variant, he believed there were innovators who could create and continued to create beautiful songs. They could do so because they were firmly grounded in tradition, and the ballad was the product of the "art of tradition" (Gerould 1957: 187–188; Gerould 1923:24).

Tristram P. Coffin and G. Malcolm Laws Jr. attested to the vitality of English, Scottish, and Irish song traditions in the United States and Canada by cataloging the instances of Child ballad variants that were collected in North America and the American ballads that derived from broadsides (Coffin 1963; Laws 1957). While not all ballads successfully crossed the ocean, the American tradition was as vital as that from which it so liberally borrowed. Furthermore, new folksongs arose in the United States and Maritime Canada—a native American balladry—that had, for the most part, no analogues in British or Irish tradition. Laws excluded from his *Native American Balladry* songs that were only collected before 1920 as well as those recently collected, on the grounds that the earlier ones might no longer be in tradition and the later ones might not enter tradition. Nevertheless, he identified two hundred and fifty American ballad types and recognized that more might eventually need to be added as other ballad collections were published (1964:10).

British ballads did not die in the New World, nor were ballad variants the result of mishearing and forgetting. In oral tradition, broadsides could acquire the unity, simplicity, and subtlety characteristic of the Child ballads (Laws 1957:115). Ballads were intentionally recomposed and improved, even if this recomposition was at times the work of ballad printers rather than ballad singers (121–122).[9]

Paull Franklin Baum assembled and commented on the "Dream Bead" story over the course of a thousand years. While his study is not evolutionary, nowhere does he suggest that later versions of the story were in any way inferior to earlier ones. Instead he writes, "One is struck by the variety of tunes that have been played on a few notes. . . . The story has maintained itself intact since before the time of Petrus Alphonsi" (Baum 1917:407–408). Similarly, W. Norman Brown's study of "The Silence Wager" (AT 1351) betrays no sense of superiority or inferiority of the versions he considers. He looks for the earliest versions and tries to identify the likely place of origin and general paths of dissemination. He notes the various subtypes of the story and which elements drop out or develop in which regions. There is no intimation, however, that the story has degenerated since its earliest literary manifestation in the fifth century C.E. (Brown 1922).

Given the ways in which the devolutionary premise has been defined and the data with which it has been evidenced, serious questions may be raised about the reality of a devolutionary premise in folklore theory. Devolution appears to be less an objective fact than a concomitant of the definition process. If one is allowed to reckon devolution in any number of ways, devolution is likely to be identifiable in theoretical orientations of various stripes.

The question of whether folklore is actually disappearing is also likely to rest on matters of definition. Dundes himself is aware that the devolution he identifies in folklore theory is inextricably linked to a definition of what constitutes the *folk:*

> Of course, the gloomy reports of the death of folklore are in part a result of the misguided and narrow concept of the folk as the illiterate in a literate society, that is, the folk as peasant, as *vulgus in populo,* as isolated rural community. Since the majority of folklorists in Europe and Asia continue to restrict the concept of the folk in this way . . . it is easy for them to believe that gradually the folk are dying out. With the devolutionary demise of folk or peasant culture, the deterioration of folklore was a matter of course (Dundes 1965:13).

If the folk are the peasants, and the peasants are disappearing, then the lore, which is the possession of the folk, must disappear as well. In other words, devolution ceases to be a theoretical bias and becomes an irrefutable fact.

The peasants are not the folk according to Dundes, however. The folk are "*any group of people whatsoever* who share at least one common factor" (1965:2). Consequently, there are all kinds of folk groups: religious folk groups, ethnic folk groups, occupational folk groups, and so on. "Who are the folk, among others, *we* are," he famously stated (Dundes 1977:34). Peasants were one possible folk group, but there were innumerable others.[10] New folk groups were continually being created. The folk were not some residual historical category but a constant, diverse, and ever-changing social presence.

Not only did Dundes subscribe to a different definition of *folk*, but he held a different conceptualization of *lore* as well. Dundes first provided an enumerative definition of lore: e.g., myth, tale, proverb, dance, recipe, costume, instrumental music, fence types, mnemonic devices, and even conventional sounds to summon animals (1965:3). Later, he shifted his definition of folklore from a list of forms to the forces shaping those forms: forms that exist in multiple versions as a result of continual transformation in the course of transmission (Dundes and Pagter 1975:xvii).[11] But Dundes is wrong to suggest that W. J. Thoms—the coiner of the word *folklore*—similarly offered an enumerative definition of the term, although Thoms does list "custom," "legend," "tradition," and "ballad" (Thoms in Dorson 1968a 1,:53; Dundes 1965:4). For Thoms, the term *lore* implies a teaching, a doctrine, a religious and moral philosophy of olden times that is preserved in bits of belief and practice in the present day. Thoms urged English folklorists to collect these bits and pieces in an effort to do for Britain what Jacob Grimm had done for Germany—reconstruct the system of mythology and religion of the heathen folk before the arrival of Christianity (Thoms in Dorson 1968a, 1:52–54). Lore, for Thoms, is not the enumeration of idle verbal, behavioral, and artifactual forms but the remains of a primeval philosophy. That is why Thoms modified the forms he enumerated with such adjectives as "neglected," "fading," "local," and "fragmentary" (53).

The notion that folklore consists of fragments of ancient philosophies that have disappeared with the evolution of culture and the emergence of science is a problem of definition, not devolution. The popularity, vitality, and aesthetics of jokes or folk speech in Western societies today cannot serve to evidence the devolutionary bias of earlier scholars (1969:15, 19).[12] Jokes were known in the nineteenth century; they just weren't—except in rare cases—considered folklore. Had jokes been regarded as encapsulating elements of ancient belief and practice, they would have been studied as folklore. But even had they been studied by earlier folklorists, those folklorists would have paid little attention to either their aesthetic qualities or their vitality in contemporary times.[13] They would have been studied as relics, and relics are important for their connection to the past, not the present. Early folklore scholars were studying—or thought they were studying—*antiquities*. To impute a devolutionary premise to such folklorists is to criticize antiquarians for studying antiques or to suggest that antiques may be very new rather than very old.[14]

Although definitions come and go, it seems perverse to criticize one definition as devolutionary on the basis of another. Dundes thinks of folklore as aesthetic forms that diversify in the process of their communication. In these terms, new folklore and new genres of folklore can be and are constantly being created. However, the work of scholars who saw folklore as a survival from a prehistoric past or as a tradition of venerable lineage will prove devolutionary by definition. They are operating in a different conceptual universe.

Dundes characterizes those who viewed the peasants as the folk as "misguided and narrow" (1969:13). But this presumes that particular definitions of folklore are somehow right or wrong rather than constructive or ineffectual in particular circumstances. What Dundes does not recognize is that the definition and redefinition of folklore is itself an attempt by folklorists to escape from the seemingly inescapable fact that the folklore they were studying—defined in terms of antiquities, survivals, peasant culture, or tradition—was bound to disappear. As definitions changed, previous orientations rooted in other concepts could be regarded as devolutionary. In other words, the *definition of devolution has depended on the evolution of definition*. And Dundes was deeply implicated in the evolution of folklore definition. In fact, Dundes redefined *folk* and *lore* precisely to escape the inevitability of a dying subject to which earlier, historically-oriented definitions condemned him. If the folk could be anybody, and the lore could be anything that was repeatedly transformed in communication, folklore could never and would never die. Devolution, therefore, is not a theoretical bias but an artifact of the process of definition. Devolution is what one sees when units of evolution are allowed to shift, when devolution is assessed according to various criteria, and when one examines the works of scholars who are operating with completely different definitions of the field. It is a phantom concept which may be apprehended as real and may not easily fade, even in the light of the morning sun.

11. Transmission and Degeneration

Experiments are usually associated with the "hard" sciences—e.g., biology, chemistry, and physics. There is, however, a robust field of experimental psychology, and economics—at least behavioral economics—routinely involves the design of experiments about human decision making (Levitt and Dubner 2005; Ariely 2008). Sociology and anthropology are perceived as more ethnographic and less experimental, but experiments are conducted in these fields as well (Nadel 1937; Friedman 1942; Pelto and Pelto 1978). In fact, there is no sharp divide between observation and experiment. Experiments do not require laboratories or specialized equipment, nor do they even demand a manipulation by the observer of the processes being observed. Experiments are simply controlled and systematic observations. They are designed (Kaplan 1964:144–147). Folklore is not commonly thought of as an experimental field, but as folklore is usually defined in terms of its materials, there is nothing that prohibits these materials from being systematically observed. In fact, there are experiments in folklore that often are not regarded as such because they are statistical (Poggie, Jr. and Gersuny 1972), clinical (Burns with Burns 1976), or field rather than laboratory experiments (Goldstein 1967). The few laboratory experiments in folklore that have dealt with the process of folklore transmission have only yielded equivocal results (Anderson 1951; 1956).

> *Everything degenerates in the hands of man.*
> —Jean Jacques Rousseau

EXPERIMENTATION HAS been fairly limited in folkloristic research. Folklorists have been hesitant to commit themselves to the task of controlling variables and observing the effects of such control. Nevertheless, one aspect of the folkloristic inquiry has aroused a modicum of interest—the process of transmission. Even in this area, however, folkloristic experimentation was primarily a response to, and a reflection of, earlier experiments performed by psychologists concerning the processes of remembering and the reliability of testimony. Perhaps the most thorough and influential of these earlier experiments were those performed since 1913 by Frederic C. Bartlett which culminated in his work *Remembering* (1932). Bartlett's investigations did not escape the attention of folklorists, because he utilized folklore materials in his experiments and made his findings known in an article in the journal *Folklore* (1920) which Alan Dundes reprinted in his widely-read anthology *The Study of Folklore* (1965).

Bartlett performed two kinds of experiments. One involved the repeated reproduction of material by the same individual over a course of time. Another involved the serial reproduction of material; that is, texts communicated by one individual to another to yet another and so on along a chain. Bartlett's subjects read and wrote out the materials in question and did not communicate orally with one another.[1] In his experiments, Bartlett employed visual material, a Native American and an African folktale, as well as other prose materials drawn from books and newspapers.

Bartlett described several principles of change that could be abstracted from his experimental data on the folktale materials: rationalization; dramatization; the omission of the unfamiliar, the irrelevant, and the unpleasant; the dominance of a word, phrase, or event; the persistence of trivial linguistic formulations (1920:32–28). All of these were noted by folklorists and correlated with their own observations of folklore traditions (Abrahams and Foss 1968:12–26; Burns 1970).

Nevertheless, Dundes criticized Bartlett's experiments as they related to folklore transmission. His criticisms were: (1) the subjects that Bartlett used were isolated individuals rather than members of a folk group; (2) the folklore materials utilized in the experiment were foreign to those individuals who were required to transmit them; (3) the tales were written and read rather than communicated orally; (4) there was no possibility in the experimental procedure for the operation of "self-correction"; (5) the time intervals for reproduction were artificially short (Dundes 1965:243–247)[2].

Dundes called attention to differences between Bartlett's experimental environment and the natural environments of most folklore transmissions. But such differences are not in themselves a basis for criticism. Most experimental environments differ from their natural counterparts because experiments attempt to reduce the number of variables under consideration. Differences between experimental and natural environments become problematic only when experimental results differ from those in the situations they purport to model. In other words, if an experiment fails to replicate natural processes, criticisms may be directed at variables introduced into or eliminated from the experimental procedure that may have affected the results. However, the types of omissions and transformations that took place in Bartlett's experiments did mirror those that occur in natural folklore transmission. The perceived distortion of natural transmission processes in Bartlett's experiments that Dundes criticizes is based on the fact that the folklore materials Bartlett employed *invariably* seemed to degenerate in experimental transmissions. "Bartlett's final versions . . . revealed degenerative change" (Dundes 1965:245). Of course, folklore can degenerate in oral transmission (Ortutay 1959:180, 184–185). But it does not invariably degenerate, and the "incredible stability of folk narrative" has been remarked upon by many observers (e.g., Krohn 1971:122).

It is difficult to know how many folklorists have attempted to reformulate and perform Bartlett-like experiments that incorporate the modifications suggested by Dundes. If one may judge from oral reports (and this is certainly to beg the question since it is the validity of oral reports that these experiments were initially designed to measure), many teachers of folklore in the United States have found a modified transmission experiment useful in classes if only as a pedagogical tool. Unfortunately, few of these experiments have been reported in the literature.

One notable exception is an experiment in which an anti-legend was introduced into an already existing folk group that was communicated in an oral-aural fashion (although subjects actually heard the version they were to reproduce from a tape recorder rather than from the previous subject). Nevertheless, in the second reproduction of the anti-legend, the subject changed the word "coffin" to "casket" and thus destroyed the punchline of the narrative in its original telling. The third subject when called upon to relate the narrative found it rather "pointless" (Clements 1973).

My own classroom experiments support Clements's findings. Experiments I and II involved the single-chain transmission of jokes. The joke employed in Experiment I resembled the following:[3]

184 *Just Folklore*

> A Madison Avenue advertising executive, who had a hectic morning, went into a fashionable bar for lunch. He sat at the bar and ordered a martini. As he was sipping his drink, a beautiful woman, tall and blonde, walked into the establishment. Everyone in the bar noticed her. She hesitated a moment near the doorway, and then walked toward the bar and sat down on a vacant stool right next to the advertising executive. Many eyes followed her as she adjusted herself on the seat next to him. The advertising man felt a bit nervous, having such a beautiful and striking woman sitting next to him, and decided to smoke a cigarette. He put a cigarette in his mouth and then discovered that he had no lighter. Nervously, he turned to the woman next to him, leaned over, and softly said, "Excuse me, do you have a match?" Whereupon the girl turned toward him and shouted, "I will not sleep with you!" Heads turned and people began to murmur. The fellow was terribly embarrassed. He couldn't figure out what had happened. What had he done to elicit such a response? He picked up his drink and crossed the room and settled into a booth at the rear of the bar. He sat there sipping his drink, muttering to himself, trying to figure out what had just happened. After about five minutes, the girl got up from the bar and came over and sat down with him in the booth. "Allow me to explain what happened," she said pleasantly. "I am a graduate student in psychology at the local university, and I am doing an experiment on people's reactions to shocking and embarrassing situations." The man looked up from his drink and shouted, "Seventy-five dollars?"

This joke involves a sexual theme and employs a technique that Freud would describe as "ready repartee".[4] When the man innocently requests a match, the woman embarrasses him by making his request publicly appear to be a sexual proposition. Later, when she attempts to explain her behavior as being part of an innocent psychological experiment, he makes her explanation publicly appear to be a proposal to fulfill that fictitious sexual proposition.

The joke employed in Experiment II revolved around well-known ethnic stereotypes in American jokelore:[5]

> There was this fellow who was very much in love with a girl who is Polish. And he wants very much to marry this girl, but her parents are opposed to the marriage because the fellow is not Polish. He becomes very upset because he loves the girl very much. Finally, he hears about this doctor who can perform an operation that can

make a person Polish. He goes to see the doctor, and the doctor explains, "Yes, there is a surgical procedure that can make you Polish. It is a radical procedure, but it can be done. Essentially, what we do is cut out half your brain." The guy thinks about it for a minute, but he really loves the girl, so he decides to go through with the operation. The next week he goes in for the operation, and they open him, and while the surgeon is operating, his hand slips and instead of cutting out half his brain he accidentally cuts out three quarters. But there is nothing that the doctor can do. He finishes the operation and closes up. Later, in the recovery room, after the guy has come out of the anesthetic, the doctor comes in and says to him, "Listen there was a problem during the operation. The knife slipped and instead of taking out half of your brain I took out three quarters." The patient sits up and slaps his forehead with the palm of his hand and says, "Mamma mia!"

In American jokelore, the Pole is stereotyped either as a quintessentially stupid or dirty character.[6] This stereotype is alluded to in the above joke when the doctor suggests that he can turn normal people into Poles by excising half their brains. The point of the joke lies in the revelation that there is a figure who is even stupider and more foolish than the Pole—the Italian.

These same jokes were employed in over a dozen classroom experiments by the author, as their form and content were familiar and current among contemporary college populations. All communication was oral-aural, although each rendition was tape-recorded during the process of transmission. Situations varied from the presence of an entire class during reproduction, to more private settings with only the experimenter and active subjects present. The results were always the same; by the end of five transmissions, no recognizable joke remained, and the last subject in the chain *never* understood the materials he was attempting to reproduce (see Figure 1).

Linda Dégh and Andrew Vázsonyi have proposed a multi-conduit hypothesis to help explain the degenerations observed in transmission experiments (1975). Although the focus of their criticism has been the experimental design of Walter Anderson, their criticisms seem to apply as readily to Bartlett's, Clements's, and my own experiments. Essentially, Dégh and Vázsonyi claim that there are very

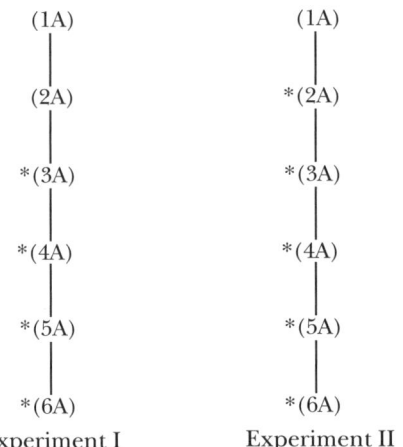

Figure 1: Single-Chain Transmission

An asterisk (*) indicates that the text performed lacked the essential elements necessary for the reproduction of the humorous structure of the narrative or that the teller was unable to understand the joke. The texts can be found in Appendices I and II.

likely many different communication channels for different kinds of folklore. When a type of folklore is communicated outside its natural conduit, it is most likely to degenerate or to cease entirely: "The extent of distortion [of a message] is likewise variable, but it is generally more frequent and exaggerated if it moves along a designated track than it is if the message follows a self-appointed spontaneous course" (1975:223). In other words, the degeneration of folklore in an experimental situation is a function of the experimental situation itself. As the materials, channels, and contexts of communication have been determined for the subjects by the experimenter, there is significantly greater probability of degeneration than in situations of natural transmission.

Thus, both Dundes and Dégh and Vázsonyi have attempted to account for the repeated degenerations of folklore materials in experimental situations by attributing the degeneration to the introduction of extraneous variables in the experimental process. In natural situations where these variables do not operate, degeneration is less likely to occur.

It might appear as though the entire issue were now closed, yet I believe that my own transmission experiments shed further light on the problem. It must immediately be pointed out that my experiments have chiefly involved the use of jokes, whereas Dégh and Vázsonyi have concerned themselves primarily with rumor and legend, and Dundes's critique stems from his consideration of Bartlett's experiment with tales. A focus on different forms of folklore may result in different conceptualizations of the problems concerning experimental transmissions and degeneration.

One aspect of my research was to establish a baseline for the natural transmission of a joke; that is, a description of what occurs to a text in oral communication that could be used as a point of reference for the experimental data. Ideally, one would hope to follow and surreptitiously record an item of lore as it was spontaneously performed and transmitted. Such a baseline, however, would be nearly impossible to obtain. What could be obtained, however, was the re-collection of an item that was spontaneously transmitted. The joke transmissions all took place before the re-collection commenced, and the joke was never intentionally introduced or disseminated for the purpose of re-collection. This baseline is short of ideal since the joke is recorded in an interview context rather than a natural situation of performance. Often, the informants' language and demeanor acutely reflected their consciousness of being recorded. Nevertheless, this re-collection may serve as a baseline if its usefulness is not pushed too far and until superior baselines are constructed. To my knowledge, no similar baselines have been published. Generally, the baseline for discussion of natural transmission has been abstracted from texts collected over considerable geographical and chronological distances with channels of dissemination hypothesized rather than demonstrated. The diagram of the channel of transmission is illustrated below in Figure 2.

I first became aware of this joke when it was told by one of the students in my class. The joke continued to be spontaneously performed both by myself and my students over the next week. When it came to my attention that the students had told the joke to others, an attempt was made to re-collect as many versions as possible. Seventeen texts were elicited, although it was quite clear that the joke had been performed for many more people. (X's followed by a numeral in the transmission diagram [e.g., X(5)] indicate the

Figure 2: The Re-Collection of a Natural Transmission

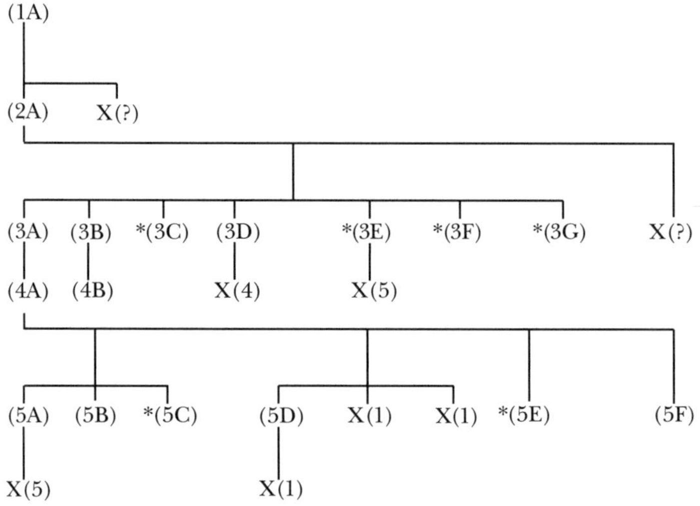

```
(1A)
 |
 ├──────────┐
(2A)       X(?)
 |          |
 ├───┬───┬───┬──────┬──────┬──────┬──────┐
(3A)(3B)*(3C)(3D)  *(3E)  *(3F)  *(3G)  X(?)
 |   |    |   |     |
(4A)(4B) X(4) X(5)
 |   |
 ├───┼────┬────┬──────┬─────┬──────┬─────┐
(5A)(5B)*(5C) (5D)   X(1)  X(1) *(5E)  (5F)
 |        |
X(5)     X(1)
```

An asterisk (*) indicates that the text performed lacked the essential elements necessary for the reproduction of the humorous structure of the narrative or that the teller was unable to understand the joke. In the above transmission, 5E realized that the performance was problematic and indicated at the end the elements that were necessary to correct it. All texts can be found in Appendix III.

number of known people who were told the joke by a particular transmitter in the course of the week, but from whom neither texts nor data concerning further transmission of the joke could be obtained). The diagram, therefore, represents only a portion of the transmission network for a one-week period.

The most significant point to emerge from this natural baseline is that single-chain transmission is not characteristic of the natural transmission network of jokes. If a person performs a joke for one person, he or she is likely to perform it for many. A joke performance begets a litter of variants, not just a single offspring. The characteristic of rapid and widespread reproduction is already familiar from biology. It is a strategy that has proved successful in maintaining the continuity of a species in which there is a high probability of mortality for individuals prior to reproduction. This type of survival strategy seems advantageous for both insects and jokes. Certain species, on the other hand, beget very few offspring, but devote considerable time and energy in overseeing their development and survival to the age of reproduction. This type of strategy has proven advantageous to members of the order of primates. It has also proven the advantageous strategy in many societies for the transmission of myth, epic, and historical chronicle, where specialists are laboriously educated in the memorization, musical accompaniment, and performance of these genres.

The baseline transmission further suggests that:

(1) If one is to perform laboratory experiments concerning folklore transmission, one should probably employ a tree-like or lattice-like model. A single-chain model may perhaps be employed if the subjects of the experiment are expert performers of the genres that are being transmitted.

(2) In the course of joke transmission certain texts have degenerated. Thus, degeneration is not in and of itself a characteristic of artificial transmission networks. It is well known that there are many that hear and appreciate jokes (or other genres), who are incapable of successfully re-performing them. Many individuals recognize their own performance disabilities. Poor performers are undoubtedly one of the major predators of good jokes. It is for this reason that competent performers must prove *fertile*. They must perform the same joke many times for different audiences if the joke is to survive. Nevertheless, there is nothing wrong with including unaccomplished tellers in the framework of a transmission experiment, so long as the results of the experiment do not exclusively depend upon their performance abilities. Single-chain transmissions usually create such dependencies.

Incompetent performers may be included in the experimental network if they are considered toward the end of a transmission series with few, if any, other tellers dependent upon their performance for further transmission. Such a construction would tend to accord with natural environments where a low probability of transmission would be assigned to poor tellers (i.e., they are not generally the source of other versions).

(3) A particular transmission sequence (not the total experiment) may be halted by the experimenter at the point the joke is no longer understood by one of the subjects. Evidence indicates that people rarely communicate jokes that they themselves do not understand

or are incapable of correcting.[7] In a natural situation, the line of transmission would be terminated. There is nothing to be gained in an experimental situation by forcing an individual to communicate such material. It will only assure a further degeneration and reduction to absurdity that is not characteristic of the natural joke-telling process. A transmission in an experimental situation is only valid when the subject accepts some of the responsibility for performance in the experimental situation. This responsibility is never accepted if subjects are forced to repeat material they do not understand.

(4) Dégh's and Vázsonyi's proposal that an acceptable experiment must give subjects *complete* freedom of choice is doubtful (1975:243). It is more surmised than demonstrated that such complete freedom exists even in natural performance environments. Furthermore, some problematic variables would be introduced into the experiment. For example, Dégh and Vázsonyi suggest that the actual items for transmission should be selected by the subjects themselves (244–247). However, this would potentially expose the subjects to the folklore materials at least twice (more if they selected materials previously familiar to them), once before the commencement of the experiment when they choose the material and again when they hear the material they are to pass on in the course of the serial transmission. Thus, Walter Anderson's Law of Self-Correction would become a variable in the experiment; a variable that Dégh and Vázsonyi go to great lengths to deny as a crucial factor in the stability of folk narratives.

(5) Such a shotgun approach to freedom is not methodologically acceptable. It may be that only freedom in a very specific range of activity is necessary to secure desired experimental results. One of the problems with the single-chain experiments that I conducted was that subjects were uncertain as to their degree of freedom in reproducing the text. Most seemed to think that they were required to repeat what they had heard from memory. Bartlett indicates that he encountered similar assumptions on the part of his subjects (1932:145). Thus, attempts at joke reproduction were based upon memorization and attempts to be accurate, rather than on attempts to re-create a communicative and aesthetically satisfying joke.[8] In different experiments, subjects indicated that they sensed something was wrong with the joke and that they knew how it might be

corrected, but they refrained from doing so because they felt they were required to reproduce only what they had heard. This freedom to re-create, I suspect, is essential in communicative competence. There are shifts to unhabitual perceptual and linguistic frameworks when attempts are made to memorize and reproduce a joke. A certain amount of "experimental sophistication" is necessary for subjects to understand that they are free to re-create a joke as they do in more natural circumstances. We may agree with Dégh and Vázsonyi that experimental subjects require freedoms to act, but it is not clear that total freedom is necessary for the simulation in experiments of characteristics of natural transmission.

(6) An experiment need not duplicate the natural environment to be useful. In fact, an experiment that completely duplicates the natural environment may no longer be a laboratory experiment. But the laboratory environment offers distinct advantages to researchers. It allows for the reduction of the number of variables that are associated with a particular phenomenon. It also allows for an increase in control over the variables present. For example, if it is felt—as Dundes feels—that more extended periods of time are necessary for an individual to absorb and master folklore materials before reproducing them, time can be varied in different experimental situations to see whether this actually proves to be the case. In experiments concerning the issue of transmission and degeneration, it should only be necessary to construct an experiment in which the degeneration of the text regularly fails to occur, to be able to identify those elements of the natural environment that are necessary and sufficient for the communication of folklore through time and space. If a text is successfully transmitted in an experimental situation in which the conduit is predetermined, then a teller's choice of audience is not a necessary variable for the maintenance of textual integrity through time. On the other hand, if it is discovered that adequate texts are generated in a forced experimental situation only when Anderson's Law of Self-Correction is operating, then it may be hypothesized that either voluntariness or self-correction is necessary for adequate transmission. In any event, the laboratory environment allows for the identification of necessary and sufficient conditions because it is not identical to the natural environment.

Needless to say, the necessary and sufficient variables for the maintenance of competent performance for particular texts or genres through time have not been experimentally identified—only offhandedly hypothesized. Nevertheless, an experimental model employed in folklore classes may help shed some light on the problem. Experiment III (see Figure 3) represents such an experiment performed with the identical joke that degenerated in Experiment I. The model was tree-like, branching out from a single source, and seemed more consonant (though by no means identical) with the pattern of the baseline re-collection discussed above. Prior to the experimental transmission, subjects were asked to identify themselves as good, average, or poor joke tellers and were distributed in the transmission sequences with the best joke tellers at the top and the worst toward the bottom. All the subjects had previously observed or participated in a single-chain transmission experiment and were thus "experimentally sophisticated." Allowance was made in four instances for subjects to hear the joke more than one time (subjects 4B, 4D, 4F, 4H). That is, they heard the joke from two different tellers before they were called upon to tell it. After the experiment was completed, subjects were surveyed to determine whether they understood the joke, whether they had ever heard the joke before, how much they liked it (on a scale from 1 to 5), and whether they thought they might tell the joke to someone else outside the experimental situation. Several remarkable results were obtained: (a) the great majority of texts were competent and intact; (b) there were a surprisingly large number of people who had heard the joke before (40+%) suggesting a potential relevance and power for Anderson's Law of Self-Correction; (c) tellers who characterized themselves as "poor" produced competent versions if they had heard the joke previously (3C, 4B, 4E, 4F); (d) tellers who had characterized themselves as "poor" and had never heard the joke before (3D, 4G, 4H) failed to produce adequate texts.

When the joke that had degenerated in single-chain Experiment II was introduced into a similar multi-chain experimental model, competent texts were produced in the fourth and fifth "generations" even though the Law of Self-Correction was not in operation (none of the subjects had heard the joke previous to the experiment).

Figure 3: Multi-Chain Transmission 1

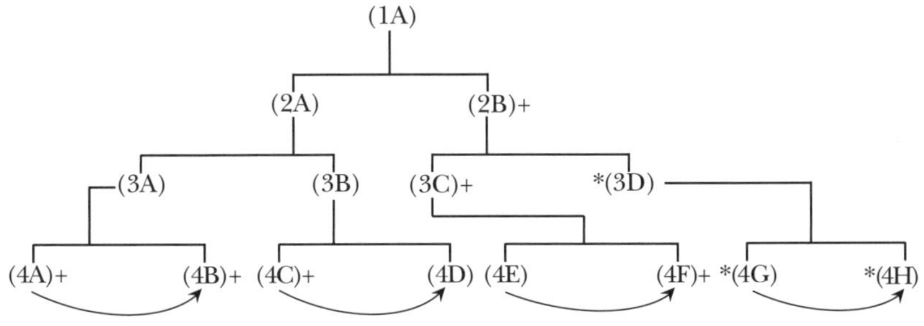

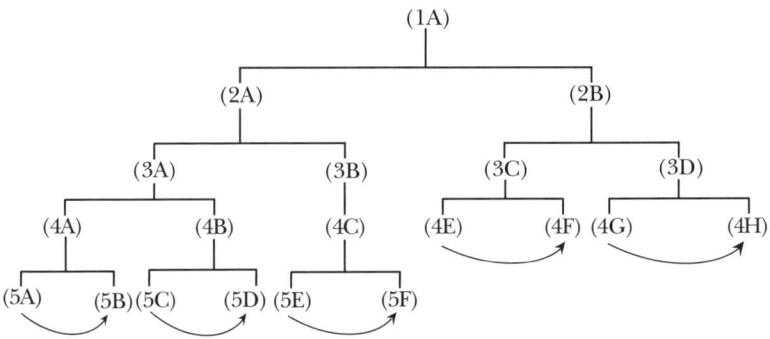

An asterisk (*) indicates that the text performed lacked the essential elements necessary for the reproduction of the humorous structure of the narrative or that the teller was unable to understand the joke. A plus sign (+) indicates that the subject had heard a similar joke prior to the start of the experiment.

Subject 2A identified himself as a *good* joke teller.
Subjects 3A, 4A, 4C, 2B, 3B identified themselves as *average* tellers.
Subjects 3C, 3D, 4B, 4D, 4E, 4F, 4G, 4H identified themselves as *poor* joke tellers.
The texts can be found in Appendix IV.

Figure 4: Multi-Chain Transmission 2

Subjects 2A, 3A identified themselves as *good* joke tellers.
Subjects 2B, 3B, 4A, 4B, 5A, 5B identified themselves as *average* tellers.
Subjects 3C, 3D, 4C, 4E, 4F, 4G, 4H, 5C, 5D, 5E, 5F identified themselves as *poor* joke tellers.
The texts can be found in Appendix V.
Despite the fact that only 4 of the 19 subjects thought that they might repeat the joke outside the experimental situation, the humorous structure in all texts was intact. This structure is intact in the texts of 4G and 4H even though they claimed not to understand the joke.

These multi-chain experiments are not definitive; only suggestive. But they are concretely rather than abstractly suggestive. First, texts do not necessarily degenerate when the intervals of reproduction are artificially short. Second, texts do not necessarily degenerate when the line of transmission is determined by the experimenter rather than freely chosen by the subject. Third, texts can degenerate in experiments even when the mode of transmission is oral/aural rather than written.

Such experiments could easily be run in any sizable class of students. One could easily alter the basic model in a number of ways to allow for or to limit the operation of particular variables. In any event, it should be clear that within the context of contemporary Western urban society, randomly organized, single-chain, folklore transmission experiments do not serve as a meaningful model of folklore transmission.

There remains one final point. It concerns the form of folklore that is employed in experimental environments. I have employed jokes almost exclusively in conducting transmission experiments. Yet, jokes are very special kinds of narratives. They involve a distinct humorous structure. Often, the loss of a single word or the transposition of a single phrase or the confusion of a single character is sufficient to destroy this humorous structure. The humorous anti-legend employed by Clements in his experiment, in which the simple substitution of the work "casket" for "coffin" destroyed the "point" of the entire narrative, may serve as a typical example. One might consider this fragility of jokes to be an argument against their use in the experimental environment. Actually, jokes offer two distinct advantages in such environments. One of these advantages has already been cited, namely they are familiar forms to the experimental groups under consideration and thus are more likely to be transmitted utilizing practiced perceptual and communicative mechanisms. But they have another great advantage. Degeneration in jokes is easily defined and identified. Jokes are artistic forms that employ a structure of appropriate incongruity (Oring 1992:1–15). When this underlying structure is no longer perceived, the humor is lost. The "point" of the narrative can no longer be understood. Thus, degeneration can be simply defined as an incompetent performance—a performance in which the basic elements necessary for the recognition of a humorous structure are no longer clearly delineated. This is not purely a distinction drawn by the observer of the experiment, for the subjects themselves recognize when essential structural elements are absent. Thus, all kinds of changes may take place in the course of a joke telling without degeneration occurring; or one minuscule change may take place which destroys the entire structure. But degeneration is clearly defined and readily discernable by both experimenters and experimental subjects.

The case is considerably more complicated in the transmission of non-humorous genres, such as tale, rumor, and legend. The criteria for degeneration for these genres (which have served as the major genres used in psychological and folkloristic experiment to date) have never been adequately defined.[9] It seems that any kind of change can be regarded as potentially, if not actually, degenerative. One cannot help but wonder as to the criteria employed by Dundes in categorizing the changes in the tales employed by Bartlett in his experiment as "degenerative." Bartlett never employed this term. In fact, in his consideration of the tales "The War of the Ghosts" and "The Son Who Tried to Outwit His Father," Bartlett spends a good deal of time discussing the increasing coherence of the tales and the points of elaboration and adornment that develop throughout the serial transmission (1932:125, 127, 128, 145).

If one compares the course of the folktale materials and the non-folktale materials utilized by Bartlett in his experiment, different dynamics are readily discernible (Graph I and Graph II). The non-folktale materials rapidly condense to less than 20 percent of their original size and show little or no potential for re-expansion or revitalization. The folktale materials never condense to such an extent however, and all show potential or actual expansion in the course of their transmission. It is true that this comparison has been done solely on the basis of word count, but it suggests that Dundes and others have been premature in the assumption that the folktales in Bartlett's experiments degenerated.

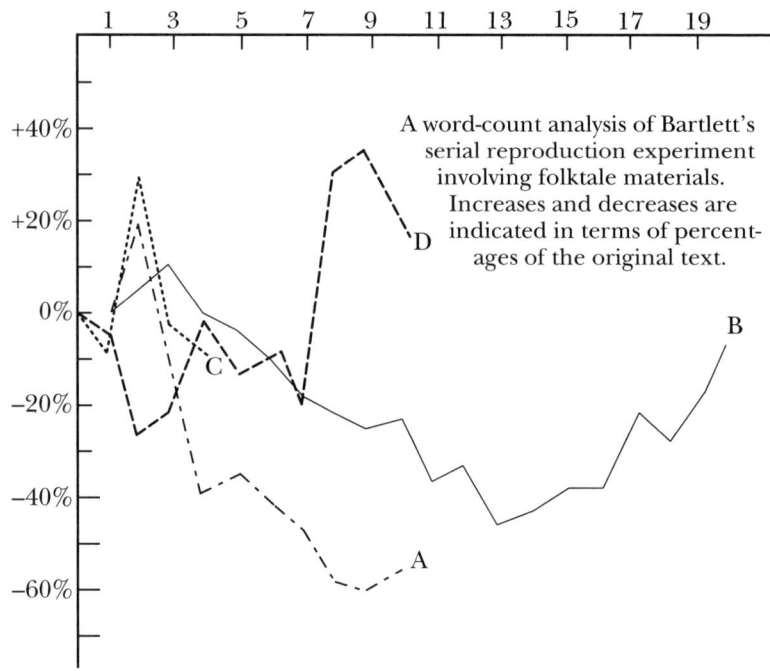

Graph I: The Folktale Materials

The curves refer to the following texts:
A = "The War of the Ghosts," (Bartlett 1932:65, 121–124);
B = "The Son Who Tried to Outwit His Father," (129–135);
C = "The Son Who Tried to Outwit His Father" (138–140);
D = "The Son Who Tried to Outwit His Father" (141–144).

If degeneration is to be defined in terms of any deviation from an original text, it is clear that texts will degenerate in the oral process. It is essential, however, to draw a distinction between change and degeneration. One should be required to delineate those criteria by which a text may degenerate, and indicate—utilizing those same criteria—how that same text might improve. As degeneration for jokes has been defined in terms of a particular structure—appropriate incongruity—it may be shown that jokes may improve artistically as they come to delineate this basic structure more clearly. In fact, such an improvement took place in several texts in the baseline re-collection (Figure 2). Instead of an ethnically unidentified protagonist, as in the original version (1A), two versions identified the protagonist as Jewish (5A, 5B). It is not

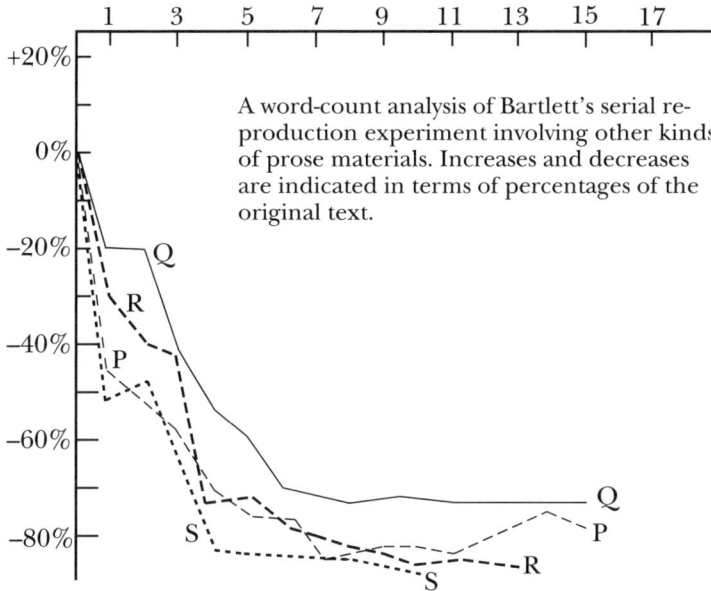

Graph II: Other Prose Materials

The curves refer to the following texts:
P = "Fine Batting at Lord's" (Barlett 1932:146–149);
Q = "The Deaf Moochi" (154–149);
R = "Air-Raid on the East Coast" (160-164);
S = "Modification of Species" (166–168).

difficult to hypothesize why the protagonist became Jewish in two of the versions: the person who transmitted the joke was Jewish and was known to be Jewish by those who heard it. In other words, two people may have made the protagonist Jewish because they identified the joke with the individual from whom they heard it. Biography aside, however, a Jewish protagonist rounds off the narrative and humorous structure aesthetically. There are now three ethnic groups specifically alluded to in the joke, and the ranking of their intelligence mirrors the scripts traditionally employed in countless other contemporary ethnic jokes. This tripartite ethnic division—Jew, Pole, Italian—helps delineate the basic humorous structure of the joke more successfully and therefore might be regarded as an improvement. (This humorous structure was not so carefully delineated in Single-Chain Experiment II. Confusion arose about the ethnic status of the protagonist, which led to the subsequent degeneration of the joke.)

In the discussion of experiments concerning rumor, legends, and tales, the criterion most frequently employed seems to have been the degree of distortion of original information. This criterion is problematic. As there is no way for a tale, rumor, or legend to regain lost information—save by self-correction or freak accident—these forms are degenerative a priori. But this is to overlook the fact that these same forms may also exhibit artistic narrative structures that may be improving while original information is being lost or distorted. In certain situations, artistic improvement may depend upon the distortion of original information. That is to say, artistic structuring may be inversely proportional to the retention of original information. In such situations, how is one to assess whether any particular text in a serial transmission is degenerating or evolving?[10]

Gordon Allport and Leo Postman recognized that art and information may be antithetical in the transmission process (1965 [1947]:146–147). But their basic research interests lay in the spread of *misinformation* in wartime rumor. Their fundamental perspective was clear. What did Alan Dundes or Walter Anderson mean by "degeneration"? What might be the perspective of contemporary folklorists whose concerns are sometimes for materials that necessarily change from some original source in the past and sometimes for materials that change as they adapt themselves to the aesthetic tastes of the present? In other words, what might degeneration mean for those whose concern is for materials that are sometimes defined as "oral tradition" and sometimes defined as "verbal art"?

APPENDIX I[11]

Experiment 1: Single-Chain Transmission

(1A)

There's this sort of Madison-Avenue type executive, works in an advertising agency, and one day—he's had a fairly hectic day—and he walks into one of these Madison Avenue bars, a really fine bar, you know, where you get a lot of executive types. He goes in there, and quite a few people are there. Sits down at the bar, orders a drink, orders a martini, and he's sipping his drink and just thinking to himself about how the day has gone, which wasn't too good, and while he's sitting there this absolutely incredible looking woman walks into the bar. You know, people notice her when she walks in; blonde, really well-dressed, beautiful. You know, people sort of turn, the ones sitting in the booths, you know, as she walks by, and notice her. She, strangely enough, walks up to the bar and sits down beside him orders a drink, and he notices her too and sort of nods, and goes on drinking his drink. And after a few minutes he takes out a cigarette and when he looks for a light, you know, he can't find his matches or his lighter. And so he turns to this girl next to him and says, uh, "Excuse me, do you have a match?" And she screams out, "I will not sleep with you!" He's absolutely baffled, he doesn't know, and everybody's turning around and looking at him and he can't figure out what's wrong. And everybody's murmuring, and he's just totally embarrassed, and he picks up his drink and he walks away from the bar and sits in a booth in the corner 'cause he's just . . . and he's sitting there wondering what the heck did I do? What went wrong? You know, it's really weird, and he's sitting there sort of sipping his drink trying to figure all, all of this thing out, you know, the whole event out. And after about five minutes, the girl gets up from the bar and walks over and sort of slides into his booth and says, "See you have to understand that uh, I'm a graduate student at New York University in social psychology, and this whole thing is part of a social psychological experiment that we're running, you know, to find out what people's responses will be to shocking situations. And he says [really loud], "Seventy-five dollars?"

(2A)

There was this businessman and as usual, he had a rough day. So, at lunch time he decided to go down to the nearby cocktail lounge to get a drink and relax. And, so he walks in, there's several people, a lot of people in there. And sits down at the counter and orders a drink. After he's been there a little while, this beautiful woman comes in. Everybody in the bar looks at her and notices her, and he notices her, and she comes up and sits down next to him. So he nods and goes about drinking up. Then he goes to get a cigarette, and he can't find his matches. So he asks her, you know, "Excuse me, do you have a match?" And she screams at him. "I will not go to bed with you!" Everybody in the bar looks, you know, everybody's staring at him. He's just shocked, you know. He was very embarrassed. He didn't know what to do so he takes his drink and kind of goes back to the, a booth in the back to sit down and think what this was about. And uh, everybody's kind of looking at him and wondering what was going on. And after a little while the girl comes over and sits down next to him, and she says, "Excuse me but I just wanted you to understand that I'm a student at the university and we're in social psychology, and this is an experiment to see how people react under stressful situations." And he looks at her and he says [loudly], "Seventy-five dollars!"

*(3A)

A businessman has had a hard day, and he goes to a cocktail lounge. He sits down to have a drink and a young lady walks in and she's good looking and the people in the bar notice her. And he notices her. And so she comes over and sits down next to him. And he's going to have a cigarette, so he doesn't have any matches on him. So he asks the girl if she has some matches. And she says, she screams, you know. And so he's kind of shocked, and everybody's staring at him, and so he kind of retreats to the back of the bar, in a booth and decides to kind of think this one out, you know. Everyone's kind of looking over at him and kind of murmuring. And so after a little bit, the girl comes over and sits down next to him and she says, "I'm a student at the university, and they're doing an experiment to see his reaction to what she had just said." And he looks over at her and says, "Seventy-five dollars," yells out "Seventy-five dollars" and that's it.

*(4A)

There's a businessman and he walks into a bar, and he takes a seat and starts having a cocktail. He takes out a cigarette and asks the girl next to him for a light. She's very pretty and everything, and everybody's aware of her. Well, as soon as he asks her for a light she screams. So he doesn't know what to think, so he runs back to the back of the bar, in a booth, and thinks he's going to think it all over. In the midst of all this everybody's kind of looking over their shoulder, watching what he's doing. And the girl comes back, sits with him back at the booth and told him she's a university student and was doing an experiment and said something about seventy-five dollars.

*(5A)

There's a businessman that walks into a bar and sits down; going to have a drink. He orders his drink, sits there a while, and this girl walks in and sits down next to him at the bar. So he pulls out a cigarette, asks the girl if she has a light. The girl screams, just screams, and so he doesn't know what's happening. So he goes back to the back of the bar. He sits in a booth back there. He thinks I'm going to think this over and see what's happening here. So he sits in the back of the bar, and everybody's sort of looking, you know? And the girl that screamed comes and sits down next to him in the back of the bar, and she says she's a university student and she was doing an experiment and then says something about seventy-five dollars.

*(6A)

A businessman walks into a bar, and he sits down and then a girl walks in. He takes out a cigarette and asks the girls for a light. The girl screams. He doesn't know what's going on. He goes and sits in the bar in a booth. Everybody's staring at him, and he's wondering what's going on. The girl gets up, and she goes to the back of the bar and tells him that she's a university student and she said something about seventy-five dollars.

APPENDIX II
Experiment 2: Single-Chain Transmission

(1A)

A joke about this fellow who's very much in love with a girl who is of Polish descent, who is very much in love with her, but the family has quite a bit of pride and the father was totally against the marriage because this fellow wasn't Polish, and he wanted his daughter to marry someone who was Polish. And he was very upset, and he was desperate and was going to do something. And he heard about this doctor who could perform an operation that would make you Polish. So he was desperate, so he went to this doctor, and the doctor said, "Well yes, there is a procedure. It's a radical procedure, but it can be done. Essentially what we do is remove half your brain." And ah, the guy thought about it a minute and said, "O.K., I'll go through with it." And they scheduled the operation for the next week, and they opened him up and then removing half a brain, and all of a sudden the doctor's knife slips during the operation and by accident he removes, he makes an extra cut, and he's forced to take out three-quarters of the brain. And there's nothing he can do. He removes it, sews the guy back up, and after the guy gets out of the recovery room, the doctor goes to see him. And he says, "Look, listen, there was a slight problem during the operation. There was a slip-up. Instead of taking out half your brain we took out three-quarters of your brain. Guys says [slaps his forehead] "Mamma mia."

*(2A)[12]

There was this guy who was of Polish descent who was just madly in love with this girl. Well, the girl was Polish, and her parents who really wanted her to marry someone who was Polish, and so this guy who was in love with the girl decided to go to a doctor. He had heard that there was this operation that you could become Polish and so the doctor said, "Yeah, it's true. It's a radical operation, and what it required was the removal of half your brain." So the guy said, "O.K." And so they went and they had the operation, and during the operation the surgeon's knife slipped, and he took out three-quarters of his brain instead of half of it. So he came up there the next day, a little after the guy recovered, to tell him that he made the slip and had taken out three-quarters of his brain instead of half the brain. So he came and the guy said [flat tone], "Mamma mia."

*(3A)

O.K. There's this Polish man who's madly in love with this Polish woman—young Polish woman—and she goes to her parents; explains they want to get married. And her parents are just emphatic that she marry a Polish man. So this guy goes to a doctor and explains his circumstances to him and his predicament. And the doctor explains to him that there is an operation by which they remove half his brain, and thereby he would be declared a Polish person or Polack. And so he goes ahead and has the surgery, and during the surgery, the surgeon's knife slips and he removes three-quarters of his brain instead of the half of his brain. And in the recovery room, the doctor wanted to find his patient to tell him what had happened. And he explained it to him and the guy turned around and said "Oh, mamma mia."

*(4A)

This Polish guy and this Polish girl wanted to get married. So the girl goes to tell her parents, and they are really happy because they want to keep it in the family. So this guy got a predicament, and he goes to the doctor and he says, "I got to marry this Polish girl. What am I going to do?" And he says, "Well, we'll fix you up real quick." And he says, "We got to perform this operation on you where we remove half your brain." And the guy says, "O.K., that's fine as long as it will make them happy." So he goes through the surgery and everything, and the doctor, he's performing the operation—he must be Polish too 'cause the knife slipped—and he cut three-quarters of the brain out and the guy only has a fourth of a brain. And he wakes up from the operation and goes to the doctor and says, "Well, how did it go?" And the doctor says, "Well, we had a little accident and cut three-quarters of your brain out." And the guy goes, "Mamma mia."

*(5A)

There's these two Polish people—one's a guy and one's a lady. They were going to get married. (It makes me nervous.) And his parents didn't want him to—his parents didn't want him to. (Wait, that's not right.) Anyways, so what happened was to satisfy their parents, her parents, he agreed to have an operation on his brain. And they were going to remove half his brain. And so he said, "God! What's going on?" and he says, "just to satisfy her parents I'll do this, you know." So when he had his operation, the doctor slipped and cut out three-fourths of his brain. The doctor is Polish too. He must have been Polish. O.K. So the guy woke up, you know, the next day, the doctor said look, ah, I have made a mistake, I cut out three-fourths of your brain instead of half of it, and the guy said "Mamma mia."

*(6A)

O.K. There's a Polish guy and a Polish girl, and they were going to get married, you understand. And so the [hesitation], yes the wife, the future wife's parents, didn't want them to get married, so the man agreed to get an operation. Have an operation that would suit her parents. So he did, and he went down and, this doctor was going to work on his brain. So, so the doctor was going to cut out about one-fourth of his brain. Just to suit the girl's parents. So he went down and had the operation and the doctor essentially cut out three-fourths of his brain. So the next morning, the guy woke up, the Polish guy woke up, and the doctor says, "I'm sorry I cut out three-fourths of your brain." He says, "Mamma mia."

APPENDIX III
The Re-collection of a Natural Transmission

(1A)

There's this gentleman, and he wished to marry this Polish lady. And he went to her parents and said that he wanted to marry her. And they immediately rebuked the poor chap and said, "No, you're not Polish, you're not of the Polish way." And he was just totally down, bummed out. So he went to his doctor. And he said, "Doctor, I really love her and I really want to marry her." So his doctor said, "Well, I think I can work something out but we're going to have to operate." Being a good neurosurgeon, he informed him of the procedure, which was going to have to remove half the guy's brain. So they're in there at the operating table—the doctor very intense—working on him. And about half way through the operation, when he's removing half the brain he slipped—he sneezed—and he slipped and he cut out damn near three-quarters of the guy's brain. So the guy is coming out of it all and the doctor's sitting there. It's after the operation and the guy's coming out of it, and the doctor's looking at him explaining what happened that during the operation he slipped and cut out nearly three quarters of the guy's brain. And the guy through all this fog comes and looks at the doctor and says, "Mamma mia!"

(2A)

There was this man who was in love with a girl, a Polish girl. And he wanted to marry her, but his father wouldn't let them get married because the guy wasn't Polish. So he went to a doctor and said, "Doc, you have to make me Polish. You just have to." The doctor says, "The only way I can make you Polish is to cut out half your brain." So he says, "Anything. I have to marry this girl." So the doctor's doing the operation, and he's ready to cut out half the brain, and just as he starts slicing, he sneezes and he takes out three-quarters of the brain instead of just half of it. "Oh now what do I tell this guy?" So he's in his room afterwards, and the guy's coming out of the anesthetic, and the doctor says, "I made a big mistake; I cut out three-quarters of your brain instead of just half your brain. I sneezed. What are you going to do?" And the guy looked at the doctor and said, "Mamma mia!"

(3A)

This fellow was very much in love with this girl, a Polish girl, and he wanted to marry her but her father forbade the marriage because he himself wasn't Polish. And he had heard that there was an operation that could be performed that would make you Polish. And he went down to see this doctor who was known to perform this operation, and asked what was involved in the operation. And the doctor said, "Essentially it's not a big problem. What we do is remove half your brain." And the guy said, "Well, I'll do it," 'cause he was really in love with this girl and he wanted to marry her at all costs. So he scheduled himself for the operation; went into the hospital. And during the operation the surgeon was operating, and during the operation his knife slipped, and instead of cutting out half the brain he cut out three-quarters of the brain. But there was nothing he could do. Then he finished the procedure and closed up. And after the guy came out of intensive care the doctor went to see him and said, "Listen there's been a slight problem. A mistake was made during the surgery. Instead of cutting out half your brain, we cut out three-quarters of your brain." And the guy goes, "Mamma mia!"

(4A)

A fellow wanted to marry this Polish girl, and he asked for her hand in marriage but her parents wouldn't hear of it because the guy wasn't Polish. So he decided to do something about it. He heard about this operation that could change him in [...?] and just about make him turn him into a Polack. So he went to this surgeon and the guy said, "Yes, we have this operation that, you know, that will enable you to become a Polack, but it involves removing half your brain." And the guy said, "Well, okay, I'll go through with it." So he enters the hospital, and they take him down to the operating room, and the surgeon starts cutting him up. And he's cutting and cutting, and all of a sudden, he slips and he cuts an extra quarter. And, what could he do? So he sews him up and they bring him back to the recovery room. And the guy's coming out of the anesthesia. The surgeon bends over and then he says, "Listen, you know I told you that we're going to remove half of your brain but we made a mistake; we actually removed three-quarters of it." And the guy looks up at him, slaps his forehead, and he says, "Ah, mamma mia!"

(5A)

This is a joke about a Polish girl and a Jewish guy. The guy wanted to marry the girl, but she wouldn't marry him because her parents thought that he should be Polish. So he went to see a doctor, and the doctor told him that it was a simple operation, and in order to get it done he had to have one fourth of his brain removed. So the guy consented. He went to surgery but while he was in surgery, the surgeon slipped and took one half instead of a fourth, you know. So when the guy went to the recovery room, he asked the doctor, "How'd the surgery go?" He said, "Fine." He said, "There was only one mistake. I took a little bit too much of your brain." And the guy's reply was, he went, "Mamma mia!"

(5B)

This is a joke about a Jewish boy who wants to marry a Polish girl and her parents object because he's not Polish. O.K. So he goes to his physician and tells him, explains the story. So his physician says they're going to do an operation in which they're going to remove half of his brain, and he goes through with it. During the operation, there was an error—a mistake, his hand slipped or something—and instead of taking a half, they took three-quarters of his brain. So when he's coming out of it, the physician bends over and tells him, "We made a mistake. Instead of removing half of your brain, we removed three-quarters of your brain." And this guy says, "Oh, mamma mia!"

*(5C)

They had this guy who wanted to marry a Polish girl, but he wasn't Polish. So he went to his friend and he said to his friend, about this great love he had for this girl. He wanted to marry her but he couldn't marry her because he wasn't Polish. So his friend told him that he knew a doctor, and he could go there and tell the doctor his problem, and the doctor would perform an operation on his brain, and when he came out he would be Polish. So he went to see a doctor and the doctor agreed to do it, and while the doctor was performing the surgery on him, he cut too much off, too much of his brain off, and he said, "I cut too much off." Anyway, the guy comes out of the anesthesia, and the doctor asks how does he feel, and he says, "Mamma mia!"

(5D)

There was a young man that wanted to marry a Polish girl and everything was fine except that the girl's parents objected to the fact he was not a Pole. And not to be dissuaded, he tried to find a way in which he could become as closely like a Pole as possible. And he consulted his doctor. His doctor informed him that they've been devising an operation whereby an average man could be converted into a man who was just identical to a Pole. Now he informed him that the operation consisted of removing half of his brain. The young man consented to the operation and surgery was carried out. However, during the surgery, the doctors made a mistake and in the course of the mistake they removed more of the brain than they'd planned. The patient recovered and during the post-op period the doctor came to inform him of the error that had been made. And he said, "Sir, I'm sorry to inform you that during the surgery we made a mistake. Instead of removing one-half of your brain, we removed three-quarters of your brain." And the patient said, "Oh, mamma mia!"

*(5E)

As best as I can recall a man is in a hospital, and the doctor speaks to him and tells him that the only way he can save his life is by removing half of his brain, which the man agrees. And somehow in surgery a little mistake is made by the surgeon and three-quarters of the brain is removed. And the surgeon is most distraught. And when the man awakens, he tells him that he is very sorry. He doesn't quite know how to tell him this but that three- quarters of his brain was removed. Incidentally, the man was Polish. And when he heard what the surgeon had to say, he said, "Mamma mia!"

(5F)

Let's see. There was a good, red-blooded American guy who wanted to marry this Polish chick. So the mother of the bride said, or the bride-to-be said, "Before you can do this, you're going to have to go through this operation so you can become Polish." Goes to the surgeon, and the whole procedure that's involved is removing a part of his brain, because everybody knows a Polish person only has half a brain. So he goes into surgery in the morning—and the surgeon is in there and has gotten stoned the night before—gets in there, kind of happy, and is cutting away, knife and fork, and he slips, and he cuts out more than he's supposed to. So he stitches up the guy anyway and sends him to recovery. And the next morning he goes in, he tells the guy, "Hey, look, in surgery yesterday I got kind of happy and during the operation, and I cut more than I was supposed to cut of your brain." The guy sits and considers it for a minute and then comes out with, "Aye, mamma mia!"

(3B)

Well, there was this Polish family, and the father, the daughter was going to marry a non-Pole. So she asked her father if it was all right and the father said, "Well, he's going to have to, since he's not Polish, he's going to have to have an operation that's going to make him Polish." So he goes down to the hospital, he decides to do it since he wants to marry her. And they tell him, "Well, this operation is going to take out half your brain in order for you to be Polish." So he consents, and he's on the operating table, and the doctor opens up his head, and his hand slips and takes more of the brain than he meant to take out in the first place. So he wakes up and the doctor tells him, "Listen, I made a big mistake. Instead of taking out half your brain, I took out three-quarters of your brain." The guy says, "Mamma mia!"

(4B)

A Polish girl brought her boyfriend home to meet her father, and the father said that they don't like the daughters to marry anyone other than a Polish person. And he said how could he get to be Polish? He would do anything to marry the daughter. So they said only one thing that they could do and that is to have an operation. And this operation was to cut out half of his brain. So he agreed because he really wanted to marry the daughter. He was all prepared for surgery, and he went in, and the surgeons came in and they worked for hours over the case. And as they were getting ready to finish, the surgeon's hand slipped and he cut out another fourth of a lobe—he cut out three-fourths all together. So when the guy woke up in the post-op room, the surgeon came in and told him he was very sorry but he'd had a slight accident, and he cut out three-fourths of his brain instead of only half. And the guy said, "Oh, mamma mia!"

*(3C)

O.K. This guy was going to marry a Polish girl, and in order to marry her he had to be Polish too. So he was wondering how to get Polish. Somebody said to go to the doctor and have an operation. So he went to the operation, to the doctor, and he said, "Well, Doc, what are you going [. . . ?]." Oh, he was going to have the operation, so he had the operation and then after it was finished he said, "Doc, so how am I?" And the doctor said, "Well, I was only going to take out half your brain, but I sneezed and accidentally took out three-quarters of your brain." He said, "Oh, mamma mia!"

(3D)

There was this Polish girl and she was going to marry this man, and the man wasn't Polish. And she had him over for dinner, and her father got kind of mad and wouldn't let them get married because he wasn't Polish. So he wanted to be Polish. And he heard of a doctor that could make you a Pole. So he went to the doctor and the doctor said, "Well, it's kind of a weird operation; we take out half your brain." The guy said, "O.K., I really want to marry this chick." So during the operation he sneezed and his scalpel slipped, and he removed an extra quarter of the brain and he was really worried. And when the guy came out of anesthesia he said, "I really made a mistake. Instead of taking out half your brain I took out three quarters." And the guy went, "Mamma mia!"

*(3E)

This guy was Polish, no, he was Italian and he wanted to marry a Polish girl. But he couldn't marry her because his parents, I mean, her parents objected to it. So he decided to have an operation. So he went to a surgeon, and he told the surgeon if he could have an operation on his brain to take out, I think a half of a brain. And so the surgeon, during the operation, he sneezed, and took three-fourths instead. And at the very end he's telling the patient, "I took out three-fourths instead of half." And the guy goes, "Mamma mia!"

*(3F)

This fellow wanted to marry a girl and he wasn't of the same nationality and decided that he would have some surgery of the brain. When the doctor operated, that is after the surgery, he said, "I made a mistake. I cut out three quarters of your brain." And so the fellow said, "Mamma mia!"

*(3G)

Somebody was going to have brain surgery to change some kind of a pattern. He was Polish? And he went into the hospital and having the surgery performed. The surgeon said to him, "I made a mistake in performing the operation and I did something to the recorders." So it seems that somewhere along the line someone said, "Don't worry about it; I feel okay." Oh, the mother, oh, he told, okay. Let's see. There was a mother in here too. He told his mother. The doctor told him, he told his mother and the mother said, "Don't worry about it. You look okay." And as a result out came, "Mamma mia!"

APPENDIX IV

Experiment 3: Multi-Chain Transmission 1

(1A)

This advertising executive in New York gets off at lunch, and he goes into this bar on Second Avenue. Very nice bar. And there's a good crowd there, and goes up to the bar and sits down and orders a martini. He's drinking his martini and, well, he's sitting there sipping his martini and a beautiful girl walks in, blonde, really good looking. In fact, a lot of people in the bar notice her as she comes in. And she walks in the door, stops, looks around for a second, and walks up to the bar and sits down right next to him. You know, and he's sitting there having his martini and decides to light up a cigarette, and he gets a cigarette out, then looks for a match and he doesn't have a match. And he turns to her in a quiet voice and says, "Excuse me, ma'am, miss, do you have a match?" And then she says at the top of her lungs, "I will not sleep with you!" The guy was just shocked. Was just shocked and he can't figure it out. And everybody in the bar turns around naturally, and he's terribly embarrassed. He picks up his drink, his hand shaking, walks to the back booth and sits down, and sitting there looking at his drink trying to figure out what the heck he did to get that kind of response. He's sitting there for about five minutes, and the blonde gets up from the bar and walks over to him and says, "Listen, I want to explain what happened over there. You see, I'm a student at the university in social psychology and we're running an experiment on people's reaction to novelty and surprise in shocking situations." And he says at the top of his lungs, "Seventy-five dollars?"

(2A)

O.K. This is New York City. This advertising executive is getting off for lunch, about lunch time he goes down to the nice bar, thought he'd have a drink for lunch, he wasn't really hungry. A nice bar around Second Avenue. A real classy place, soft lights, a piano, everything. He comes up, and he sits up at the bar and orders a martini, and he's there sipping on his martini, and this real nice-looking blonde walks in. And she's a real head turner, the whole place, just kind of a hush falls over the place, all watch her go to the bar and she sits right next to him. And he thought that was kind of strange, in the seat right next to him. And he's, gets him a little shook up, doesn't really know why she sat next to him, so he pulls a cigarette out, realizes he doesn't have any matches, pats around on his shirt, no matches, so he looks over at her and says, "Do you have a match?" And she looks at him and at the top of her lungs in this quiet bar she goes, "I will not sleep with you!" And the guy looks up, and the whole crowd looks up—looking at him like this—and it embarrassed the hell out of him. Doesn't know why she said it, so he kind of takes a pull from his martini and slinks off the bar and sits in a booth over by the wall. And he's just kind of sitting there looking like this, doesn't, trying to figure out what's going on, why she would say something like that. And she's really just shaken him up. So a little while later, she comes over and sits down next to him and says, "I want to apologize for what happened just now. Let me explain. I'm a student at the university down here and study sociology and psychology and all that, and we're doing a little experiment on embarrassing situations, and the reactions people have when they become embarrassed. And that's, and that's why I said what I did to you." So he looks around a little bit, and at the top of his lungs he goes, "Seventy-five dollars?"

(3A)

There's this advertising executive in New York City, and it's lunch hour, and he decides to go down and have a drink, so he walks into this pretty nice bar and he orders a martini. Sits up at the bar. And so he's getting his martini, and he takes a sip, and this beautiful blonde walks in, and the whole place turns around and looks at her. She's really gorgeous and all. And she walks right up and sits next to him. And he seemed pretty flattered about this, but he's wary as to what's going on. So he takes out a cigarette, trying to look cool and all and pats around because he doesn't have any matches. He looks over at her and asks her if she has a match, and she goes, "I will not sleep with you!" at the top of her lungs.

And everybody turns around you know, he doesn't know what's going on, so he slinks down in the chair, kind of sips on his drink and eventually he gets pretty embarrassed about it so he walks over and sits in a booth. And after a while the blonde walks over and sits down next to him in the booth and says, "I'd like to apologize for what I said earlier. I'm a student at a college and we're doing a sociological experiment as to how people cope with embarrassing situations. And so I just want to apologize for that. It was just an experiment, it wasn't anything serious." So the guy looks at everybody and goes, "Seventy-five dollars?"

(4A)+

O.K. There's this advertising executive in New York City, and he goes out to lunch one day and he decides to go to a bar. And he goes into a bar, sits at the bar, and orders a martini, and he starts drinking his martini. So he sits there for a while, and pretty soon this gorgeous blonde walks in—she's really pretty—and everybody in the place turns around and looks at her. And eventually she comes over and sits by him. And he's very flattered and decides that he'd better have a cigarette because he's a little bit nervous. And he doesn't have any matches. So he starts feeling around in his pockets for matches, and he doesn't have any. So he finally asks her if she has a match. And she says, "I absolutely will not sleep with you!" And he's very embarrassed because she says it so loud that everybody turns around and looks. And he sits there for a while, slumps down in his chair, and everybody's just watching him; he gets up and leaves and goes and sits in a booth. And eventually she walks over to him and says, "I'm really . . . I want to apologize for saying that to you, but I'm a student here at one of the colleges, and we're doing a sociologic experiment about how people cope with situations, and you were part of the experiment. I'm sorry if it caused you any embarrassment." And he said, "Seventy-five dollars?"

(4B)+

There's an advertising executive in New York City. He's on his lunch break. So he decides to have a drink, and walks into a bar. And he sits at the bar and orders a martini, and pretty soon a nice, beautiful girl—blonde girl exactly—walks in and sits by him. He's so flattered, and he gets nervous, so he decides to light a cigarette. But he doesn't have any matches, so he decides to ask the chick for some matches. And when he asks her for the matches she says, "I certainly will not sleep with you!" at the top of her lungs. And so he kind of gets embarrassed—everybody turns around and looks at him. And eventually he kind of leaves and sits in a booth. She comes to him later and says she wants to apologize for saying what she did because, and explains that she is a, goes to school at one of the colleges and that they're doing a sociological survey on people's reactions when they're embarrassed—what people do when they're embarrassed. And so he turns around and says "seventy-five dollars!" really loud.

(3B)

This joke takes place in New York City. There's this executive—regular working day—and he's going out to lunch. And he just felt like going to a bar, you know. Sitting around and maybe having a drink or two. So he went down to this nice, you know, swanky bar that an executive would go to natural, you know. He sits in there, sitting down at the bar. He orders a martini, just sort of sitting around and drinking his martini and this blonde walks in. You know, just a real head turner. She's really beautiful and everybody's looking at her. He's looking at her. She comes walking in, she sits right next to him at the bar, and it made him, you know, a little nervous you know. Something like that happens to him, makes him a little nervous. And he's sitting there taking a sip out of his drink and reaches for a cigarette and couldn't find any matches. So he asks the girl if she has a match. And the girl stands up and yells at the top of her lungs, "I will not go to bed with you." And the guy, you know of course, kind of made him a little nervous. And he's just sitting around like this, for a little while, taking a little sip of his drink and trying to look real small. So he kind of slithers out from the bar and goes and sits down at a booth trying to regain his composure a little bit, you know. And he's sitting there drinking his drink. A few minutes later this girl comes. And she says, "I want to explain what happened up there. I'm a student at the university and we're running an experiment in the psychology class to see people's reactions to embarrassing situations, you know, to see how they react." Just then the guy stands up and yells at the top of his lungs, says, "Seventy-five dollars is too much."

(4C)+

O.K. There was a young man, an executive, and he's tense, and he decided to after work go out for a drink, and so he chose a bar and, in New York, and he went in and sat down at the bar and ordered a martini, and was watching people. And he noticed that a young woman came in, a blonde, very attractive, walked up and sat down next to him at the bar. And he became kind of agitated then—nervous—and decided he'd have a smoke. And pulled out a cigarette and then he couldn't find a match. So he turned to the girl and asked her if she had a light, and she stood up very abruptly and said, "No, I will not go to bed with you," and embarrassed the guy to death. And he withdrew and sat there very quietly for a few minutes and then decided to very quietly and inconspicuously slip away, so he walked over to a booth that was empty and sat down. And a few minutes later, the young woman at the bar walked over to him and said, "I would like to explain what happened, what happened at the bar just a few minutes ago. I am a student at the university, and I'm performing a psychology experiment, and I'm investigating what various situations will embarrass people. And that was the purpose of it. The experience you just had." And he stands up very abruptly and says, "Seventy-five dollars is too much."

(4D)

O. K. This executive was sitting in a bar in New York and had a drink, and this lady came in, and she was very attractive, and he had a hard-on he had to take care of, and he kept drinking till he wanted to smoke a cigarette and he had no light and asked her for a match. And she got up and said, "No, I would not go to bed with you!" He got really embarrassed because that's not what he asked her in the first place. And then there was other people around, and he was really embarrassed by the situation. Anyways, after a while she came around and tried to explain things to him. And she told him that she was a student at the university, and she was doing a psychology experiment, and she wanted to see what people would do—or how they would react—to different situations. And he tried to embarrass her, so what he did, he backed up and said, "Seventy-five dollars? That's too much."

(2B)+

There's this little story about this man, Madison Avenue executive type, and at the end of a terrible day—really rotten—he just drags himself to the nearest bar, orders himself a martini; tall, cool, terrific, ahhhh. O.K. So he's there resting for a few minutes and then he notices heads swivel. He looks over, and this beautiful woman is walking in the door. Wowee! And even that, even greater than that, she comes up and sits right beside him. O.K. Well, he's getting sort of nervous about this, so he pulls out his cigarettes and tries to light them and realizes he doesn't have a lighter with him. No matches. So hmmm, "Pardon me madam, do you have a match?" And she says at the top of her lungs, "Go to a motel with you?" So he just sort of slithers down to some insignificant little place at the bar; really nervous, terrified, really nervous. "What did I do? How did I blow it?" And he's trying to think about it, and a few minutes later the girl comes over—walks over to where he's sitting—and says, "I'm sorry about the whole incident, but see, I'm a psychology major at the university here, and I'm doing this experiment on reactions to trying situations. And that's the whole thing, and I thought I should explain it do you." And the man stands up and goes, "Seventy-five dollars?"

(3C)+

There's this Madison Avenue executive type, and he's had a really terrible day at the office. So he leaves work and goes to a bar. And he sits down at the bar and orders a martini, and he starts to drink. And suddenly he notices all heads swivel. And he looks up and this beautiful, beautiful woman who's just entered the bar. And more than that, she sits down right next to him. And he is really nervous because there is this beautiful creature next to him, he doesn't know what to do. So he is nervous enough, so he decides he needs a smoke. So he takes out his cigarettes, he looks—no lighter, no matches. Looks . . . terrific opportunity. So he asks her. Turns to her and asks, "Pardon me ma'am, do you have a match?" And she turns to him and at the top of her lungs she shouts, "Go to a motel with you?" And he's scared to death. He slithers away to a table, and he sort of sits down shaking. And a few minutes later, she walks over to him and she says, "Pardon me, but I felt I just had to explain. I'm a psychology student over at the university, and I'm trying to get people's reactions to situations like this. I hope you'll forgive me." And he turns to her and at the top of his lungs he shouts, "Seventy-five dollars?"

(4E)

Well, there's this Madison Avenue executive type guy, and he had a hard day at the office. So he decides after work to go down and get himself a drink at the local bar. So he goes on down there and goes in, orders himself a drink, and all of a sudden he notices all the heads swivel. So he looks around and for a reason all of the heads swivel is because a beautiful woman comes in. And more than that, she sat down right beside him. This made him all nervous, and he reached for a cigarette. And he found the cigarette, but he didn't have any matches—a lighter, you know. He said this is a beautiful opportunity. So he asked her for a match, and she said, "Go to a hotel with you?" And this made him all—everybody look around. And she walks off. And so he sits there for a while, and she comes back and says, "I guess I should tell you. I'm a psychology student at the university and this is just kind of an experiment to see what the reaction would be in this kind of situation." And he says, "Seventy-five dollars?"

(4F)+

There's a young executive Madison Avenue, type man who had a miserable day at the office, and thinking he would like to go and relax and sit down and have a drink. He went to a local bar. And at the bar he sat down and ordered a martini, and he noticed that all the heads in the whole placed turned. And he followed their look and caught the eye of a beautiful young woman who had just walked in. And not only did she just walk in, but she came and sat down right next to him, and it made him extremely nervous. So he felt the need to smoke and pulled out a pack of cigarettes, but he couldn't find a lighter—any matches. So he figured that was an excellent opportunity to start a conversation with her. So he asked for a match. He quietly turned to the side and just spoke to her, and as he asked for a match, she exclaimed really loudly, so everyone in the place could hear, "Go to a motel with you?" And he, he was flustered, and he just got up and kind of slunk off to another table, and was mortified, and sat and kind of brooded over his martini, feeling sort of bad about the whole situation. She approached him and went over to his table and explained to him that she was a psychology student at the university and was just trying to get people's reaction to the same situation. And as she explained this to him, he stood up and said, "Seventy-five dollars!"

*(3D)

There's this man, and he worked on a, like say, a real busy street—you know—Manhattan. Anyways, so after work one day, he was going to get a margarita, you know, so he went in this real nice place. And you know, he sat down and, ah, and he ordered a margarita, all of a sudden he saw something go by, and it was this real beautiful lady. And so he says, "God! You know I'd love to get to know her." And so, somehow she ended up coming to sit next to him. So he was going to light a cigarette, and he didn't have a match or lighter, so he asked this lady—and he was real excited asked this lady said—well, he said, "Do you have a light?" She goes, "Will I go to bed with you?" So, you know, he got really embarrassed, you know. He couldn't figure out how she said that. And so, you know, he really sort of upset himself. And he went up to this man, he was talking to this man, and says, "Look I'm a psychology major, you know. I'm a psychology professor at this place, and I've been doing this experiment, you know, on why people say different things. So this man hollers out, "Give you seventy-five dollars?"

*(4G)

There was this man, and he was getting off work, so he wanted to get a drink, so he went to a bar and got a margarita. And he was sitting there drinking his margarita, and he saw somebody walk by, and it was a lady and she sat down next to him. And in the meantime he was trying to light a cigarette, but he didn't have a match or a lighter, so asked the lady, "Do you have a light?" And she said, "Will I go to bed with you?" And he went, "What?" He didn't—"how did she get that out of what I said?" So he was all upset, you know, and everything, so he started to talk to this man that was a psychologist. And this man was a psychologist. And he said he was doing experiments on why people say things, and so, then he yelled out, "Will I give you seventy-five dollars?"

*(4H)

There was this man that worked in a real busy place, and he was getting off work, and he wanted to go get a margarita. And he goes to some bar and as he's sitting there, this beautiful woman goes by. And he's real attracted to her, and he wants to see how he can get to meet her—talk with her. And just by chance, she happens to sit close to where he's sitting. And they start talking, and–I don't know who's lighting what. Anyways, something about—let me see, yeah, she's going to light her, she's going to smoke a cigarette, but she doesn't have a lighter or a match or anything to light it with, and so he's going to come and help her, and so he says, "Can I light your cigarette?" And she says, "What? Will I go to bed with you?" And then he starts perplexing, because he just can't figure it out, you know. How could she have misunderstood something like that? So he leaves, and starts talking to this other man. Turns out this man is a psychologist, and he's been working on this type of stuff, you know, people who say things that don't make sense. And so the poor man keeps on talking to him and then, ah, somehow the psychologist says, "What? Will I give you seventy-five dollars?"

APPENDIX V

Experiment 4: Multi-Chain Transmission 2

(1A)

O.K. I'm just going to tell you this joke and you'll be called upon to repeat it a little later on. It's about this guy who falls in love with a girl and she's Polish. And he's very much in love with her and wants to marry her, but her parents are very much against the marriage because he isn't Polish. They have a lot of ethnic pride and they want her to marry a Polish guy. He's very upset—wants to marry her—and finally he hears that there's this doctor who's capable of performing an operation that can turn a person into a Pole. So he goes to see the doctor, and the doctor tells him, "Yeah, we can do it. It's essentially a procedure that involves cutting out half your brain." The guy thinks about it, but he's really in love with this girl, so he decided he'd go through with it. And they scheduled the surgery. The next week they're operating and in the operating room. While the surgery's being performed, the doctor slips—the knife slips—and instead of cutting out half of his brain, he cuts out three-quarters of his brain. Well, nothing to do. He finishes the operation. And when the guy's waking up from anesthesia in the recovery room, the doctor comes in to see him and says, "I'm sorry, you know. There was a mistake made during the operation. Instead of removing half your brain we removed three-quarters of your brain." And the guy goes, "Aye, mamma mia!"

(2A)

There's this young man who's madly in love with a beautiful, young girl but she's Polish. And he really wants to marry her, but her parents are really against it because he is not Polish. And they really want her to marry a Polish man. But he hears of a doctor who will make him into a Polish man by an operation. So he's really excited, and he goes to see the doctor and he says, "Doctor, can you help me?" He says, "Sure I can help you, but it requires removing half of your brain." So the guy goes, "I don't care. I really love her. Take half my brain." So the operation is scheduled, and the doctor operates on the man, but during the operation he cuts out three-quarters of his brain by accident. So the doctor can't do anything now. So he sews him up, and the man's in the recovery room, and the doctor goes to see him. He goes, "Hey, look. I'm really sorry. I removed three-quarters of your brain, not half." The guy goes, "Oh, mamma mia!"

(3A)

This is a story. It's a true story. It really happened about this girl that was Polish. She was a Polack. And she was going to marry this guy because she was really very much in love with him. And the only problem is, is her parents were very much against her marrying him because he wasn't a Polack. She was a Polack, and she didn't know what to do, and he didn't know what to do. He was very upset. So he found out through doctors that he can get an operation—a special operation—to make him into a Polack. You know, it was a very heavy operation, but he was so in love with the girl that he decided he'll do the operation. So he went to the doctor, and the doctor said, "Well, the operation consists of taking half your brain out." And the guy that wasn't a Polack, you know, wanted to be a Polack. He said, "Listen. I love this girl so much, it's O.K. Take out half my brain." So the doctor said, "O.K., we'll do the operation." A couple of weeks later he had the operation and the doctor made a mistake. He took out three-quarters of the brain. Really felt, really felt, really. . . . "God! What did I do to this guy? You know I took out more of his brain than I should have." So finally, the guys comes to, and the doctor says to him, "Listen. I really don't know how to say this, but I made a mistake. I didn't take out half. I took out three-quarters of your brain." He says, "Ayayai . . ."—no wait—he says, "Mamma mia!"

(4A)

O.K. This is a true story. It's about this Polish girl, and she was very much in love with this guy. But the thing was, she was Polish and he wasn't. And her parents were against her getting married to him because he wasn't Polish. And they didn't know what to do. So they discussed it, and then he found out that there was an operation that he could have performed on him to make him Polish. So he went to the doctor, and the doctor told him that in order to become Polish, he'd have to have half his brain removed. And so he talked with the doctor, and he decided well, you know, he really loved the girl and so he'd do it. He'd have half his brain removed so he could marry her and become Polish. So they had the operation, but the doctor made a mistake and he removed three-quarters of the brain. And so when the guy finally came to, when the guy finally came to, the doctor said, "I'm so sorry. What can I say? But I removed three-fourths of your brain." And the guy said, "Mamma mia!"

(5A)

There was this couple that wanted to get married, and they were very much in love with one another, and the girl was Polish. The boy wasn't. So they had a problem with the family because her parents didn't want him to marry her if he wasn't Polish. So they talked it over, and they found out that there was an operation he could have to make him Polish. So they went to the doctor and talked it over, and the doctor said, "Well, the operation consists of removing half your brain to make you Polish." And he decided that he loved the girl very much so, therefore, he would have the operation. So he had the operation. He's over with the operation. The doctor comes in. He apologizes to him. He says, "I'm very sorry, but I made a mistake. Instead of removing half of your brain, I removed three-fourths of it." And then the man says, "Mamma mia!"

(5B)

It's a true story about a guy and a girl who fell in love with each other, and they decided to get married. The girl is Polish and her parents didn't agree to the marriage. So he found out there is a way he can become Polish, which, making an operation taking half his brain away. So he went and he decided to get the operation done because he loved the girl. And he went to the doctor and he got the operation done. And finally the doctor came in, and he was apologizing to him that he took three-fourths of his brain and not half of it. So the man says, "Mamma mia!"

(4B)

There was this young couple that wanted to get married. They were really in love. And the parents of the girl objected entirely to it because the family was Polish and he was not, and they were against the intermarrying. So he couldn't understand that, and then he found out that there was this doctor that could make him into a Polack. So he went and talked to him, and he decided to go ahead with the surgery, but the problem was that he had to take half his brain out. And he says, "Well, I really love this girl a lot, so I'll go ahead and have the surgery done." So he went into the hospital. He had the surgery done, and the doctor ended up making a mistake. He took three-quarters of his brain out. And after the post-op and his recuperation and stuff, he told him. He says that, "I really goofed. I'm sorry. I took out three-quarters of your brain instead of half." And the guy's reply was, "Mamma mia."

(5C)

There was this young couple who were really in love, and they wanted to get married. But her family was against it because they were Polish and his family wasn't. So he decided to go to a doctor and find out if he could get transformed into being Polish. And the doctor said, "Yeah, I can help you, but I'll have to take half of your brain out." So he decided since he really loved her and really wanted to marry her that he'd go ahead with the operation. And so he went to the hospital, and the doctor during the operation made a mistake and took three-quarters of his brain out instead of only half. So after he recuperated and everything, the doctor came in and broke the news and told him, "Listen. I'm really sorry I made this mistake. Instead of taking half your brain out to make you Polish, I took out three-quarters." And the guy goes, "Mamma mia!"

(5D)

There's a young couple that wanted to get married. They're very much in love, only the boy's family was not Polish and the girl's family was. But he heard of this doctor that transformed people into Polacks by removing half of their brain. So he decided to go along with this because he really loved the girl and wanted to marry her. However, during the operation, the doctor made a mistake and took out three-quarters of the brain instead of half. After post-op, he informed the patient of this and the patient went, "Oh, mamma mia!"

(3B)

There was this man who was very much in love with a Polish woman. And they wanted to get married. But her parents were Polish, and they only wanted her to marry another Polish person—a Polish man. So he was really beside himself, and he didn't know what to do. And he heard from someplace that there was a doctor that could make him Polish. So he went to the doctor, and they talked about it, and the doctor said it was a very serious operation, and was he sure he wanted to go through with it. And he said, "Yes." "Well, it will entail taking out half of your brain." And the guy thought about it for a while—and he really wanted to marry this girl—so he said, "O.K." So he went through with the operation. During the operation, by mistake, the doctor took out three-quarters of the brain by accident. And he didn't know what to do. He couldn't put it back. So he just sewed the guy up, and he was in the recovery room. And when the guy came to, the doctor told him, he says, "By accident I took out too much of your brain." And the guy says, "Mamma mia!"

(4C)

There's this man that's madly in love with this Polish girl, and he really wants to marry her bad. And she's in love with him, but her family has forbidden her to marry anybody that's not Polish. So he's really heartbroken. So he's walking around wondering what he can do about it. And he hears about this doctor that can make you Polish. So he goes in and talks to the doctor, and the doctor explains to him that it's a very serious operation. Does the guy really want to go through with it? He says, "I don't care what it is. I want to be made Polish." And so the doctor said, "Well, O.K. It involves cutting out half of your brain." And so the guy says, "O.K." He goes ahead, through the operation. And the doctor by mistake cuts out three-quarters of the guy's brain. And the doctor is sitting there because he doesn't know what to do because he can't put a quarter back. And so he sews the guy back up. In the recovery room he comes in and tells the guy, "You know, I really want to apologize about this, but I cut out three-quarters instead of half your brain." And the guy goes, "Mamma mia!"

(5E)

There was a man who fell in love with a Polish girl, and he really wanted to marry her. She was also in love with him, and she wanted to marry him. Unfortunately, her parents wouldn't allow her to marry anyone that wasn't Polish. This poor man was upset, and he found out about a doctor who could perform an operation that would make him Polish. So he went to this doctor, and the doctor told him about it. And he said this was a very serious operation. And the guy said, "I don't care. I want to be Polish. I want to do it." "Well, the operation involved cutting out half of his brain. [Teller claims that she can't go on and laughs.] Unfortunately, the doctor cut out three-quarters of his brain instead of half his brain. And when he went to the recovery room, he tried to explain it to him. And he said, "I'm really sorry but instead of taking just half of your brain, I took three-quarters." And the guy looked up at him and said, "Mamma mia!"

(5F)

There was a man who was very much in love with a Polish girl. And she was in love with him too. But she couldn't marry him because her parents wanted her to marry somebody who was Polish. And so the guy went to a doctor who was supposed to have been able to perform an operation that could make him Polish. And even though it was very serious, he went ahead on the operation. But the doctor took out three-quarters of his brain instead of half of his brain, which is what he was supposed to have done. And in the recovery room, the doctor told the man that he had taken out three-quarters of his brain instead of half, and the man said, "Mamma mia!"

(2B)

There was a man and a woman and they were in love, and they wanted to get married. But they didn't have the consent of the girl's parents because she was Polish and they wanted her to marry a Polish guy. So the man was very distraught and wanted to do something about it. So he heard there was a doctor that could perform an operation to make you Polish. So he goes to see the doctor, and the doctor told him, the operation, he could do it, no problem. "It involves removing half your brain." So the man goes, "O.K. doctor, I'll have the operation." The doctor takes him, they're performing the operation, and the doctor during the operation accidentally slips and makes a slight mistake and cuts out three-quarters of the man's brain instead of only half. So when the man wakes up, the doctor goes into the room and explains to the man, "I'm sorry but we made a mistake. We cut out three-quarters of your brain instead of only half." And the guy goes, "Oh, mamma mia!"

218   *Just Folklore*

(3C)
There was a young couple that wanted to get married and there was a catch to it because she was Polish and he wasn't. So they had to do something in order to be able to get married, being one Polish and not the other. So they heard of a doctor that could perform an operation to make him Polish. He consented to it, and he went for the operation, and the operation was that they would cut out one half of his brain in order to make him Polish. So the doctor made a slip. Instead of cutting out one half of his brain, he cut out three quarters. So when the fellow—after the operation when he was coming to—they said to him, "We are awful sorry, but we made a mistake and instead of cutting out half your brain we cut out three quarters. And the patient said, "Oh, mamma mia."

(4E)
There was a couple. One of the couple was Polish and they decided to get married. In order to get married they decided they both had to be Polish. So the procedure was to get an operation in brain surgery. So the guy went to the surgery and the operation was to be following: they had to cut half of his brain off. After the operation was through they found out they cut three-quarters instead of half so when he came to they told him and his response was, "Oh, mamma mia."

(4F)
There was a couple who wanted to get married, but they had a problem because one of them wasn't Polish and so they had to . . . someone said they knew of a doctor who could fix the situation and make him Polish. In order to do this they had to remove half of his brain. And he submitted to the operation, and they made a mistake. Instead of removing half of his brain, they removed three-quarters of his brain. When they called him in to tell them about his mistake he said, "Ah, mamma mia!"

(3D)
There was a couple and they wanted to get married. But her folks did not want her to marry him because he was not Polish. So they heard of a doctor who could perform an operation and make him Polish if he removed half of his brain. So he consented to this. The scalpel slipped during the surgery. So when the man was recovering in the hospital, the doctor came in and said, "I'm sorry. The scalpel slipped and we removed three-fourths of your brain rather than half, and the patient said, "Oh, mamma mia!"

(4G)
There was a couple. They had a daughter who wanted to get married, but the parents objected because the man she wanted to marry was not Polish. So there was a surgeon who could perform an operation to remove half of his brain to make him Polish. While the surgeon was performing the operation, the scalpel slipped and three-fourths of his brain was removed. When the patient was recovering, the doctor says, "I'm sorry but I removed three-fourths of your brain by mistake." And the man put his hand up to his head, "Oh, mamma mia."

(4H)

There was a couple and their daughter wanted to be married, but they were against it because the man she wanted to marry wasn't Polish. So they searched and they found a surgeon who could perform an operation to make him Polish. And the operation was that they would remove half of his brain. So they went in for the operation, and while the surgeon was busy working on him, the scalpel slipped and he accidentally removed three-quarters of the brain instead of half. And when he came to, they informed him of what had happened and he said, "Oh, mamma mia!"

12. Thinking through Tradition

The word tradition *is itself traditional in folklore studies. John Aubrey used it in his* Miscellanies *in 1696. In 1777, John Brand identified tradition—indeed, oral tradition—as central in the preservation of the rites and opinions of the common people (Brand in Dorson 1968a, 1:8). W. J. Thoms referred to "local traditions" in his 1846 letter to the* Athenaeum *where he proposed his neologism "folklore" (Thoms in Dorson 1968a:53), and E. Sydney Hartland characterized folklore as the "science of tradition" in the last years of the nineteenth century (Hartland in Dorson 1968a, 2:231). Tradition has remained central to most definitions of folklore since (Brunvand 1998:3). It is considered one of a few "keywords" in folklore studies (in addition to the terms art, text, group, performance, genre, context,* and identity *[Feintuch 2003]). But what is the status of tradition in folklore studies? What role does it play and what achievements can the field attribute to its deployment?*

> *Tradition is a matter of much wider significance.*
> *It cannot be inherited, and if you want it you must*
> *obtain it by great labour.*
> —T. S. Eliot

IN HIS 1984 ESSAY, "The Seven Strands of Tradition," Dan Ben-Amos identified a variety of ways that folklorists have used *tradition*: as lore, canon, process, mass, culture, langue, and performance. "Lore" refers to past knowledge of a society that has inadvertently survived but is in danger of dying out (104). "Canon" refers to that body of literary and artistic culture which has gained acceptance in a particular social group (106). "Process" refers to the dynamics of cultural transmission over time (117). "Mass" refers to what is transmitted by tradition. It is not the result of a superorganic process but rather is changed by those who transmit it (118). "Culture" suggests that tradition is synonymous with the anthropological conception of thought and behavior in social life (120–121). "Langue" refers to the concepts, categories, and rules that engender culture. As in Ferdinand de Saussure's linguistics, it refers to the abstract system that underlies and generates speech and behavior (121). "Performance" refers to enactment, and although enactment is always in the present, tradition always exists in the minds and memories of people as a potential (122–123).

These differences in the uses of the term *tradition* are not always crystal clear, but Ben-Amos was trying to sort out the usages of the term by folklorists from different periods and publications. His was an attempt to construct a descriptive history of the term. He found that folklorists did not use *tradition* consistently nor did they examine their usages critically. Curiously, Ben-Amos states at the conclusion of his essay that none of the uses of the term *tradition* is more adequate or proper than any other. Tradition, he states, is a metaphor that guides folklorists in dealing with "an inchoate world of experiences and ideas" (1984:124). Simon Bronner, writing a decade and a half later, was perhaps less forgiving. He characterized the use of *tradition* in folklore as reflecting "multiple meanings" and betraying a "conceptual softness" (1998:10).

Can a "science of tradition" be based on a concept that is so scattered, inchoate, and soft? Ben-Amos's seeming unconcern with the ways that the term *tradition* was deployed probably stemmed from the fact that he had no personal investment in the concept. He had eliminated tradition from his definition of folklore more than a decade before. For him, folklore was "artistic communication in small groups" (1971:13). Tradition played no part. Ben-Amos nevertheless claimed that folklorists think *with* the term *tradition* even if they did not think much *about* it. Do folklorists think with *tradition*? Is tradition an analytical concept that helps folklorists to perceive, explore, and explain the world? These are some of the questions addressed below.

Tradition as Process and Product

The word *tradition* comes from the Latin roots *trans* + *dare*; literally "to give across," that is, to hand over, deliver, or transfer.[1] Thus, *tradition* involves the notion of transferring or transmitting and has been applied to the *act* of handing over or handing down as well as to those *objects* that are handed over or handed down. Consequently, *tradition* refers to both processes and products.

Although folklorists have consistently noted the duality of the term (Final Discussion 1983:241; Ben-Amos 1984:116–119; Vansina 1985:3; Gailey 1989:144; Sims and Stephens 2005:65), they have focused almost exclusively on the products of tradition.[2] They have been drawn to the field by quilts, proverbs, remedies, legends, songs, and tales. The study of folklore has always been rooted in the study of particular traditions, and the study of those traditions only sometimes turned towards the question of the means by which they were passed on.[3] Folklore did not begin with a study of process and then turn to the outcomes of that process. The process was used to label objects of interest and set them apart. The process itself, however, has always remained somewhat opaque.[4]

Dan Ben-Amos's survey of the uses of *tradition* noted that the term was employed to denote both process and product, but the distinction was obscured as he listed all seven uses indiscriminately. Process is listed with six other uses that refer to products of tradition: lore, canon, mass, culture, langue, and performance (1984:102–125). These products are the ideas, knowledge, objects, behaviors, or rules that are transferred and transmitted through time. Had Ben-Amos arranged the categories taxonomically, however, with the first distinction drawn between *process* and *product*, the fact that the other six categories were—or dealt with—product would have stood out more clearly. Then the deficiency of attention to tradition as process would have been underscored, since "process" would have included no further categories.

Tradition
|
lore
canon
process
mass
culture
langue
performance

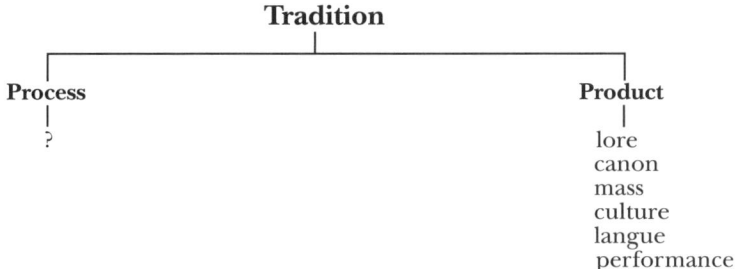

The collapse of "process" and "product" into a simple list obscures the fact that process is not just another entry. It does not constitute a mere one-seventh of the meanings of tradition. It represents a fundamentally different conceptualization.

Process is more fundamental than product. Traditions are traditions only by virtue of some process that makes them so. Process creates product. Without the process, traditions would be indistinguishable from all other cultural ideas and practices.

What then is this process? The process of tradition, I contend, is the process of *cultural reproduction*. Cultural reproduction refers to the means by which culture is reproduced in transmission and repetition.[5] It depends on the assimilation of cultural ideas and the reenactment of cultural practices. Reproduction may be accomplished in an act of transmission from one person to another. Or it may be accomplished when individuals produce something they have reproduced before, such as singing a song they have sung in the past (Bartlett 1932:63, 118). The use of *cultural reproduction* refers to a much broader sphere of activity than that addressed by Pierre Bourdieu in his study of French educational institutions. The term should not be restricted to school learning or the learning of "high" or "official" culture. A study of cultural reproduction need not focus on the ways that it preserves social stratifications (Bourdieu 1973; Bourdieu and Passeron 1977). Indeed, folklorists should be more interested in how social organizations enable cultural reproduction than the reverse. In reality, cultural reproduction is achieved through a number of different processes. *Cultural reproduction* is merely an umbrella term for these processes. It is these that are the processes of tradition.

It is even possible to identify some of these processes within Ben-Amos's essay. When Ben-Amos discusses the sense of tradition as "canon," for example, he talks about creativity and how folklorists view creativity as necessary to the maintenance of tradition. Creativity—or better, *re-creation*—would then be one of the processes of tradition. Canons are products, but *canonization* is a process, so it might be included as well. Beyond Ben-Amos's essay other processes spring immediately to mind: *education, memorization, rehearsal, comparison, performance,* and *traditionalization*.[6]

Tradition and Creativity

Everything changes. What comes from the past mutates, is modified, transformed, or disappears. There are two possible approaches to the past and change: take the past as given and describe and explain change; or take change as given and describe and explain that which perseveres. The attention of contemporary folklorists is unequally distributed with respect to these approaches. For the most part, folklorists take the past as given and address themselves to variation (Ben-Amos 1984:114). Each instantiation of a tradition is regarded as a performance with its own peculiar variables. Rather than being something handed down, it is highlighted as something new and unique.[7] It has even been claimed that "tradition is change" ("Final Discussion" 1983:236; Toelken 1996:7).

Of late, the attention of folklorists has been directed to one type of change: change that is deliberate, crafted, and aesthetic. The terms for this type of change are "innovation," "improvisation," and "creativity."[8] Folklorists hold that it is creativity that keeps tradition alive by making an inheritance from the past relevant in the present (Ben-Amos 1984:113; Glassie 1995:395). There are several problems with this proposition, however.[9]

(1) There is a presumption that the changes that occur to past ideas, expressions, and behaviors are *necessary* ones: "Folklore lives through a generally selective process that ensures . . . that traditions will maintain their viability, or change so they can, or die off" (Toelken 1996:43). "Only those forms are retained that hold a functional value for the given community" (Jakobson and Bogatyrev 1980 [1929]:6).

"Creative storytellers are the ones who modernize and renew the folktale tradition to make it attractive for current consumption" (Dégh 1995:44). "The creative impulse speaks to the fact that tradition is not and has never been something static, the most stable aspect of any tradition being its ability to change in response to changing needs" (Neulander 1998:226). The claim is that all changes are necessary for the survival of a tradition. But this is mere assertion. Change and adaptation have not been assessed independently but defined in terms of one another. The change of past forms is required for survival in the present; survival in the present demands change in forms from the past.[10] However, without some empirical determination of what constitutes necessary and incidental change, what has been proposed is tautology: the changes that have occurred to an expression from the past enable its survival; expressions from the past that have not survived did not change appropriately to suit current conditions. In other words, that which survives, survives; that which has not, has not.[11]

(2) "Creativity" is a term for a process that is applied to a product. Because creativity is a process, it is conflated with the process of tradition itself. But the process of tradition, whatever its particular characteristics, must conceptually relate to a process of cultural reproduction, not innovation. Things from the past can be altered. Things from the past are altered. Things from the past are "creatively" or otherwise revised. But to call this the process of tradition is to largely ignore continuity and stability. Continuity and stability depend on what people preserve—for good or ill, consciously or unconsciously—of the thought and behavior of the past. To study tradition, folkloristics must come to understand the means by which cultural reproduction is accomplished; to grasp the forces that direct the present through the conduit of past practice.

The notion of creativity as employed by folklorists is not the process *of* tradition but a process *acting upon* particular traditions (Bronson 1969:144–145). For example, would the creative refashioning of a ballad or folktale constitute the operation of tradition or an operation performed on a traditional expression? The use of a single term to at once refer to both process and a product is probably the source of many problems with the term *tradition*. Some statements that might be true about tradition as product (e.g., "traditions change") are ambiguous, meaningless, or false when applied to tradition as process (e.g., "tradition is change"). Some statements that might be true about tradition as process (e.g., "tradition never dies") are ambiguous, meaningless, or false when applied to a product (e.g., "traditions never die").

(3) Contemporary folklorists have been trapped by tradition. Like Ben-Amos (1971), they have moved away from the concept. Unlike Ben-Amos, they did not consciously or precipitously abandon it. Almost alchemically, they transformed it. The continuity of the past was regarded as a given. The focus was on change, particularly creative change, which became the touchstone of tradition: "Tradition . . . is an innovative adaptation of the old" (Glassie 1995:395); "The artist's own unique talents of inventiveness within the tradition . . . are expected to operate strongly" (Toelken 1996:37); "The pattern of creative activity within the forms of one's own society is valid not only in such folk arts as pottery or storytelling, but equally in the most extreme forms of self-expression in modern European painting" (Crowley 1966:136); "The linking of creativity and tradition . . . succeeds the Romantic notion of art as the domain of exceptional and cultivated minds" (Bronner 1992:2). Tradition was thus made to exhibit the quality that defines art in our culture—it was dynamic, innovative, original, and creative. In other words, *"creativity" was the means by which folklorists recuperated tradition as art.*[12] Tradition, consequently, has been something of a "survival" in contemporary folkloristics. It has lost much of its original meaning and has made its way into "a new state of society different from that in which . . . [it] had . . . [its] original home" (Tylor 1874, 1:16). Yet the older sense of the term haunts the discipline like an unlaid ghost, and it indexes, ironically, the influence of tradition in the operation of contemporary folklore scholarship.

Tradition: Etic and Emic

Where an etic and superorganic notion of tradition dominated folklore scholarship in the past—under theories of evolution, diffusion, function, and structure—an emic sense of tradition is privileged today. Richard Handler and Jocelyn Linnekin dismiss the idea that *tradition* might refer to a core of culture traits inherited from the past, and regard it solely as a symbolic construction—an interpretation of the past enacted in the present (1984:273). The traditional is what people claim their traditions to be. Whether those claims can be substantiated by empirical evidence is another matter entirely.[13] Barry McDonald, writing in response to Henry Glassie's essay on tradition is more forgiving. He feels that practitioners and folklorists need to negotiate "some mutually intelligible core meanings for the concept" (Glassie 1995; McDonald 1997:52). The meaning of the term, he feels, should not be determined by the folklorist's critical viewpoint alone.

Both propositions seem problematic. Handler and Linnekin base their claim for an interpretive concept of tradition on their independent investigations of particular cases in Quebec and Hawaii. But the cases only evidence that tradition can be constructed and deployed for symbolic purposes—for purposes of cultural identity. Identity formation and maintenance are important uses made of the past and the perceived past—or what might be called "the rhetorical past."[14] But they hardly seem to exhaust the possible roles that past ideas, objects, and practices might play in contemporary affairs, nor do they engage at all with tradition as process.[15]

What would happen to the field of folklore were it restricted only to those practices that were deemed by their practitioners to be traditional? Many people tell jokes, cure illnesses, dance, sing, and make quilts, simply to engage in those activities. Tradition may have nothing to do with the reasons for the performance. That the joke is a funny one, the remedy an effective one, the song a moving one, the dance a sensual one, and the quilt a warm one is often more than sufficient justification for the endeavor. People may know the joke, the remedy, the quilt pattern, the dance, and the song have been around for a while, but it may have little to do with why they joke, heal, sing, dance, and stitch. In fact, it is often the folklorist who raises questions about the past and introduces traditionality into folk consciousness and discourse. In any event, much of what folklorists consider to be folklore would evaporate overnight were *folklore* defined as tradition and *tradition* defined in terms of people's claims about what constituted the practices of their ancestors.

And what might be achieved by McDonald's notion of a negotiated concept of tradition? It is quite possible—indeed likely—that scholars and the people they study will have different, sometimes radically different, notions of the past. The scholar certainly needs to be aware of these differences. It may be that etic and emic concepts illuminate one another or talk past one another, but what exactly is to be negotiated? How would the outcome of such a negotiation be decided? Why should etic and emic concepts of anything agree? What would be gained from such agreements, and more importantly perhaps, what would be lost? It is precisely in the disparities between the assessments of scholars and practitioners that some of the most fruitful questions about human thought and behavior are engendered.[16]

Traditions can be unconscious. Ideas, knowledge, and behaviors can be received and acted upon without an awareness on the part of the recipient of their nature, origin, or consequences. Some hold the idea of unconscious tradition as "theoretically 'deficient' and potentially offensive to its practitioners" (McDonald 1997:58). Wherein lies the deficiency and offense? Is all knowledge consciously acquired and accessible to consciousness? If so, why is it that the native speakers usually cannot describe the rules that govern their language production? They clearly follow rules but often have a hazy grasp, if any grasp at all, of what those rules are. People, ourselves included, often do not know exactly what they are doing, how they do it, or how they acquired the means to do it.

The unconscious aspects of cultural practice—the principles that seem to be operating outside the awareness of cultural actors—are the most fascinating part of a cultural system. This proposition is not cultural paternalism. It is not some imposition upon subaltern peoples. Cultural analysis is most trenchant when it identifies a pattern of thought or behavior governing our *own* culture of which we are unaware.[17] Victorian folklorists regularly pointed to behaviors in their own society that seemed devoid of sense and showed that these derived from the beliefs and practices of earlier times. Diffusionists showed that ideas and behaviors that were central to a cultural system often—usually—came from the outside (Wissler 1926). Evolutionary and diffusionist perspectives have long been abandoned, but they demonstrated that numerous forms of behavior are rooted—unbeknownst to their practitioners—in forms from other times and places (Linton 1937). A strong case has been made, in fact, that real tradition consists of tacit rather than explicit knowledge (McKeon 2004).

Folklorists need to be attentive to the uses of the word, or any words, that serve to denote the relation between past and present. They need to record what people select from the panoply of past belief and practice as "traditional"; describe how claims of traditionality are negotiated; and understand the effects of such attributions in specific situations and in society more generally. Understanding tradition emically is to understand something significant about the conduct of human affairs both large and small. How people imagine their pasts contributes directly to the maintenance and modification of past beliefs and practices. However, there may be other forces beyond an individual's or group's ken that influence thought and behavior. Folklorists cannot ignore the emic notion of tradition, but the view that tradition is a symbolic construction only allows for the exploration of the ways we make use of the past; it does not allow for an understanding of the ways that the past makes use of us.[18]

Tradition and Modernity

Tradition has not only been applied to products and processes. The term has also been used to designate periods of time. *Tradition* has been used to label what is conceived to be the predecessor and opposite of modernity. *Modernity* (from the Latin *modo* meaning "lately") is a term that postulates a radical break with the past. It designates that period in which technology, social and economic organization, aesthetic expression, values, and lifestyles were utterly transformed from what they had been. Modernity is marked by industrialization, capitalism, nationalism, individualism, rationalized and secularized social institutions, and parliamentary democracy. It is defined against tradition: the "pre-modern," "old," "old-fashioned," "antique," "conservative," "classic," "primitive," "feudal," "folk," and "traditional." In this framework, *tradition* cannot be defined except from within modernity. *Modernity* and *tradition* consequently, are not simply descriptive terms but comparative and evaluative ones (Anttonen 2005:13–14, 28). Whether tradition in this formulation takes a positive or negative value depends on whether one takes a positive or negative view towards contemporary society and culture. Modernity may be seen as something to be escaped—in which case tradition may be celebrated and venerated—or modernity may be seen as something to be embraced—in which case tradition is a shackle from which society needs to be freed.[19]

This discourse on "tradition versus modernity" has profoundly shaped the field of folklore from its inception. Folklore was born, after all, in the concern for how the past might serve to improve and invigorate an anemic present (Wilson 1989:27). Even for folklorists today, tradition often figures as the opposite of and as an alternative to modernity. Folklorists often identify, describe, and attempt to preserve traditions because they feel that bygone ways of life are valuable, beautiful, and ultimately more humane. The work of folklorists has, in large part, been an effort to engender respect and sympathy for past or marginalized ways of life (Hofer 1984:133; Gailey 1989:159; Feintuch 1988:1–16; Abrahams 1992:25). Consequently, the studies, publications, and exhibits of traditions become homilies whose purpose is the aesthetic and moral edification of the citizens of modern society. Scholars who adhere to this approach to folklore cannot ignore how their reactions to modernity shape their scholarly perspectives, or how their scholarly perspectives participate in the response to and critique of modernity.[20]

Tradition and modernity are just one of many polar categorizations of society and culture: folk/urban, mechanical/organic, religious/secular, oral/literate, status-based/contractual, communal/societal, highbrow/lowbrow, local/global. They often prove evaluative concepts as well. As such, they probably obscure as much as, if not more than, they clarify. Few would contest that urban life in a first-world country in the twenty-first century is qualitatively different from life on a European feudal manor in the ninth. There are fundamental differences in their technologies, social organizations, and world views. However, a folkloristic definition of *tradition* is not something that can only be accomplished in relation to modernity, nor need the definition necessarily engage the value of either past or present.[21] Defined as *cultural reproduction*, tradition can be value neutral. One can investigate how cultural continuities are created and disturbed independently of whether the continuities or transformations are for better or for worse. There is no society, regardless of how "modern," in which tradition—as a process of cultural reproduction—plays no great part.[22] Similarly, there is no society, no matter how "traditional," in which there is uniformity of belief and practice determined by the automatic and exact reproduction of past ways of life and thought. In every society, there is innovation and deviation.[23]

Folklore and Tradition

Since everything is necessarily derived to some extent from the past, so that everything is to some extent traditional, what part of tradition constitutes folklore? Is folklore some special sort of tradition? Henry Glassie maintains that it is. He regards tradition as a matter of people keeping "faith with the past" and "with themselves." Tradition is a responsibility that individuals voluntarily assume (1995:402; also Noyes 2009:248). Those who do what others make them do are mere "slaves." Oppression is the opposite of tradition (Glassie 1995:396).[24] Barry McDonald, who disagrees with Glassie on a number of points about tradition, also regards tradition as rooted in choice and a "personal relationship" (1997:57–58). Both seem to privilege tradition as a kind of cultural reproduction rooted in particular relationships and responsibilities.

Undoubtedly, such relationships and responsibilities inform the maintenance of certain traditions. But is there justification in limiting the application of *tradition* to this sphere alone? One can think of situations—religious beliefs and practices immediately come to mind—in which the maintenance of the past can be a matter of imposition and oppression. Belief is scrutinized, behavior is supervised, threats are made, and punishments and rewards meted out in the maintenance of conformity. Should such situations be exempted from the category of tradition a priori? Would it not be better to include all instances of cultural reproduction within *tradition* and then distinguish them by type, organization, and motivation?[25]

Glassie's and McDonald's conceptions are consonant with the notion that traditions represent the good and beautiful that survive in the modern world and that goodness and beauty can only be forged through free and humane practice. Folklorists have focused almost exclusively on traditions that reflect positive value: traditions that evidence creativity, resilience, cooperation, commitment, and community. Studies of racist, classist, and even sexist traditions are, for the most part, absent in the folklore literature.[26] This evaluative approach to tradition significantly narrows the scope of inquiry and severely limits the possibility that folkloristics can participate in a general science of tradition.

If a limitation is to be imposed on *tradition* for the folklorist, it should be that the term avoid the invocation of evaluative and moral criteria. Let folklore be those parts of tradition that deal with the oral or handmade, that are transmitted face-to-face, and are, to a great extent, aesthetic in nature.[27] This limitation in scope presumes nothing about the goodness or morality of the products of tradition or the goodness or morality of the process of their reproduction. It is true that the concern of folklore studies with oral, face-to-face communication came about because these were the touchstones of those communities eradicated or marginalized by industrial and market forces. The loss was felt to be a moral one. But if folklore as a field was founded in concerns over the costs of modernity, the field need not remain rooted in that accounting. Folklore can define itself without privileging the oral and face-to-face morally and without presuming that its study must serve as a critique of modern life.

In limiting themselves to aesthetic reproduction achieved through oral and face-to-face channels, folklorists could not claim to be scientists of tradition at large nor claim to be the only scientists of tradition. There are many areas of cultural reproduction in which folklorists have no interest or expertise and about which they have had little to say. Most prominent are those broad areas of language and social organization to which folklorists—at least American folklorists—have paid little or no attention. While folklorists have been interested in linguistic products—tales, riddles, and proverbs—they have not concerned themselves with language systems as a whole; with the means by which lexicons, morphologies, grammars, and pragmatic rules are acquired and maintained. Nor have they worried about the reproduction of institutional and bureaucratic organizations and practices. While these areas may fall outside the folklorist's purview, at some level they still need to be noted in order to grasp the larger questions of cultural continuity to which the study of folklore can contribute. In exploring such questions, all kinds of traditions need to be examined: oral and literary; contemporary and ancient; conscious and unconscious; individual and institutional; artistic and ordinary. The folkloristic focus on the oral, the face-to-face, and the aesthetic is likely to contribute to an understanding of tradition only within this larger frame. Consequently, folklorists will have to become informed about these other areas of reproduction, even if they do not stand at the center of their researches.

Tradition as a Contemporary Subject

The raison d'être of folklore studies was that traditions were dying and should be observed and recorded before they vanished entirely. Once gone, these traditions would be beyond documentation and understanding. Some scholars have scoffed at folklore's claim that tradition was dying, because folklorists had been using the same justification for more than three centuries (Bauman and Briggs 2003:306). Of course, no one ever claimed that tradition was dying—if what is meant by tradition is the process of cultural reproduction—but only that particular traditions die out, which is demonstrably true. In addition, societies that perpetuated traditions almost exclusively through oral and face-to-face transmission were disappearing or rapidly changing—also demonstrably true. The relatively isolated societies rooted in face-to-face, oral communication and hand- rather than machine-work were, in fact, vanishing in Europe and America where the discipline of folklore developed.

It is claimed that folkloristics' myopic concern with dying and marginalized practices can only serve to marginalize it as a discipline. Barbara Kirshenblatt-Gimblett felt that folklore must struggle "to find a truly contemporary subject, one that is not just *in* the present, but truly *of* the present (1995:70). But is the value of a field to be based on the contemporaneity of its subject matter? Are archeology or paleontology somehow deficient as disciplines because they engage the ancient or prehistoric? Are classical and medieval history inadequate because they deal with periods and peoples long past? The answers to these questions should be obvious. Nevertheless, there is no barrier to folklore engaging a fully contemporary subject. *The contemporary can only be defined in terms of what it replaces, marginalizes, or renders superfluous.* A focus on the persistence and disappearance of past practices is, therefore, an utterly contemporary matter. The field of folklore would prove of inestimable value to the study of society in being able to describe and explain how and why the persistence and replacement of cultural ideas and practices occur. Furthermore, the attention to cultural maintenance and replacement does not demand a commitment to either the practices that are maintained or those that are being replaced. The old and the new need not be conceptualized positively or negatively. They need not be moral categories. The need is to understand why the new replaces the old, when it does, and how and why certain past practices continue even when everything else seems to be changing around them.[28]

The Force of Tradition

The claim that tradition could not be understood as a core of inherited traits, but as a symbolic construction (Handler and Linnekin 1984:273–290) was related to larger moves in the humanities and social sciences in the 1970s and 1980s: moves away from notions of essence, description, cause, universality, and science to notions of resemblance, interpretation, motive, contingency, and the literary. One book that was particularly influential in encouraging a change in the view of tradition was *The Invention of Tradition* edited by Eric Hobsbawm and Terence Ranger. A series of essays demonstrated how much of what had been presented as an inheritance from the ancient past was, in fact, no more than the invention of comparatively recent times. Even when the content of a tradition was not entirely factitious, the claim for its continuity was, since much tradition was a deliberate revival and reformulation rather than a continuous handing down. Thus, the traditions which people cherished and around which they rallied—those traditions whose perusal might be said to be the very reason for folklore studies—were often invented to provoke those sentiments and to provide a point about which people could come together. The traditions with which folklorists were concerned turned out to be the result of deliberate crafting—often for transparent political purposes (Hobsbawm and Ranger 1984:9).[29]

Nevertheless, the concepts of tradition as inheritance and as invention are interrelated. The power of invented traditions—which is considerable—is rooted in the belief that what is inherited from the past matters. Traditions that have been invented, revived, or reformulated can only have force if what is handed down from "previous generations" is thought to have bearing in directing, supporting, and validating current thought and action. An invented tradition is consequently engendered by the same forces as a genuine one.

The relation of invented traditions to genuine traditions is somewhat analogous to the relation between truth and lie. Lies are employed to achieve specific ends. They have functional value. But lies can only function effectively if they are represented and accepted as truth. Lies are utterly dependent on the power of truth. Invented traditions, though they may be crafted for particular purposes, depend on the same warrant that genuine traditions possess.

Consequently, some very basic questions about tradition—whether inherited or invented—remain the same: How does the past acquire and assert its authority? How is the past sustained in the present? How is following precedent made to seem necessary or desirable?[30] When does the past trump contemporary experience, and under what circumstances, and in what ways does contemporary experience substitute new rationales for past ideas and behaviors? Why and how do new rationales succeed, and why and how do old rationales fail? In what areas of thought and behavior in contemporary society is the inherited past still appealed to, and in what areas does it continue to operate? (These may not be the same.) Conversely, in what areas does the past lose its power as a model for present thought and action, and why?

Directions in the Study of Tradition

Tradition needs to be approached on a number of levels: social, psychological, and aesthetic, although these are not entirely separate. The approach can be both etic and emic. Approaching reproduction on the social level would involve ascertaining the fields of choice available in a social group. It would also require a close examination of the kinds of pressures—personal, social, religious, political, legal, aesthetic—that engender conformity and the preservation of precedent (Thompson 1953:592). Furthermore, the extent to which ideas and behaviors are embedded in or attached to other forms and practices that constrain the possibility of their variation needs to be examined.[31] Attention to the conditions and circumstances in which individuals and groups invoke *tradition* is, likewise, needed.

The psychological level would involve, for example, some investigation of the processes of memory. Folklorists have pretty much avoided a confrontation with the question of memory and of learning more generally. Folklorists would have to make themselves familiar with some of this literature as it helps to understand the process of tradition which begins as a process of learning.[32] The aesthetic and the psychological are closely intertwined, and psychologists, folklorists, anthropologists, and oral historians have made contributions to such research (Bartlett 1920; Anderson 1951, 1956; Oring 1978; Vansina 1985; Rubin 1995). The theory of oral formulaic composition did turn folklorists and literature scholars to the question of how traditions are remembered and reproduced (Lord 1960; Foley 1988). Much of this work focused on the study of poetic narratives, but it seems there is a lot more to do.[33] The codes and symmetries in the particular forms of folklore that serve as aids to memory and guides to reproduction need to be identified (Rubin 1995).[34] Folklorists need to understand what parts of an expression or practice are relatively fixed and what parts are free—and under what conditions (Bronson 1954:6, 1969:151; Smith 1986:6; Glassie 1995:406). The critical responses of audiences need to be observed and described in order to see whether and how they affect subsequent performance. Folklorists have talked about this, but they have not done very much in the way of reporting, let alone analyzing, it (Bauman 1977b:11; Glassie 1995:407; Toelken 1996:39).

Because it has often been thought of as some accumulated mass of belief and custom—some lifeless, superorganic entity—tradition has not usually been thought of in ethnographic terms. The presumption has been that one can do an ethnographic study of particular traditions but not of tradition itself. As cultural reproduction, however, an ethnographic approach to tradition is possible. Henry Glassie has described tradition as a keeping of faith—a faith, among others, with deceased teachers (1995:402). But where are the close descriptions of the relationships through which traditions are learned and maintained? Glassie is undoubtedly right that student artisans in Turkish ateliers do not receive much in the way of formal instruction but "breathe the air of experience" (408). But what does this involve? The folklore literature is remarkably thin on the description of interactions of teachers and students or students with their fellow students.[35] When "influences" are written about, they are often inferred from texts and performances rather than from observations of formal and informal situations of instruction.[36] Likewise, there is little or no ethnographic data on performance review, self-assessment, and rehearsal.[37] These are areas to which folklorists might give considerably more attention. The observation and analysis of these micro-processes might prove unique and important contributions to the study of tradition.[38]

The Problem of Tradition

Despite claims for the centrality of tradition in folklore, tradition has not served as an analytical concept; that is, it has not helped folklorists think about the materials that they study, nor has it provided an orientation for their investigations. Folklorists do not study tradition but tradition*s*. They are interested in tales, quilts, ballads, and proverbs to be found, primarily, in certain—largely marginal—social groups. The focus is on the objects themselves rather than on what the study of such objects and practices contribute to an understanding of a process of "handing over" or "handing down."[39] The traditions that folklorists focus upon are regarded as *expressions*. Even traditionality itself has most often been regarded in expressive terms (Oring 1994:243); that is, as a sign and symbol of individual and community (e.g., Radin 1935, 15:62–67; Gailey 1988; Johnson 1998:658–659; Jones 2000; Antonnen 2005; Sims and Stephens 2005:66–67). Folklorists, therefore, have been interested in discovering the meanings and functions of the traditions that they collect. Only rarely have they broached the questions identified above that might be regarded as central in a study of tradition as process: how are beliefs and practices taught and learned; what is the source of the authority of tradition and how does its force make itself felt; how do past practices continue to operate in the present, and how and why do new practices come to destroy or marginalize the old? Folklore fieldwork can speak to these questions in important ways, but for the most part, it does not. It is not surprising, therefore, that folklorists have written no major treatises on tradition, and those that have been written are by scholars in other fields (Shils 1981; Hobsbawm and Ranger 1984; Boyer 1990; but see Bronner 1998; 2011). These works make little use of folklore research—much to the consternation of folklorists (Bendix 2002:110).

Contrary to what Dan Ben-Amos suggested in his 1984 essay, folklorists do occasionally think *about* tradition,[40] but rarely do they think *with* it. *Tradition* is a word they frequently *use* but largely to mark territory. Something called a "tradition" or "traditional" is deemed to fall within the folkloristic purview.[41] It becomes something which folklorists feel justified observing and discussing.[42] However, only when folklorists start attending to tradition as a process of cultural reproduction will the term acquire a measure of conceptual depth.[43] This is not to suggest that folklorists stop studying the particular traditions with which they are enamored and about which they have some interesting things to say. Nor does it suggest that folklorists should ignore change or creativity. Tradition, however, has been regarded somewhat like inertia: an object in motion tends to stay in motion; an object at rest tends to stay at rest. This may prove adequate for classical physics, but it does not seem adequate for the study of folklore. Folklorists need to grasp the means by which thought and practice are reproduced over time (Phillips 2004:25). Tradition needs to be regarded as a problem and not simply a given. In fact, *the major problem of tradition in folklore studies is that it has not sufficiently been regarded as a problem.* Only when the term *tradition* directs folklorists to frame substantive questions, can it gain any conceptual value for the discipline.

One hundred and twenty-five years ago, Joseph Jacobs noted, "We shall have to go more minutely into the modus operandi of tradition" (1893:237). It would seem this note is long past due. Perhaps when folklorists have come to understand the modus operandi of tradition better than they do now, they will be closer to making tradition a concept with which they can truly think. Only then will folklore be able to claim to participate in the "science of tradition" that E. Sydney Hartland envisioned.

13. Generating Lives: The Life History of a Life History

In the 1970s and 1980s, a revolution occurred in the human sciences. The authority of grand theories that been rooted in the processes of history, the structure of society, and the structure of the human mind was undermined. In anthropology, folklore, and sociology, there was a realignment of focus to context, contingency, intention, meaning, and the inescapable messiness of social life. This revolution was not only directed at the theoretical paradigms but at the epistemologies of these disciplines. There arose a "crisis of representation"; a concern with not only how, but whether, social reality could be adequately represented (Marcus and Fischer 1986:8). Ethnography was not an effort of detached observation and objective documentation. It was a solitary and unverifiable experience shaped by the position of ethnographers both within and outside the societies they were endeavoring to represent. The very presence of the ethnographer, in fact, was a critical determinant of the life being observed and described. Yet in traditional ethnographies, this determinant of the social scene was almost entirely overlooked. Except for the occasional anecdote, the ethnographer remained almost entirely invisible. Furthermore, a culture or society was not a thing in the world, but the result of an act of writing. And what was written was the product of Western literary convention. The cultures depicted in ethnographies were not transparent representations of social life.

Two responses to this crisis were reflexivity and experimental writing. Ethnographers increasingly put themselves in the ethnographic picture observing, being observed, and observing themselves being observed while registering all these observations in their descriptions. They also attempted to break the conventions of ethnographic reportage by inventing new genres and even anti-genres (e.g., Lau 2002). Below is a reanalysis of a traditional life history as it was conceived and carried out at a time before ethnography was seriously interrogated. The reanalysis revives the interaction between informant and interviewer that was disguised in the original text, and displays some of the negotiations necessary to construct a text meant to represent a life.

> *When are you coming to see us?*
> *I am thinking of my life in terms of chapters now.*
> —Igor Slatz

"PERSONAL DOCUMENT" is a term scholars often use to designate those expressions that can throw light on lives of individuals and their worlds. Personal documents include autobiographies, diaries, letters, paintings, dream reports, and life histories. Life histories, however, unlike letters and diaries, are comprehensive and retrospective compositions. Unlike dream reports, the events and situations reported in life histories are recounted and entertained as actual and true occurrences. Unlike paintings, life histories are verbal and are sequentially structured. Unlike autobiographies, life histories are elicited by another person. They are not self-initiated or entirely self-actualized reports (Watson and Watson-Franke 1985:2). Of course, these categories overlap considerably. Dreams may appear in life histories and autobiographies, letters and diaries may involve lengthy retrospectives, and many autobiographies have been initiated by others.

This essay focuses on the life history of one individual. The life history is an unpublished, ninety-nine page, double-spaced, typewritten text compiled from five interviews conducted between 18 October and 20 December 1966. Each of the interviews lasted between one and one-and-a-half hours. The first four interviews were tape-recorded. The subject of the life history, Igor Slatz (a self-chosen pseudonym), was a twenty-three-year-old male graduate student. He was married, had no children, and lived with his wife in university student housing, where all but the fifth interview took place. The history begins with his birth in Chicago, outlines his early upbringing in a rural community in central Illinois, his high school years in Goshen, Indiana, his participation in a medical experiment at a hospital in Philadelphia, his employment at a mental hospital in lieu of military service, and concludes with his marriage and return to the university to complete his undergraduate and commence graduate study (which he was doing at the time the interviews took place). I have chosen to discuss this life history because I participated in all phases of its production. Furthermore, as a piece of work done decades ago when I was a beginning graduate student, I no longer feel defined by it. I believe I can discuss it dispassionately and without the feelings of exposure that might otherwise attend the discussion of more contemporary work.

As a cultural document, "A Life History of Igor Slatz," as it was titled (Oring 1966), is not particularly significant. It certainly does not measure up to the many rich and compelling documents published in the anthropological literature. Indeed, it is the product of some rather naïve notions of life history and curious conditions of research. However, I have chosen to discuss this life history, not for what we can learn about Igor Slatz, but more for what it might teach about the process of representing a life.

Considerable attention has been devoted to anthropological methodology—how ethnography should be conceptualized and carried out. Considerably less attention has been devoted to describing how it actually has been carried out. Ethnography is presently viewed less as a prescriptive program for controlled observation and recording than as occurrences of talking and writing. In other words, ethnography refers to and is itself communication. This perspective leads to a conceptualization of fieldwork as an engagement in dialogue, and ethnographic writing as a literary effort (Dwyer 1977; Clifford and Marcus 1986). Life history, therefore, is but one of the ethnological "genres." To understand anything about the life to which it purportedly refers, we must understand something of the life history's construction (Langness and Frank 1981:98). Yet very few researchers have written about the actual "doing" of life history (Plummer 1983:116). I hope what follows will contribute to this discussion.

The issues that are addressed in the construction of "A Life History of Igor Slatz" are: (1) the impetus that gave rise to this life history project, (2) the ideological ambience in which the project was framed, (3) the selection of the informant, (4) the interview, and (5) the editing of the text. The conclusion makes some general statements about the kinds of performances life histories seem to be.

The Impetus to Life History

The impetus to document the life history of Igor Slatz was an assignment in a graduate folklore fieldwork class in 1966. The major requirement for a grade in the class was the production of a written life history. Thus, the major force directing the production of this life history was a force from the outside. It originated neither with the "informant" nor with the "fieldworker." Had the professor not demanded a life history, it would never have come to be. This situation is perhaps idiosyncratic with respect to the life histories in the published literature. Nevertheless, in my own case at least, the completion of the life history project was in part a reflection of the instructor's power to make a student complete a life history project. As such, the life history of Igor Slatz was born, to some extent, in resistance. Not an absolute resistance, since the instructor's power derived from a particular social structure and value system to which I had voluntarily subscribed—the institution of the university. But the life history project engendered, at the very least, the kind of resistance that attends those activities conceptualized as *work*. To this extent, my life history was probably not idiosyncratic. I can only wonder about the possibly different nature of a life history composed in some non-work-defined frame—if such life histories exist.[1]

The compulsory aspect of the life history framed the project from its inception. My informant agreed to participate in what I explained to be the fulfillment of a course requirement. As a fellow graduate student, he understood and empathized with my situation. In fact, it was because he understood my situation as a fellow graduate student that he agreed to participate in the project in the first place. I am uncertain whether he would have agreed to participate so readily if I had merely expressed some vague personal interest in recording an account of his life.

In fact, in the first few minutes of the first taped interview, the informant clearly indicated that his responses were directed toward my needs. In response to a question about the town in which he was raised, he replied, "But just about everyone was connected with Block's [fertilizer and seed-corn company]. Well that's only about 200 people, but that was really the only industry in the town. *Let's see, what else do you want to know?*" [I/20, my emphasis].[2] Igor posed this question several times throughout the course of the interviews. Towards the end of this same interview, he asked what I was going to do with the taped material. When I explained that I had to transcribe the tape and type it up, he went on to express his disbelief over the scope and tedium of my assignment and commiserated with my situation [I/129–131]. Unfortunately, as he began this inquiry into the specific requirements of my project, I turned off the tape recorder since at that time I felt these questions and comments to be extraneous; irrelevant to the "data" I was gathering. Again, in the fourth interview, the informant concluded his comment on the disenchantment of his generation with the church with the disclaimer, "But that's beside the point, this isn't my interview" [IV/110]. In other words, throughout the interviews the informant was aware that his talk was to help me fulfill my assignment. This is not to say that the interviews were necessarily painful for him or that he gained nothing from talking about his life, but it seems that through the entire interview process he conceptualized the project as mine and not his.

An anthropologist or folklorist usually chooses to pursue a life history project. A life history project, on occasion, may be promoted by an informant (Strathern 1979:x). Yet the external constraints under which I labored were perhaps not so unusual. To what extent is the impetus to life history the explicit demand of a dissertation advisor, the implicit demand of a granting agency, or the logical demand of some ethnographic paradigm? To what extent does an informant comprehend these impetuses and commiserate with them? To what extent do informants identify what we call *their* life histories as *our* compulsory projects? Even when an impetus is explicit, its impact on the life history may be difficult to gauge. What are the effects of motivations that are not explicit, external, or formal demands, and how do these shape the life history? The answers to such questions are fundamental to the conceptualization of life history and to what one is actually doing when an attempt is made to produce it.

The Ideological Ambience

The life history project in which I was engaged was conditioned by the ideology of the academy and its various sub-disciplines. I believe the members of the fieldwork class were taught to view life history primarily as an ethnographic document and secondarily as a psychological one. Actually, I recall considerable uncertainty in the class as to what kinds of information we were supposed to be getting. The uncertainty some of the students felt about the nature of our life history assignment was succinctly characterized by one student who queried the professor as to whether we should be asking our informants, "How does one milk cows?" "How do you milk cows?" or "How do you feel about milking cows?" Nevertheless, the primary framework informing these life histories was the ethnological, and my own interview guide outlined areas of inquiry about the informant's childhood community in solid ethnological terms: its physical organization in space; its economic, religious, political, and educational institutions; the presence of minority populations; community cooperation and conflict; music, folklore, etc., as though I were preparing to do a study of a culture at a distance. Nevertheless, whether the basic orientation was ethnological or psychological, the shared orientation that was never questioned was that we were gathering *data* through the elicitation of a life history, and this data would relate to concepts of culture as well as personality. The individual's reported experiences—whether framed as cultural, psychological, emotional, or moral—were fundamentally *facts* for analysis and interpretation.

During the fieldwork and editing, all sorts of classroom discussion revolved around whether we were getting "good data" and whether we might formulate keener questions to elicit more data or to delve "deeper." Since our life histories were not informed by any hypothesis we were trying to invalidate, what constituted good data was never explicitly defined. It was clear, however, that good data were specific and detailed. We were to focus upon specific topics, and we were to ask specific questions (Maccoby and Maccoby 1954:456). We were to avoid asking the informant general "Why?" questions, because it would put the informant in the role of the analyst. That was supposed to be our job. The informant was to supply the data; we ethnologists would interpret it. In other words, scholars and scientists were to ultimately negotiate the meaning and significance of the life history materials. But the data had to be specific if there was to be any hope of performing productive analytic or synthetic operations.

In addition, "good data" often seemed to be of the kind that was hidden or difficult to obtain. While some data were on the surface and easily accessible, other data were "deeper" and accessible only through particular techniques. Some of these techniques—such as the use of euphemism, indirection, or face-saving phraseology— were designed to minimize ego defenses. Other techniques were meant to overpower these defenses, such as assuming the lowest valued behavior of informants and placing the burden of denial upon them (Maccoby and Maccoby 1954:457). An example that I find written in my course notebook is: "ASK: 'When was the last time you slept with a rabbit?' NOT: 'Do you sleep with rabbits?'"

I still recall an example provided by the instructor from his own field experience. As I remember it, he told us, how in driving from his village to the city, he picked up a hitchhiker who turned out to be a member of the national police. In the course of their conversation, the professor had no success in eliciting from this policeman any but the most positive descriptions of how the police treated those they arrested. Finally he asked the policeman, "Surely when you have a prisoner who is giving you a hard time and subjecting you to all kinds of abuse, you know how to handle him. After all, you guys are pretty tough yourselves." The policeman's response to this statement-question was, "Of course!"

Whether or not we subscribed to this particular technique, all in the class clearly understood that informants were the possessors of vast stores of information. Some of it they could articulate and would readily impart. Some they would divulge only in the face of the most sophisticated interrogative techniques. We were constantly made aware that there were secrets to be uncovered, and that it was our task to uncover them (Schwartz and Jacobs 1979:72). Perhaps the assumption that a good life history is in large part an effort to elicit secrets is itself a legacy of Augustine and Rousseau who characterized their personal histories as "confessions."[3]

In truth, many of the secrets we were charged to uncover were not deliberate concealments. Much simply lay beyond the everyday awareness of informants. Informants possessed important knowledge that they could only articulate if they were made aware of the fact that they possessed it. Our questions were often designed to encourage such awareness. Through judicious questioning, the informant's knowledge could be made explicit. On several occasions, the members of the class were directed to peruse sections of published life histories and segments of their own interview transcriptions and formulate further data-eliciting questions. The class never failed to generate a plethora of potential questions. Invariably, these questions asked the informants to think about their knowledge and behavior in new ways—to assume a different orientation and perspective toward the material provided in previous statements. The questions offered new structures for examining the familiar. It would seem that much of our task was to get our informants to talk about familiar topics in ways they never could or would if left to their own devices (Pelto 1970:95). It almost seems that our job was to "relativize" our informants—to make them into culturally and psychologically reflective beings. But, in the act of relativizing informants, in bringing them to a perspective above their culture and personality, the character of the informant is altered. The informant is no longer informing. Of course, such relativization is a characteristic of all interviewing (Briggs 1986:121-133), but its significance seems magnified when the ostensible object of research is the life of the informant rather than some abstract social institution. The ways that interviewers urge informants to talk about their lives profoundly alters the lives that they are documenting.

It does seem curious that once our class's life histories were edited and typed, we were never asked to perform any serious analysis or interpretation of them. With the composition of the final text, the assignment was over. The text itself was a document of what we had or had not accomplished. We had either captured the life of an individual, broadly and deeply, or we had not. The result, I imagine, was supposed to be self-evident. Of course, the absence of analysis was not a peculiarity of the life history projects of our class alone. Critiques of anthropological life history have repeatedly remarked on the absence of sustained analyses (Mandelbaum 1973:179; Frank 1979:71; Langness and Frank 1981:64). I shall return to this point.

The Selection of the Informant

On the first page of my notebook from my fieldwork course, immediately below the office hours of the professor, is a notation that we must "prepare a fieldwork project." Apparently, it was not clear at that early date that the project would be a life history. Immediately below the notation of the assignment I wrote, "The possibility of investigating the existence of 'beggar culture', traditions, social groupings, etc." In the back of that notebook are eight bibliographic references to beggars with Library of Congress call numbers that I clearly had gone out of my way to obtain. It is now difficult to recall what was going through my mind. I certainly had no experience with beggars, and it could not be said that I had any personal inclination towards beggars as a group. Perhaps this interest was influenced by then emerging trends in anthropology to conceptualize the study of American culture as the study of deviant groups within it, a characteristic of anthropological research in the United States for the past several decades (Varenne 1986:35; Caughey 1986:232; Plummer 1983:15). In any event, after the life history had been formulated by the professor as the fieldwork project in the class, I recall walking through the town center and seeing an older man sitting against a wall playing a banjo. Somewhere on his person, I believe, was a tin cup for monetary donations. I no longer recall whether he was blind or not. I still remember thinking to myself that here was my chance to make contact with an individual who could not only serve as the informant for my life history, but who also could potentially satisfy my curiosity, however superficial, as to the existence and character of beggar culture. I could not bring myself to approach this man, however. Something in me resisted the idea of approaching and developing a relationship with a man begging in the town square in order to fulfill a fieldwork assignment. I would like to think I was reluctant to make the acquaintance of someone just to use them as an informant, but I doubt that my disinclination was morally grounded. I am certain it was sheer cowardice. I simply was not ready to walk up to a total stranger—let alone one whom I had classified as somewhat deviant—and negotiate the relationship necessary for carrying out a life history project.

I can no longer recall what other potential candidates I considered for my life history. However, my failure to approach the banjo-playing beggar in the town square convinced me that if I were to complete my assignment on schedule, I would have to seriously attend to identifying an informant with whom I felt I could work. This realization led me to approach Igor. I had met Igor and his wife socially several months earlier and found them warm, outgoing, and humorous. They were people I liked and whose company I enjoyed. I wanted to get to know them better. I knew I would feel comfortable explaining my assignment to Igor, and I also felt I would enjoy hearing him talk about his life. In fact, I felt the experience of recording Igor's life history would help me to learn more about him and accelerate our developing friendship. Although it is not always the case, anthropologists frequently choose friends as the subjects of life histories.[4] In retrospect, however, it would seem that in the act of choosing Igor, I was willing to somewhat compromise the ideological aims of the fieldwork project to interests of sociability and friendship.

I recall feeling that there was an expectation that our informants would somehow be culturally exotic. I can no longer identify the cues that led to this feeling, but I do not believe it was explicitly stated as a fieldwork requirement. Nevertheless, I sensed that in selecting a university student, a born and bred American at that, I was not entirely fulfilling expectations of exoticism. In my estimation, however, Igor was to some extent exotic. Igor was raised a Mennonite and identified himself as one. Mennonites for me were a complete unknown. They were Christian, primarily rural, and pacifist. I was none of these.

I had come to the Midwest and graduate school from New York City. Despite New York's image of worldliness and sophistication, it can be a fairly provincial place in some respects. I, for example, upon being accepted at a midwestern state university, had to look up the state on a map to see exactly where it was in relation to New York. I seem to recall being surprised that I had to drive through Ohio to get there. I had thought Ohio to be further away. Despite New York's fantastic ethnic and cultural mix, I had been raised within a fairly delimited ethnic and religious environment. I was Jewish, my home was Jewish, my relatives were Jewish, my best friends were Jewish, and virtually all my formal affiliations were with Jewish institutions. I participated in "mainstream" American culture through books, newspapers, radio, television, theater, concerts, and phonograph records. Even the population of the municipal university I attended was largely Jewish. In fact, at my university graduation, a minister who was charged with giving the benediction blessed the graduating class in the name of "Our Lord and Savior Jesus Christ." When I commented to the friend sitting next to me, "Let us hope that God is a better sociologist," laughter emanated from two adjacent rows of complete strangers.

In coming to a large university in the American midwest, I sensed I would have to develop a new sociological and cultural awareness. The mechanisms of understanding and adaptation that had served me in New York would no longer prove entirely appropriate. I recognized that my own ethnic identity would have to be reexamined and to some extent renegotiated. In this frame of mind I entered my first semester of courses, including the one in fieldwork. In this frame of mind I chose Igor to be my informant. I cannot help but think now that this choice was in some sense an effort to see how another individual from an equally and perhaps even more parochial ethnic and religious background negotiated his identity in what was now our common world; an effort perhaps to see what and how I myself was doing.

Before closing this discussion on the selection of an informant, I should note that in one of our class meetings, we were instructed by the professor to describe to our fellow students something about our informants and how we had come to select them. One Chinese student, whose English was difficult to understand and who was still far from fluent, stood up and told the class how she had made the acquaintance of an old banjo player in the town square. She went on to complete her life history project with great success.

The Interview

Only after studying the transcripts of my interviews in preparing this essay did I come to realize how the ideology that I had absorbed in class became an object of negotiation between Igor and me. The ideology I had absorbed was that a life history was a discovery procedure—a program for eliciting data. Furthermore, I (and my "scientific colleagues") would be the final arbiters of the meaning or significance of that data. As I look back now, Igor seemed more cognizant of this program than I was myself. Consider the following exchange sequence early in the first interview:

> Q: Do you also have a younger sister?
> A: I have two younger sisters.
> Q: Two younger sisters and one older sister. And you were the only boy?
> A: Yup! No conclusions on that?
> Q: I don't draw conclusions, I just ask questions.
> A: All right, why the snicker [I/28–29]?

The above exchange all took place in the spirit of play, as clearly marked by the informant's laughter at its conclusion. But it also shows his acute perception of a threat—a perception that, in the context of creating a life history, the meanings of his circumstances and experiences might not remain within his control. In a world of events, having three sisters is a fact and not necessarily a sign. In an elicited life, in the context of the life history program, there were other possibilities. These other possibilities were highlighted by what I thought at the time to be a mere error-checking question, "You were the only boy?" At that moment he discerned that our programs were actually different. Igor, my willing and helpful friend and informant, suddenly appreciated the potential of his life as *object*. Paradoxically, for Igor to recognize that our interests diverged, he had first to conceptualize my interests and identify with them. Only then could he appreciate the extent to which he was not entirely in control of his recounted life. Who was to know what might be done with his facts and memories? What elaborate theory might be enlisted to impose some new meaning on his life's events? It would seem that in deliberately calling attention to the possible psychological ramifications of his all-female sibling set, Igor was reasserting control over the meaning of his life's events. After all, what could I see that he could not see himself? My insights were unlikely to be any more informed, compelling, or convincing than his own. In effect, Igor was co-opting the privilege of the academy to authoritatively ascribe significance. He was challenging my anthropological program and my exclusive claim to the position of observer and interpreter.

Later in this same interview, Igor described a scandal that had occurred in his small town when he was eight years old. He related how his mother took him aside to explain why boys shouldn't sleep together. Igor recalled not understanding what she meant. "I didn't understand it. . . . And that was the first clue that I got that you no longer crawl in the same bed with the same sex. . . . I knew what screwing meant. I knew that ever since I can remember anything. But I didn't make the connection at all with the homosexual activity; at least not consciously. It could be I repressed it" [I/133,136,137]. Here, Igor once again foregrounds potential psychological interpretations, but without the humorous frame. Interestingly, in highlighting the psychological construct of repression, Igor is offering to entertain the possibility of his latent homosexuality. What he seems unwilling to entertain, however, is the claim that I could understand his life in a way that he was incapable of understanding it.

In the second interview, this negotiation took a new turn. Igor had been talking about the pacifistic orientation of his Mennonite home, and he mentioned his mother's initial resistance to his joining the Boy Scouts. His mother, he said, felt the Boy Scouts were a form of socialization for the military. I then said, "You were a Boy Scout? . . . You see how things come out" [II/23–24]. Here I was joking about his being a Boy Scout by suggesting that his Boy Scout membership was a secret best kept hidden. This mild witticism is actually fairly complicated. It is based on the recognition of the propriety and wholesomeness of the Boy Scout image. For many people in the United States, Boy Scouts conjure up ideas of obedience, conformity, duty, charity, and an entire array of Victorian virtues symbolically at odds with the often revolutionary images projected by many university students in the 1960s. Of course, no normal, mature adult would truly be embarrassed by their childhood affiliation with the Boy Scouts. Thus, by saying to Igor, "You see how things come out," I was suggesting that my interview program was indeed capable of revealing deep, dark secrets. Of course, the message was clearly ironic. No real secrets had been revealed at all. In effect, therefore, I think I was reassuring Igor that no serious exposure was likely to occur in the course of our interviews, nothing more embarrassing or beyond his control than the revelation of his membership in the Boy Scouts, which of course was neither a revelation nor truly embarrassing.

By the third interview, we clearly had reached an accommodation on the issues of the discovery of secrets and the monopoly on authoritative interpretation. Igor was telling about the hospital where he served as a volunteer and described a psychiatric social worker who also was employed there. According to Igor, the social worker had the young volunteer staff in a real panic. At weekly staff meetings, he would challenge their motives for working in a mental hospital, question their mental stability, and contest their conceptualizations of their relationships with their parents. Igor claimed this social worker really frightened him:

> A: He scared the hell out of me. I didn't know what he was gonna say next. And there were some things I didn't want brought out in my past, you know, that I didn't want talked about, and I wasn't sure that he wasn't gonna talk about them.
> Q: Did I get those?

Again my comment was a joke, and laughter followed. But this joke was also an acknowledgment of Igor's privacy and my acquiescence to his control. My question, "Did I get those?" it would seem, signified that: (1) I had not been pursuing any of Igor's secrets, and (2) that if, in fact, he had told me any, I had not even recognized them. He would have to be the one to tell me which were his secrets; that is, he would have to tell me which of the events in his life he deemed so significant as to qualify for him as secrets. In effect, I was saying that, at least as far as our relationship during the interviews was concerned, he was the arbiter of his own life. I would not deliberately attempt to mislead him into revelations or ascribe meanings to events that he could or would not ascribe himself.

If I had acknowledged Igor to be the arbiter of his life in one sense, in another sense it was largely beyond his control. Perhaps the single most striking fact to emerge from a review of the transcripts of my interview tapes is that Igor's brief life story was the result of approximately 450 question-answer exchanges. In truth, these are only the exchange sequences that were recorded on tape and transcribed. In my last interview with Igor, I did not use a tape recorder, and although I still have the interview guide I employed, I have no recollection of how many supplementary, subsidiary, or tangential questions I asked. And there were all the things that were said when the tape recorder was turned off, or not yet turned on, as well. Therefore, 450 verbal stimuli were the very minimum number employed to elicit the material that came to shape Igor's life history. Actually these 450 exchanges could not accurately be called question-answer exchanges. Frequently my verbal input would not be a question, but some other type of comment, and a good number of Igor's responses were not answers to my questions. In fact, it is not even clear that they could all be called exchanges, as some of his responses did not proceed from my immediate questions or comments. However, I will continue to call them question-answer exchanges for the convenience of it all.

As might be expected, most of my questions could be categorized as requests for information about the informant's life. A full 67 percent of my comments were either requests for information, requests for clarifications, checks on information received, or efforts at channel maintenance. However, approximately 21 percent of my verbal utterances were comments on the informant's previous remarks. Another 4 percent were joking remarks, and 3 percent were what might be called meta-statements, which commented on the situation of the interview itself. (My utterances could often be assigned to more than a single category.)

Why so many questions? In American culture, there are few occasions in which individuals are permitted to talk about themselves for extended periods of time. Psychiatrists, anthropologists, folklorists, and perhaps fortune-tellers are among the primary providers of arenas for such protracted autobiographical discourse. My 450-plus verbal stimuli were probably necessary to sustain what would otherwise have proved a short and self-limiting monologue. Also, eliciting the life history had been defined as "work." I was being trained to ask questions. By asking questions, I was doing my job.[5]

My questions, however, were more than signals to the informant that he was permitted to continue, and they were more than the fulfillment of my role responsibilities. The "life" of Igor Slatz was determined by the questions I asked as much as by his experiences, his memories, or his narrative abilities. The shape of his life as represented by the life history text is as much a construction of mine as his (Freeman 1979:398). The questions I asked, even the questions that seemingly requested the recall of what one might consider "objective" information, defined, structured, and even interpreted the life history text (Dwyer 1982:214).

Below is a short sequence from the life history text in which the informant tells about listening to radio programs during his youth. The section includes a few bracketed words and phrases in the manuscript, indicating that the enclosed words were not the informant's own but added by the editor.

> There used to be a lot more programs on radio than there are now. Now its just music practically the whole time. But we used to listen to stuff life *Amos and Andy, Baby Snooks, The Great Gildersleeve, One Man's Family, Beulah.* We weren't supposed to listen to *Gunsmoke* or the *Cisco Kid.* I guess *Gunsmoke* wasn't on but *Cisco Kid* and *The Lone Ranger* [were] on. I got an old radio from my Grandpa, and I used to listen upstairs in my bedroom under the covers [to these programs] (Oring 1966:29).

This would appear to be a coherent and organized recollection. However, this recollection proceeded from the following exchanges:

> Q: What kind of radio programs did you used to listen to?
> A: There used to be a lot more programs on the radio than there are now. Now it's just music practically the whole time, but we used to listen to stuff like *Amos and Andy, Baby Snooks.*
> Q: [bursts out] *Baby Snooks,* oh good boy.
> A: *The Great Gildersleeve.*
> Q: *The Great Gildersleeve, Beulah?*
> A: *Beulah. One Man's Family.* Those national shows I guess everyone.... We weren't supposed to listen to *Gunsmoke* or *The Cisco Kid.* I guess *Gunsmoke* wasn't on but *Cisco Kid* and *The Lone Ranger* was on.
> Q: That's right, yeah.
> A: And we weren't supposed to listen to this sort of stuff.
> Q: Did you ever listen?
> A: Yeah, I got myself an old radio from my grandpa and I used to listen upstairs in my bedroom under the covers [II/38–42].

My initial question about the radio programs proceeded from Igor's comment that he and his sister used to fight about which radio programs they were going to listen to. When he began to mention specific programs, he managed to awaken memories of my own. *Baby Snooks* was one of my favorite radio programs as a child. Although I could recall almost nothing about the show itself, the reawakening of a fond, if vague, childhood memory provoked an enthusiastic, if unprofessional, outburst on my part (Plummer 1983:96; Titon 1980:276). Following the outburst, I managed to return to my life history program to find out whether he listened to Westerns like *The Cisco Kid* and *The Lone Ranger* despite the fact that their violent formats should have made them unacceptable entertainments in a good Mennonite home. In any event, it was my inspiration to ask about specific radio programs, my enthusiastic response to the mention of specific shows, and my concern as to whether he obeyed his parents that precipitated this almost classic description of an American youth growing up with radio in the 1950s.

As it is difficult to understand the "flow" of the informant's history without attending to the numerous questions that precipitate that history, it is often difficult to comprehend the "flow" of my questions without attending to the responses of the informant. For example, the following are a sequence of three questions that I asked in the course of the second taped interview:

> Q: Did they ever hunt for sport?
> Q: Are there Mennonite Negroes, Negro Mennonites?
> Q: When did you find out you were going to leave Septicville? [II/29–31].[6]

The logical connections between these questions are obscure, and one would have to imagine the use of some avant-garde interview guide to account for the sequence in this inquiry. Of course, the flow of the questions is directed by the flow of the responses as much as the flow of responses is directed by the flow of the questions. The first question was directed at Mennonite pacifism and its relationship to hunting or shooting animals. After telling me how he was allowed to shoot pests like rats and starlings, Igor then returned to our earlier discussion of the Boy Scouts. When he mentioned his Boy Scout troop, he mentioned that it was "integrated"—meaning that it included both Mennonites and Christian Apostolics. He then pointed out that it was not integrated in the sense of race. That triggered my next question about black Mennonites. In answering that question, he suggested there may have been a black Mennonite in his high school in Goshen, Indiana, which then led to my question about his leaving Septicville and moving to Goshen.

On one occasion [II/16], the informant enumerated a variety of his father's side occupations while he was minister of the Mennonite Church in Septicville. Often, Igor would aid him in these enterprises. At one time or another, they sold auto jacks to gas stations, raised geese, bred pedigree dogs, and raised rabbits. When Igor mentioned the rabbits I said, "Tell me about the rabbits." I asked this question not because of any desire to learn about raising rabbits. I was certainly no more interested in rabbits than I was in geese or dogs. The question was something of a joke. In John Steinbeck's novel *Of Mice and Men*, the character Lennie constantly badgers his companion George to tell him about the rabbits they were going to raise when they got a farm of their own. Lennie was a simpleton. Lennie liked rabbits because they were soft and cuddly. Perhaps I made this joke because I was beginning to feel like a simpleton asking all my questions. Perhaps I was merely trying to impress Igor, a student of American literature, with my ability to make literary allusions. Whatever my motive, Igor missed the reference and proceeded to tell me about how they raised, butchered, skinned, and sold rabbits. This description now holds some small place in his life history; selling auto jacks, breeding dogs, and raising geese do not.

Both interviewers and informants respond to each other and create new areas of inquiry and recollection. My questions were structures of meaning which stimulated recollection and demanded focused talk. Igor's talk created yet other areas of meaning which stimulated new questions. What we had was something of a *pas de deux* in which the interviewer and the informant were engaged. The life of Igor Slatz, as represented by the life history text, was based upon a recollection and verbalization of significant events—but that significance was rooted not in the nature of the events themselves nor in Igor's conceptualization of some life narrative or drama. The significance of the events was rooted, rather, in the relationship between his accessible memories and the emergent framework of the interview dialogue.

The Editing of the Text

"A Life History of Igor Slatz" is a constructed and edited text. Although the text is primarily composed from Igor's own words, insertions in the text, deletions from the interview responses, the total obliteration of the interview questions, and the frequent concatenation of responses from different parts of the interviews reflect significant editorial intervention. A greater part of this editorial process is not deducible from the text itself; it is nevertheless clear from the text that it is an edited one. Words inserted to increase readability and comprehension are enclosed in brackets. Brief responses to questions are turned into complete declarative statements. The text below represents a fragment of transcribed interview:

> Q: Did any farmers live in town or did they tend to live . . .
> A: No, they lived in their own, on their own, almost invariably in their own house on their farms.
> Q: Were there any differences, do you remember any differences between the kind of people who lived in town and the farmers?
> A: Yeah, I suppose. We were town boys, you know, and we never had anything to do after school. We would get together and play football or cops and robbers or something. The farmer boys always had to go home and milk [I/24–25].

These exchanges are represented by the following piece of edited text:

> [The farmers] lived almost invariably in their own house on their farms. I suppose [that there were differences between town and farm people]. We were town boys and we never had anything to do after school. We would get together and play football or cops and robbers or something. The farmer boys always had to go home and milk [Oring 1966:4].

Additions to the text are noted in brackets although deletions and ellipses are not noted. Occasionally, a phrase would be inserted with a question mark to indicate that I could not be completely certain if the addition was the intention of the informant. For example, "[It would be] about a forty minute talk. Sometimes he would go regularly through [the Bible?]" [II/20]. Even though it was quite clear to me that Igor meant the Bible, I included a question mark since neither he nor I had explicitly mentioned the Bible." When my constructions were even more tenuous, I attached two question marks to the bracketed phrase.

The order of the interviews was not followed exactly in editing the text. I felt free to concatenate materials that I felt belonged together. Overall, the structure of the life history text follows the order of the interviews. The text was divided into four chapters, and these chapters are largely congruent with areas covered in the four taped interviews. The fifth interview was not taped and was basically an interview designed to fill in what I perceived to be "gaps" in my record. I never completed asking the questions I had formulated for this fifth and last interview because I ran out of time. Those answers I did get were inserted into the text in their chronologically or topically "appropriate" positions.

It is not difficult to indicate in gross terms the mapping between the order of the interviews and the order of the edited text. There are five interviews labeled Roman numeral I through V respectively. The verbal exchanges within each interview were numbered sequentially with Arabic numerals. Thus, each chapter can be accurately indexed in terms of the interview sources from which they were derived.

Chapter 1: **I**: 1, 2, 3, 5, 6, 7, 9, 10, 11, 12, 13[8], 14, 15, **V:** 4, **I:** 17, 19, 20, 21, 22, 23, 24, 25, 26, 30, 31, 32, 34, 36, 37, 38, 39, 40, 42, 46, 47, 48, 50, 51, 52, 53, 56, 57, 58, 59, 60, 61, 62, 63, 66, 67, 68, 69, 70, 71, 72, 75, 76, 77, 79, 80[*], 82, 86, 87, 89, 91, 92, 94, 95, 96, 99, 100, 101, 102, 103, 104, 106, 107, 108, 109, 111, 113, 114, 115, 117, 118, 119, 126, 127, 132, 133, 135, 136, 137, 139,, 140, 142, 144, 145, 146, 147, 148, 149, 152, 153, 154, **II:** 10, 11, 13, 14, 15, 13, 17, 18, 20, 21, 22, 24, 25, 26, 27, 28, 29, **I:** 155, 156, **II:** 29, 30, 1, 2, 3, 4, 5, 6, 38, 39, 40, 44, 37, 45, 47, 48, 49, 50, 51, 52, 53, 54, 55, 57, 58, 59, 60, 31, 32, 33, 34, 35.

Chapter 2: **II:** 8, 61, 62, 63, 64, 65, 66, 67, 68, 69, 70, 72, 73, 75, 68, 75, 80, **V:** 1a, 1d, 1c, 1e, 1b, **II:** 80, 81.

Chapter 3: **II:** 80, **III:** 8, 14, 15, 14, 16, 17, 31, 32, 33, 34, 36, 37, 39, 18, 6, 7, 19, 20, 21, 22, 23, 24, 26, 27, 29, 30, **II:** 80, 81, **III:** 9, 10, 12, 41, 42, 43, 44, 45, 46, **II:** 81, **III:** 48, 47, 49, 50, 61, 62, 63, 64, **V:** 3, **III:** 67, 69, 81, 82, 74, 100, 75, 77, 78, 101, 102, 103, 104, 105, 106, 108, 109, 110, 111, 113, 114, 115, 116, 188, 119, [*], 120, 122, 132, 80, 86, 87, 90, 93, 95, 96, 97, **IV:** 5, 6.

Chapter 4: **IV:** 12, 13, 14, 15, 16, 20, 23, 24, 25, 18, 31, 33, 34, 46, 55, 56, 57, 58, 60, 61, 62, 63, 64, 67, 70, 84, 85, 87, 89, 91, 93, 67, 70, 71, 72, 73, 75, 77, 78, 79, 80, 82, 83, 95, 96, 97, 98, 99, 100, 101, 102, 103, 104, 105, 108, 110, 111, 114, 115, 114, 116, 119, 120, 131, 133, 134, 136, 122, 126, 127, 128, 129, 136, 137, 138, 141, 142, 144, 146, 148, 149, **II:** 76, 78, 79, **IV:** 152, 154, 156, 157, 160, 161, 162, 163, 164, 166, 167, 171, 173, 175, 176, **II:** 75.

Despite a general adherence to the sequence of the interviews, it is clear that the maintenance of this order was not a goal in and of itself, for I abandoned the interview sequence far too often. The extent to which the edited text follows the order of the interviews is primarily the extent to which my interview questions imposed a chronological organization on Igor's responses.

My editing procedures lead me to a couple of general observations: I never made any attempt to go beyond the interviews in creating Igor's life history. The information from which the history was composed was drawn exclusively from the domain of discourse explicitly framed as "interview." No effort was ever made to gather other materials from family or friends. During the period of the life history project, I spoke to the informant on numerous occasions for great lengths of time about all manner of things, but none of these conversations found their way into the life history. Even in the interviews, only the explicit verbalizations within the interview context were considered. Postures, grimaces, and gestures were ignored. Even the laughter that occurred during the interviews and was clearly noted throughout the transcriptions is nowhere indicated in the life history text. It is as though we understood that the history would be composed from materials that we both were specially noticing at the same time. This focus may have been the consequence of our surreptitious negotiation about privacy and authority, which I described earlier, but it is my impression that in composing life histories, many anthropologists and folklorists also respect the boundary of the interview frame.

Although the folklorist is committed to an accurate representation of an informant's words, in the life history these words must be made readable and comprehensible. Insertions, deletions, and transpositions seemed preferable to a difficult text. Such editing is directed toward servicing the reader at the expense of the informant. In other words, the access of the reader to the text takes precedence over the precise and accurate representation of the interviews. While it is necessary to consider the influence of the potential reader on the shape of life history, I do not think editing is simply an accommodation of the reader. I believe the editorial process is intended to serve the informant as well. It intensifies the focus and impact of the informant's spoken words. The editing process is meant to create a frame for the conceptualization of and empathy with a life. It is by no means clear that the most careful transcription of interviews can achieve these ends. Lives are not transcriptions of events. They are artful and enduring symbolic constructions which demand our engagement and identification. They are to be perceived and understood as wholes. They are texts.

The structure of these texts is not the structure of the informant's memories, nor is it the structure of the interview in which these memories are recalled. It is, rather, the structure of history. History is a chronological conceptualization of events and experiences. History is but one of our paradigms of coherence.[7] A text demands organization and coherence even when a life does not. And it is only to the extent that we can conceive of life as organized and somewhat coherent that we can even begin to conceive of a life at all. Life history, therefore, is not merely one of the genres of literature; it is one of the genres of self. To even say that there lived an Igor Slatz at all, one must move from transcription to inscription of an historical or some other kind of coherent text (Clifford 1986:113).

Reflections

All in all, it would appear that "A Life History of Igor Slatz" is an ethnological/psychological document of questionable value. It would seem that I shaped this history as much as did Igor. It would be convenient if we could attribute the problems of this life history to the naïveté and ineptitude of student fieldworkers but we cannot. While some of the problems with the life history of Igor Slatz are perhaps flagrant, they are not in any sense unusual (Brandes 1979). Perhaps they appear flagrant only because we are rarely shown the process by which life history, or any type of ethnography for that matter, is actually accomplished. The accounts regularly contained in anthropological and folkloric monographs are metaphors of and not descriptions of fieldwork (Pratt 1986:27–50). The involvement of the fieldworker in a life history is deep and unavoidable. And this involvement cannot be merely dismissed as "interview error" or "bias" (Maccoby and Maccoby 1954:103–104). A "life" is not an entity that good fieldworkers, with a minimum of interference and distortion, extract from helpful informants. "The story of a life is not a *fait accompli* of consciousness but is a form that emerges in discourse" and in the composition of a written text (Frank 1979:86).

If life history is something that emerges in talk between people, it would seem that this talk needs to be preserved as fully and accurately as possible. Perhaps life history should attempt to be no more than a transcription of dialogue. Certainly this position is advocated by anthropologists of widely different generations and theoretical persuasions (Kluckhohn 1945:97; Dwyer 1982:xxii). To the extent that the original talk of an informant is provoked, abridged, transposed, and recombined in life history, we are removed from the informants' subjective image of their own lives (Brandes 1979:9). Thus, the original words, syntax, questions, repetitions, digressions, tones, postures and gestures must be preserved if we hope to penetrate to the individuals behind the talk. Furthermore, some anthropologists feel the dialogue of the ethnographer and informant needs to be preserved if we are to come to an awareness of the human relationships upon which ethnography is founded (Crapanzano 1980:11; Dwyer 1982:278).

But if it is recognized that a life history does not represent *the* story of *the* life of *an* individual, why has it been so prominent in the ethnological armamentarium? Why must some scholars *push* for the publication of such transcriptions and dialogues in their stead? It would seem that the answers to these questions depend upon what, if anything, life history achieves as a genre; as a literary, if not a scientific, enterprise.

It seems to me that life histories attempt to create *voice* (Lewis 1970:xiv; Plummer 1983:1). Life history is constructed in such a way that we must necessarily confront our informants' speech as communication before we can reduce it to mere data. In other words, the informant is granted the same privilege that we grant ourselves—the privilege to speak through coherent and authoritative texts. As texts, life histories are articulate, controlled, and compelling communications, and they rival other modes of ethnological discourse in scope, depth, and authority.[8] I believe this commanding voice of the informant establishes what has been called the "self-evidence" of the life history text (Frank 1979:72; Plummer 1983:119).

In the transcription of an interview, an informant's voice is mainly reactive. Numerous questions invoke a voice and at the same time fragment it. Its authority is undermined by its pauses, false starts, digressions, mishearings, and misunderstandings. While a transcription of an interview may seem preferable as data, it cannot serve as an adequate representation of voice. Voice is more than an accumulation of words. This essay is not some unedited account of my confrontation with the topic of life history. It is not a chronicle of my thoughts, feelings, and behaviors over a period of time. It is, rather, a severely censored, highly edited, repeatedly restructured communication. It represents a voice. In that sense, it is as much a life history text as the life history text it purportedly describes.

It seems that voice is what we attempt to create with life history. It seems unfair to represent our informants by a mere transcription of their words. In life histories, others are given voices and are permitted to speak to us as persons. To speak to us, these voices must have the same presence, coherence, and authority we imagine our own voices to have. To achieve such effects, ethnographers must in great measure disguise (at least at the surface) their own creative involvement in the text.

Of course I am not suggesting that we must eschew alternative or more avant-garde means of representing lives. Such representations, however, simply enact alternative genres; they are not inherently better. It is by no means clear that the alienated modern novel supersedes the *Bildungsroman*, for example (Crapanzano 1977:7). There is no reason to abandon one genre for the other when both seem capable of holding our interest.

The past reluctance to analyze life history, it seems to me, has been a result of three interrelated factors. First, ethnographers' sense of their own dramatic participation in the construction of the text made them wary of analyzing it as the unadulterated expression of an individual or the representation of a culture. Second, life history is first and foremost a product of synthesis. As such, life history stands opposed to analysis. As analytic efforts involve refiguring life history as *data*, they vitiate the generic motivation of creating a voice allowed to speak without interruption. Finally, to the extent that an authoritative voice has been successfully created in a life history, an analyst is at risk of commenting less significantly about a text that already appears coherent, compelling, authoritative, and full of significance (Plummer 1983:17).

One of life history's central purposes was defined some time ago. Life histories were to remind us of the human subjects that lurk behind ethnological objects (Mandelbaum 1973:177; Georges and Jones 1980). They were to reveal that behind such constructs as modal personality, agnatic lineage, and mother's brother, there exist *people* who have something to say to us (Jay 1974). For people to have something to say, we must have more than their words. Their words must be articulated in a voice we can understand and with which we can identify (Pascal 1960:8). The people whom the ethnographer has come to know in the world must somehow be reconstituted as persons in text. Life history, therefore, is one of the prominent performances of such personhood in our culture.

14. Victor Turner, Sigmund Freud, and the Return of the Repressed

In the early twentieth century, Sigmund Freud profoundly changed the way folklore was understood. Folklore was made up of symbols. The figures, objects, and episodes of folklore did not correspond to realities in the outer world but represented inner psychic dispositions. Myths and folktales were like dreams, and they could be interpreted in a similar manner. A number of psychoanalysts and folklorists produced provocative interpretations of narratives, superstitions, and rituals (Rank 1952 [1909]; E. Jones 1964; Dundes and Falassi 1975; Dundes 1984). Even Freud made his own small contributions to the enterprise (Freud 1958 [1913], 12:281–287; 1958 [1911], 12:177–203).

One of the problems with such interpretations is that they depend upon the acceptance of an array of psychological processes and conditions posited by psychoanalysis as universal: repression, projection, identification, displacement, Oedipus complex, anal-eroticism, penis envy, castration anxiety, and so on. As the applicability of this metapsychology came to be questioned, especially in non-Western cultures, psycho-symbolic interpretation languished. In the 1960s, Victor Turner (1920–1983) generated considerable excitement among anthropologists and folklorists with his studies of African ritual symbols. Turner's interpretations were rich, subtle, and linked to the specific culture that he was studying. He proposed a general method for the interpretation of symbols in society. Later in his career, he acknowledged that his approach owed something to Freud's style of interpretation.

Symbolic interpretations can be found in a number of the essays in this volume. The meanings that are proposed, like Turner's, are largely social. Folklore is usually considered to be an expression by a group, for the group, and about the group. However, interpretations of folklore linked to individual psyches have their place as well (e.g., Burns with Burns 1976; Oring 1984; Jones 1989).

> *Perhaps we would be wise to reread*
> The Interpretation of Dreams.
> —Melford Spiro

FIVE YEARS BEFORE his death, Victor Turner published an essay titled "Encounter with Freud: The Making of a Comparative Symbologist" (Turner 1978). In this essay, Turner states that it was during his fieldwork among the Ndembu in Northwest Zambia in mid-1953 (then Northern Rhodesia), that he "rediscovered" the works of Sigmund Freud which opened his eyes to many of the properties of Ndembu ritual symbolism. Yet Freud's work, Turner stated, was more of an inspiration than a direct influence: "I consider my encounter with Freud's work, particularly *The Interpretation of Dreams*, to have been decisive in arriving at an independent theoretical position. It was his *style* of thinking and working which gave me encouragement rather than his actual inventory of concepts and hypotheses" (1978:582).

Turner's little essay is curious on a number of counts. First, Freud does not figure at all in Turner's writings on symbolism in the 1950s. Only later, as Turner began to formulate and reformulate his approach to the analysis and interpretation of ritual symbols, is Freud mentioned. Even then, the references are spare and, for the most part, tangential. In *The Forest of Symbols: Aspects of Ndembu Ritual* (1967), a collection of ten essays, nine of which had been previously published, there is only a single mention of Freud (37). Indeed, none of Freud's works are cited in the bibliographies of any of the ten essays in the volume.[1]

Freud is just as sparingly cited in the rest of Turner's writings, and when Freud or psychoanalysis is referred to in the body of the text, it is usually to register some limitation or problem with the approach (Turner 1968:21–22). For example, Turner criticizes psychoanalysis for dismissing native commentaries on rituals as mere rationalizations and for universalizing findings that derive solely from Western European clinical practice. He dismisses a psychoanalysis of ritual symbols which assumes that ritual symbols have "the same properties of dream symbols" (1967:34). In fact, while discussing Freud, Turner actually warns against the "crude interpretation of cultural symbols by psychoanalytic concepts" (Turner 1975:30).

A second curious aspect of Turner's "Encounter with Freud" essay is that the concepts that he claims to derive from Freud—wish fulfillment (1978:565), repression (576), compromise formation (1967:37), sublimation (1978:574) projection (1978:579), and ambivalence (1978:579)—are rather specific. Their application, even to novel ethnographic materials, betrays an indebtedness to more than a mere "style" of thought. It is difficult to see how Turner could claim that he was "not basing [his] analysis on Freud's system, but rather using certain of his concepts analogously and metaphorically" (Turner 1975:576).

Turner's highlighting *The Interpretation of Dreams* as critical to the formation of his own perspective also seems odd. A number of the psychoanalytic ideas cited by Turner find little or no place in that work. While the "multivocality" of dream symbols, wish fulfillment, compromise formation, and repression are certainly emphasized by Freud in his study of dreams, sublimation and projection are not mentioned at all, and ambivalence barely in passing (Freud 1953 [1900], 5:431). Rather, these last three concepts are developed elsewhere in Freud's work.[2]

Finally, it is strange that Turner should only turn to a serious consideration of his indebtedness to Freud in 1978.[3] Turner characterized his first rediscovery of Freud during his 1953 fieldwork in Zambia as following "about twenty years' latency period!" (1978:573). It would seem that another latency period of twenty-five years would elapse before he would bring himself to confront Freud's role in the development of his own theoretical approach to religious symbols. A latency period is, after all, a period in which intense repression brings about an amnesia (Freud 1953 [1900], 5:521). What then was Turner repressing? Exactly what had he forgotten?[4]

There is more here than meets the eye. There are too many questions that serve to undermine Turner's characterization of Freud's role in the formation of his own theoretical approach. I would suggest that a closer inspection of the relations between Victor Turner's work on symbolism and Sigmund Freud's own psychoanalytic approach is warranted.

Turner's contributions to the study of ritual symbolism are threefold. Of course, there are his extraordinarily rich and detailed descriptions of Ndembu ritual symbolism and behavior. Without doubt, Turner's fieldwork established new standards in the ethnography of ritual practices. Turner did not merely describe Ndembu symbolism, however; he also offered trenchant interpretations of that symbolism. He was concerned to demonstrate the relationships of Ndembu symbolism to the structure of their society and the substance of their thought. In effecting these interpretations, however, Turner was led to articulate a *hermeneutic* of ritual symbols—that is, a generic interpretive method applicable to symbols whenever and wherever they might be found. This hermeneutic has been regarded as Turner's most significant contribution to the anthropological discourse on symbols (Manning 1990:172), but it is this hermeneutic, I would also argue, that is most directly influenced by Freud's own symbolic approach.

Turner has outlined his hermeneutic in any number of books and essays (e.g., 1966; 1967; 1969a; 1976), but perhaps most succinctly in "Symbols in African Ritual" first published in *Science* in 1973 and widely anthologized thereafter (Dolgin, Kemnitzer and Schneider 1977; Freilich 1983; Lehmann and Myers 1985; Appelbaum 1987). In the essay, Turner sets out his notion of a ritual symbol's semantic structure—that is, the ways meanings are encoded in ritual symbols—and the process for unraveling those meanings. Ritual symbols, according to Turner, are so constructed that: (1) they have multiple meanings (significata, referents); (2) there is a unification of apparently disparate significata in the symbol that are connected by analogies and chains of association; (3) there is a tremendous condensation of objects, actions, and relations in the symbol which are simultaneously represented; and (4) there is a polarization of significata in that the referents tend to concentrate around opposite poles. Social and moral ideas constitute an "ideological" or "normative" pole of symbolic meaning while concrete objects and processes that excite the emotions constitute a "sensory" or "orectic" pole of meaning. Thus, the Ndembu *mudyi* or milk tree symbolizes breast milk and the mother's breast at the sensory pole of meaning, but it also symbolizes motherhood, womanhood, and the mother-child bond at the ideological pole of meaning (1973:1100). All in all, ritual symbols, are dense, multi-layered expressions with both cognitive and affective dimensions that cannot be reduced to any single level of meaning.

Undoubtedly there are many who would see in Turner's conceptualization of the ritual symbol a dramatic advance over Freud's psychoanalytic symbolism with its single level of meaning—invariably sexual—which remains constant in dream, myth, and folklore through time and across cultures (Freud 1953 [1900], 5:351). But this notion of symbol was only one small part of Freud's theory of symbolism. In fact, this notion of the symbol had no place in the first edition of *The Interpretation of Dreams*. The material on symbolism was added only in the 1909 and 1911 editions of the work (5:350n).

Of course, many have employed Freud's roster of unvarying sexual symbols to decode dreams, rituals, and folklore. Freud, however, remained highly skeptical of such interpretations. He explicitly warned against "over-estimating the importance of symbols in dream interpretation" (Freud 1953 [1900], 5:359–360), and he found many symbolic interpretations to be "scientifically untrustworthy" (350). In fact, the very title *The Interpretation of Dreams* [*Die Traumdeutung*] was intended by Freud as a sarcastic allusion to ancient divinatory manuals and those popular dream books sold at carnivals and fairs that offered readers such symbolic interpretations.[5]

Symbols with unvarying sexual referents were only one kind of symbol for Freud, and he devoted only 55 of 627 pages in *The Interpretation of Dreams* to this kind of symbolism. These kinds of symbols were definitely secondary to the other kinds of symbols that appeared in dreams and for which he had formulated a lengthy and complicated interpretive procedure. One of the reasons the invariant symbols assumed such prominence in popular, and even scholarly, notions of Freudian symbolism is that Freud reserved for this type of symbolism the term "*Symbolik*" [symbolism]. But Freud was more concerned with what he labeled *Vorstellungen* [ideas] or *Darstellungen* [representations]. *Vorstellungen* and *Darstellungen* were symbols whose relations to their referents were variable. They were highly condensed representations linked to their underlying thoughts through highly complex and idiosyncratic chains of association. They could never be mechanically translated. Each symbol could only be interpreted in the context of the dreamer's experiences and recollections.

This concept of the symbol is a lot closer to that of Turner's, and I would argue that Turner's concept of the ritual symbol derives directly from it. Even Turner's terminology often reflects standard English translations of Freud's nomenclature. That dream symbols can have multiple meanings is an axiom of Freud's (Freud 1953 [1900], 4:149, 279, 283–284). These meanings, however, are in large part distorted through the process of "condensation" [*Verdichtung*] (1953 [1900], 4:284), the very term employed by Turner. In Freud's "Dream of the Botanical Monograph," the image of the botanical monograph is linked to Freud's own monograph on the plant coca; to Dr. Königstein who introduced cocaine in ophthalmic surgery; to the figure of Professor Gärtner [gardener]; to the "blooming looks" of Gärtner's wife; to the favorite flowers of Freud's wife; and to artichokes, which Freud jokingly referred to as his own "favorite flowers" (4:170–172). Thus, the botanical monograph is a highly condensed image in which numerous trains of thought converge.

Turner's notion that there is a "unification of apparently disparate significata" in ritual symbols also can be found in Freud. Thus, the similarity of two different persons may be represented in a dream by representing only one of the persons but placing him in situations and circumstances that are characteristic of the second. The similarity may also be represented by combining elements that are unique to each of the individuals in a composite figure. In Freud's terminology, both are forms of "unification" which is a type of condensation (Freud 1953 [1900], 4:320–321).[6]

Turner mysteriously attributes his use of the term "condensation" to Edward Sapir's essay on symbolism (1934 14:492–495) rather than Freud's *The Interpretation of Dreams* (Turner 1967:29). Considering the extensive discussion by Freud of "condensation," it is a striking instance of Turner's amnesia. "Unification," however, appears only in Freud; it does not appear in Sapir's essay.

The significata unified in a single symbol might be so disparate as to prove contradictory according to Turner (1973:1101). Thus, the *mukula* or blood tree which secretes a red gum can, in Ndembu ritual, represent the blood caused by violence as well as the blood that accompanies the birth of a child. It can, in other words, symbolize both life and death (Turner 1967:40–41). Freud also asserted that dream images could represent diametrically opposed thoughts.

Dreams, Freud noted, "show a particular preference for combining contraries into a unity or for representing them as one and the same thing" (Freud 1953 [1900], 4:318). Thus, in "The Language of Flowers" dream, a woman dreams she is holding a blossoming branch of red flowers. On the one hand, associations to this image—the figure of an angel holding a spray of lilies in paintings of the Annunciation, and white-robed girls in Corpus Christi processions—refer to *sexual innocence*. On the other, the red flowers refer to menstruation and *La dame aux camelias* (who wore a camellia to indicate when she was sexually available) and signify the contrary idea of *sexual sinfulness* (4:319).

If there is no equivalent in Freud's terminology to the sensory and ideological "polarization of significata" of a symbol, the concept is clear enough. Interpreting the dream of a girl in which her brother promised to give her a feast of caviar but whose legs were covered all over with black grains of caviar, Freud remarked: "The element of '*contagion*' (in the moral sense) and a recollection of a *rash* in her childhood, which covered her legs all over with *red* spots, instead of black ones, had been combined with the *grains of caviare* into a new concept—namely the concept of '*what she had got from her brother.*'" In this example, the polarization of the sensory referent—the rash—and the ideological referent—the moral pollution—is made abundantly clear (Freud 1953 [1900], 4:325). In the interpretation of "A Dream of Bismarck's," the action of seizing his whip and striking the rock before him refers, on one level, to Bismarck's attempt to liberate an ungrateful people, but on another level it refers to the act of masturbation (5:378–381). In yet another dream, diving into water represents not only the physical act of birth but spiritual rebirth as well (5:400).

Those who hold a narrow view of Freud's symbolism invariably believe that he was only concerned with the sensory pole of symbolic meaning: knives, daggers, and pikes symbolize the penis; boxes, cases, and chests—the uterus; and so forth (1953 [1900], 5:354). Turner goes to some length to distinguish the anthropological from the psychoanalytic approach to symbolism on the basis of the latter's total neglect of the ideological pole of meaning (1967:36–37). While it is true that Freud was concerned to demonstrate the coarse sexual thoughts underlying seemingly innocent dreams, he recognized that many dreams satisfied other than gross erotic desires (Freud 1953 [1900], 5:396). Many dream representations have referents that cluster around the ideological pole: a broken bone may represent a broken marriage (5:409); right and left in dreams may be understood in an ethical sense; luggage can refer to the burden of sin (5:357–358); infanticide may represent the failure to conceive a child (1953 [1900], 4:155–156); the top floor of a building may signify superior social position (4:287). The ideological pole of meaning which Turner highlights in his own interpretations of Ndembu symbols was well recognized by Freud in the dreams of his middle-class Viennese patients.[7]

Underlying ritual symbols and their significata are to be found, according to Turner, dynamic affirmations and cultural themes—Morris Opler's terms for the declared or tacit postulates and ideas that control activity and stimulate behavior in a society and which are the keys to its "character, structure, and direction" (Turner 1973:1100–1101). Ultimately, it is the task of the anthropologist to lay bare the affirmations and themes of a society through the judicious interpretation of its ritual symbols.[8] So the ritual symbol for Turner has a tripartite structure; the symbol; its significata; and the underlying cultural themes (although on occasion there may be a conflation of significata and themes, since themes might be significata [1100–1101]).

This tripartite structure is precisely mirrored in Freud. In his view, there is the "manifest content" [*manifeste Trauminhalt*] of the dream; that is, the objects, actions, settings, and words that appear in the dream and are retained in memory; the "latent content" [*latente Trauminhalt*] of the dream, the unconscious referents of the manifest content; and the "dream thoughts" [*Traumgedanken*], the unconscious thoughts which motivate the dream (Freud 1953 [1900], 4:277). Like Turner, Freud conflates the latent contents and the dream thoughts, but it is quite easy to distinguish the two levels; the latent contents are the referents of the symbol; the thought, however, is a proposition that underlies the range of symbols in the dream and is ultimately congruent with the wish. Thus, in Freud's "Non Vixit" dream the phrase "*non vixit*" ["he did not live"] was part of the manifest content of the dream but referred to an inscription on the Kaiser Josef memorial—its latent content. The dream thought, however, was that Freud's friend, to whom he applied the phrase, deserved a memorial for his contributions to science (Freud 1953 [1900], 5:423–424). The dream thought is an articulated expression, not merely a specific referent.

Given the virtually homologous conceptualization of the semantic structure of the symbol by Turner and Freud, it was inevitable that their interpretive methodologies would also prove substantially similar. In Turner's scheme, the interpreter must confront a symbol in its exegetic, operational, and positional dimensions. The exegetic dimension consists of the explanations that actors in the ritual system give the anthropological investigator. Thus, in the Ndembu *Isoma* ritual, informants explain the name of the ritual as deriving from *ku-kosoma,* meaning to "slip out of place." The slipping out of place seems to relate to the condition the ritual is designed to cure, which is repeated miscarriage. The child is thought to "slip out" before it is ready to be born. *Ku-kosoma* is also explained by the Ndembu as meaning "to leave one's group" which Turner relates in his interpretation of the ritual to the forgetting of matrilineal attachments (Turner 1969b:15–16).

Of course, in Freud's decipherings of dreams, exegetic commentaries were absolutely crucial and interpretation could scarcely proceed without them. Wrote Freud, "We are not in general in a position to interpret another person's dream unless he is prepared to communicate to us the unconscious thoughts that lie behind its content" (1953 [1900], 4:241).[9] These unconscious thoughts are communicated by the dreamer through his "associations" [*Assoziationen*] to the content of the dream. A dreamer is obligated to communicate every idea or thought that occurs in connection with the subject matter of a dream, suppressing no thought, no matter how trivial or meaningless (4:101). Associations are properly elicited with respect to the details of a dream rather than for the dream as a whole (4:103), much as one might ask a Ndembu the meaning of a ritual's name or the significance of some ritual medicine. Free association was the method Freud devised to decode dreams. It was Freud, therefore, who first explored what Turner has called "the exegetic dimension" of symbols, and who transformed the rote character of dream interpretation that had been inherited from ancient times (4:98–100).

The operational dimension of a symbol refers to the meanings communicated in the way a symbol is used, the relations that are organized around it, and the behavioral and accompanying emotional responses that it elicits. Freud, of course, saw in the use of a symbol a clue to its significance. The use might refer to the disposition of an object in the dream itself, or the use of something in real life. Thus, in Freud's "Open Air Closet" dream, the feces he encounters covering the seat of the outhouse produces no sense of disgust, but he cleanses the feces from the seat with a stream of his own urine. The reference is to the cleansing of the Augean stables by Hercules and to Freud's wish to be assured of his own greatness after a day in which he felt his psychoanalytic endeavors had been of little or no value (Freud 1953 [1900], 5:468–471).

In *The Psychopathology of Everyday Life*, where Freud addresses the symbolic significance of ritual behaviors rather than dream images, his attention to the operational dimension of a symbol can be even more clearly discerned. A man occupied a subordinate position at a particular institution where the front door was kept locked. Consequently, he was always forced to ring the bell to gain admission to the premises. On a number of occasions, however, he found himself trying to open the door with his own house key. The behavior, Freud noted, expressed the desire to have a key as did the members of the institution and to feel as though he were "at home" there (Freud 1960 [1901], 6:164). Here it is the place and the manner in which the key is employed—its operational dimension—that reveals its underlying meaning.

The positional dimension of a symbol's meaning, according to Turner, is discerned by considering the position of an object or activity in relation to an assemblage of objects and activities. Such relations tend to highlight one of a symbol's potential meanings. Thus, in Ndembu girls' puberty ceremonies, the grass hut constructed for the novice has a frame whose principle laths are made from both the *mudyi* (milk tree) and the *mukula* (blood tree). Although the *mudyi* and *mukula* have a broad range of meanings within the Ndembu ritual system, when opposed to one another in the context of the puberty ceremonies, the *mudyi* represents the girl and the *mukula* the groom whom she will marry after the ceremonies are completed (Turner 1973:1101–1102).

The binary oppositions of Claude Lévi-Strauss are the strongest influence in Turner's conceptualization of the positional dimension of the symbol (Turner 1969a:12–13; 1973:1101). Nevertheless, Freud also considered the relation of symbols to one another. Statements about the meaning of particular dream elements could "carry conviction only if ... treated in the context of the interpretation of the dream as a whole" (Freud 1953 [1900], 5:405). In one dream reported by Freud, a young unmarried man imagined being seated with his companions in a restaurant as several people appeared to arrest him. He told his companions he would be back but they dismissed him with, "That's what they all say." When he left, one of his table companions called out, "There goes another one." He was taken to a room in which a woman sat holding a child. He was introduced to the police inspector as Herr Müller and the inspector thumbed through a bunch of cards repeating the name, "Müller, Müller, Müller." The inspector finally asked the dreamer a question to which the dreamer responded, "I will."

Freud interpreted this dream as a fantasy of marriage. Being called away from his companions who express skepticism at his return, being called to a room with a woman carrying a child, and uttering the phrase "I will" to the official's question *conspire* in an allusion to marriage. Even the official's thumbing through cards and repeating the dreamer's name resembles the reading of the bundles of cards and telegrams at wedding festivities which are all addressed to the same name. The notion that he was being arrested referred to the qualms that the young man felt about marriage; the idea of losing his freedom (1953 [1900], 5:494–495). Freud never actually analyzed this dream. He noted it down sketchily and had no occasion to elicit associations from the dreamer. His interpretation depends almost entirely upon examining the various components of the dream in their relations to one another.

Again, the positional dimension was emphasized in Freud's famous interpretation of an instance of forgetting a quotation from

Virgil's *Aeneid*. The word forgotten was the indefinite pronoun "*aliquis.*"[10] Freud extracted a chain of associations to the word from the forgetter which ran from "liquid" [*Liquid*] and "relics" ["*Reliquien*"], saints, and blood libels, to the liquefaction of the blood of St. Janarius on a given holy day and the commotion of the people if the miracle failed to occur on schedule. Freud argued: "*The calendar saints, the blood that starts to flow on a particular day, the disturbance that takes place when the event fails to take place ... [is] a brilliant allusion to women's periods*" (Freud 1960 [1901], 6:8–11). The allusion to women's periods can only be deduced, however, if the associations to *aliquis* are considered in relation to one another—that is, positionally.[11]

The meaning of a symbol, according to Turner, is constructed by analogy and association on three foundations; the nominal, the substantial, and the artifactual. In other words, in establishing symbolic meaning an investigator must attend to the name of the symbol, to the physical properties of the symbol, and to the way the symbol is transformed in the course of a ritual. Turner illustrates these distinctions with the medicine of *undumila* employed by the Nyakusa of Tanzania in girls' puberty ceremonies. The nominal basis of *undumila* is its derivation from the word *ukulumila*, meaning to "bite or be painful." The substantial basis of the symbol is the root's pungent taste. The medicine is pushed through the tip of a funnel made of a leaf of a barkcloth tree that is filled with salt. The girl takes the tip of the root in her teeth and pulls it inward causing the salt to trickle into her mouth. The root and the leaf funnel, as well as their use, constitute the artifactual dimension. All the dimensions of the symbol—nominal, substantial, and artifactual—contribute to the symbol's meaning which is sexual intercourse between husband and wife (a meaning that is confirmed by native exegesis [Turner 1973:1103–1104]).

Freud also closely attended to nominal, substantive, and artifactual aspects of symbols. Freud was always keenly interested in the nominal aspect of a symbol—that is, its existence as a word and its relations to other words. The connection between the forgotten word *aliquis* and "liquid" and "relic" discussed above indicates Freud's particular emphasis on symbols in their nominal foundations. In fact, Freud recognized that the meanings of actions and objects in dreams might depend entirely on those objects' and actions' nominal relations. Thus, a woman who dreamed of having animals thrown at her was dreaming, according to Freud, about "hurling invectives" since animal names are commonly used as slurs (1953 [1900], 5:405–406). In an analysis that Freud was conducting in French, Freud appeared in the patient's dream as an elephant. The significance of this image was based on the French word *trompe* for an elephant's trunk, and the patient's thought that Freud was deceiving her—*vous me trompez* (5:413).

The substantial or physical dimension of symbols was certainly recognized by Freud. Most of his inventory of sexual symbols depends upon some physical analogy between the symbol and the symbolized sexual part. Flowers represent human sexual organs probably because flowers contain the sexual organs of plants (Freud 1953 [1900], 5:376). Elongated objects such as sticks, tree trunks, and umbrellas stand for the male organ. Containers and other kinds of hollow objects often symbolize the vagina and uterus (5:354). Freud took issue with Wilhelm Stekel who held that any of these genital symbols might be employed for either the male or female organs. Freud argued that the imagination did not admit long, stiff objects as representations of female genitalia (5:358–359), thereby emphasizing the substantive basis of these symbols.

The artifactual aspect of the symbol was also employed by Freud in interpretation. In *The Psychopathology of Everyday Life*, Freud recounts a time when his eldest daughter had been ill and he had given up hope for her recovery. When he heard that her condition had greatly improved, he gave way to an impulse to hurl one of his slippers against the wall which caused a little antique statute of Venus to fall from the wall and break into pieces. Wrote Freud: "My attack of destructive fury served therefore to express a feeling of gratitude to fate and allowed me to perform a *'sacrificial act'*—rather as if I had made a vow to sacrifice something or other as a thank-offering if she recovered her health!" (Freud 1960 [1901], 6:169). Here, it is clearly Freud's behavior toward the object, the way it was transformed in the course of usage—its artifactual basis—that is essential to establishing the underlying meaning of sacrifice.

It is possible to see the nominal, substantial, and artifactual foundations of symbol meaning operating in a single dream symbol. In the "Wagner Opera" dream, the conductor of the opera stood on a high tower surrounded by an iron railing. The woman who dreamt this dream had a great deal of concern for a musician whose career was cut short by insanity. Nominally, the tower signified the "*Narrenturm*" or "Fool's Tower"—an old name for the insane asylum. Artifactually, the tower represented the dreamer's social elevation of the young musician above everyone else (Freud 1953 [1900], 5:342–343). Substantially, the tower represented the phallus and the dreamer's sexual interest in the young man.[12]

Each and every aspect of Turner's ritual symbol—its nominal, substantial, and artifactual foundations; its exegetical, operational, and positional dimensions of meaning; as well as its sensory and ideological polarization—is easily derived from Freud's theory of dream representations. It is no wonder that Turner emphasized the particular influence of *The Interpretation of Dreams* on his work. What he neglected to reveal was the extent of his indebtedness. He did not borrow a few psychological concepts from Freud, but an entire theory of symbols.

Given Turner's rather substantial debt to Freud (Paul 1989:187), why did he play down this indebtedness in his writings? Why did he acknowledge his indebtedness only in 1978, and even then, why so incompletely? Why did he claim indebtedness only to the *style* of Freud's thought when he was so clearly influenced by its substance as well? I believe the answers to these questions in some measure depend upon three factors: (1) Turner's structural-functionalism, (2) his metaphysical orientation, and (3) tendencies within the anthropological discipline as a whole.

Despite the fact that Turner rarely mentioned Freud in his writings, they nevertheless betray a distinct Freudian flavor. Thus, Turner sees in the human organism and bodily experience the "*fons et origo* of all classification" (Turner 1967:90). He is comfortable talking about the inevitability of repression, sublimation, and guilt in the conditioning of the individual by society (1968:235–236). He is willing to entertain the idea that early capitalism was fueled by competition repressed within the puritanical Protestant family (1967:277). More specifically, he comments on the emotional "ambivalence" engendered in mothers and daughters by competing sociological principles (1968:79); the rich symbolism of "oral aggression" in *Kayong'u* and *Ihamba* rituals (1967:146,366); the "masculine protest" dissolved by *Nkula* ritual (1968:86); and the "castration" symbolism of *Mukanda* songs (1967:276). Nor is he averse to commenting on the "passive homosexuality" (1968:192) or "unconscious grudges" (1967:150) of particular informants.

But if a Freudian flavor permeates Turner's work, Freudian psychology does not frame or organize it. Turner's approach is grounded in the structural-functional tradition in which he was trained. It is the corporate body and not the physical body that is his concern. The Freudian roots of Turner's work are transformed by this structural-functional perspective. Psychological concepts metamorphose into sociological ones. In fact, Turner so thoroughly "socializes" (F. Turner 1990:150) Freudian ideas, that by the time Turner comes to reflect on his debt to Freud, he seems incapable of recognizing anything substantive, only elements of style.

For example, Turner introduces the term "situational suppression" as a substitute for the psychological notion of "repression" (Turner 1967:39–43; 1978:576–577). Situational suppression is meant to characterize the suppression of ideas within particular social contexts. In rituals highlighting a certain ideological principle—such as the unity of the Ndembu matrilineage—participants behave as though no conflicts within the matrilineage existed. It is not that Ndembu are unaware of such conflicts, but reference to such conflicts is suppressed within the ritual. No one speaks of them and no one seems to recognize them, even when they find expression in the symbols of the ritual itself (Turner 1967:39–43; 1978:576–577).[13]

What is suppressed, in Turner's view, is itself social—knowledge about the arrangements of society. Furthermore, the reason for the suppression is likewise social—to promote the celebration of certain principles upon which the integration of society depends. Finally, the suppression itself is a social rather than a psychological mechanism. It is a condition of not mentioning rather than not knowing. For what is suppressed is not inaccessible or categorically forbidden to consciousness.[14]

"Sublimation" is also socialized by Turner. For Freud, sublimation was the diversion of an unconscious sexual instinct toward nonsexual—indeed toward socially and culturally uplifting—forms of activity (Freud 1963 [1917], 16:345). As the sexual meanings of symbols among the Ndembu were often conscious rather than unconscious, Turner expanded the notion of sublimation so that it referred to more than the transformation of an instinct. In Turner's sense, sublimation was a process by which emotion came to permeate abstract sociological ideas. Thus, the various, and even conflicting, emotions aroused by the image of blood among the Ndembu—the blood of hunting, of circumcision, of menstruation, and of birth—infuse the principle of matrilineage loyalty that the *mukula* or blood tree signifies.[15] Although emotions are, at root, human physiological responses—they are not necessarily of biological origin. Society "charges" symbols in the circumstances of their use. The drumming, dancing, and singing that attend the display and manipulation of a symbol, and the emotion that such activities evoke, infuse a symbol with a power that can be channeled to the moral and jural principles of society (Turner 1978:575). In other words, sublimation, in Turner's sense, is the direction of emotional energy that is often social in origin toward sociological ends.

"Ambivalence" is treated similarly. Rather than regard ambivalence as a fundamental contradiction in human attitudes and feelings—the coexistence of love and hate in a single individual for a single object (Laplanche and Pontalis 1973:26–29)—Turner attributes the contradictions exhibited in ritual performances to contradictory principles of social organization (Turner 1967:56–57). Ambivalence has a sociological rather than a psychological origin.

Finally, Turner provides a sociological rather than a psychological theory of symbols. He exploits Freud's conception of the structure of symbols and his method for their interpretation, while rejecting or ignoring most of Freud's metapsychology—at least as it purported to identify the forces that underlie and give rise to ritual symbolism. In Turner's view, ritual symbols reflect society and its particular arrangements, not the contents and structure of the unconscious mind (Turner 1967:39). Rituals are communications. They constitute society's commentary on itself. That ritual symbols might also reflect individual endopsychic processes was a matter for the psychoanalyst, not the anthropologist. Beyond recognizing that such processes could infuse a symbol with additional power, anthropologists need not be overly concerned with them (Turner 1967:36). They are not what the symbolism is really about.

Turner seems to have trouble recognizing or acknowledging Freudian ideas once they have been filtered through a structural-functional membrane. Following Max Gluckman, Turner viewed society as an organization of conflicting groups, interests, and principles. He saw rituals, which gave expression to the forces of conflict and rebellion, as basically integrative, transforming the conscious and unconscious hostility to the social order into loyalty and allegiance to the norms and values of that order (Turner 1955:54). But hostility and conflict are also at the root of Freud's idea of ritual. Not the ritual behaviors of neurotics which are motivated by repressed sexual impulses, but religious rituals which originate in aggressive impulses—in "self-seeking, socially harmful instincts" (Freud 1959 [1907], 9:125). In Freud's view, taboo and religious ritual control the conflict that inevitably proceeds from the impulse of "attacking, of getting control, and of asserting oneself" (Freud 1953 [1913], 13:73). To the extent that religious ritual is capable of controlling such impulses, it allows men to maintain their social arrangements. While Turner criticizes those who hold ritual to be "an obsessional defense mechanism . . . against culturally defined illicit impulses and emotions" (Turner 1978:578), it is an idea that he clearly endorses (1968:236–237). Engaging conflict and competition from a Durkheimian perspective strikes Turner as something of a novelty (1968:272–273). It is probably this sense of novelty that prevents Turner from recognizing his Freudian roots as clearly as he might.

Nevertheless, Turner has resisted some of the more extreme tendencies of the structural-functional perspective. Turner rejects the idea that within native commentary is to be found the whole of symbolic meaning. S. F. Nadel argued that when native informants could not confirm a meaning that the anthropologist had adduced, the symbol necessarily lacked such meaning and it, therefore, could play no part in an anthropological understanding of the ritual (Turner 1967:26). In Turner's view, there was more to the meaning of a ritual than what an informant might be able to, or care to, articulate at any particular moment. While the commentaries of informants should evidence anthropological interpretations, they could hardly be expected to reproduce them. If Turner is unwilling to fully engage Freud's notion of the individual unconscious, he is equally unwilling to recognize symbolism as an entirely explicit mode of representation.

It is not merely Turner's sociological emphasis that contributed to the blurring of his vision of Freud. Turner conceived of the symbol as having a fully conscious *manifest* sense, a marginally conscious *latent* sense, and a completely unconscious *hidden* sense (Turner 1968:81). Turner directed the greatest part of his descriptive and interpretive energies to the first two of these. He was ambivalent about the third. On the one hand, he viewed the hidden sense of the symbol as psychological in nature, firmly rooted in infantile experience (1962:79); on the other it was ontological, concerned with the nature of reality and human existence (1962:80). Social and psychological categories, however, are incapable of corralling this deep sense of the religious symbol which, in Turner's view, proceeds from an "intuition of a real and spiritual unity of all things" and the wish "to overcome arbitrary and man-made divisions, to overcome for a moment—a 'moment in and out of time'—the material conditions that disunite men and set them at odds with nature" (1968:21–22). This spiritual quest that Turner glimpsed at the core of ritual symbols was clearly at odds with Freud's psychology of religion. If rituals symbols were fundamentally ontological, they could not be reduced to sexual or aggressive instincts and their vicissitudes. And if Turner's sense of the metaphysical nature of symbols freed him from Freud's psychology, he probably felt relieved of his debt to Freud's symbology as well.[16]

In conclusion, it should be noted that Turner's "repression" of Freud was really not all that idiosyncratic. It was part and parcel of a more general repression of Freud's thought in anthropology as a whole. Beginning about the time that Turner did his fieldwork among the Ndembu, psychological anthropology in general, and psychoanalytic anthropology in particular, became increasingly marginalized (White 1989:506–509). In 1958, Weston La Barre documented the inhospitality of anthropology to Freud's thought, and things do not seem to have changed very much since then. Of the twenty-eight selections included in the anthology *Symbolic*

Anthropology (Dolgin, Kemnitzer, and Schneider 1977), none is by Freud.[17] The third and fourth editions of *Reader in Comparative Religion*, edited by William A. Lessa and Evon Z. Vogt (1979), likewise include no selection by Freud although one had been included in earlier editions. Instead, they include two reviews by Alfred Kroeber of Freud's *Totem and Taboo* which largely attend to criticizing Freud's thesis that totemism and exogamy begin with some primal parricide. In some sense, it seems the whole of Freud's work has been condensed to this notion of primal parricide, and to the extent that this particular idea has offended anthropological sentiment, everything has been tabooed. How else can we comprehend a 306-page book titled *Freud and Anthropology* (Wallace 1983) that deals exclusively with *Totem and Taboo*? The fact that the hypothesis of the primal parricide is only a small section of *Totem and Taboo* or that many of Freud's other works—*The Interpretation of Dreams, The Psychopathology of Everyday Life, Jokes and Their Relation to the Unconscious, The Future of an Illusion, Civilization and Its Discontents, Group Psychology and the Analysis of the Ego*—are anthropological and bear directly on the analysis and interpretation of culture seems scarcely to be recognized. Perhaps this disciplinary repression of Freud's ideas and works provides a context within which Turner's own amnesia can be explained.

Melford Spiro invited Victor Turner to organize a symposium on symbolism for the 1969 annual meeting of the American Ethnological Society. As the discussant of the papers in that symposium, Spiro bemoaned the participants' neglect of their spiritual ancestors—those who had blazed the trail of symbolic analysis and interpretation (Spiro 1969:208–209). Ironically, it was just such neglect of ancestors that brought misfortune to the Ndembu camp and provoked those rituals that first inspired Victor Turner in his quest for symbols and their meanings. And perhaps for the same reasons that the Ndembu were drawn to confront their neglected ancestors and confess their neglect in the context of their therapeutic rituals, Victor Turner was drawn to his reencounter with Freud in the context of his 1978 essay. Repression, after all, is never complete. What is repressed is always destined to return—if only in distorted fashion and in the form of a compromise.

15. Missing Theory

In previous centuries, evolutionist, diffusionist, psychoanalytic, functional, and structural theories were proposed to explain the origins, development, spread, and operation of culture. In the second half of the twentieth century, the belief in a theoretical science of culture began to break down. The principles on which the study of culture was conducted began to be questioned. The methodological, philosophical, and moral aspects of anthropological and folkloristic practice were scrutinized. Radical, reflexive, deconstructive, and postmodern perspectives coalesced to destabilize knowledge and undermine the possibility of description, explanation, and interpretation of that knowledge (Hymes 1974; Marcus and Fisher 1986). The production of knowledge was politically, economically, and historically situated, and it became the task of the anthropologist and folklorist to grasp the conditions of knowledge production. Anthropological and folkloristic efforts increasingly turned to a critique of its disciplinary practices. Yet critique may employ the same descriptive, analytical, and explanatory procedures as the practices at which it is directed. It may entail the very same problems it attempts to identify and resolve.

> *If law is anywhere, it is everywhere.*
> —Edward Burnett Tylor

AT THE END OF her oft-cited article "Mistaken Dichotomies," Barbara Kirshenblatt-Gimblett urged folklorists to close the divide between academic and public-sector folklore. In her view, folklorists of both stripes were members of powerful elites, were instrumental in the construction and distribution of folklore, but were largely indifferent to the political economy that shaped their enterprise. Once they understood where they were coming from in political and economic terms, the divisions between theory and practice, the academy and the public and applied sectors, could be transcended (Kirshenblatt-Gimblett 1988:141, 152). In other words, folklorists needed to study themselves. Theories and methodologies were the products of social, political, and historical circumstance. The study of folklore—or the study of anything—was at root a political act, and folklorists needed to scrutinize the political and economic interests that shaped their scholarly practice.

The political nature of scholarship has been a concern in anthropology and folklore for almost half a century. Beginning in the 1960s, profound doubts began to be raised about the ethnographic and analytic projects of anthropology and folklore. Theorists questioned the possibility of representing culture in writing; recognized ethnographic writing as yet another literary genre, explored its tropes and conceits, and experimented with new forms; scrutinized their complicity in the generation of cultural data; and explored the positions from which they generated their analyses and interpretations. Reflexivity was the watchword: scholars were to be as attentive to what they were doing as to the ethnological objects themselves.[1] Grand theories were finished. The turn was from the theories of society and culture to the critique of those theories: that is, to theorizing about theoretical and methodological practices. Where commentaries on expressions and behaviors of particular people had once been the object of attention, the commentaries on these commentaries moved to a central position.

Much of value was produced in this inward turning, and there is no need to review these accomplishments here. But there were some definite losses to be reckoned along the way. Knowledge not only became uncertain—for it had always been uncertain—but nigh impossible (Tyler 1987). Nervousness pervaded the scholarly enterprise as scholars brooded over assumptions that they might have been making that betrayed their philosophical naïveté. They had assumed that social groups and structures were real, that data could be representative, that texts recorded in speech events were similar to those performed when the ethnographer was not around, that texts were meaningful and that these meanings could be glimpsed, and that what they were reporting was more reflective of the ethnographic object than the ethnographer.

The turn to the political implications of folklore scholarship involved identifying the political foundations of the folklorists' role in fieldwork, text making, and analysis. However, the purpose of engaging in this political analysis was not to make the folklore enterprise more "objective"—which is regarded as a naïve and impossible task—but to reveal the manner in which power infuses scholarly research and writing (Briggs 1993:389). Scholarly practices participate in the reproduction of the inequalities of race, gender, and class. Consequently, it was claimed that the knowledge that the folklorist produces is to be regarded "*more as a mode of legitimating social inequality than as an objective mode of illuminating the world*" (Shuman and Briggs 1993:115, my emphasis).

Scholarship, however, is not politics. Scholarship is scholarship. Scholarship may be politically motivated, politically situated, and have particular political effects. Politics is a perspective on behavior and expression and not behavior and expression itself. Almost anything can be viewed in political terms, much as almost anything can be viewed in social, economic, aesthetic, ethical, or spiritual terms. One can explore the politics of art, as one can explore the art of politics. Political analysis, like any other kind of analysis, can be illuminating, whether it is directed at the expressions and behaviors of the members of a particular "folk" group, or at the expressions and behaviors of someone who studies a particular folk group. Sometimes it is interesting to analyze behavior in terms of access to and deployment of power. Sometimes it is not. When it is claimed, however, that a perspective is relevant to the analysis of everything, it tends to be relevant to the analysis of nothing. It is only when a perspective is partial that it is likely to contribute to any sort of understanding.

Is it really naïve to hope that the folklore enterprise might be made more objective? Is the effort truly impossible?[2] While I would concede that one cannot expect complete objectivity, it must be presumed that *greater* objectivity is itself realizable. For if it is possible to introduce *less* objectivity into fieldwork, into text making, and into analysis—for example, by writing about people one has never met, creating texts in the absence of observation or documentary procedures, or by producing analyses tied to absent facts or facts unequivocally misread—then it is clearly possible to create greater objectivity. Whatever "complete objectivity" might mean—if anything—it would at least seem possible to utter statements that correspond to the world more and to our wishes of how we might like the world to be less. After all, what could be the value of even a political critique that did not to some extent reflect and have relevance for the real world: one that failed to approximate actual conditions and had no possible consequences for practice?

If politics is in fact the underlying shaper of scholarly discourse, one would expect that greater ethnographic attention might be paid to the actual politics of scholarly production in the university. There is little such description. Theoretical orientations may be adopted for political and economic reasons, but the process is rarely described or discussed. How is the theoretical orientation of a young scholar shaped? What are the forces that direct a scholar towards a particular subject matter, methodology, or theory? What are the rewards and punishments for choosing one over another, and how are they meted out? What are the differences between those who leave and those who remain in the academy? If the political foundations of theory and practice are to be understood, it would seem that a close description and analysis of power in the academy might be an important first step.

The political views of faculty in folklore programs, anthropology departments, and in the humanities in general tend to be liberal or leftist. Where is the articulation and analysis of these views and their impact on scholarly conceptualizing, theorizing, and teaching? If academic theorizing cannot be beyond ideology, political interests, and economic concerns (Kirshenblatt-Gimblett 1988:141), how do we account for the fact that folklore and anthropology programs are filled with liberal Democrats while political science and economics departments tend to attract more than their fair share of conservative Republicans? What are the differences in the social and economic locations of folklorists, political scientists, and economists that lead to such divergences in political outlook?

Even so, to what extent do the social and economic positions of the scholars determine the character of their scholarly production? Must institutions constructed and maintained by the "dominant classes" necessarily promote their "sponsors' privileged positions" (Kirshenblatt-Gimblett 1988:144)? Can institutions speak and act against their own interests? If the answer is necessarily "no," then the proposition is a tautology. Expression and self-interest are not separate variables but a single one. Do institutions always promote their own privileged positions? Do they always recognize their own interests? Are these interests unified and coherent? Do institutions necessarily speak with one voice? If not, which voices represent the interests of the institution, and what is to be made of those that do not? And what of the reactions and responses to what institutions promote? Do responses actually coincide with what is promoted? Do people receive the same or different messages than the one intended by the institution?

Should scholarship prove to be merely an epiphenomenon of the social and economic position of the scholar, what then can be said for the social and economic locations of critique? What interests and positions do such critiques promote, and how do these critiques escape recapitulating the very problems of the conceptualizations and practices under scrutiny?

The fragmentary quality that Kirshenblatt-Gimblett characterizes as a central attribute of the ethnographic object in her essay on museum display is no less fragmentary than her own essay; an essay which alludes to, refers to, and cites a world of absent text (Kirshenblatt-Gimblett 1991:388–394). Similarly, the analyses of the metadiscursive practices of folklorists about which Richard Bauman and Charles Briggs (2003) have written at length are themselves metadiscursive practices: discourses that seek to "shape, constrain, or appropriate other discourses" and exercise power over them (Briggs 1993:389–390). Those who would interrogate the basis for the scholarly authority of a particular text invariably must establish authority for their own critical assessments. And if fieldworkers do influence what is performed and control what is presented in their scholarly texts (Briggs 1993:406), the critics of those texts likewise choose what aspects are to be critiqued, from what standpoints, and which authorities are to be invoked. Even reflexivity, which is supposed to lead to an awareness of oppression, recapitulates the self-examination, confession, and quest for internal truth that has been regarded as one of the most powerful forms of surveillance and subjugation (Foucault 1990:60). Critics who seek to identify those interests that belie the descriptive, analytical, and theoretical work of folklorists should be equally undone by their own interests. What validity, after all, could a necessarily self-interested critique possess? "Give me a place to stand, and I will move the earth," Archimedes was supposed to have said, but there is no such place. The critique of folklore scholarship has no claim to privilege per se (Oring 1994:245–246).

Critique that purports to identify the hidden interests that underlie scholarly discourse seems a dubious enterprise. Such critique seems less like inquiry and more like puzzle solving. That is to say, critics know where they have to start—with the scholarly text—and where they have to wind up—with the revelation of hidden interests. It is a matter of going from point A to point B with the beginning and end points known in advance. At times, the process may require some ingenuity, but it is hardly a voyage of discovery. Hidden intentions may be helpful in speculating about why a particular statement may be off base, but that explanation can only arise *after* it has been determined that the statement is indeed off base—that is, found wanting in terms of its descriptive, explanatory, or predictive value. Thus, the standing of the assertion that in the "big lie there is always a certain force of credibility" and that the masses "more readily fall victim to the big lie than the small lie" (Hitler 1942:134) is independent of who formulated it, used it, and for what reasons. What matters is whether populations are more persuaded by big lies than small ones, and whether they are an effective propaganda technique.[3] The answer to this question does not depend upon the character or purposes of the claimant but upon observations of and experiments in the real world.

If folklorists can say anything worthwhile about the types of expressions they call *folklore* and the people who produce and purvey them, and create understanding by situating folklore in its social, economic, and political contexts, then certainly folklore scholarship must be open to the very same kinds of analysis. About that there should be no disagreement. Scholarship is no more created *ex nihilo* than is folklore. But the inverse is also true. If something insightful and meaningful can be said about scholarly ideas, practices, and institutions, then something insightful and meaningful can be said about folklore expressions in society. The warrant for one is as strong as the warrant for the other. I fear, however, that the value of folklore research and interpretation is increasingly regarded—even by some prominent folklorists—as mere fodder for critical analysis and without value in its own right (Oring 1998:333).

I am particularly suspicious of critique that claims to unmask the legitimization of inequality. I presume "inequality" refers to the existence of differences between people and groups in their abilities to command particular political, economic, and symbolic resources.[4] If history teaches us anything, inequality in this sense has been structured into human society from the very beginning, and it is not clear that it will go away anytime soon, no matter how much we claim we wish it might.[5] It often seems to be the case that the eradication of one form of inequality results in the creation of another.

I do not doubt that there are scholarly conceptions and practices that might contribute to the legitimization of certain forms of inequality. I also do not doubt that certain scholarly conceptions and practices serve to contest and undermine certain forms of inequality. (And I do not doubt that there are scholarly conceptions and practices that have little or no impact on the state of the world at all.) The question is: what should be the motive for the production and distribution of scholarly knowledge? Should folklorists devote themselves to developing concepts and practices that they believe to be beneficial or liberating (for certain people)? Or should they devote themselves to concepts and practices that help to describe and understand the world as best as they know how, even if they cannot be certain of what their effects might be?[6]

Invocations of inequality in a critique claim the moral high ground for that set of critical practices that decenter and deconstruct the concepts of folklore. If it seems reasonable to speak of a commitment to a "rhetoric of loss" or a "poetics of disappearance" as has been frequently done for folkloristics (Briggs 1993:436; Kirshenblatt-Gimblett 1998:300–302), it would not seem unreasonable to speak as well of a commitment to a "rhetoric" or "poetics" of inequality. After all, who dares speak against equality? Who would speak against a mode of analysis that claims to identify hidden forms of subjugation and oppression? Yet, the move seems paradoxical because to recognize oppression and to do something about it requires a solid understanding of the situation on the ground, as well as a genuine faith in a set of abstractly conceived forces that might be marshaled to overcome it. If the production of knowledge is more a mode of creating and legitimating social inequality than an objective mode of illuminating the world, where could an assessment of inequality come from and how would the means to amend it be conceptualized and implemented?

All this leads to the title of this essay—"Missing Theory." I think theory has been missing from folklore studies for quite some time. What I mean by "theory" is not simply the recourse to abstract statements. Nor is it to be equated with a critical scrutiny of folkloristic concepts and practices. Theory is a type of statement about the world that has several distinct properties. It is: (1) interesting, (2) plausible, (3) generalizable, and (4) testable. The first two properties need little elaboration, but the last two—generalizablity and testability—might. Folklorists do need to stop—or at least reduce the frequency of—flitting from curious expression and custom to curious expression and custom. They need to ask larger questions and address them in such ways that the answers are not preordained. An insight into a specific custom needs to be examined for its broader applicability. A statement that is restricted to only a single example is not a theoretical statement at all. Thus folklorists have to be constantly on the alert as to how they can generalize their intuitions, insights, and understandings about particular folkloric events.

Generalization is not enough. A generalization should be testable. Folklorists need to formulate *hypotheses* that propose alternate possibilities to explain phenomena under scrutiny. Research would then eliminate some of these hypotheses. What would be produced is knowledge: knowledge which our experience of the world might not verify, but knowledge that our experience of the world would not, as far as we can tell, falsify.

Too often, there is a wholesale application of a theoretical perspective to social and cultural phenomena without an effort or concern to establish the limits of such application. No theoretical formulation accounts for everything. A theory is not a philosophy. A theory must necessarily fail, and in exploring the extent of its applicability and the situations of it failure, both its *limits* and its *value* are established. Setting out to demonstrate the applicability of the formulations of some prominent thinker to some set of ethnographic data is more frequently an exercise in acrobatics than inquiry. If a theorist is to be engaged at all, it should be through opposition. Data should be marshaled to test the limits of theoretical propositions rather than happily confirm them.

If all this sounds like a move towards "science," so be it. The negative valuation of science that has become conventional over the past few decades is largely a result of a literary turn (and a literary megalomania) in anthropology and folkloristics. The dismissal, however, does not seem to have been rigorously reasoned and may be more a matter of style than substance (Reyna 1994). Science is no more than the attempt to explain observations of the world in terms of the formulation of general propositions from empirical research which are in turn tested against other empirical data. If this is a colonial perspective, it is one that many in the world have adopted.[7]

I am not against a politics of folklore. But if political theories are to be employed, I would prefer to see them directed to explaining folklore on the ground rather than to the folkloristic conceptualizations of the academy.[8] I want to see theory, any kind of theory, directed to engaging the stuff of folklore. Interpretation, performance, and other moves towards extreme contextualization that have been prominent for four decades in folklore studies have led to a kind of microscopism in analysis. It is difficult to get beyond the individual case.[9] A comparative perspective in folklore studies needs to reemerge, in new forms with new problems. There has been almost a half-century of reflection on the tropes of scholarly discourse. It is time to move back to theory rooted in the scrutiny of our purported subject matter more than in the scrutiny of ourselves. While I welcome the "extra edge of consciousness" that self-scrutiny affords (Williams in Kirshenblatt-Gimblett 1998:320), I can't but agree that to "choose doubt as a philosophy of life is akin to choosing immobility as a means of transportation" (Martel 2001:6).[10] We need to get back to the field with a renewed sense of confidence that we do not know what we are doing, probably never have, and probably never will. Nor, it would seem, does anyone else. In that understanding lies a possible formula for success. I would like folklorists to go out there and say something truly significant about folklore *before* criticism emerges to say why it can't be said, can't be done, or may be too dangerous to even contemplate.

While I think theoretical formulations have *some* relation to the socioeconomic conditions in which they emerge, I do not feel that these formulations are determined by them. I am somewhat astonished that those who suggest that academic conceptualizations are the product of the positionality of their creators seem to overlook the essentializing that necessarily underlies such a perspective. Theory—indeed all culture—is the product of an internal dynamic as well as an external one. Cognitive processes are dialectical and a theoretical formulation is as or more likely to emerge as a reaction to a previous theoretical formulation than it is from a set of social, economic, or political interests (Harris 1968:71). We cannot foresee where theory will be in a hundred years, fifty years, or even twenty-five years. The most acute critical perspectives cannot tell us either, except—as we already know—that theory will be different from what it is today. Whatever the shape and thrust of that theory proves to be, I think it will be made by those who engage folklore in the world, who attempt to make the best sense of it that they can, and who do not freeze when they look over their shoulders and glimpse their own shadows.

I would return to Kirshenblatt-Gimblett's suggestion that the dichotomies between academic and public sector folklore were mistaken and would disappear if only folklorists of both stripes would come to grips with the political economy of the field. It is noteworthy that Kirshenblatt-Gimblett invokes political economy, not to explain a division between folklorists, but to suggest that reflexive knowledge of it is the means to ameliorate conditions and remedy the divide. This is typical of the critical stance.[11] Rather than attempt to account for the ways things actually are, it proposes instead to direct attention to the way things ought to be.

16. Folk or Lore? The Stake in Dichotomies

For some time, a divide has been recognized between what has been called "academic" folklore and "public-sector" folklore. Academic folklorists work in universities where they teach classes, undertake research, and publish results in scholarly journals and in books issued by university presses. Public sector folklorists tend to work for government-funded arts and humanities councils, museums, and non-profit corporations. Public folklorists engage traditions to record them and feature them in exhibits, concerts, films, festivals, and catalogues. Both academic and public-sector folklorists do fieldwork, publish, and teach—although the teaching is conducted in different venues, for different groups, with different methods, at different depths, over different periods of time. The key difference between academic and public-sector folklorists is that public-sector folklorists study folklore to bring about particular results. They endeavor to make communities aware of their traditions, engender respect for those traditions, and help communities counter the forces that threaten their ways of life. Theirs is an activist agenda (Baron and Spitzer 1992:3). It is based in a concern for particular individuals and groups—a folk. Academic folklore begins with a search for an understanding of the structures, functions, and meanings underlying an array of cultural expressions—a lore.

> *If he had been asked whether he liked or didn't like the peasants, Konstantin Levin would have been absolutely at a loss what to reply. He liked and did not like the peasants, just as he liked and did not like men in general.*
>
> —Leo Tolstoy

FOLKLORISTS WILL probably view the choice between "folk" and "lore" a strange one; after all, the two go together. You can't have the lore without the people who create and purvey it, and when you encounter the folk in any sustained way, you will inevitably come up against their lore. The choice that I pose, however, relates to the question of where the emphasis of folklore studies lies and the motives which induce folklorists to enter and persevere in the field. Is it basically an attempt to encounter a folk—that is, people of a particular, and often marginalized, social class, occupation, religion, or ethnicity; or is it to pursue questions about lore—questions about tradition, transmission, artistic creativity, and identity? The use of the opposition between "folk" and "lore" is purely indexical; it is meant to point to differences in perspective that guide the folklore enterprise.

There are those who feel it is a folklorist's job to "tell stories." Martha Norkunas, for example, tells the story of her own mother, who, with her five children, left her husband when she learned that he had a mistress in the city where he worked. She gave up wealth and position for a life of economic uncertainty and the stigma then associated with divorce and a broken home (Norkunas 2004:105–106). Norkunas feels that silences—such as her mother's—need to enter the historical record and that "stories of resistance" need to be heard.

Similarly, Debora Kodish sees the job of the folklorist as bringing into memory that which has remained outside. Tap dance, for example, with its connotations of "Uncle Tom," and more especially women's tap dance, has, according to Kodish, been left out of histories and festivals and overlooked by funding panels. Hortense Allen was invited by producer Larry Steele to produce shows at Club Harlem in Atlantic City. According to Allen, she produced three shows a day, choreographed two to three numbers each week for the chorus line, and danced in front of the line in production numbers. She sewed costumes for the show as well. But she was not credited for her work because Larry Steele had neglected to tell the Harlem Club backers that Allen was brought to the club to produce. Consequently, Ms. Allen was only remembered for her dancing, not her producing. Ms. Allen did not want to be remembered as a "shake dancer." She wanted to be remembered as a choreographer and producer. She said that she only did her dance act to help Steele fill out his show. She wanted Kodish and the Philadelphia Folklore Project (PFP) to correct these errors.[1] Kodish remarked, "Now people can say that truth is relative (and of course it is).... This is the truth: She WAS Club Harlem. She WAS Larry Steele" (1997:7).

Kodish sees the job of the PFP as rectifying such distortions of memory. She wants to write histories that work for "equity and justice" (5). History should be looked at "from the point of view of those most forgotten" (8). Ms. Allen's accomplishments had been overlooked and minimized. In the PFP film "Plenty of Good Woman Dancers," Ms. Allen was given the opportunity to speak and set the record straight. As Kodish notes, "We set things right" (8). There is a politics of exclusion that gives unequal status to some folk groups, and folklorists' definitions of folklore should consider "political tasks and practical effects" (1993:200).

For Norkunas, eliciting and documenting stories of resistance is essential. Without resistance one "traffics in discourses abhorrent to the spirit . . . [and] allow[s] others to control the present through their interpretations of the past" (2004:115). Norkunas sees progress in the movement away from a history that is "primarily white, male, celebratory, and heroic" (117). But a history that is merely ethnic and female—equally celebratory and heroic—seems less like progress than revenge. Norkunas for example, lauds the chief historian of the National Park Service's efforts to interpret Civil War sites within the context of a war that was fundamentally about slavery (118).[2] How does that reckon, however, with the many "folk" (or even professional) voices that would argue it was not? What voices get silenced so that others may be heard (Stoll 1999:244)? Why would Norkunas favor *any* particular interpretation of the Civil War knowing that such an interpretation would invariably lead to the silencing of certain voices? Short of making some deliberate and reasoned assessment as to what caused what, no particular view is likely to have any claims to privilege (Stoll 1999:244).

Life history and oral history are among the provinces of the folklorist. In their interviewing, folklorists necessarily confront personal experience stories, family histories, and statements of values and principles that express their informants' sense of the world and where they stand in it. It is only through exposure to such accounts that scholars can grasp the subjectivities that lie behind such abstract sociological categories as immigrant, plantation, chairmaker, missionary, or wife. It is only by coming to terms with memories, traditions, and values that folklorists can begin to penetrate some of the mysteries of their informants' knowledge and art. Folklorists need to know how people perceive and comprehend their worlds.

It does not seem to me that the folklorist can be satisfied in merely eliciting oral reminiscences and family histories and publishing them in books, displaying them in museums, or recording them on videotape—at least no more than a folklorist today can be satisfied with collecting a corpus of folktale texts and publishing them in a collection. If folklorists publish a collection of tales, there is a call for an accompanying historical, structural, functional, semiotic, political, performance-based, or other kind of analysis. That is, the folklorist's encounter with folk expression should be critical. A folklorist's encounter with oral history should likewise be critical. Oral history should be more than a matter of presenting informants' pronouncements, recollections, and traditions. Oral history is more than giving people a voice—regardless of who those people might be. Oral accounts need to be assessed and evaluated either as documents in the creation of a critical history (whether of slavery, immigration, factory labor, or tap dance) or as a reflection of individual or community worldview (Wilson 1979:460–66). A personal narrative or family tradition is not necessarily fanciful or out of step with the course of human events. Like any historical document, however, it requires scrupulous appraisal to evaluate it as a record of past events (Vansina 1965; Stoll 1999:61). Even when oral history is employed to reflect worldview, that worldview needs to be elaborated and related to the conditions and experiences that engender and sustain it. Folklorists cannot be content to allow oral testimony to stand on its own. They cannot simply put "another's truth before their own" (Lindahl 2004:176).

In 1974, David Kerr went to the University of Zambia to take up a position in Drama and Literature. As he believed that a powerful drama could only be built on indigenous expressive forms, he allied himself with an ongoing project to collect the performance traditions of the Chewa people. He focused on spoken and sung narratives that he hoped would become a foundation for the theater being created at the university. His research was very much motivated by a salvage ideology, and consequently he collected an eclectic array—from riddles to rites—of traditional forms. He encountered some resistance in his efforts to elicit certain expressions because the interview situations were not always conducive to their performance.

Once, a village elder formally requested that he and his team intercede on behalf of the village with the President of Zambia concerning economic conditions in the region. His inability to be an effective conduit for this message caused him to lose enthusiasm for the collection of traditional narrative. He deposited his tapes and transcriptions in the University of Zambia library, and began taking drama students from the university to rural villages to create improvisatory plays in the local language. Some of these were based on local stories and songs, but there was no attempt to scientifically record or study the local traditions they were employing. The purpose was to create performances "that would help rural communities . . . to understand and mediate the socio-economic changes occurring in Zambia" (Kerr 1991:53). This effort led to his being involved in other theater projects in Malawi that utilized improvisatory performances that rural people could use to improve their own lives even when they had no tradition of indigenous spoken drama. Kerr and his researchers did not come to these rural villages as "remote academics" (56). They came to the villages as equals, as fellow artists. They participated in the songs and dances. The communities were enthusiastic because the performances provided space for the discussion of important community issues (58).

The models of folk theater that Kerr and his associates employ derive in part from theories of Third World Popular Theater (57). Kerr believes the work of the folklorist should be compatible with progressive social development. And who could dispute it? Folklore can be used for any number of purposes—some of them good. But even if Kerr wanted to abandon his original focus on the study of traditional narratives and pursue more interventionist and politically engaged activities, why could he not study his own engagement? Which local narratives worked in activist theater? Which did not? How were they transformed in the course of use? To what extent were the plays and their messages shaped by university students or by local audiences? Where did conflict arise between them? What were the consequences of these theatrical productions in the rural communities, and how did they lead to changes in life on the ground?

The formulations proposed by Norkunas, Kodish, Kerr, and others (e.g., Botkin 1953:204; Davis 1992:109; Hawes 2002:70–71; Lomax 1977:130; Lawless 2001; Payne 2004:341) are rooted not in critical assessment but in ethical response—the crafting of a project that can be used in the creation of a "humane and just world" (Norkunas 2004:120).[3] The impetus to fieldwork is not so much to learn something as to be able to teach something. What is being taught is known before the research even commences: that minorities often have little power, their voices have not been heard, and they are overlooked or discounted by elites in powerful institutions. This is a kind of social work.[4] The task of the folklorist, then, is recognizing "the existence of various publics and their need to obtain cultural equity in a situation in which various sectors of society are contending for scarce resources," and to assist "groups to receive . . . respectful attention within their own community and beyond" (Abrahams 1992:25). History research and presentation is meant to be reparative. The task of the folklorist is to amplify, broadcast, and validate the voices of the folk—or, at least, *some* folk—in an effort to redress the grievances of the past and ameliorate the injustices of the present.[5]

There is another model of folklore study, however. It is a model that places *inquiry* before empathy, before equity, and before healing. This kind of folkloristics is driven by questions: questions about history, art, culture, communication, and mind. In studying folklore and the people who purvey it, folklorists hope to answer questions small and large. Why does "Springfield Mountain" still hold a place in oral song repertoires hundreds of years after its creation? To what extent is it a product of the past or a creation of the present? What is to be made of the variability of the song over space and through time? What is the relation of this song to other songs in the singer's repertoire? How does the song create and reflect the character of the individuals or communities that sing it? Why do people sing some songs but not others? Why do people sing?

The distinction I am making is not so much between academic and public sector folklore, although some of this difference will tend to distribute itself along these occupational lines, as much as it is between a folkloristics driven by questions and one driven by answers. It seems to me that questions are the more important. Beyond, "What can we do to help these people?" I don't know what the questions of an ethical history or ethical folkloristics are.

Somehow the discussion has devolved into what is the most moral thing to do. Who demonstrates the greatest concern for their informants? Who helps their research communities the most? Who sacrifices the most on behalf of their informants? I am not in principle against helping people. I agree with Debora Kodish (1997:5–6) quoting historian Howard Zinn (who in turn paraphrases Albert Camus) that in "a world of victims and executioners, it is the job of thinking people . . . not to be on the side of the executioners."[6] I might point out, however, that I am not sure that the world breaks down neatly into those two groups (Stoll 1999). And even when it does, it may at times be difficult, even for thinking people, to know who are the victims and who the executioners when both are blindfolded and well armed. But I appreciate Zinn's emphasis on "thinking people." Somehow Zinn implies that thought precedes and engenders ethical practice.[7] In any event, for one to be a thinking person there have to be questions to think about. If our questions lead to inquiry and our inquiry to conclusions—provisional though they may be, as all human knowledge is—are we to respect these conclusions when we are thrust up against a situation that pits the interests of a community against our own laboriously won knowledge?

In 1996, Barre Toelken returned some sixty hours of recorded tapes of his Navajo informant Yellowman to Yellowman's wife. The tapes included Coyote stories, Yeibichei songs, hunting ritual instructions, discussions of traditional crafts, some episodes of the Emergence Myth, as well as oral history and personal anecdotes. Although Toelken had first heard some of these materials in 1956, he only began to record them in 1966. The performance of much of the material is seasonal: Coyote stories, for example, are told in winter between the first killing frost and the first lightning strike (1998:381–382).

Toelken began to wonder about what would happen to the tapes after his own death. Even if he deposited them in a library or archive, the tapes could be played out of season, and the release of the words of the stories into the air might cause injury. Because Toelken felt that Navajo belief should be respected, he brought the problem to the attention of Yellowman's widow (Toelken's sister by adoption). She suggested that Toelken give her the tapes so that she could destroy them (1998:385, 389).[8]

It is not Toelken's desire to respect his informant's beliefs that bothers me. But he seems to have raised the problem of the tapes before his Navajo family expressed any concern about them. Even then, it does not seem that he made much of an effort to suggest ways that the tapes might be protected to satisfy his Navajo family's concerns. Was the destruction of the tapes really the only solution?[9] One would think that the tapes could have been transcribed and translated. The English translation would not be a problem because the English language does not have the destructive power of Navajo. Indeed, translations of some tales have already been published (Toelken 1998:387). Even if a transcription of the stories were made, it could only be sounded out by someone proficient in the Navajo language. Such a person would be likely to respect a request not to read the transliteration aloud in the wrong season. An archive could put restrictions on the recorded materials so that tapes or CDs could only be listened to in certain seasons or with earphones.

But Toelken does not seem to feel the effort to secure the tapes worthwhile. He plays down their value in the preservation of Navajo culture stating that the tapes are at best an artifact of the culture and not the culture itself. He further argues that Navajo culture is very much alive and the Coyote stories continue to be told by Navajo. But these are red herrings. Toelken did not collect these stories in order to save the culture, nor did, I suspect, Yellowman narrate them for that reason. And even though Navajo storytelling is very much alive (although Yellowman's children do not seem to have taken it up [1998:386]) and may have good prospects for the future, what might be learned from comparing stories and storytelling situations in the years 1966, 1996, and 2066? Toelken collected these stories for what they could teach about Navajo storytelling and about Navajo culture. He collected these stories in context. Navajo storytelling may go on, but how will it change? How will it adapt? Without the kinds of documents that Toelken collected, no one—not even the Navajo themselves—will ever know.

Toelken characterizes his research as part and parcel of elite power and the colonialism in fieldwork (1998:386). He agonizes over all the benefits that have accrued to him as a result of his work with Yellowman. After all, it was Toelken who "wrote the essays and published them, and happily received whatever academic advantages came from those efforts, including, of course, tenure, advancement in rank, and pay raises" (389).[10] It is, of course, true that Toelken received these advancements: but they were for his *good work* on Navajo folklore. I presume he would not have received them for bad work on Navajo folklore. I imagine that he would have received similar benefits for having done good work on the Child ballads or Beowulf, even if he did not himself elicit these ballad and epic texts from cooperative informants. And why did Yellowman tell Toelken his stories and allow and even ask for them to be recorded? One can only wonder about what Toelken gave Yellowman and his family in return that either Toelken is not owning-up to or does not himself recognize. Knowing Barre Toelken as I do, I would venture that it was considerable.

Toelken is certainly right when he acknowledges that he should have discussed the ultimate disposition of the tapes with Yellowman (1998:388). There are serious ethical issues in working with informants. But there is a serious ethical issue as well when workers in the academy deny the value of what they do. If folklorists cannot respect what scholars do and what they do as scholars, I wonder why they don't find another line of work. Deeply rooted in the psyches of many folklorists and anthropologists is an antipathy for their own culture. A discussion of the sources and consequences of this antipathy are probably worth at least an article, if not several books. Nevertheless, one can only wonder about the nature of the respect folklorists profess for other cultures when it seems to emanate from a profound disrespect for their own.

In 1990, a letter was published in the *American Folklore Society Newsletter*. The letter reports a trial that was going on in St. Albans, Vermont, concerning Abenaki fishing out of season in order to promote their claim as an Indian nation. The writer of the letter, Dr.

Joseph Bruchac, is a storyteller who claims some Abenaki ancestry.[11] He was called to testify as an expert witness in the case. He said that certain of the tales, "to our minds," reflected the "longstanding relationship of the Vermont Abenakis to the land and their continuance as an Indian people." He then told two tales and was cross-examined by the state attorneys. These attorneys tried to get Mr. Bruchac to admit that such stories—like the traditional stories of peoples everywhere—were likely to be ethnocentric and biased, and they would have been substantially altered in their transmission over the years. The attorney likened oral transmission to whispering something to someone, who in turn whispered it to someone else until what was said emerges as greatly changed. At this point, according to the account, the judge stepped in and said that they were talking about oral history and not a game of "Telephone." Mr. Bruchac's letter concludes with, "In any event, it was a good day for storytelling, and I think it was a good day for the Abenaki people" (Bruchac 1990).

I do not dispute Dr. Bruchac's claim that it was a good day for storytelling and for the Abenaki people.[12] My question is whether it was a good day for folklore? After all, if folklorists have established *anything* at all in their years of study, it is that oral traditions are malleable. Art, memory, creativity, and desire can reshape expression in profound ways (e.g., Burns 1970). Should folklorists celebrate the fact that the judge in the case was unwilling to entertain testimony on the nature of oral traditions and their propensities to change?

Now it might be supposed that Mr. Bruchac's letter was sent to the *American Folklore Society Newsletter* and the editor felt responsible to publish it even if it did not reflect considered folklore opinion. But, in fact, Mr. Bruchac's letter was *not* sent to the newsletter. It was published in the spring 1989 issue of *Atlatl: Native Arts Update* and permission was requested by the AFS newsletter editor to reprint it. The republication of the letter was meant to be congratulatory and celebratory. The question is why should folklorists celebrate the outcome of a court case—whether it confirmed or denied an individual's or group's claim—that negated or ignored what folklorists have painstakingly established about the processes of oral transmission?

The field of folklore has an ethic as does scholarship more generally: sustained and patient research, careful reporting, detailed analysis, insightful and creative commentary. Test concepts against evidence. Relate what has been found to what others have found. Build on the similarities and thrash out differences. Folklorists should criticize, respond to criticism, and produce knowledge. They should value that knowledge, make that knowledge known, and predicate action upon knowledge. This is not an ethic, however, that one can live by twenty-four hours a day, seven days a week: it is a situational ethic, and there are many situations when it has to be scrapped. But there are situations when each one of the Ten Commandments might have to be scrapped as well. In and of itself, this scholarly ethic is not a guide for living a virtuous life, but as it goes, it seems a good one: but only to those who view the activities of scholarly research as worthwhile.

Are there dangers in scholarly pursuits? Of course there are. What words or actions do not court danger? But I doubt the dangers of these pursuits are any greater than deliberate efforts to help people. In helping people, the intentions may be pure, but the outcomes may prove uncertain and profound. Folklorists, of all people, should know what the road to hell is paved with.

Most people want to be of some help, but the question, "How can I help?" can be asked by carpenters, engineers, and journalists as well as folklorists. The question is not in any way peculiar to folklore and does not define a folkloristic enterprise. Questions about tradition, memory, art, identity, and society should define folklore study, and there should be some commitment—an ethical commitment—to seriously formulating and responding to such questions.

Am I suggesting that folklorists stop doing activist folklore, stop being concerned with their informants, or stop turning their knowledge and practice toward the betterment of the communities in which they work or the world at large? I am not, I cannot, nor do I wish to. What I hope to do is call attention to a difference between an ethical and intellectual approach to doing folklore. By an ethical approach, I do not simply mean being ethical in the treatment of informants. Everyone should behave ethically in the treatment of people all of the time. Folklorists should be as ethical in their dealings with shopkeepers, gardeners, and neighbors as with their informants. By an "ethical approach," I mean an approach that puts the motive of service above that of inquiry—that puts the pursuit of social justice before the acquisition of knowledge. When the ethical approach is ascendant, folklore work becomes another form of social work. While I have no problem with the existence of social work as a field or with social workers as a group, one should not be surprised if a divide arises in the folklore community that parallels the divides between sociology and social work or between experimental and clinical psychology. The separation between these perspectives is real and consequential for the field of folklore. Contrary to what some folklorists have suggested, I do not see any benefit from attempting to bridge the gap, close the circle, or eradicate the dichotomies (Seeger 1966:6; Kirshenblatt-Gimblett 1988:152). Dichotomies help to keep positions clear and people honest.

17. Anti Anti-*Folklore*

The definition of folklore *has always been something of a problem, but that problem was exacerbated by both conceptual and economic upheavals at the end of the twentieth century. Changed conditions impelled some folklorists to reconsider the value of the term* folklore *both theoretically and practically. They questioned its usefulness in continuing to designate the work of scholars and the courses and programs in which students were trained. These suggestions were more than idle musings. The point was central in the 1996 American Folklore Society Presidential Address (Beck 1997:134). The term* Volkskunde *had been abandoned at a number of German universities. To date,* folklore *continues to be employed by scholars in the United States. The field, journals, and scholarly societies use* folklore, *although there are scholars who trained and received degrees in folklore who no longer characterize themselves as folklorists.*

> *My name, dear saint, is hateful to myself,*
> *because it is an enemy to thee.*
> —William Shakespeare

WHEN W. J. THOMS coined the word *folklore* in 1846, it moved into the vocabularies of various languages with surprising rapidity: not only into languages in the Indo-European language family, but into other language families as well.[1] However, a century and a half after the term was first invented, folklorists began to call for its elimination.[2] Two folklorists central in calling for the end of *folklore* were Regina Bendix and Barbara Kirshenblatt-Gimblett. Their arguments against the term were at once practical, theoretical, and moral, although these three impulses were anything but distinct.

The practical argument for changing the name *folklore* is that it fails to communicate. It fails in registering the discipline's accomplishments and insights with "broader communities of thought and action" (viz., other disciplines, granting agencies, government bureaucrats). Consequently, the name stands in the way of getting jobs both in and out of the academy (Bendix 1998:236). Folklore departments and programs, the argument runs, are stagnating if not shrinking, and public folklore and folklife programs are falling under government budgetary axes. The more the corporate model of management is adopted by institutions of higher learning, the more folklorists need to think in terms of their product and their position in the market. If folklorists wish to be players in this transcultural and commodifying postmodern age, *folklore* will not and cannot serve their purposes. The name does not provide the desired product recognition, and any market analyst would have advised folklorists to change their name decades ago (237).

In fact, a market analyst would first have done market research. A market analyst would find out what the reaction to the name was before suggesting a change. Are folklorists failing to get jobs in and outside the academy? The question can only be meaningfully answered with hard data. That data first and foremost depend upon folklore programs tracking their M.A. and Ph.D. students after graduation. Programs need to know what kinds of employment their students have sought, what they have found, and whether they feel their folklore training directly, indirectly, or negatively affected their abilities to gain employment.[3] Were such data forwarded by folklore degree programs to the American Folklore Society for amalgamation and analysis, folklorists would be in a much better position to ascertain the extent to which folklore training translates into jobs, the types of jobs folklorists hold, and where folklore studies stands in relation to other advanced-degree programs in the humanities. The perception of crisis in folklore studies cannot be rationally addressed if there are no means to ascertain how that perception maps onto reality. The field of anthropology has also regarded itself as in "crisis" (Ortner 1984:126; Appell 1992:193; Weiner 1995:14). Do folklore graduates students fare worse than graduates in anthropology?

Is the problem of folklore studies one of product recognition as Bendix argues? Or is the problem one of *name* recognition; the recognition of the name *folklore* as standing for a quality product. If folklore suffers from marketing problems, it suggests that there are possible marketing solutions—

solutions that do not require a change to the name of either the product or the scholarly engagement with that product.

Marketing problems may have practical solutions. Moral-theoretical problems are more insidious. The most serious charge against *folklore* is that the term itself is tainted: tainted by virtue of its origin and the vicissitudes of its history. Folklore is made, not found, says Kirshenblatt-Gimblett. It is not something out there waiting to be discovered. Folklore is rather something that is created in the act of naming and conceptualization (1996:245). Furthermore, folklore is a "discipline predicated on a vanishing subject," established on the expectation of imminent disappearance (249). Folklorists regard this disappearance as located in the real world, but in fact, says Kirshenblatt-Gimblett, it is part of their disciplinary subject. The moment of death is constant, shifting its location from one impending extinction to another. The constancy of this "eleventh hour" in folklore studies "indicates that it is our disciplinary subject, and with it our discipline, that is threatening to disappear" (249).[4]

It is hard to imagine that any discipline can escape the charge that its subject matter is constructed. In what respect are business, art, culture, politics, history, or mathematics any more "found" and any less "made" than folklore? The definitions of fields of study are always problematic. Basic terms elude neat formulation. Is mathematics the manipulation of numbers? What then is to be done with geometry which includes no numerical component? Even objects that we tend to feel are really out there in the world are often no more than categories constructed in particular historical and cultural settings. What, after all, is a "tree"? Do all societies unanimously lump together those objects that we consider to be "trees" under a single term? They do not.

Folklore has been concerned with the disappearing subject as Kirshenblatt-Gimblett claims; not exclusively, but perhaps disproportionately when compared with some other disciplines.[5] Even the collection of the most contemporary joke cycle or piece of photocopy or computer lore is motivated in part by a sense of its ephemerality—the sense of its imminent extinction. However, cultural disappearance is not a mere artifact of the folkloristic imagination. Death, unfortunately, is a fact, and not merely a fiction, of life.[6] Institutions, languages, practices, beliefs, and peoples do disappear.[7] In addition, folklore's affinity for the "eleventh hour" hardly evidences that the disciplinary subject, and consequently, the discipline of folklore is disappearing. Particular cultural forms disappear, but disappearance does not disappear. Disappearance is forever.

The discipline of paleontology is not threatened by its focus on the biologically extinct. What truly could threaten paleontology is not its obsession with extinction, but the resurrection of extinct reptiles.[8] Were such to occur, paleontology would be wholly absorbed into zoology. What would truly threaten a discipline devoted to cultural marginalization and disappearance would be a pervasive and indissoluble cultural persistence. A concern with disappearance in-and-of itself does not delegitimize folklore. Rather than discount a discipline rooted in a disappearing subject (and through some perverse logic, call for that discipline's disappearance), one might first attempt to theorize disappearance.[9] If folklore studies is concerned with disappearance, it suggests that the field has a unified subject and that field has an important mandate: accounting for the why, how, and consequences of cultural disappearance.[10]

For Kirshenblatt-Gimblett, cultural studies is the antithesis of folklore studies. Cultural studies is the discipline of the contemporary, situated where the "new politics of difference—racial, sexual, cultural, transnational—can combine and be articulated in all their dazzling plurality" (Grossberg in Kirshenblatt-Gimblett 1996:251).[11] Cultural studies focuses on difference, folklore studies on diversity; that is, on community, solidarity and tradition.[12] Assuming for the moment that this characterization is correct, is the world finished with community, solidarity, and tradition? Is the academy finished with community, solidarity, and tradition (Ortner 1984:157)? To the extent that a discipline of the contemporary can be imagined, so should a discipline of the disappearing. The contemporary can only be said to exist in relation to some marginalized and disappearing past. What could "contemporary" possibly mean in the absence of disappearance (Köstlin 1997:263)?[13] The old and the new are inextricable intertwined. As opposite sides of the same coin, it is difficult to grasp why an understanding of one could be more valuable than an understanding of the other.

According to Kirshenblatt-Gimblett, disappearance is not only a conceptual problem but a moral problem as well. Folklore is a function of collecting, remembering, and preserving only as a prelude to forgetting. The customs, beliefs, and expressions that excited the interests of the antiquaries of the seventeenth and eighteenth centuries and the folklorists of the nineteenth were out of step with the times. Whimsically quaint at best, vulgar errors at worst, the description and study of these customs were in fact preliminaries in a program of annihilation.

Kirshenblatt-Gimblett cites a number of instances in which the interest in, and the presentation of, culture functioned as a ritual of eradication: "The object . . . was not to understand . . . culture, but to perform it in a paradoxically selfconsuming fashion" (Mullaney in Kirshenblatt-Gimblett 1996: 246). Thus, folklore has been absorbed in a process of cultural eradication from its very beginnings. In its claim to study what is past, it has explicitly and covertly presented it as "falsity, wrongness, fantasy, and distortion" (Dorson in Kirshenblatt-Gimblett 1996:246). It is no wonder that the term *folklore* has failed to escape connotations of error in the public imagination. It is an idea which has been deeply implicated, according to Kirshenblatt-Gimblett, in the folklore project since its inception.

While there are certainly occasions when folklorists continue to promote the notion of folklore as error, it is hard to agree with Kirshenblatt-Gimblett's overall view of folklore studies.[14] In the first place, if there are any charges to be filed against contemporary folklore studies in its treatment of the past, it is not that it trivializes the past and underscores the error of it all. Rather, it is that folklore studies romanticizes the past and celebrates the value of it all. There are various ways of viewing the past; as something to be escaped or something to be reclaimed. Certainly both views are implicated in folklore studies, but if there is one that seems most problematic, it is the tendency to see the past as a resource to be conserved, reclaimed, and revitalized.[15] The romantic view of folklore has been the predominant one in folklore studies. Folklorists of a romantic bent are not satisfied to regard the past as past; they are impelled to describe, present, and valorize this past and to offer it up as an antidote to the present. Not only are they not engaged in a program of eradication, they endeavor to sustain and even resurrect dying arts, customs, and practices (Evans 1988; Jabbour 1989; Eff 1990). As even Kirshenblatt-Gimblett acknowledges, "Folklore is the champion of conservation" (1996:249).

That folklore studies has arisen in state societies implicated in the suppression and destruction of other societies and cultures does not bind folklore's project to the policies and programs of state organizations. The degree to which folklore studies aid and abet or undermine state interests is a matter for investigation. To assume that there is, and has been, a unanimity of program and purpose is to accord state societies an unwarranted degree of homogeneity—a homogeneity now disputed even for small scale hunting and horticultural communities. Folklorists did not set out to obliterate the past. Nor did they describe and study the past in order to forget it. As Laurence Gomme characterized folklore: "If investigation of the past be not wholly vain, wholly meaningless, then surely that branch of it which gives us the most intimate contact with the minds and hearts and souls of countless generations who otherwise would perish from our ken . . . may claim some need of recognition and respect" (Gomme in Dorson 1968a, 1:260).

Bendix is in full agreement with Kirshenblatt-Gimblett on folklore's "taint," although she is concerned with quite another blemish on its escutcheon: the one acquired through ethno-nationalistic uses of folklore and tradition to promote exclusionary, fascist, and sometimes murderous agendas. "The ideology inscribed in the field of folklore has . . . latently or . . . overtly assisted in a horrifying number of deaths." If folklorists would only accept responsibility for the term *folklore*, Bendix urges, folklorists would be able to distance themselves from the abuses to which the term has been put. Bendix lauds those German folklorists that turned away from the term *Volkskunde* because that discipline fueled a racist program. "Volkskunde will always be associated with the *volkisch* ideology of the Nazis no matter how much rehabilitation the discipline undergoes" (Bendix 1998:240). Consequently, Bendix endorses the change of program name in German universities from *Volkskunde* to "Europäische Ethnologie" (European Ethnology) and "Empirische Kulturwissenschaft" (Empirical Cultural Science).

Are such name changes appropriate? A change of name is, effectively, an act of forgetting: the suppression or repression of disturbing reminiscences. The past should be remembered. Folklore—all disciplines—need to be reminded of the uses to which they have been put and may be put again. Anthropology is not called upon to change its name because in the nineteenth- and twentieth-centuries "anthropologists" were steeped in racialist programs of inquiry (as were the practitioners of virtually every field of human science).[16] Nor should the horrors that have been committed in the name of "medical science" be forgotten. We need to remember and acknowledge unsavory tendencies in our disciplinary pasts. But this is not to concede that these tendencies continue to govern. Nazi ideology is no more inscribed in folklore studies than it is in the steam locomotive. That folklore has been used to promote extreme nationalisms does not make the stuff of folklore inherently nationalistic or folklorists extreme nationalists (Ben-Amos 1998:271). In the past decade, the word "inscribed" has become quite fashionable, but it should be used—like materials of folklore themselves—with circumspection. Notions of "tainted" and "inscribed" disciplines should be repudiated by those who would otherwise be suspicious of such essentializing.

What is perhaps most peculiar in Kirshenblatt-Gimblett's critique of folklore is that it recapitulates the very charge that she lays at the door of folklore studies. In trying to characterize the negative ways in which folklore studies were implicated in the obliteration of their subject, she relies upon Mona Ozouf's notion of "shameful ethnology" (1996:247); that is, the displaying and shaming of traditional beliefs and practices. Kirshenblatt-Gimblett points to a nineteenth-century German-Jewish magazine, *Sulamit*, which ran a column titled "Gallery of Obnoxious Abuses, Shocking Customs, and Absurd Ceremonies of the Jews" which was meant to malign various traditional religious and social practices. Religious reform in Germany was conducted through a process of stigmatization and embarrassment. The new refined and civilized practices would be defined and promoted in relation to the stigmatized ones. Curiously, Kirshenblatt-Gimblett does not seem to recognize that what the German Jews did to the practices of traditional orthodox Judaism, she is now doing to folklore. She has selected a few characteristics of the field and held them up for shameful display. The shame of folklore studies, according to Kirshenblatt-Gimblett, is that they themselves have been deeply implicated in a process of shaming as prelude to cultural obliteration.[17] But it is folklore studies that are in fact being held up for shame; a shame that should both impel and justify folklore's own obliteration. In the eyes of cultural studies, folklore studies should be excised from the academy as an absurd and harmful relic of a barbarian past. Like the orthodox customs maligned in the Jewish magazine, they are good for nothing but collection, study, and display. And this is precisely what cultural studies does to folklore; it scrutinizes the history and interrogates the practices of folklore studies. But it will have nothing to do with folklore or folklore studies concepts in-and-of themselves.[18]

Kirshenblatt-Gimblett assures that change in disciplines is natural. It has been going on for centuries and will continue. Ceasing to employ the term *folklore* to designate a field of study is simply part and parcel of the ordinary course of change. The discipline Kirshenblatt-Gimblett uses to illustrate her point is the omnibus discipline of geography. Geography once claimed all on the earth's surface: geology, meteorology, oceanography, botany, zoology, as well as what we now call anthropology and folklore. Every university had a department of geography. Today very few departments of geography remain and the field has largely shrunk to urban planning and environmental studies on the one hand, and the phenomenology of space on the other (1996:249–250). But as Kirshenblatt-Gimblett also tells us, folklore is one of the fragments of what once was philology. Folklore never was an omnibus discipline. In the United States, its life in the academy is somewhat over sixty years.[19] In England, Australia, and other English-speaking countries, it has had no such life. "Disciplines are aging," as Kirshenblatt-Gimblett says, but an academic discipline dead at sixty?

I am less sanguine than Bendix and Kirshenblatt-Gimblett about the postdisciplinary world into which folklore studies would be absorbed. I believe in the existence of social forces which impact upon the community and the individual and which may, and in some cases must, elude human control. Although I have great respect for the human imagination, the world is not simply the happy space of our own imaginings. Utopias always fail, not for want of imagination or will, but from a failure to recognize that the social and psychological are not entirely matters of human agency (Schudson 1997:50–52). My sense is that there will be disciplines and departments as long as scholarly and scientific research is based in bureaucratic institutions. I suspect that the "postdisciplinary formation" that Kirshenblatt-Gimblett envisions folklore becoming (1996:252) will be no formation at all.[20]

Why should anyone want to call for an end to the name *folklore*? Who would benefit and how from giving up the name? As far as I can tell, those who would favor relinquishing the name have already done so. They have merged with the programs with which they are affiliated. They have become literary critics, historians, linguistic anthropologists, or cultural studies or performance studies practitioners. They are not bound by the term *folklore* or the concerns of "folklorists." Certainly, few who are active in cultural studies today have degrees in it. They have become cultural critics by virtue of their theoretical, research, organizational, and literary affiliations. In any event, no one asks to see your Ph.D., and if most folklore degrees look anything like mine, there is not even an allusion to the folklore program in which one was trained. As far as I can tell from looking at my degree, I am a philosopher. To my mind, that is as it should be. Philosophy is, and has been, the umbrella term for the intellectual work that academics in all disciplines do.

Why would those who have abandoned the folklore agenda and name be interested that others give up the term as well? How would they benefit? Why should the American Folklore Society "support the efforts of its members to seek the best possible way to support the field within their given institutional setting" (Bendix 1998) if that field is not the field of folklore? And if it is the field of folklore, why abandon the name and the strength that might be derived from its affiliation with a broader body of practitioners in a centuries-old endeavor? And what benefits would accrue to those who call themselves "folklorists" by giving up the name? Once the name is abandoned, who is the "we" that would move on? Folklorists exist only as long as the term "folklore" continues to exist.[21] After *folklore*, "we" are no more.

Can those in other disciplines actually see some value in the termination of folklore studies? Would cultural studies realize some gain in bringing the handful of folklore M.A. and Ph.D. programs to an end? Are resources being squandered on the work of folklorists? If what folklorists are doing is commensurate with the work that is being done in other disciplines, what matter if it goes under the name *folklore*? And if folklore studies is truly not "with it," at the so-called cutting edge of cultural inquiry, should not our difference be tolerated, even appreciated, by fields that claim to be dedicated to difference, diversity, and marginality? Where, after all, is that sense of the "dazzling plurality" that cultural studies would claim to valorize? Do not read this as a rationale for bad work. But it is a repudiation of the notion that folklorists must adopt the theories, methods, and concerns of cultural studies wholesale and be absorbed into its program. I reject Bendix's injunction that our knowledge production should be directed toward "the negotiation of global transcultural relationships" (1998:242). If that is what a folklorist wants to do, fine. But folklore studies is not about "late capitalism" (Jameson 1984), "fast capitalism" (Agger 1992:148), or "flexible accumulation" (Harvey 1990:147). It is about people—individuals and communities—and their aesthetic expressions.[22] To the extent that peoples' arts are affected by global economic and political changes, the folklorist has cause to be interested. But to ask folklorists to abandon the forms and peoples they have traditionally studied for a current fashion? And what will happen when the fashion passes?[23] There are people, behaviors, and expressions that will not be examined, or even observed, by those who are focused on cultural commodification, computer mediated communication, and transnational exchange. Cultural studies will never know how "folk" communities and their expressions might challenge its own comfortable theorizing, unless there are folklorists to tell them.[24]

In fact, there is no percentage for the "larger whole" that Bendix speaks of (1998:243 n5) if everyone joins the compact majority. Humanistic inquiry is not some Los Alamos project that can be brought to a successful resolution with the proper equations, computations, and engineering. Opposition, resistance, and marginality are necessary.²⁵ If there is no place for folklore studies anywhere in the academy, then there are bigger things to worry about than the fate of folklore. It will be the academy that is in jeopardy.

There never was a golden age of folklore studies (Ben-Amos 1998:262). There probably will never be one.²⁶ Nevertheless, I am content to live a marginal scholarly existence. But I will not be happy to exchange marginality for termination. And strangely, I hear no calls from outside folklore studies for its destruction. I confess to being somewhat at a loss to explain the calls from within. As individuals and as a society, we have not even made the beginnings of an attempt to register the contributions of folklore research to philosophical inquiry. In this the American Folklore Society has been a failure, and I would further suggest that a great number of folklorists have been cowards. We have not identified ourselves as folklorists, we have not identified our best work as springing from our folklore training and interests, we have not vigorously defended folklore studies when occasion demanded, and we have been timid in labeling bad work in folklore as unmitigatingly "bad." We live in an age when everyone is coming out of the closet, save folklorists, who are rushing in. It seems we operate with a deep sense of shame.

I cannot quite get Kirshenblatt-Gimblett's reference to German Jewry out of my mind. In 1893, Theodor Herzl, worried by the continued non-assimilation of the Jews, proposed the mass conversion of all the Jewish children in the Austro-Hungarian Empire. A mass conversion, Herzl reasoned, would overcome the shame that attached to the individual Jew who wanted to convert. Herzl and other community leaders would accompany the children to the doors of St. Stephen's in Vienna, but would remain outside. They would not convert. But the place of the next generation of Jews in Central European society would be assured. The "Jewish question" would be finally resolved.²⁷ The editors of the *Neue Freie Presse* for whom Herzl worked—both assimilated Jews—talked him out of publishing his proposal, and he gave up the plan (Elon 1975:114–117). Two years later, he had a very different idea.²⁸

18. Theorizing Trivia: A Thought Experiment

The catalog presented in the Introduction as to why folklore has been dismissed and seems dismissible needs amendment. Folklore constitutes such a miscellaneous assemblage of beliefs, practices, and artifacts that no coherent sense of the domain can be easily formulated let alone theorized. In other words, folklore emerges as a list of trivial forms. Can there be any justification for a field embarked on an encounter with trivialities? The concept of trivial, however, is not transparent. Are things trivial in themselves or are they trivial by virtue of context or perspective? The meditation below entertains the idea that the things that folklorists call folklore *might be trivial, but in acknowledging that triviality, one is led to confront matters of great significance.*

> *What mighty contests rise from trivial things.*
> —Alexander Pope

IF THERE IS A SINGLE problem that has plagued folklore as a field of inquiry since its inception, it has been the reconciliation of subject diversity with conceptual unity. While *antiquities*—the precursor of *folklore*—were relatively well-defined as a category, that category constituted a miscellany without conceptual integrity. Antiquities included, as Francis Grose pointed out, "monuments, statues, coins, manuscripts, and customs" (Grose in Dorson 1968a, 1:2). Certainly all these materials derived from the ancient past, but the individual antiquities coalesced into no coherent whole. Grose argued for the importance of antiquarian knowledge to the divine, jurist, statesman, soldier, architect, and gentleman, but other than the fact that antiquities offered the opportunity to learn from the past, *what* could be learned from the past was exceedingly diverse. The divine might uncover the foundation of his religious ceremonies as the jurist might discern those customs in which common law is rooted. The soldier might grasp the significance of past battles from an assessment of ancient ordnance; the statesman or legislator might learn the causes of the subversion of kingdoms; the architect might learn the proper way to repair an ancient church; the gentleman might learn appropriate costuming for a masque (3–4).

Popular antiquities focused upon the rites, sports, and opinions of the common people (John Brand in Dorson 1968a 1:6–8). This subset of antiquarian activity was not haphazard, as it was held to reveal connections to past ritual and belief (11). Although popular antiquities consisted of assorted and sundry materials, these materials were theoretically unified. They derived from—and consequently spoke to—the religious and philosophical doctrines of ancient times.

In *Deutsche Mythologie,* Jacob Grimm revealed the systematic nature of these doctrines and demonstrated a method by which they could be reconstructed. W. J. Thoms's felicitous phrase captured the theoretical unity of the Grimm's inquiry. To study folklore was to pursue past knowledge and doctrine ("lore") surviving in the idioms and practices of common people ("folk") and to restore its intellectual integrity as a systematic body of knowledge. The success of the term *folklore* rested upon severing popular antiquities from other objects of antiquarian study and registering the common thread uniting an otherwise great assortment of objects, expressions, and behaviors.

Folklore studies has continually been faced with the challenge of identifying a conceptual unity within the diversity of its subject matter. When the unity established by the Victorian folklorists under the banner of the survival of religious and philosophical doctrine began to weaken, new conceptualizations were required to hold the field together. Concepts of "tradition," "art," "orality," the "face-to-face," and the "quotidian" were invoked to register an underlying unity and to demonstrate that these materials were matters of consequence (Ben-Amos 1971:12–13). As these centralizing concepts came to be questioned in more recent times (Handler and Linnekin 1984; Shuman 1993), folklore was described as facing a disciplinary "crisis" (Kirshenblatt-Gimblett 1994:237).

What if folklorists were to abandon the quest for conceptual integrity and study "manners, customs, observances, superstitions, ballads, proverbs &c" (Thoms in Dorson 1968a, 1:53) with the full understanding that it is a miscellany lacking any conceptual integrity? What if folklorists were to accept at face value Thoms's characterization of the materials as "a mass of minute facts, many of which when separately considered, appear trifling and insignificant" (1968a, 1:53). What if folklorists confessed their passion for the overlooked and otherwise ignored; the flotsam and jetsam of disciplinary inquiry? What if folklorists unabashedly declared themselves students of the trivial? Where might this lead?

Postmodernists would be pleased. Folklorists would have acknowledged "the death . . . of a subject that is unified, stable, and centered" (Kirshenblatt-Gimblett 1994:234). They would study materials with no inherent connections to one another and subsumed under no essentializing concept. Each item would be studied individually. Eventually, the items would be situated in some other disciplinary discussion and made meaningful in the context of that discourse.

In effect, that is already happening. If one looks at a typical program from the American Folklore Society annual meeting, one is struck by the enormous variation in the materials studied as well as the analytic approaches taken. Nevertheless, there is an overall strategy, which is to take a piece of seeming trivia and show that it is somehow important. Thus, an Afro-Brazilian game is part and parcel of Yoruba philosophy. Dissimilar performances of *Pretty Polly* by two brothers reveal "the importance of musical diversity in the community." An annual jeep safari fosters a "sense of brotherhood" and "equality." Photocopy lore is deeply implicated in "the politics of class and gender." A children's counting-out game is a "classic puzzle in mathematics" (American Folklore Society 1995). And so it goes. In each case, the oddity is allied to concepts in some other discourse that confer legitimacy. But shouldn't the study of these individual items properly be left to those disciplines in which they are legitimized and made meaningful? Could there be any rationale for maintaining such trivia under the umbrella term *folklore*? Is there any way to theorize a miscellany of trivia while continuing to recognize their miscellaneous and trivial nature?

There would seem to be another possible approach. The kinds of trivia that have been traditionally called *folklore* are regarded as *interesting*. Even laypersons who have no knowledge of folklore theory or the various attempts to define folklore find the stuff of folklore fascinating (Georges 1991:6). What is it that makes some things interesting? The notion of "interesting" has not been sufficiently explored, but at some level, what constitutes the interesting is that which challenges our "routinized taken-for-granted world of everyday life" (Davis 1971:311). If folklore is interesting, this miscellany, in some manner, must disturb presumptions about the way the world appears and is understood. To the extent that scholars find the materials of folklore interesting, these materials must throw up some challenge to a subset of everyday scholarly assumptions.

Of course, the attempt to characterize the way in which these materials counter the taken-for-granted world of either scholars or laypeople would involve a re-theorization of folklore—something that we initially set out to avoid. Consequently, we can only extend the insight that the kinds of trivia that folklorists study resist dominant assumptions and understandings.

The only recourse, it would seem, is to cast the study of trivia as a program of counterinsurgency against the propositions and theories that hold sway in the world and in the academy. Folklorists would become academic guerillas attacking and undermining the prevailing theoretical paradigms using knowledge derived from a close analysis of some part of their miscellany of trivial cultural forms. Folklorists would constitute some sort of perpetual loyal opposition in the parliament of ideas. Folklore and folklorists would only be conceptualized in relation to the constantly changing intellectual fashions they critique.

Given the marginality of the materials and peoples that folklorists study, and the marginality of folklorists in the world of scholarship, it might make some sense for folklorists to turn that marginality to useful ends. Rather than complain that they "don't get respect" (Pimple 1996:20), they would proclaim that they aren't seeking respect at all. What they want is an argument in which closely examined, if trivial, materials are employed as critical counter-examples to grand and not-so-grand theorizing broadcast from disciplinary centers. Folklorists would generate the kinds of anomalies that provoke the crises that drive conceptual revolutions (Kuhn 1962:82).

Of course, if trivia might serve to fuel a state of constant theoretical revolution, one wonders how the study of trivia could in any sense be regarded as trivial. Just as essentializing concepts inevitably seem to undo themselves, so it would seem that efforts at undoing inexorably lead back toward the center of things. From trivia, we are directed to matters of gravity and consequence. The periphery does not hold. And why should it?

There really are no such things as trivia, because things are not trifling in-and-of themselves. Knowledge only appears trivial absent a context. What is the value of simply knowing that the half-life of carbon 14 is 5730 ± 40 years? In isolation, it is a piece of trivia. In the context of the dating of artifacts, however, it fundamentally changes the reckoning of history. The word *trivia* itself was once steeped in matters of consequence. In the late Middle Ages, trivia constituted those three liberal arts—grammar, rhetoric, and logic—basic to university education. The word itself derives from the "joining of three roads" (*tri* + *via*). *Trivia* designated a crossroad, a place both feared and respected, through which all travelers must eventually pass.

Notes

Introduction

1. See Jeffrey Mazo (1996) on an alternative origin of the word *folklore*.
2. The concept of survivals preceded evolution and could operate independently of it.
3. It was born again in anthropology during the 1950s and 60s (White 1949, 1959). Evolution experienced no such rebirth in folklore studies, however.
4. Sociology, psychoanalysis, and linguistics were not oblivious of history. But the forces motivating human behavior and institutions, even if they were the result of historical factors, operated in the present.
5. Although many psychoanalysts wrote about folklore, including Sigmund Freud, few folklorists extensively or doctrinally utilized psychoanalytic theory, Alan Dundes (1935–2005) being the notable exception.
6. These views entered both folklore and anthropology through functionalism. The functionalism in anthropology had its roots in the works of Durkheim (1858–1917) and was promoted by anthropologist A. R. Radcliffe-Brown (1881–1955). The functionalism in folklore studies, however, was psychoanalytically inflected and was inspired by the work of anthropologist Bronislaw Malinowski (1884–1942).
7. There are art historians and collectors who do employ the term *folk art*, but it is rooted in notions of excellence and connoisseurship, not in the social or psychological.
8. Students who enrolled in my folklore classes initially associated the places where folklore was to be found with remote geographies—e.g., the Appalachians, the Ozarks—and the "backward" peoples who inhabited them.
9. Furthermore, marginal social groups are often products of centralized social processes (Dorson 1959; Bauman 1983). Federal spending on defense and immigration legislation, for example, had an enormous impact on the formation of African-American communities in the United States during and in the wake of two world wars.
10. One example is an analysis of the jokes that followed the explosion of the space shuttle Challenger in 1986 (Oring 1987) that was later generalized to a theory of sick humor about celebrity deaths and public disasters (Davies 2001).
11. I have defined Jewish humor as that which has been labeled "Jewish humor" (Oring 1992:112-121), without abandoning an interest in analyzing and interpreting the humor itself.
12. It would be limited to scrutinizing past conceptualizations and approaches, as there would be no justification for further efforts in grappling with the materials themselves. After all, the materials are not folklore. What folklorists study would be folklore. Since the study of folklore would be the study of what folklorists study, it eventually would become the study of folklorists studying what folklorists study since that is what folklorists are now studying. And so on.

1. The Arts, Artifacts, and Artifices of Identity

1. Two years later it appeared in the title of another essay in the same journal (Oring 1973).

2. Identity is related to a host of other concepts—self, ego, individual, person, persona, character, personality—but the relations are often vague and remain to be mapped (Fogelson 1982:92).

3. Sigmund Freud, who throughout his life labored to uncover the workings of the unconscious mind, never employed the term or conceptualized identity in his psychological works. But he did, in addressing the members of the B'nai B'rith, use the term "inner identity" to refer to a consciousness of kind that was accompanied by powerful, emotionally-charged forces that bound him to Jewry and the community of Jews (Erikson 1959:101–102; S. Freud 1959 [1929], 20:273–274). These forces were "dark" and "inaccessible to any analysis" (E. Freud 1960:376, 428).

4. Although the distinctions I am making have long been noted, the terms for these concepts vary, and the same terms may be applied to different concepts (Whittaker 1992:198–201).

5. When Erik Erikson wrote his essay "Reflections of American Identity," he employed, perhaps unsurprisingly, American folklore to help establish the contours of this identity (Erikson 1963:297–306).

6. Note Edward Spicer's distinction: "An identity system thus develops independently of those processes by which a total cultural pattern, a set of particular customs and beliefs constituting a way of life, is maintained" (1971:798). Nevertheless, the confusion is often made (see Carpenter and Vidutis 1984:233).

7. Jacob Grimm, however, was quite aware that Christianity had done much to preserve ancient heathen practice (Grimm 1966, 3:xxxv–xlvii).

8. Both Herder and the Grimms felt that the primary expression of national identity was to be found in language. Now, what was being called *folklore* was accorded this privileged position.

9. Which is not to say that the folklorists thought of primitive culture as being entirely without worth or that something was not lost in the process of civilization. In this respect, they shared the romantic view of Herder and the Grimms.

10. Survivalists, however, could relate their discussions to ethnic and regional groupings. In the debate as to whether English political institutions were of Roman or Anglo-Saxon origin, Laurence Gomme suggested that since primitive democratic assemblies were not found among all the Aryan nations, they might harken back to a more ancient Celtic period (de Caro 1972:206–216). Otis Mason acknowledged that "place, race, or people" might give rise to particular "lore areas" (1891:102).

11. Actually, Gottlund was not at all pleased with Lönnrot's success. In the first place, Gottlund himself hoped to get the credit for rescuing Finnish folk poetry from oblivion. Second, Lönnrot received the professorship in Finnish language and literature for which Gottlund had applied. Third, Lönnrot stated in his introduction to the *Kalevala* that no one had thought of editing the individual poems into a larger epic whole, although Gottlund had previously written on this matter (Anttila 1931–1935, 1:242–244; 2:104–115; Hautala 1954:95–101, 119, 148–149).

12. Perhaps Lönnrot, to some extent, had glimpsed this fundamental equation as well when he claimed that variants and variation were the touchstone of authenticity (Wilson 1976a:41).

13. Gummere ends his book *The Popular Ballad* with the observation that it "is no individual that speaks out his thoughts, his hopes, his fears in the ballads" and invokes Herder's appellation of folk songs as the "Voices of the Nations" (Gummere 1959:344).

14. In truth, American folklorists were not always as sensitive to the processes of tradition as they might have been. Many tended to overlook the idea of selection as an active affirmation of the past, and regarded continuities over time simply as part of an inexorable inheritance. Thus, they were able to maintain an artifactual sense of folklore while, at the same time, defining folklore in terms of the re-creative process. They did not see that folklore might reflect identity, whether it was traditional or transformed. In some sense, folklore's relation to identity was bifurcated. If it was innovative, identity emerged from the creative process; if it was traditional, identity was lodged in the communal past. The conflict that is often represented in folklore studies between "tradition" and "change," between "dynamism" and "conservatism" is, in fact, a conflict between paradigms of identity and its expression. Only in the late twentieth century did folklorists begin to imagine both continuity and change as contemporary choices (Ben-Amos 1984:116).

15. Yet, only about thirty-five monographs have relied upon the method (Goldberg 1984:16 n1).

16. Kaarle Krohn, who had maintained his father's position on the development of the Kalevala poems, reversed himself in *Kalevala Questions* in 1918. He maintained that the poems had not been borrowed, that they had originated as wholes which had later fragmented, and in pagan rather than Christian times (Wilson 1976a:81).

17. To demonstrate that folklore crosses national or other group boundaries ultimately confronts the issue of identity, if only by calling the relationship between folklore and identity into question. For example, since aspects of the Spiritual could be traced to both European and African song traditions, a debate arose over whether they were essentially white or Negro. The debate, in other words, was: to whom did the songs belong and whose "voices," "aspirations," and "genius" did they reflect? See Wilgus's outline of the controversy (1959:345–364).

18. Timothy Cochrane (1987:48) does not understand why folklorists have not made more use of the oicotype concept that they have so openly advocated. The answer would seem to be that folklorists have simply assumed a unique relationship between the traditions they study and the groups in which they are found. Since contemporary folklorists rarely study a song or tale type but a constellation of songs and stories, this assumption has greater plausibility. But ultimately, it is simply easier to claim uniqueness than to demonstrate it.

19. William A. Wilson has drawn attention to the connection between Dorson's attempts to define and characterize an American folklore and the romantic-nationalistic projects of emerging European nations (1989).

20. Such variation, rather than orality per se, came to be employed as the touchstone of genuine folklore. Photocopy lore, though mechanically reproduced, was considered to be genuine folklore: "One result of multiple existence is

variation.... Each person (and ultimately each society) makes the item of folklore his own by consciously or unconsciously placing his personal interpretive stamp upon it" (Dundes and Pagter 1975:xvii).

21. Dorson had to reframe his conceptualization of folklore. Rather than being defined in terms of oral tradition, it was regarded as the "culture of the people ... lying in the shadow of official civilization" (Dorson 1968b:37). Of course, much of this shadow culture was still traditional, composed of "age-old lore" absorbed from parents and peers (37). But folklore was not tied to tradition by definition. Nor was it tied to any particular group of people. "We are all carriers and conveyers of expressive culture" (Dorson 1978b:267) when we are not acting in our "official" roles and capacities.

22. Some modern theorists seem more reluctant to dispense with the concept of tradition; see Abrahams (1971:30) and Kirshenblatt-Gimblett (1983:208–213).

23. This presentist orientation in contemporary folklore studies was in large part influenced by functionalism with its synchronic perspective. It is worth noting, however, that functionalism in folklore studies was almost invariably of the Malinowskian variety—that is, psychologically expressive rather than sociostructurally utilitarian (e.g., Bascom 1954; Abrahams 1971:18).

24. History has proved a particular problem for the performance approach as it can only deal with cultural production, but not cultural reproduction (Bauman and Briggs 1990:79).

25. Geertz is specifically cited by Abrahams (1977:94–95).

26. The issue here is not whether folklore is generated among individuals who share or do not share identities, but that identity is conceived as central to the production, and consequently, to the meaning of folklore.

27. What has been called performance theory is, in fact, a research strategy. Performance theory explains nothing. It only tells where one should look for certain kinds of explanations.

28. It is instructive to look at Sandra Dolby Stahl's attempt to make the case for personal experience narrative as a legitimate folklore genre. Her first effort involved a series of acrobatic maneuvers to demonstrate the "traditionality" of such stories. Ultimately, she finds that the tellers of such stories belong to "reference groups" whose "shared attitudes" are expressed in personal experience stories. Thus, she attempts to legitimate these stories in terms of their expression of a collective identity (Stahl 1977:22). Later, she abandons this strategy and simply accepts personal experience narratives as artistic constructions that express "part of the 'inner life' of the storyteller" and express those "'categories of value' of most concern to the tellers and listeners" (Dolby-Stahl 1985:47, 50).

29. All sorts of ironies emerge from this perspective. Often those who were most faithful to tradition were most radically affected by the commercial forces. Those who replicated antiques were acting on the same premises as those who conferred value on the originals (Bausinger 1990:128).

30. Glassie would employ the term in another, more robust work on Turkish art (1993b:336, 338–339, 602, 829–831, 862).

31. For example, Michael Owen Jones sees folklore as essentially part and parcel of the study of organizations (1991); that is, as the study of society. Jay Mechling characterizes folklore as part of communication studies (1991).

32. For example, "Earlier definitions of folklore were clouded by romantic mists and haunted by the notion of 'popular antiquities'" (Ben-Amos 1971:4). Or: "Ours has been an antiquarian, or historically oriented discipline, devoting its efforts to the preservation of performance so that we may study the way in which they were constructed and the paths by which they have been disseminated" (Abrahams and Kalčik 1971:228).

33. "Wahrheit und Ausdruck" (Schütze 1920:65). Of course, concepts of identity have changed since the time of Herder. Identity may not be regarded as an essential and enduring entity, but as a contingent construction, born in interaction and achieved through performance (Workman 1993; Fine and Speer 1992). Identity may be fragmented, conflicted, compartmentalized, or negotiated (Oring 1981, 1984, 1992:67–80), and may not cohere according to any single, unifying principle. Margins and boundaries, rather than the centers of social and cultural groupings, may be highlighted as key sites of identity formation and expression (Abrahams 1981; Baumann 1971b). More emphasis is placed on identity as self-conscious reflection rather than unconscious expression (Bauman 1988; Fine and Speer 1992), and more attention is being directed to personal, not just collective, identity (Jones 1989; Kirshenblatt-Gimblett 1989; Stahl 1989). These changes in the conceptualization of identity, however, do not alter the fundamental commitment of folklore studies to the identity project.

34. When the concept of identity is explicitly confronted, the greatest emphasis has been given to sociological markers, rather than orienting values, goals, and meanings (e.g., Badone 1987; Coggeshall 1986). While such markers are relevant to a study of identity, they are not central to it.

2. Whaling Songs and the Context of Fantasy

1. For examples of those who saw natural phenomena as the ultimate inspiration for folklore content, see Max Müller (1871–1876), Angelo De Gubernatis (1872), or John Fiske (1872).

2. Wish fulfillment is a concept central to Sigmund Freud's theory of dreams, linguistic and behavioral errors, psychoneuroses, and folklore. See Freud (1953 4:121–134). Boas attended Freud's lectures at Clark College in 1909.

3. Benedict was aware that some distortion could be attributed to cultural lag. Zuni tales recount entrance to houses by means of ladders descending from the roof. Ladders had once been used, but by the late nineteenth century, most houses had doors. At the time of Benedict's collection of stories, doors were universal. Only kivas were entered by ladder (Benedict 1935: 1:xiv). Marc Galanter noticed something similar in lawyer jokes in the 1990s. In the United States, the jokes reflected the condition of legal practice in a previous era. In India, a joke might describe an attorney arguing before a jury, although jury trials had not been conducted in India for more than a century (Galanter 2005:154, 254).

4. For an exception see Bullen (1899:1–6).

5. Even the outfitters came to use the term "landsharks" for themselves, and the New Bedford Outfitters' Association had to impose fines on members who employed the term during their own meetings (Hohman 1928:97–98n).

6. The captain brought a medicine chest on board and acted as ship's surgeon, but the crew members were charged for the cost of the medicines (Hohman 1928:137, 264).

7. This was to prevent men who had been shanghaied from escaping.

8. Huntington believes that this is a song the whalers sang, and he includes music with the verse although he admits that he borrowed the music from a different song (1964:20). Elmo Paul Homan feels that this was a poem composed by H. T. Cheever for the epigraph of a chapter of his book (Hohman 1928:214n). The language of the song appears more characteristic of a literary effort than the product of oral transmission.

9. Right and bowhead whales generally produced more oil than sperm whales of the same size, and right whales could be obtained with voyages of shorter duration (Hohman 1928:284n).

10. There is one song of the Greenland fishery that mentions trying out the whale. The song is found on the phonograph record *Thar She Blows* (Lloyd and MacColl 1956) but as is noted, "the song collector . . . heard fisher girls in northeast Scotland sing the melody in the 1880s." In the 1880s, tryworks would have been more commonly used in the British Greenland fishery.

11. Beside the forty-four point compass and the compression of the harpooning and lancing sequence, only one other significant distortion appears in the songs. In two of the songs about the Greenland whale fishery (Lloyd and MacColl 1956: side 1, bands 4, 5), there is a mention of sperm whales. Sperm whales, however, were found mainly in tropical and sub-tropical seas and did not frequent the northern seas (Ashley 1938: 141; Chatterton 1930:15), although they might occasionally be found on the fringes of the Arctic and Antarctic. Furthermore, another song (Lloyd and MacColl 1956: side 1, band 1) is called "Sperm Whale Fishery" even though it deals with the Greenland fishery, and there is no mention of sperm whales in the song. Possibly, the use of "sperm whale" in reference to the Greenland fishery is an idealization as sperm whales were considered a more dangerous, valuable, and prestigious catch. Employing the term might have been meant to endow the Greenland industry with greater standing.

12. It is estimated that ten percent of the whales harpooned were not captured. There was an average of one death per voyage—a mortality rate of over three percent (Hohman 1928:316).

13. There are two songs that deal with the unusual experience of being swallowed by a whale. The songs are "Paddy and the Whale" and "Jack was Every Inch a Sailor" (Greenleaf 1933:138, 252). There is no indication that these songs were actually sung by whalers, but the former does appear on *Thar She Blows* (Lloyd and MacColl 1956: side 2, band 2).

3. Totemism and the A.E.F. Revisited

1. For an analogous, although not identical, relationship with a rooster, see Granot (1969).

2. The term "grunt" was originally restricted to Marines but later was extended to combat troops in general (Herr 1975:100). There are two traditional connotations to the term "grunt" that make it relevant to combat soldiers: (1) a pig (as in

"grunter"), and (2) a habitual grumbler or complaint (Farmer and Henley 1970; Berry and Van Den Bark 1947).

3. Structuralist terminology would distinguish the mongoose as *metaphor* and Bruce as *metonym* (see Leach 1976:14).

4. Note that dead men are not a social group but a natural species. The mongoose may also be considered as the representative of a species, rather than as an individual, since it never acquired a name. It was simply referred to as "the mongoose."

4. The Structure of a Joke Repertoire

1. The members of particular units would go on to claim that their unit was the elite of the Palmach.

2. This joke is not enjoyed, in large part, because it has to be explained. If one does not undergo the process of rapidly recognizing an appropriate incongruity, the humor may be understood but not experienced and enjoyed.

3. "Levantine" means "of the Levant," the lands east of the Mediterranean Sea.

4. A script is "a chunk of semantic information surrounding a word or evoked by it. The script is a cognitive structure internalized by the native speaker and represents the native speaker's knowledge of a small part of the world" (Raskin 1985:81).

5. Eli Yassif, in his review of my book *Israeli Humor*, categorized my analysis as based on "the binary oppositions of Lévi-Strauss" (1982:142). Although I was very aware of Lévi-Strauss's work, the structure actually emerged from the analysis of the appropriate incongruities in the chizbat repertoire. I was not trying to replicate Lévi-Strauss's methods.

5. Forest Lawn and the Iconography of American Death

1. These numbers were provided by administrators at Forest Lawn and mentioned in its brochures. I suspect they are stock numbers. The figure of fifty-thousand weddings was already cited some forty years ago. The number is repeated again in St. John (1959). The figure of a million yearly tourists also shows up regularly. Although Forest Lawn counts entrances to the Mausoleum and sometimes to the Hall of the Crucifixion, they do not monitor the number of entries into the park itself.

2. Forest Lawn Memorial Park, Glendale, was only the first. Other Forest Lawns—Hollywood Hills, Cypress, Covina, and most recently, Long Beach—were subsequently established.

3. For those familiar with Protestant cemeteries, this will not prove surprising, as explicit Christian symbolism (e.g., crosses, Bibles, biblical figures and scenes) is often meager.

4. There are several of these throughout the park, however.

5. Entombment in the Memorial Court of Honor in the Great Mausoleum, which is determined by the Trustees of Forest Lawn, is one such exception.

330   Notes to Pages 77–90

6. The quotation is originally from John C. London's *On the Laying Out, Planting and Managing of Cemeteries* published in 1843 and is quoted in French (1975). Also see Gillon Jr. (1972:v–xiii) and Harris (1966:200–208).

7. For good overviews of Victorian culture see Howe, ed. (1976); particularly the essays by Howe and Coben.

8. For an excellent description of this consolation literature see Douglas (1975).

9. Also see his "Asides to the Reader" (Bode 1959:ix–xv) where he develops some other points concerning Victorian culture.

10. Hubert Eaton's first acquisition for Forest Lawn was Elizabeth Barrett Parson's bronze *Duck Baby,* which he saw at the 1915 Pan-Pacific International Exposition in San Francisco; (St. John 1959:105). For the influence of the exhibition complex on Hubert Eaton, see Rubin et al. (1979:1–12).

11. Forest Lawn can legitimately be linked with Hollywood and Disneyland to the extent that all have been motivated by the same Victorian tastes and values. For an exploration of one aspect of the attempt to suppress Victorianism, see Oring (2003:71–84).

6. Dyadic Traditions

1. For example, see Nickerson (1974), Danielson (1977), Lawless (1983).

2. The very same claim had been made almost three-quarters of a century before by Joseph Jacobs (1893:237).

3. Jay Mechling (1989) has argued that there are traditions established between humans and animals and even "solo folklore" (2006).

4. Dyadic traditions fall within the concept of "idioculture" defined by Gary Alan Fine. However, dyadic traditions are conceptualized by the dyad as unique properties of the unit or unique enactments of more widely shared properties (Fine 1979a). My notion of tradition does not accord with that of Edward Shils, who requires two "transmissions" over three "generations" for a pattern to be considered a tradition (Shils 1981:15). Dyadic traditions require a minimum of two transmissions, but not over generations. Dyadic traditions are oscillating rather than linear transmissions. They are created and passed back and forth but, for the most part, they are not passed on.

5. Fine has described the "triggering events" for the creation of an idioculture as potentially infinite and hence unpredictable (1979a:742–743).

6. They did not get the quote exactly right. They told me that the proverb was: "*Ḥayyim ve-mavet be-yad ha-lashon.*"

7. Love and hate are acute, transitional states, so that "there is no contradiction in expecting the best of friends to be temporarily annoyed with one another, a circumstance that should motivate mirth from witnessed disparagement" (Zillman 1983, 1:91).

8. It is clearly not my own idiosyncratic experience, however. See Regina Bendix (1987); Paolo Tavarelli (1987–88); Bell et al. (1987).

9. For a discussion of the relation of sentiment and humor, see Oring (2003:71–84).

7. Legend, Truth, and News

1. There is no necessary connection between genre and perspective. Any genre can be approached from either perspective. One can investigate the ideology underlying traditional ballads or the aesthetics of legend communication.

2. I do not mean this in the same sense that Carl Lindahl uses "double credibility" in his discussion of the legend (1986:6).

3. The lack of objective truth used to be a formal criterion in legend definition (Littleton 1965:22). Now it is simply an undeclared value of the categorizer. For a discussion of truth and the legend see chapter 8 in this volume.

4. While folklorists acknowledge that legends can turn out to be true (Dégh and Vázsonyi 1976:95), rarely do they proceed to study what they believe to be true as if it were legend.

5. For the antithesis between art and information, see chapter 11 in this volume. Jan Brunvand provides an example of a particularly artful urban legend that is first regarded as untrue and later reconsidered as potentially true (1986b:122–125).

6. The other major arguments that proceed from the broad distribution and variation of folklore is that it is "popular"; that it is the "culture of the people" (Dorson 1968b:37) and represents their "main concerns, values, tensions and anxieties, goals and drives" (Dorson 1973:xiv). Thus, folklore is often claimed to speak for a "silent majority" that is almost never described in quantitative terms.

7. Although "legend" originally referred to something written—stories about the lives of saints—that was meant to be read for edification and emulation.

8. Some emphasis has been given to the uses the media make of folklore (e.g., Denby 1971). The television medium has been approached in terms of the traditionality of its texts, performance style, situation, and audience (Burns 1969). There are no significant structural or content differences between oral and printed accounts of apparition visitations and both might equally serve the aims of ideological analysis (Danielson 1979). In the 1970s, a general program was outlined for an encounter with the mass media that extended beyond the identification and use of folklore; it has been largely unheeded (Bird 1976).

9. News would constitute the boundary of the "modern" or "urban" legend. At the boundary of the older type of legend is *history*.

10. The recognition of the strong relationship between the newspaper and folklore is found in Helen MacGill Hughes (1940). Hughes was a student of the sociologist—and former newspaper reporter—Robert Park. Park viewed the newspaper as a natural evolution in the movement from community to society. In his view, the first newspapers were little more than devices for organizing gossip. See Hughes (1940:106, 162) and Park (1923). Michael Schudson disputes Park's view, but Schudson may be overemphasizing the role of the commercial and political press (1978:39–42).

11. The word "news" only comes into common usage in England after 1500, that is, shortly after the introduction of printing (Shaaber 1966:1).

12. How news is framed in the newspaper is an interesting and important question. Marshall McLuhan suggests that real news is bad news, whereas advertising is good news (1964:187–188).

13. Most prominently was Michael von Aitzing's *Relatio Historica* sold twice yearly at the fair in Frankfurt am Main from 1588 to 1593. Also, Janos Manlius's *Newe Zeitung aus Ungarn* was published in the 1580s. There are those who claimed that King Matthias's summaries of events published in *Dracola Waida*, begun in 1485, to be the oldest news periodical. See Smith (1979:9) and Shaaber (1966:3, 309–311).

14. With the exception of local news which was not covered until the beginning of the nineteenth century (Shaaber 1966:9).

15. In the sixteenth century, however, readers were perhaps more likely to see copies of official documents than they are today (Shaaber 1966:173).

16. A "relation" was a term for a prose account. "Discourse," "declaration," "description," "narration," "examination," "dialog," "articles," "ballad," "ditty," "song," "sonnet," as well as "news," could serve to characterize a prose or poetic account of recent events (Shaaber 1966:12).

17. Editorial and opinion are published on the only pages of the newspaper—other than the front page—that are devoid of advertising. This supports the contention that advertising somehow serves to frame news and other features of the newspaper (see note 12). Advertising was once the main feature of the mercantile press, and four-fifths of newspaper space, including the entire front page, was devoted to it. These were not ads in the modern sense. They were notices of goods and services for sale, much like contemporary "classifieds," rather than appeals to the imagination (Weisberger 1961:74–75).

18. Factuality and objectivity are relatively recent developments in the popular press. Before 1830, little premium was placed upon objectivity in reporting. Political newspapers were partisan and represented the point of view of those parties that financed them (Weisberger 1961:33–63; Smith 1978:157–159). Various forces, however, came to promote standards of objectivity in reporting. The most notable development was the rise of the penny press, a cheap daily press which sold news to an anonymous mass of readers rather than to a social network of paid subscribers (Schudson 1978:15, 18, 25). Unlike the numerous political and commercial presses of the day, the penny press was independent because it was ignorant of its audience. "Objectivity" was a value that could be explicitly promoted to such an anonymous mass, and the penny press congratulated itself for paying reporters to seek out the news and report it "correctly" (Schudson 1978:21, 23–24).

The invention of electronic media also contributed to the honing of objectivity as a journalistic value. Telegraphic communication made words expensive, so news had to be transmitted in a terse, unaugmented style. The development of wire services in the middle of the nineteenth century which sold news to a variety of newspapers demanded that the news be sold in a form that any newspaper, regardless of its political persuasion, could use (Carey 1986:164–165).

The idealization of empirical inquiry—the scientific method—as the sole means to a true knowledge of the world and the progress of its inhabitants served to enhance the prestige of facts. "Facts" became a watchword of journalism and were, in a sense, regarded as self-justifying (Schudson 1978:74–75, 77). That human beings were among the objects of this empirical inquiry had been incontrovertibly established by Darwin.

While the rise of factuality and objectivity in newspaper reporting may not be accurately depicted by a smoothly rising curve, factuality and objectivity nevertheless remain core values in contemporary journalism (Henry III 1984; Rosenblatt 1984).

19. Despite the complexity and size of news organizations, they are only sometimes the eyewitnesses of events. Reporters must rely upon sources that are anything but objective or factual. See Sigal (1986:9–37) and Chefets (1985). Robert Darnton (1975) gives some insight into how the news is created. Events are also staged to be reported by the news media. Daniel Boorstin characterizes such events as "pseudo-events" (1964). A good example of such an event was the flight of a human-powered airplane from Crete to the island of Santorini. The plane was name Daedalus and its flight was deliberately conceptualized to model the escape of the mythological hero from his island prison (Gorman 1988:67). Newspapers continue the practice of copying news from other newspapers (Shaw 1984). Curiously, while the multiplicity of versions in oral channels often undermines the truth of the account, a multiplicity of versions in the media argues for it.

20. Several interesting studies by folklorists have compared court records, newspaper accounts, and folklore. Peter R. Aceves saw an ideological conflict between the written record and oral accounts (1971). Likewise, Roger E. Mitchell noted different emphases in the official, media, and oral accounts (1979). Anne B. Cohen, however, noted the similarities between newspaper and ballad accounts and how both, over time, tended to move toward a single stereotype (1973).

21. The telegraph is thought to have something to do with the development of the inverted construction and the presence of the "lead." There was a need to condense the story so that all the key facts could be communicated in the first paragraph with details following (Warren 1959:84). But it seems that orally formulated news accounts also employ the same inverted construction.

22. Appropriately, human interest stories are thought by reporters to be of less significance and consequence (Warren 1959:84).

23. Susan Kalčik (1975) and Moira Smith (1984) suggest that inverted construction is peculiar to women's narratives. However, it may be that the women they studied were communicating news and the nature of the stories determined the form of construction.

24. This is the distinction between an *image base* and *verbal report* (Zan 1989:209–210; also Bauman 1986:5). Despite differences in the construction of news and folktales, they are often similar. In prescribing the attributes of the television news story, Edward J. Epstein virtually recapitulated Axel Olrik's epic laws of folk narrative. Television news, according to Epstein: (1) should be conveyed in "palpable images" (Olrik: *tableaux scenes*); (2) there should be "highly dramatic conflicts between clearly defined sides" (Olrik: *Law of Contrast*); (3) "stories should have a rising action, a climax, and then a falling action, and a seeming resolution (Olrik: *Law of Opening* and *Law of Closing*). The "high value placed on action" that Epstein emphasizes is so basic to the notion of folk narrative as to be merely assumed in Olrik's laws (Epstein 1981; Olrik 1965 [1909]).

25. Dorson, however, viewed the Mathers as collectors of "legends" rather than collectors of "news" (1973:17).

26. Herbert Gans has suggested that more literary analysts apply their insights and methods to news stories (1980:7). I concur with this view.

Although they have been the focus of this essay, I do not wish to suggest that attention only be given to accounts of ironic or uncanny occurrences (what the French call *fait-divers*). Economic and political stories can also be read for their underlying ideology, although I would think that folklorists might be drawn to the cultural rather than particular partisan perspectives that might shape these accounts.

27. Except perhaps for public sector folklorists who emphasize celebratory modes in their engagement of folklore (Kirshenblatt-Gimblett 1988:151).

8. Legendry and the Rhetoric of Truth

1. David Buchan (1981:5) characterizes the range of legends somewhat differently: happy, merry, horrific, unusual, unlucky, and group lore tales.

2. See Fine (1992) and Turner (1993) for legends affecting major corporations. The government and press were more concerned with rumor and legends about hurricane Katrina ("About Those 'Sniper Attacks'" 2005; Pandey 2006; Pawlaczyk 2005), the World Trade Center (Dunbar and Reagan 2006), and AIDS (Fine and Turner 2001:166; Goldstein 2004).

3. That is why Linda Dégh can characterize legends as expressive of "fundamental ideas concerning human existence" (1991:19), and Bill Ellis can see them as "the communal redefinition of worldview" (1987:34). Many legends, however, seem to do no such thing.

4. It "calls for the expression of opinion on the question of truth and belief" (Dégh and Vázsonyi 1976:119). I prefer the truth part.

5. I do not mean to imply that truth-making practices are necessarily the same in all cultures. I focus almost exclusively on Euro-American examples. See Cooperson (2005) and Rushforth (1992) for discussion of the legitimization of truth claims in non-Western societies.

6. Inferences can be made about the surprise-party legend and the baby-sitter legends as well: don't trust young baby sitters because they are likely to use drugs or be otherwise irresponsible. The "Surpriser Surprised" legend might lead some to infer that when it comes to engaging in some type of embarrassing behaviors, one should take special precautions to insure that no spectators are present. These inferences, however, are not necessary to interpret the events in the story. The inferences are didactic—morals in the Aesopian sense.

7. Aristotle recognized that rhetoric and dialectic could be "acquired by habit" (1991:29).

8. And, of course, the rhetoric I elucidate is purely descriptive, whereas Aristotle's is meant to be prescriptive.

9. However, many legends may be based on media sources that were intended as fictional, humorous, or ironic. See Dégh and Váyzsoni (1976:99), for example.

10. There is some disagreement on the use of the term "memorate." Some would reserve it exclusively for first-person accounts, while others would apply it to accounts told even at two or three degrees of distance (Dégh and Vázsonyi

1974:225–228). I find this latter extension of the term unhelpful. A memorate should apply to a first-person account, even if that designation only identifies a rhetorical distinction. If degrees of distance are important, we might start using subscripts to indicate the distance the narrator measures between event experiences and narrative realization. A legend$_0$ would refer to a first-person account. Legend$_1$ would refer to an account that a narrator claims was heard from a person who experienced the event in question. ("Messages from the Dead" would be a legend$_1$.) Legend$_2$ would refer to a narrative heard from someone specifically known to the person who told it to the narrator. In cases where the chain of transmission is unspecified, the legend might be regarded as legend$_x$ and the standard "friend-of-a-friend" narrative might either be characterized as legend$_x$ or, perhaps, as legend$_{ff}$. I doubt, however, that this type of notation will be adopted.

11. Narrators often use this perception of responsibility to create tall tales and other kinds of humorous accounts whose purpose is to deceive the listener.

12. Interestingly, the narrator's wife made all sorts of remarks through the first-person narration questioning the ghostly interpretation that the narrator attributed to the event. Although at the outset of his narration she asserted that the story was "absolutely true," it is possible that she reacted negatively to the personalization of the story that she had previously heard only in the third person (Slotkin 1988:99–105).

13. The account of the reporter checking the letter writer may be as remote as the account of the payment for the color television. Georgina Smith (1981:170) cites the account in *The Guardian* by Michael Parkin, who was not the reporter who checked the original story. In other words, the newspaper report of narrative distance involves the same distancing as the story it reports.

14. It remains unclear, however, why the narrator would avoid the ghostly interpretation, when he so meticulously prepared for it and when his interviewer seemed so willing to accept it.

15. "Some legend, it doesn't matter which, is necessary to justify the traditional ritual [of legend tripping]" (Ellis 1982–83:63). In other words, the legends underlying legend tripping are merely the excuse for the trips; they are not what the trip is about.

16. Such expressions of concern are also likely to suggest that a narrative is true because if it were not, there would be nothing to be concerned about (logos). They also heighten the fears of the audience members (pathos).

17. When interviewed and recorded at a later date (M. Omidsalar, 22 January 2006), the narrator admitted that he actually had not witnessed the second operation. He also admitted that when he was shown the cancer, he simply believed what was pointed out to him. He was not trained to recognize it (although he claimed, in this account, that the surgeon called the anesthesiologist over who confirmed the pervasiveness of the cancer). In this later retelling, the narrator was laughing throughout the story as well.

18. This narrative also illustrates that the account is just one instance of a class.

19. The folklorist's questions shaped much of the interaction in this narration, but the example shows how a narrator can invite responses and support for the truth of the account.

20. While it is indeed worthwhile to compare stories that were told to be believed and those told to be discounted, it may be problematic to base a comparison on only two examples. Bennett picks this up again in later work (1993).

21. Without the explanation and dialogue, the tale is reduced to the following: a woman was sleeping in a caravan driven by her husband. When he stops to urinate, she also goes out, but he drives on, not realizing she has left. Standing in her nightie, she is picked up by a motorcyclist who overtakes the husband, who is very surprised to see her. This, of course, is not narrating but summarizing.

22. Bennett may believe that the circular pattern she describes and the riffle and pool technique are similar because both slow down the delivery of the story. It seems to me, however, that the techniques are quite different. The circular technique is not linear; the riffle and pool presentation is.

23. Bennett calls attention to this defensive function (1984:83).

24. The Leicester materials that she collected involved longer interviews—from three-quarters of an hour to an hour-and-a-half—and were conducted in the women's own homes, but these women were still strangers to her (G. Bennett 1999:181).

25. Tedlock (1983:165) has called attention to the use of paralogism in Zuni narratives, albeit fictional ones.

26. The sword is a Swedish one of a pattern that was only introduced after 1685 (Johnsen 1989:159).

27. The willingness of narrators to discount specific evidence and claims, although not a general belief, enhances their credibility. They demonstrate judgment and do not accept any and all testimony to establish their case.

28. The inscription on the stone, however, states quite clearly that Floyd E. Pruett is buried there. Furthermore, it seems that Floyd Pruett died before his wife (Dégh 2001:333).

29. There is an old tradition that angels do not eat or drink (Ginzberg 1968, 1:234).

30. The "whodunit" was first invented in 1841 by Edgar Allan Poe in "The Murders in the Rue Morgue." The significance of story elements is revealed to the reader only at the story's conclusion.

31. Barnes (1986:74) actually compares the future-directed legend more closely with the joke because the end line is in direct discourse and seems closer to a punchline. It seems, however, that the concealed-function form parallels the techniques of jokes in general.

32. The instruction to store food came from church leaders, and they expected it to be followed because it was a revelation to the leadership. Instructions to the entire church were not supposed to be private communications initiated by supernatural agents (W. Wilson 1975:86–87). Even though the legends ratify church directives, they ignore church authority. Thus, the legends conform to a folk rather than an ecclesiastical theology.

33. They are even offered as testimony at sacrament meetings. See W. Wilson (1986:250–252).

34. In removing the criterion of truth from the definition of the legend, I am not suggesting that folklorists never need to ascertain what is true and what is not. Everyone has to make such a determination. I am only suggesting that such a determination should not predefine the legend genre.

35. What constitutes a traditional motif is itself a problem.

36. This is not the case, however. The appearance of a Nephite is unusual even for Mormons, and the accounts are considered extraordinary.

37. The study of legend would then begin to approach a "social psychology of knowledge" (Hobbs 1989:71).

9. On the Tradition and Mathematics of Counting-Out

1. "Now it is quite a usual thing in the world for a game to outlive the serious practice of which it is an imitation" (Tylor 1874, 1:73).

2. For example, Lev. 15:7–8. Josh. 7:13–26; Jon. 1:7, Homer *Iliad* 7:171.

3. Bolton claims one instance of such a linkage between a well-known English and American rhyme and a Romany stanza that "is virtually a *gypsy magic spell*" (1888:44, emphasis in original). Bolton's source for the Romany stanza would seem to be a personal communication from Charles G. Leland, and it is difficult to ascertain why it is "virtually," rather than "actually," a magic spell. The translation of the rhyme (provided by Leland?) suggests nothing magical about it—it sounds like a typical game rhyme and includes a mention of "play."

4. Bolton pointed out that counting-out is a process of exclusion, and the ancient Hebrews' practice of casting lots also proceeded by exclusion. He also noted that the Hebrew word for lot, *goral*, also means "pebble" and pebbles play a part in the casting of lots by a number of savage tribes and groups of children. (1888:41–42). Although the identification of the criminal described in Joshua was exclusionary, it was different than that practiced in children's counting-out. In the biblical case, first the tribe of Judah was identified as *containing* the guilty party, then the lineage of the Zerahites within Judah, and then the head of the Zabdi family among the Zerahites, and finally the guilty party Achan, "the son of Carmi, the son of Zabdi, the son of Zerah, of the tribe of Judah" (Josh. 7:16–18).

5. The connection to ancient Celtic practice was also argued by Charles Taylor in *The Magpie: or Chatterings of the Pica* (Glasgow 1820).

6. Yet, the Knapps do cite Goldstein's work and recognize that the process can be manipulated (Knapp & Knapp 1979:28).

7. I have not seen a copy of this manuscript.

8. Although there is no evidence he was born in Paris, his claim to be Parisian may simply be based upon his residence there (Flegg, Hay, and Moss 1985:14).

9. Unfortunately, these are not provided in the mathematical study of Chuquet's manuscript (Flegg, Hay, and Moss 1985).

10. Mnemonics also exist in German ("Gott schlug den Mann in Amalek; Den Israel bezwang") and English ("From numbers' aid and art; Never will fame depart") (Ahrens 1901:289).

11. It also came to be known as *Josephsspiel* in German and *Peder's Lek* in Swedish. In Japan, it is known as *Mameko-date* or the stepchild problem (Smith and Mikami 1914:84).

12. The Slavonic version contains passages relating to John the Baptist, Christ, and the early Christians which are believed to be late Christian interpolations (Josephus 1927:xi).

13. I cannot help but feel that in some original form of the problem it was the

first wife, and not the second, who proposed reversing the order of the count at the point that only one of her sons remained. This balance in the story would have made it more engaging as the second count would appear as a justifiable retaliation.

14. While the insights are Tait's, the diagrams are modeled after those of I. M. Richards (1991) because they are easier to understand.

15. It is accessible only in a bibliographic sense. There are numerous mathematical papers that relate to the problem that I cannot read let alone understand. They include Ahrens (1901:286–301); Mac Fhraing (1948); Robinson (1960); Jakobczyk (1973); Herstein and Kaplansky (1974:120–128); Odlyzko and Wilf (1991). A computer algorithm is provided by Knuth (1973:158–159).

16. Some have suggested that the Roman punishment of decimation (*decimatio*) in which every tenth soldier (or twentieth [*vicesimatio*] or hundredth [*centesimatio*]) was selected for death because the cohort or legion had mutinied or panicked was accomplished by a method of counting-out (Smith 1917:67). However, there is no clear evidence for it in the literature.

17. Perhaps the sheer elaborateness of the ritual led to its abandonment. As counting-out is a preliminary to game, it should progressively be relinquished as children become more interested in the game than in its ceremonial introduction. There are ways of choosing for play that are both quicker and fairer.

10. Definition and Devolution

1. Clearly, not all these figures could be identified as folklorists although all dealt with materials that would be called folklore today.

2. In this sense it bears some relation to the idea of tradition.

3. Extinct forms can be used by scientists to evidence the evolution of life and culture from the simple to the complex or to evidence the degeneration and destruction of more elaborate forms of life and culture, as some theologians would have it. A concern with extinction does not uniquely index one or the other view.

4. This is related to, but not identical with, Dundes's observation that as peasants became fully civilized, they "evolved out of folklore" (1969:12). Dundes, however, distinguishes this from folklore itself evolving. The evolution of folklore presents the very same problem. Classical composers were enormously influenced by folk music and based their compositions on folk melodies and styles. Should the works of Bedřich Smetana (1824–1884), Antonín Dvořak (1841–1904), Edvard Grieg (1843–1907), Zoltán Kodály (1882–1967), Jean Sibelius (1865–1957), Percy Grainger (1882–1961), or Aaron Copland (1900–1990) be considered the devolution or evolution of folk music?

5. Tylor never included a chapter on folklore in any of his works.

6. He did consider, however, artifacts, beliefs, and behaviors to be species whose distribution and transmission should be traced (1874, 1:8).

7. Not to be overlooked is Lucretius's *De rerum natura* (On the Nature of Things) written in the first century B.C.

8. Nevertheless, Barry was concerned that folk music was in peril as folk musicians abandoned the traditional music to copy ersatz mountain music made in Detroit and broadcast over the radio (1961:74). Why did he feel that singers

could re-create printed texts but mountain fiddlers could not re-create tunes heard over the radio and from the phonograph?

9. With competition from radio broadcasts and phonographic recordings, it is true that neither Laws nor Coffin was sanguine about the future of oral balladry. This is perhaps more a comment, however, on the future of singing in small groups rather than any necessary deterioration of the songs in oral tradition.

10. Peasants as a whole probably did not constitute a folk group even for Dundes, because unstated in his definition is the notion of a consciousness of kind that crystallizes around the shared trait. He would not have regarded merely statistical groupings—such as people who wear size nine shoes or eat popcorn—as folk groups (Oring 1986b:1). Only to the extent that peasants could conceive of themselves as a group could they be considered a folk group. Peasants in neighboring villages may have had a consciousness of kind in relation to landlords, townspeople, and strangers and so have constituted a folk group for Dundes, but peasants as a social class he probably would not have considered a folk group.

11. This redefinition was an attempt to justify "photocopy lore"—which has no oral existence—as a form of folklore. This redefinition has some problems of its own that are unnecessary to address here.

12. Dundes actually made more of jokes in his original oral presentation than he did in his published essay.

13. Nevertheless, Tylor recognized the possibility that myth might evolve artistically: "The development of Myth forms a consistent part of the development of Culture. . . . Savage mythology may be taken as a basis, and then the myths of more civilized races may be displayed as compositions sprung from like origin though more advanced in art" (Tylor 1874, 1:284).

14. What is thought to be antique, however, can prove to be newer than anyone imagined (Hobsbawm and Ranger 1984).

11. Transmission and Degeneration

1. This choice was undoubtedly governed by the absence of recording devices at the time the experiments were initially performed and the need to have an accurate record of each reproduction.

2. Similar criticisms were offered of Walter Anderson's transmission experiment (Goldstein 1967).

3. The actual text can be found in Appendix I.

4. Underlying ready repartee is the process of "unification." The ready repartee involves the establishment of an "unexpected unity between attack and counterattack" (Freud 1960, 8:66, 68).

5. The actual text can be found in Appendix II.

6. For a full discussion of these characteristics, see Davies (1990).

7. There is an exception to every rule. In re-collecting the natural transmission, it was discovered that subject 3E attempted to tell the joke to five friends at a party, although she could neither understand the joke nor perform it competently.

8. It has been suggested that degeneration observed in classroom experiments may be deliberate and stem from the "delight of the 'degeneration' and

the 'corruption' of the message" (Jones 1976:224). That certainly takes place in "Telephone" and other serial transmission games played by adolescents. This factor was not observed in my experiments, and because jokes were generally performed before an audience of class members who had heard all the performances in the series, attempts to deliberately corrupt the transmission would have been noticed.

9. Dégh and Vázsonyi allude to this issue but accord it little discussion. The proper definition of degeneration is critical, however, if the term is to have any meaning.

10. The various criteria that can be employed to define degeneration have been discussed in chapter 10.

11. Texts are transcribed from a tape, but there is no attempt to preserve the exact pronunciations of the tellers. While most contractions are preserved, such formulations as "coulda" or "gonna" are transcribed as "could have" or "going to." Performance markers are also absent, although these may have a significant effect on ability to memorize and reproduce a coherent joke.

12. Despite the confusion in this joke about who was supposed to be Polish, all the experimental subjects did sense that becoming Italian was the point of the joke, although no one ever corrected for the anomaly of the guy initially being Polish.

12. Thinking through Tradition

1. The meanings of "surrender" or "betrayal" which exist both in Latin and English (*OED* 1989: s.v. "tradition") should be noted as well. In English, the related term "traduce" not only means "to transfer" but also to "speak falsely," "misrepresent," "betray," and "bring into disgrace" (s.v. "traduce").

2. The products are what Hermann Bausinger called objectified cultural "goods" (1986:28).

3. In a folklore encyclopedia entry on "Tradition," the term "traditions" is referred to by the second sentence. The entry goes on to note that *tradition* is an adjective modifying specific genres (Allison 1997, 2:800).

4. It is important to note that John Brand, who first used the term "oral tradition," did not think it constituted a special type of process or demanded particular kinds of social relations for its operation. Rather, the public written record had been censored to remove references to the rites and ceremonies of earlier times. Oral tradition was important because it was not so censored (Brand in Dorson 1968a, 1:6–12). Here is the root of the notion of folklore as "unofficial culture" (Dorson 1968b:37) and the "culture of resistance" (Rodriguez 1998).

5. Cultural reproduction need not be regarded from the perspective of "cultural capital" or "symbolic violence" (Bourdieu 1973; Bourdieu and Passeron 1977).

6. "Comparison" refers to checking what one has learned against other sources. "Performance" involves taking aesthetic responsibility for an action. To the extent that a performance depends upon the reproduction of something from the past, a performer might be censured for what is regarded as excessive or inappropriate deviation. Performance might then be less a matter of individual creativity and more a process of learning and faithful reproduction. "Traditionalization" refers

to the human propensity to turn experiences and texts into traditions by linking them to the past (Hymes 1975:353–354; Bauman 2004:146–149) or by creating the desire, need, and conditions for their future reproduction.

7. Since all culture is subject to constant change, it has been argued, there can only be what is new. "Tradition," consequently, becomes an interpretive term applied to ideas and practices that are new that take on symbolic value as "old." Conversely, as everything is necessarily derived from the past, everything is to some extent old, but it takes on symbolic value under the term "new" or "modern" (M. E. Smith in Handler and Linnekin 1984:273; also see Noyes 2009:245). While one can view "new" and "old" as interpretive categories, it seems extreme to regard "new" and "old" strictly as designations. Such an approach depends on the utter disconnection of all ideas and practices from one another so that they exist only in the present and are "old" or "new" by arbitrary attribution. There are, however, thoughts and behaviors that are relatively new, and thoughts and behaviors that are very close reproductions of earlier models. In the early twenty-first century quantum computing seems very new, even if electronic digital computing may now seem somewhat old.

8. What kind of changes count as creative is unclear. Does "creativity" indicate a qualitative evaluation of a particular change, and if so, who makes the determination? Definitions are rare, and when they are occasionally offered—e.g., "a heuristic process, of an expressive character, put into service of direct aims and results in the development of personality" (Voigt 1983:181)—they do not clear anything up.

9. Ben-Amos pointed to the inherent contradiction in this formulation. Changing the past, paradoxically, is what keeps the past alive (Ben-Amos 1984:114–115).

10. This claim is, in fact, belied by actual experience. Bertrand Bronson points out that there is objective evidence to suggest that many changes—creative or otherwise—meet with no community support. They simply remain in the province of the individual singer and produce curious clashes when that community performs together (1969:148–149).

11. See Bronson's critique of "selection" (1954).

12. Glassie, for example, attempts to find tradition in Ben-Amos's otherwise traditionless definition of folklore (1995:400–401).

13. Max Radin (1935, 15:62–63) felt that "tradition" should be distinguished from "custom" because traditions were judged as valuable by their bearers. They were symbolic. Walter Hävernick (1968) proposed a distinction between "tradition" and "continuity" with the former relating to the symbolic elements of social groups and the latter to the elements of an unconscious unsymbolic past.

14. Social identities may also coalesce around things that are not traditional—or regarded as traditional—at all; for example sports teams.

15. In fact, the construction of tradition in Handler and Linniken's formulation would be a process, but they are more interested in the functions of the products constructed.

16. Imagine a case in which an individual's sense of his childhood is filled with pleasant and loving memories. Is it not possible that this individual suffered greatly in childhood and that his personality might have crystallized around those negative childhood experiences? Might not the fond memories—the symbolic past—be a mask and serve as compensation for a real past? The memories of childhood are a symbolic construction, but to accept them as the only notion

of that individual's past would be to abdicate the ability to understand that particular construction of childhood or understand anything that might have been conditioned by actual childhood experience.

17. A simple example: in American culture, food picked up with a utensil is to be placed entirely in the mouth; food picked up with the hands can be taken away from the mouth and brought back to the plate. Which foods qualify as hand foods and utensil foods is a separate problem. What is theoretically deficient or offensive in this observation?

18. Twenty-five years ago, I attended a psychoanalytic seminar. The speaker was a psychoanalyst working with adolescent delinquents with whom the analyst claimed some success. In discussing one case, the analyst indicated that his patient believed that his father was trying to kill him. I asked whether his father was indeed trying to kill him, as that would seem to make a difference in his evaluation and treatment. If his father was actually trying to kill him, it might explain important aspects of the patient's problem. At the very least, his belief about his father would not be a symptom but a fact. The psychoanalyst could not seem to grasp the distinction. In his view, everything that one imagined about oneself and one's world was open to analysis and psychological amelioration. This seemed a dangerous theory; especially if the patient were killed when he got home.

19. This is not an all-or-nothing proposition. One can take a negative view of some aspects of modernity while being totally committed to others. It is difficult—perhaps impossible—to find someone who is opposed to all aspects of the modern world.

20. The centrality of folklore scholarship in the construction of national, ethnic, and other social identities is a particular case in point (Anttonen 2005:124–177).

21. The use of *tradition* to denote something handed down—usually orally—from the past is found in English in 1380 (*OED*). The Hebrew word *masoret* means "tradition" and goes back at least to the 6th century C.E. It is a close analogue of *tradition* since it is based on the root *masar*—to "give over" or "transmit." Interestingly, *masor* means "informer" or "traitor"—one who betrays someone over to the authorities, and thus is analogous to the word "traduce" to which *tradition* is related (Jastrow 1950). *Masorah*—a word found even in ordinary English dictionaries—relates to the information employed to insure the faithful reproduction of the biblical text as well as to the text itself. There is no hint of an opposition between modernity and tradition in these uses—only the sense of a faithful reproduction of the past.

22. It is more than ironic that the great replicative technologies—printing, machine manufacture, photography, analog recording, broadcasting, digitization—are technologies of modernity. The close reproduction of cultural knowledge and practice is made possible by these contemporary technologies. The technologies of the past—oral transmission, customary example, and writing—seem a more uncertain basis for cultural reproduction in the long-term. Yet modernity is thought of as opposed to convention; as a world of innovation rather than of mindless reproduction.

23. DaBore didn't believe in lightning balls, although all the men of his society fervently set to dig them up after lightning strikes and used them in garden magic. This was the only part of the belief system of the Gururumba of New Guinea in which DaBore did not believe. He built a spirit house in his garden

and assigned misfortunes to witches, ghosts, and sorcerers like everyone else. His view of lightning balls was completely idiosyncratic (Newman 1965:104–105).

24. A similar view was put forth by Bengt Holbek (Final Discussion 1983:240). Bourdieu feels, however, that cultural reproduction depends on "symbolic violence" (Bourdieu and Passeron 1977:4–68).

25. In fact, folklore needs to concern itself with "tradition," "custom," "habit," and even "fad." These terms raise similar questions and involve some of the same processes.

26. An exception to this rule might be found in the work of Alan Dundes. Because Dundes adopted a psychoanalytic perspective on folklore, he sought out the unseemly side of folklore and explored its racism, classism, and sexism (1984; 1997ab). Although a major figure in the discipline, his psychoanalytic interpretations had little influence and were sometimes ridiculed. Other exceptions are Montell (1986) and Bronner (2008).

27. To label something "aesthetic" does not presume it is of "good" quality; only that it is structurally distinct and conspicuous with respect to its background—a proverb in relation to ordinary speech, for example. On the question of whether folklore should be limited to "*oral* tradition," see Smith (1975).

28. The study of why the new replaces the old is commonly known as the study of "social change." The persistence of the old—even when under pressure by new practices—might be termed the study of "social unchange" (see Noyes 2009:239).

29. "I contend that Tradition is always being created anew, and that traditions of modern origin are as much within our province as ancient ones," wrote E. Sidney Hartland more than a century ago (Burne, Alvarez, and Hartland 1885:120). G. Malcom Laws indexed American ballads which were recent New World creations (1964). It was the political manipulation of tradition that shocked folklorists in the late twentieth century; not the idea that new traditions were being created.

30. This has been termed the "normativeness" of tradition (Shils 1981:200). Bauman has approached certain aspects of this question in his discussion of "authorization"—the process of making discourses authoritative (2004:150–158).

31. Constraints may be internal or external. An internal constraint relates to performance; the way that meter, rhyme, or music might constrain certain lexical choices in a song, for example. External constraints would condition the performance as a whole, as when certain ritual occasions demand performances of a certain kind. How certain institutional practices are a function of other practices involves something like functional analysis, but not the type familiar from past folklore theory (see Cancian 1960).

32. There is a whole subfield in linguistics on language acquisition, but there is precious little in folklore on tradition acquisition.

33. A notable exception is Henry Glassie's work (1975) on the re-creation of folk housing.

34. A code is something that "preserves a message and aids its communication" (du Sautoy 2008:282). Mozart's ability to memorize Gregorio Allegri's *Miserere*—a piece which the pope had prohibited being copied or played outside the Vatican—owed much to the musical symmetries in that work (253–254).

35. This is a textured view of what is called "the social organization of tradition" (Bauman 2001:15821).

36. "If the preferred terminology of 'stability' and 'change' is to have any validity in the future, it must be understood in the concrete particularization of the relationship between singers. It is simply not enough to pursue the sterile exercise of comparing songs solely with each other or with their supposed predecessors" (Russell 1987:336).

37. A recent article on "coaxing" and the *corrido* has some relation to rehearsal, but it is viewed from the perspective of performance and not from how performers conceive the song that needs to be reproduced (McDowell 2010).

38. Henry Glassie has probably attended more to the ways folk artists learn their skills than most, but not in close detail (Glassie 1989:92–110). Understandably, it is difficult to reprise the learning processes of individual artists who are encountered by the folklorist in their mature years. But it suggests that folklorists might attend as much to novices learning their crafts as well as to "stars." See Glassie's description of carpet-weaving sisters in Ahmetler, Turkey (1993b:669–677).

39. Paul Smith is an exception. He has thought about tradition as a learning process and developed models of what might affect the stability of any particular tradition in its transmission (Smith 1974; 1975; 1978; 1986). Smith's essays were published in a somewhat obscure journal. Nevertheless, the extent to which they have been ignored—even by those writing on the concept of tradition—evidences the lack of interest of folklorists in process. Ian Russell has also developed a model of folksong transmission that identifies both continuity and change. Nevertheless, he addresses change more than continuity (1987:331).

40. For example, Jacobs (1893); Gomme (1910); Bausinger (1986 [1969]); Smith (1974, 1975, 1978, 1986); Opie (1963); Honko (1983); Handler and Linnekin (1984); Gailey (1989); Finnegan (1991); Glassie (1995); McDonald (1997); Bronner (2000ab); Baker (2000); Jones (2000); Klein (2000).

41. Thirty papers at an American Folklore Society meeting contained "tradition," "traditions," or "traditional" in their titles (American Folklore Society 2005). These words were embedded in such phrases as "oral tradition," "shy tradition," "tradition of religious songs," "folk traditions," "traditional beliefs," "traditional foodways," and "traditional and popular culture." Judging from the abstracts of these papers, the terms were mainly employed to refer to knowledge and practices connected to the past that are maintained or reintroduced into contemporary life and literature. The term, however, seems to have little or no analytic, or even descriptive, value. This is not to suggest that the papers presented at the conference did not have something worthwhile to say. They just don't seem to have said it with *tradition*.

42. The effort to corral Internet communication within the folkloristic domain is but another example of the use of *tradition* to claim territory (American Folklore Society 2009:56; Blank 2009). If tradition can be said to exist on the World Wide Web, then the Web becomes an object for folkloristic scrutiny. In this way it can be claimed that folkloristics does not only attend to the flotsam and jetsam of a fading past but is, in fact, a scrupulously contemporary discipline. As it has been argued above, however, folkloristics would be a contemporary discipline with a contemporary subject without having to attach itself to any contemporary technology or medium.

43. It may be that cultural reproduction is close to Hermann Bausinger's suggestion that folklore, as the study of tradition, might be conceived as "diffusion research," which would possess a dynamic, processual character (1986:34).

13. Generating Lives: The Life History of a Life History

1. Perhaps Wilson (1991) might be an example of work undertaken for more personal rather than professional reasons.

2. The Roman numeral indicates in which of the five interviews the quoted material appears; the Arabic numeral indicates the position of that material in the sequence of questions and answers within that interview.

3. This view of life histories is made explicit in Dégh (1975:vii).

4. James Freeman was neither a friend nor admirer of his informant Muli (1979:34), but see Mandelbaum (1973:178) and Plummer 1983:138–140).

5. Interrogation has been a prominent mode of discourse in the academy since Socrates. For New Yorkers, it is a frequent means of showing interest and signaling friendliness (Tannen 1981:31).

6. "Septicville" was the informant's pseudonym for his hometown.

7. See Wilson (1991:140).

8. Anthropologists, folklorists, psychologists, and sociologists should acknowledge that they may not always be able to better the observations and insights of their informants (Plummer 1983:17).

14. Victor Turner, Sigmund Freud, and the Return of the Repressed

1. Rather, Carl Gustav Jung's *Psychological Types* (1949) and Otto Fenichel's *The Psychoanalytic Theory of Neuroses* (1946) are cited in the bibliography of the essay in which Freud is mentioned (Turner 1967:47).

2. Ambivalence, projection, and compromise formation are dealt with rather substantially in Freud's *Totem and Taboo*, a work much better known to anthropologists than *The Interpretation of Dreams*.

3. Turner had previously noted that Freud's symbology tempered his own structural-functional perspective on a number of occasions, but only in passing (Turner 1965:159; 1975:30). "Encounter with Freud" is his only sustained reflection on his indebtedness to Freud.

4. It is also curious that Turner should see his encounter with Freud as the "making of a comparative symbologist." Turner only occasionally engages in a truly comparative study of symbols (e.g., Turner 1962:82-96; 1967:81–88). For the most part, his symbolic studies are not comparative. Even when he explores the symbols of two cultures within the framework of a single essay, it is to show that his conceptualization of symbols as multivocal, condensed, unified, polarized, and tied to basic themes applies in both instances (Turner 1969c, 1976). All in all, Turner is a particularist committed to unraveling the meaning of symbols within a single culture.

5. *Die Traumdeutung* is a literal translation of Artemidorus Daldianus's second-century work *Oneirocritica*. Freud often jokingly referred to *Die Traumdeutung* as his "dream book" or "Egyptian dream book" as though it were merely another in a long list of efforts to translate dreams (Masson 1985:366). Books of dream symbols that were sold at local fairs were often titled "The Interpretation of Dreams" as well, and Freud was fully aware of this (Clark 1980:180).

6. What is translated as "unification" in *The Interpretation of Dreams* is actually two different phrases in German—*"Zusammenziehung zu einer Einheit"* in one

case, and *"Vereinigung"* in another. The English term may therefore have a more technical cast than was intended. However, in *Jokes and Their Relation to the Unconscious* (Freud 1960 [1905], 8:35,39), "unification" is the translation of a more technical term—*"Unifizierung."*

7. A clearer formulation of the sensory-ideological dimensions of a symbol in psychoanalysis comes from Freud's disciple Ernest Jones, who distinguishes between symbols and emblems. Rice, for example, is a *symbol* of semen but an *emblem* of fertility. (Jones 1964, 1:11, 44–45).

8. Although affirmations and themes underlie all aspects of a culture, they are expressed particularly well in ritual (Turner 1973:1101).

9. The exception, of course, is when the dreamer makes use of invariant symbols in the content of the dream (Freud 1953 [1900], 4:241n).

10. "Exoriar(e) aliquis nostris ex ossibus ultor" [Let someone arise from my bones as an avenger"] (Virgil, *Aeneid* IV, 625).

11. It is surprising that Freud made no use of the sense of this phrase in his interpretation of the slip. After all, the quote emphasizes that vengeance shall arise from the body of the aggrieved—the very retribution exacted by a woman who informs her lover that she has missed her period.

12. Freud does not actually make use of the tower qua phallus in his interpretation of this dream, but it is entirely consistent with the the secret love Freud says the dreamer felt for the musician.

13. Actually, Freud also held that much that escaped consciousness was "preconscious" rather than "unconscious"; "suppressed" rather than "repressed." Suppressed thoughts remained accessible to consciousness (Freud 1953 [1900], 4:593-94). Turner is fully aware of this (Turner 1978:578).

14. Consequently, the meaning of rituals is not beyond the grasp of participants, and the interpretations of these rituals can be substantially confirmed by the commentaries of informants. Anthropological interpretations of symbolism need not rest solely on some felicitous correspondence observed between the structure of ritual and the structure of society. In this respect, Turner's concept of suppression may avoid some of the criticisms that have been directed at repression (Grünbaum 1984:216-239).

15. In fact, this charging of ideas with emotional energy—what Turner also calls the "transference of affectual quality" (1955:54) is exactly what Freud meant by "cathexis" [*Besetzung*] which describes the investment of psychical energy in ideas, objects, or parts of the body. The energy that is invested may derive from sources quite removed from the ideas or objects in which it is invested (Laplanche and Pontalis 1973:62-65).

16. It would also explain why Turner tends to cite Jung when discussing the nature of symbols rather than Freud (e.g., Turner 1962:80; 1967:26; 1968:45).

17. Freud is briefly discussed in the "Introduction" and is credited, as Turner credits him, with recognizing the unconscious and multiple significance of symbols. But students are warned that, "Much of Freud's explication of the details of these processes [of symbol formation]—particularly his statements about the importance of instinct or of sexuality, or about the psychology of women—is now either dismissed or the subject of great debate: and much of this questioning has been the result of the comparative work of anthropologists" (Dolgin, Kemnitzer, and Schneider 1979:5). Why the psychology of women, which has never played

any significant part in anthropological analysis, is mentioned is certainly strange. As for the rest, it would be hard to identify any theory of symbols which is not the subject of great debate.

15. Missing Theory

1. This was not the first time that ethnographers had been concerned with the nature of their intrusion into the anthropological record. Anthropologists once wondered whether they should be psychoanalyzed before going into the field. Alfred Kroeber was psychoanalyzed and worked as a lay analyst until 1922, although he did not allow his psychoanalytic interests to influence his cultural theorizing (Steward 1973:11–12).

2. I am always reminded that certain scientists reacted to the proposal of the "Star Wars" type programs of missile defense as "impossible": difficult, yes; costly, yes; a program that might easily be countermanded by an enemy, yes; but impossible?

3. In *Mein Kampf*, Hitler accused the Jews of using the big lie. He did not advocate its usage. The promotion of the big lie as a propaganda technique is often attributed to Joseph Goebbels, but there is no clear evidence for this attribution. He seems to have referred to it as a technique employed by the British ("Big Lie" 2006).

4. However, when a group that previously did not have command over these resources gains control of them, there will be some people in the group who have access and control and those who do not.

5. If someone asks me whether I am for equality, I would say, "Perhaps. What kind of equality are we talking about, and what is it going to cost?" A corollary of this second question is, "Where do you send your kids to school?"

6. This issue is raised by David Kerr (1991) who abandoned any attempt to collect traditional narrative in Zambia and became involved in adapting narratives for highlighting health and other development issues in village theatrical productions. Kirshenblatt-Gimblett seems to approve of this turn (1998:304), but since Kerr does not suggest that he attempted to document the narratives that were collected and adapted for the theater—which succeeded, which did not, and why—I don't see why it should meet with any more approval than any intervention carried out in the interest and with the participation of local folks.

7. Is promoting access to and participation in scientific perspectives a sign of Western hegemony, or is denying peoples access to and participation in these Western perspectives evidence of such hegemony?

8. In the special issue of *Western Folklore* titled, *Theorizing Folklore: Towards New Perspectives on the Politics of Culture*, there are fourteen essays, of which only two could be said to deal with folklore on the ground. The remainder address folklore concepts, categories, and practices (Shuman and Briggs 1993).

9. Even the story of Cohen and the sheep that Clifford Geertz presents as an example of "thick description" (1973), depends upon concepts of contract, honor, patronage, justice, the subordination of religious minorities, and the disruption by colonial authorities of local patterns of traditional life. These categories describe a reality beyond their significance in the story. Colonial

power, for example, may have a regular—even predictable—impact on client relations in certain types of social organization. Patronage may vary regularly with particular social structures.

10. "I'm not sure it will get us anywhere. Philosophy rarely does. Perhaps it exists to remind us that we haven't gotten anywhere" (Pippin 2004:428).

11. Including this essay.

16. Folk or Lore? The Stake in Dichotomies

1. Curiously, Kodish reports that Ms. Allen's old friend Libby Spencer disputed the idea that anyone but Ms. Allen ever characterized her as a shake dancer (1997:7), but for some reason Kodish discounts this information.

2. I wonder why slavery should be identified uniquely in the interpretation of a Civil War *site*. I would think a site figures most significantly in the playing out of the war and less in its causes. Of course, there are many mainstream books that make slavery a primary cause of the Civil War, for example, Davis (1996).

3. Kodish actually speaks of "ethical theory" (1997) but I don't quite know what part of her theory is ethical and what part of her ethics is theoretical. The term has been used to refer to reflection on the concepts and principles that have or can be used in the consideration of any moral question or issue. But Kodish is not engaged in ethical philosophy. Her use of "ethical theory" is also different from Mark Goodale's ethnographic application of the term to refer to the normative ideas operating at a particular site that are the result of the interaction among universal human rights declarations, local ethical standards, state law, and the activities of regional and non-governmental organizations (2006:29). His point is that such ethical theories can be studied and analyzed.

4. The only essay that I know of in which a folklorist explicitly identifies folklore work as "social work" and characterizes folklore as "a helping profession" is Proschan (1992). Despite the quantity of social work that actually goes on under the name of *folklore*, Proschan's own example seems far from it. Although he identifies the great amounts of time and energy that he devoted to helping various individuals in the Kmhmu refugee community in which he worked, what he describes is the kind of personal involvement that any fieldworker has with informants when conducting sustained fieldwork. In each instance, the service and support he offers lead to deeper understandings of the social structure of the community. His "social work" is not the goal of his research—at least not as he describes it—although it is an inescapable aspect of doing fieldwork.

5. It may be that some of this approach is the reluctance to treat informants as mere "organisms" but to see them as whole "persons." See Jay (1974).

6. Camus' character Dr. Rieux in *The Plague* said, "All I maintain is that on earth there are pestilences, and there are victims, and it's up to us, so far as possible, not to join forces with the pestilences" (quoted in Zinn 1970:40).

7. I am less sure. It seems that both thinking people and non-thinking people can be ethical or unethical.

8. Actually, Toelken gives different accounts as to what led to the return of the tapes. In his 1998 essay, he says: "I brought up these concerns about the proper disposition of Yellowman's tapes" with Yellowman's widow (385). In his 2004 essay, he states: "About eight or nine years ago, my sister insisted that the stories should be returned to her, so she could destroy them" (443).

9. Apparently, they have not yet been destroyed. In fact, one was sent back so that Toelken could continue to use it as a demonstration tape in his folklore class (Toelken 2004:443).

10. This goes back to a concept of "scientific colonialism" in which the acquisition of knowledge about a group of people is located outside that group and—like any raw material—is "manufactured" into books and articles (Galtung 1967; Hymes 1974:49).

11. He is a storyteller of traditional tales of the Adirondacks as well the native peoples of the Northeast. He holds a B.A. from Cornell University, an M.A. in Literature and Creative Writing from Syracuse University, and a Ph.D. in Comparative Literature from the Union Institute of Ohio. http://josephbruchac.com/bruchac_biography.html.

12. The case was decided in favor of the Abenaki but was later overturned by the Vermont Supreme Court ("Supreme Court" 1992).

17. Anti Anti-Folklore

1. It moved into Hungarian and Hebrew, for example. Languages resistant to foreign borrowings for nationalistic reasons—French and Icelandic, for example—had their own terms: *tradition populaire* (popular tradition) and *þjóðfræði* (national studies; i.e., ethnology).

2. It began with a panel titled "What's in a Name? A Consideration of the Term 'Folklore' at Age 150" at the American Folklore Society meeting in Austin, Texas in 1997.

3. It would also be useful to learn, if possible, how much they earn and what benefits are concomitants of their employment.

4. The same might be said of "modernity," which is predicated on the new and emerging.

5. Folklore studies might also be characterized in terms of its concern with everyday aesthetic expressions.

6. Of course, death can be a fiction and operate powerfully as fiction.

7. In a parallel consideration: "One achieves theoretical consistency concerning the constructed nature of even 'history' at the cost of our unshakable commonsense certainty that *some things happened and other things did not*" (Boyarin 1996:871, my emphasis).

8. As was made quite plain in the film *Jurassic Park* in which the paleontologist says, shortly after seeing the living dinosaurs, "We're out of a job."

9. History is likewise concerned with disappearance. John A. Andrew, one of the foremost historians of American conservatism, challenged the explanation that historians know so little about conservatism because historians are primarily liberal. His argument was that conservatism was too robust: "They're

not dying. . . . When they do, their papers will become available. People writing dissertations will begin exploring them to understand why conservatism was so significant" (Perlstein 1997:26).

10. Unfortunately, folklore studies has not really attempted to theorize and understand disappearance. See chapter 12 in this volume.

11. One must see "contemporary" not merely as a point in time but as a marker of value. What is considered contemporary is what is attached to particular social groups—elites—in particular locations at a particular point in time. Folklorists have usually focused their studies elsewhere.

12. Konrad Köstlin (1997) sees folklore as a "highly modern discipline" (264), although its passion for the whole is a product of modernity's own ambiguities; a reclamation of the imagined wholeness of childhood (273).

13. The ephemeral is the prototypical product of postmodernity (Harvey 1990:288–292).

14. Legend research is one area that is deeply implicated in characterizing folklore as untruth (Oring 1990; 2008), but American folklorists have largely been attending to legends in their own society and usually in their own social and cultural milieux. See chapter 8 in this volume.

15. However, the stigmatization and valorization of the past were engaged by much broader segments of society than folklorists.

16. Anthropology is not without problems (Geertz 1988:133–138), but no one is asking that it change its name.

17. Although, as I have said, I would strongly contest this characterization.

18. Kirshenblatt-Gimblett notes that the stigmatized Jewish customs came in time to serve as a basis for a critique of the Jewish respectability that condemned them. Although she believes that this is only the case when respectability has succeeded in "archaizing the 'errors'" (1996:248), the resurgence of orthodoxy in Judaism may suggest that this is not entirely the case. Reform Judaism now engages in previously repudiated practices for spiritual, and not merely nostalgic, reasons. Perhaps the same dynamics will prove true for cultural studies.

19. Warren Roberts earned the first American Ph.D. in Folklore from Indiana University in 1953 (Bronner 1986:88).

20. According to an urban legend, the Department of English in a particular university appealed to the central administration to change its name to Cultural Studies. A host of departments in the university immediately petitioned to change their names to the Department of English.

21. See Dan Ben-Amos (1998) on the importance of the name of the field. While I agree with Bendix that the knowledge we seek to produce is meant to contribute to a "larger whole," I cannot understand how abandoning the term *folklore* would demonstrate "a collective sense of purpose" and make any sort of collective contribution to some larger whole (Bendix 1998, n6). Good work under the name *folklore* will contribute to the "larger whole"; bad work, by any name, will not.

22. "The link of 'folk' and 'lore' established a connection between people and creation, implying a functional relationship between social order and creative action . . . which positions us at the exact center where the social sciences and humanities become one amateur endeavor" (Glassie 1996).

23. Criticisms of the cultural studies agenda have already been registered (Brown 1997; Schudson 1997).

24. And as for the "bad name" that *folklore* seems to have in the academy, Henry Glassie is perhaps right: "It might help us stay honest, edgy, and angry" (1996).

25. See Oring (1996a; 1996b).

26. This is true as far as the place of folklore in the academy. There was a golden age for folklore in England in the second half of the nineteenth century when research on and interpretation of folklore and mythology were matters of public interest and debate. However, folklore studies never established itself as an academic program in Britain.

27. Hitler, of course, would prove such thinking wrong.

28. In 1895, Herzl published *The Jewish State*, which laid the foundation for the Zionist movement and the creation of the state of Israel.

References

"About Those 'Sniper Attacks'—Urban Legends Spread Like Water in the Big Easy." 2005. *The Commercial Appeal* (Memphis, TN), 28 September, final edition.

Abraham, Hilda C., and Ernst L. Freud, eds. 1965. *A Psycho-Analytic Dialogue: The Letters of Sigmund Freud and Karl Abraham, 1907–1926*. New York: Basic Books.

Abrahams, Roger D. 1968. A Rhetoric of Everyday Life: Traditional Conversational Genres. *Southern Folklore Quarterly* 32(1):44–59.

———. 1971. Personal Power and Social Restraint in the Definition of Folklore. *Journal of American Folklore* 84(331):16–30.

———. 1977. Toward an Enactment-Centered Theory of Folklore. In *Frontiers of Folklore*, ed. William R. Bascom. Pp. 79–120. Washington DC: American Association for the Advancement of Science.

———. 1979. Folklore in Culture: Notes toward an Analytic Method. In *Readings in American Folklore*, ed. Jan Harold Brunvand. Pp. 390–403. New York: W. W. Norton.

———. 1981. Shouting Match at the Border: The Folklore of Display Events. In *"And Other Neighborly Names": Social Process and Cultural Image in Texas Folklore*, ed. Richard Bauman and Roger D. Abrahams. Pp. 303–321. Austin: University of Texas Press.

———. 1992. The Public, the Folklorist, and the Public Folklorist. In *Public Folklore*, ed. Robert Baron and Nicolas Spitzer. Pp. 17–27. Washington, D.C.: Smithsonian Institution Press.

———. 1993. Phantoms of Romantic Nationalism in Folkloristics. *Journal of American Folklore* 106(419):3–37.

Abrahams, Roger D., and George Foss. 1968. *Anglo-American Folklore Style*. Englewood Cliffs, N.J.: Prentice-Hall.

Abrahams, Roger D., and Susan Kalčik. 1978. Folklore and Cultural Pluralism. In *Folklore in the Modern World*, ed. Richard M. Dorson. Pp. 223–236. The Hague: Mouton.

Aceves, Peter R. 1971. The Hillsville Tragedy in Court Record, Mass Media and Folk Balladry. *Keystone Folklore Quarterly* 16(1):1–38.

Agger, Ben. 1992. *Cultural Studies as Critical Theory*. London: Falmer.

Ahrens, W. 1901. *Mathematische Unterhaltungen und Spiele*. Leipzig: B. G. Teubner.

Alexander, Hubert G. 1967. *Language and Thinking: A Philosophical Introduction*. Princeton, N.J.: D. Van Nostrand.

Alligator. 1980. Directed by Lewis Teague. 94 min. De Luxe Group1/Alligator Associates. Videocassette.

Allison, Randal S. 1997. Tradition. In *Folklore: An Encyclopedia of Beliefs, Customs, Tales, Music and Art*, ed. Thomas A. Green. 2 vols. Santa Barbara, Calif.: ABC-CLIO

Allport, Gordon W., and Leo Postman. 1965 [1947]. *The Psychology of Rumor.* New York: Russell and Russell.

Alon, Yigal. 1970. *The Shield of David: The Story of Israel's Armed Forces.* New York: Random House.

———. 1971. *The Making of Israel's Army.* New York: Bantam.

American Folklore Society. 1995. *Program and Abstracts.* Arlington, Va.: American Folklore Society.

———. 2005. *Program and Abstracts: Folklore, Equal Access, and Social Justice.* Columbus, Ohio: American Folklore Society.

———. 2009. *Program and Abstracts: Examining the Ethics of Place.* Columbus, Ohio: American Folklore Society.

Anderson, Walter. 1951. *Ein Volkskundliches Experiment.* FFC Communications No. 141. Helsinki: Suomalainen Tiedeakatemia.

———. 1956. *Eine Neue Arbeit zur Experimentellen Volkskunde.* FFC Communications No. 168. Helsinki: Suomalainen Tiedeakatemia.

Anderson, Walter Truett. 1990. *Reality Isn't What It Used to Be: Theatrical Politics, Global Myths, Primitive Chic, and Other Wonders of the Postmodern World.* San Francisco: Harper and Row.

Anttila, Aarne. 1931–1935. *Elias Lönnrot: elämä ja toiminta* [Elias Lönnrot: Life and Work]. 2 vols. Helsinki: Suomalaisen Kirjallisuuden Seura.

Anttonen, Pertti J. 2005. *Tradition through Modernity: Postmodernism and the Nation-State in Folklore Scholarship.* Helsinki: Finnish Literature Society.

Appell, George N. 1992. Scholars, True Believers, and the Identity Crisis in Anthropology. *Reviews in Anthropology* 21(3):193–202

Applebaum, Herbert, ed. 1987. *Perspectives in Cultural Anthropology.* Albany: State University of New York Press.

Ariely, Dan. 2008. *Predictably Irrational: The Hidden Forces That Shape Our Decisions.* New York: HarperCollins.

Aristotle. 1982. *Poetics,* trans. with an intro. by James Hutton. New York: W. W. Norton.

———. 1991. *On Rhetoric: A Theory of Civil Discourse,* trans. George A. Kennedy. New York: Oxford University Press.

Art Guide of Forest Lawn with Interpretations. 1941. Glendale, Calif.: Forest Lawn Memorial Park.

Ashley, Clifford W. 1938. *The Yankee Whaler.* Boston: Houghton Mifflin.

Bachet, Claude-Gaspard. 1874 [1624]. *Problems plaisants et delectables qui se font par les nombres,* ed. and suppl. A. Labosne. 3rd ed. Paris: Gauthier-Villars.

Badone, Ellen. 1987. Ethnicity, Folklore, and Local Identity in Rural Brittany. *Journal of American Folklore* 100(396):161–190.

Baker, Ronald L. 1982. *Hoosier Folk Legends.* Bloomington: Indiana University Press.

———. 2000. Tradition and the Individual Talent in Folklore and Literature. *Western Folklore* 59(2):105–114.

Ball, W. W. Rouse. 1960 [1908]. *A Short Account of the History of Mathematics*. New York: Dover.
Ballard, Linda-May. 1980. Ulster Oral Narratives: The Stress on Authenticity. *Ulster Folklife* 26:35–40.
_____. 1988. Three Local Storytellers: A Perspective on the Question of Cultural Heritage. In *Monsters with Iron Teeth*, ed. Gillian Bennett and Paul Smith. Perspectives on Contemporary Legend III. Pp. 161–182. Sheffield: Sheffield Academic Press.
Baring-Gould, Sabine. 1913. *A Book of Folk-Lore*. London: W. Collins.
Barnard, F. M. 1965. *Herder's Social and Political Thought: From Enlightenment to Nationalism*. Oxford: Clarendon Press.
Barnes, Daniel R. 1986. Interpreting Urban Legends. *ARV: Scandinavian Yearbook of Folklore* 40:67–78.
Baron, Robert, and Nicholas R. Spitzer. 1992. Introduction. In *Public Folklore*, ed. Robert Baron and Nicholas R. Spitzer. Pp. 1–14. Washington D.C.: Smithsonian Institution Press.
Barry, Phillips. 1933. Communal Re-Creation. *Bulletin of the Folk-Song Society of the Northeast* 5:4–6.
_____. 1936. The Psychopathology of Ballad-Singing. *Bulletin of the Folk-Song Society of the Northeast* 11:16–18.
_____. 1961. The Part of the Folk Singer in the Making of Folk Balladry. In *The Critics and the Ballad*, ed. MacEdward Leach and Tristram P. Coffin. Pp. 59–76. Carbondale: Southern Illinois University Press.
Barthes, Roland. 1972. The Structure of the *Fait-Divers*. In *Critical Essays*, trans. Richard Howard. Pp. 185–195. Evanston: Northwestern University Press.
Bartlett, Frederic C. 1920. Some Experiments on the Reproduction of Folk Stories. *Folklore* 31(1):30–47. Reprinted in Dundes 1965:243–258.
_____. 1932. *Remembering: A Study in Experimental Social Psychology*. Cambridge: Cambridge University Press.
Bascom, William R. 1954. Four Functions of Folklore. *Journal of American Folklore* 67(266):333–349.
_____. 1955. Verbal Art. *Journal of American Folklore* 68(269):245–252.
_____. 1965. The Forms of Folklore. *Journal of American Folklore* 78(307):3–20.
Bateson, Gregory. 1972. *Steps Towards and Ecology of Mind*. New York: Ballantine.
Baughman, Ernest W. 1966. *Type and Motif Index of England and North America*. The Hague: Mouton.
Baum, Paull Franklin. 1917. The Three Dreams or "Dream Bread" Story. *Journal of American Folklore* 30(117):378–410.
Bauman, Richard. 1971a. Differential Identity and the Social Base of Folklore. *Journal of American Folklore* 84(331):31–41.

———. 1971b. Introduction. *Journal of American Folklore* 84(331):v-ix.
———. 1975. Verbal Art as Performance. *American Anthropologist* 77(2):290–311.
———. 1977. Settlement Patterns on the Frontiers of Folklore. In *Frontiers of Folklore*, ed. William R. Bascom. AAAS Selected Symposium Series 5. Pp. 121–131. Washington DC: American Association for the Advancement of Science.
———. 1977. *Verbal Art as Performance*. Prospect Heights, Ill.: Waveland.
———. 1983. Folklore and the Forces of Modernity. *Folklore Forum* 16(2):153–158.
———. 1986. *Story, Performance, and Event: Contextual Studies of Oral Narrative.* Cambridge Studies in Literature 10. Cambridge: Cambridge University Press.
———. 2001. The Anthropology of Tradition. In *International Encyclopedia of the Social and Behavioral Sciences*, ed. Neil J. Smelser and Paul B. Bates. 26 vols. Pp. 15819–15824. Amsterdam: Elsevier.
———. 2004. *A World of Others' Words: Cross-Cultural Perspectives on Intertextuality.* Malden, Mass.: Blackwell.
Bauman, Richard, and Charles L. Briggs. 1990. Poetics and Performance as Critical Perspectives on Language and Social Life. *Annual Review of Anthropology* 19:59–88.
———. 2003. *Voices of Modernity: Language Ideologies and the Politics of Inequality.* Cambridge: Cambridge University Press.
Bausinger, Hermann. 1968. Folklore Research at the University of Tübingen: On the Activities of the Ludwig-Uhland-Institut. *Journal of the Folklore Institute* 5(2–3):124–133.
———. 1986 [1969]. A Critique of Tradition: Observations on the Situation of Volkskunde. In *German Volkskunde: A Decade of Theoretical Confrontation, Debate, and Reorientation (1967–1977)*, ed. and trans. James R. Dow and Hannjost Lixfeld. Pp. 26–40. Bloomington: Indiana University Press.
———. 1990. *Folk Culture in a World of Technology.* Bloomington: Indiana University Press.
Beck, Jane C. 1997. Taking Stock: 1996 American Folklore Society Presidential Address. *Journal of American Folklore* 110(436):123–139.
Becker, Howard, and Ruth Hill Useem. 1942. Sociological Analysis of the Dyad. *American Sociological Review* 7(1):13–26.
"Bee Careful!". 1988. *Santa Rosa (Calif.) Press Democrat*, 15 June, A6.
Bell, Robert A., Nancy L. Buerkel-Rothfuss, and Kevin E. Gore. 1987. "Did You Bring the Yarmulke for the Cabbage Patch Kid?": The Idiomatic Communication of Young Lovers. *Human Communication Research* 14(1):47–67.
Ben-Amos, Dan. 1971. Toward a Definition of Folklore in Context. *Journal of American Folklore* 84(331):3–15.

---. 1984. The Seven Strands of Tradition: Varieties in Its Meaning in American Folklore Studies. *Journal of Folklore Research* 21(2–3): 97–131.

---. 1998. The Name is the Thing. *Journal of American Folklore* 111(441):257–280.

Bendix, Regina. 1987. Marmot, Memet, and Marmoset: Further Research on the Folklore of Dyads. *Western Folklore* 46(3):171–191.

---. 1998. Of Names, Professional Identities, and Disciplinary Futures. *Journal of American Folklore* 111(441):235–246.

---. 2002. The Uses of Disciplinary History. *Radical History Review* 84:110–114.

Benedict, Ruth. 1935. *Zuni Mythology*. 2 vols. New York: Columbia University Press.

---. 1959 [1934]. *Patterns of Culture*. Boston: Houghton Mifflin.

Bennett, Gillian. 1984. Women's Personal Experience Stories of Encounters with the Supernatural: Truth as an Aspect of Storytelling. *ARV: Scandinavian Yearbook of Folklore* 40:79–87.

---. 1988. Legend: Performance and Truth. In *Monsters with Iron Teeth*, ed. Gillian Bennett and Paul Smith. Perspectives on Contemporary Legend III. Pp. 13–36. Sheffield: Sheffield Academic Press.

---. 1989a. Are Legends Narratives? *Talking Folklore* 6:1–13.

---. 1989b. "Belief Stories": The Forgotten Genre. *Western Folklore* 48(4):289–311.

---. 1989c. Playful Chaos: Anatomy of a Storytelling Session. In *The Questing Beast*, ed. Gillian Bennett and Paul Smith. Perspectives on Contemporary Legend IV. Pp. 193–212. Sheffield: Sheffield Academic Press.

---. 1991. Contemporary Legend: An Insider's View. *Folklore* 102(2):187–191.

---. 1993. The Color of Saying: Modern Legend and Folktale. *Southern Folklore* 50(1):19–32.

---. 1999. *Alas, Poor Ghost! Traditions of Belief in Story and Discourse*. Logan: Utah State University Press.

---. 2005. *Bodies: Sex, Violence, Disease, and Death in Contemporary Legend*. Jackson: University Press of Mississippi.

Bennett, W. Lance. 1978. Storytelling in Criminal Trials: A Model of Social Judgment. *Quarterly Journal of Speech* 64(1):1–22.

Berger, Peter L., and Thomas Luckmann. 1967. *The Social Construction of Reality: A Treatise in the Sociology of Knowledge*. New York: Anchor.

Berry, Lester V., and Melvin Van Den Bark. 1947. *The American Thesaurus of Slang: A Complete Reference Book of Colloquial Speech*. New York: Thomas Y. Crowell.

Best, Joel. 1987. Rhetoric in Claims-Making: Constructing the Missing Children Problem. *Social Problems* 34(2):101–121.

Best, Joel, and Gerald T. Horiuchi. 1985. The Razor Blade in the Apple: The Social Construction of Urban Legends. *Social Problems* 32(5):488–499.

"Big Lie." http://en.wikipedia.org/wiki/Big_Lie.

Bird, Donald Allport. 1976. A Theory for Folklore in the Mass Media: Traditional Patterns in the Mass Media. *Southern Folklore Quarterly* 40(3–4):285–305.

Blank, Trevor J., ed. 2009. *Folklore and the Intrenet: Vernacular Expression in a Digital World*. Logan: Utah State University Press.

Blehr, Otto. 1967. The Analysis of Folk Belief Stories and Its Implications for Research on Folk Belief and Folk Prose. *Fabula* 9(1–3):259–263.

Boas, Franz. 1916. *Tsimshian Mythology*. U.S. Bureau of American Ethnology Thirty-first Annual Report, 1909–1910. Washington, D.C.

———. 1935. *Kwakuitl Culture as Reflected in Mythology*. Memoirs of the American Folk-Lore Society Vol. 28. New York: American Folklore Society.

Boatright, Mody C. 1958. *The Family Saga and Other Phases of American Folklore*. Urbana: University of Illinois Press.

Bode, Carl. 1959. *The Anatomy of American Popular Culture, 1840–1861*. Berkeley: University of California Press.

Bohannan, Laura. 1966. Shakespeare in the Bush. *Natural History* 75(August–September):28–33.

Bolton, Henry Carrington. 1888. *The Counting-Out Rhymes of Children*. New York: D. Appleton.

Boneh, Dan. 1987. Mystical Powers of Hyenas: Interpreting a Bedouin Belief. *Folklore* 98(1):57–64.

Boorstin, Daniel. 1964. *The Image: A Guide to Pseudo-Events in America*. New York: Colophon.

Botkin, Benjamin A. 1953. Applied Folklore: Creating Understanding through Folklore. *Southern Folklore Quarterly* 17(3):199–206.

———. 1958. We Call It "Living Lore." *New York Folklore Quarterly* 14(3):189–201.

Bourdieu, Pierre. 1973. Cultural Reproduction and Social Reproduction. In *Knowledge, Education and Cultural Change*, ed. Richard. Brown. Pp. 71–112. London: Tavistock.

Bourdieu, Pierre, and Jean-Claude Passeron. 1977. *Reproduction in Education, Society, and Culture*. SAGE Studies in Social and Educational Change, Vol. 5. London: SAGE.

Boyarin, Jonathan. 1996. Narratives of Jewish Identity. *American Anthropologist* 98(4):869–872.

Boyer, Pascal. 1990. *Tradition as Truth and Communication*. Cambridge: Cambridge University Press.

Boyes, Georgina. 1984. Belief and Disbelief: An Examination of Reactions to the Presentation of Rumour Legends. In *Perspectives on Contemporary*

Legend, ed. Paul Smith. Proceedings of the Conference on Contemporary Legend, Sheffield, July 1982. Pp. 46–78. Sheffield: University of Sheffield.

Brandes, Stanley. 1979. Ethnographic Autobiographies in American Anthropology. *Central Issues in Anthropology* 1(2):1–17.

Briggs, Charles L. 1985. Treasure Tales and Pedagogical Discourse in Mexicano New Mexico. *Journal of American Folklore* 98(389):287–314.

_____. 1986. *Learning How to Ask: A Sociolinguistic Appraisal of the Interview in Social Science Research*. Cambridge: Cambridge University Press.

Bronner, Simon J. 1986. *American Folklore Studies: An Intellectual History*. Lawrence: University Press of Kansas.

_____. 1992. Introduction. In *Tradition and Creativity in Folklore: New Directions*, ed. Simon J. Bronner. Pp. 1–38. Logan: Utah State University Press.

_____. 1998. *Following Tradition: Folklore in the Discourse of American Culture*. Logan: Utah State University Press.

_____. 2000a. The Meanings of Tradition: An Introduction. *Western Folklore* 59(2):87–104.

_____. 2000b. The American Concept of Tradition: Folklore in the Discourse of Traditional Values. *Western Folklore* 59(2):143–170.

_____. 2005. "Gombo" Folkloristics: Lafcadio Hearn's Creolization and Hybridization in the Formative Period of Folklore Studies. *Journal of Folklore Research* 42(2):141–184.

_____. 2008. *Killing Tradition: Inside Hunting and Animal Rights Controversies*. Lexington: University Press of Kentucky.

_____. 2011. *Explaining Traditions: Folk Behavior in Modern Culture*. Lexington: University Press of Kentucky.

Bronson, Bertrand H. 1954. The Morphology of the Ballad-Tunes (Variation, Selection, and Continuity). *Journal of American Folklore* 67(263):1–13.

_____. 1969. *The Ballad as Song*. Berkeley: University of California Press.

Brown, Michael F. 1996. On Resisting Resistance. *American Anthropologist* 98(4):729–735.

Brown, W. Norman. 1922. The Silence Wager Stories: The Origin and Their Diffusion. *American Journal of Philology* 43(4):289–317.

Bruchac, Joe. 1990. Storytelling: Oral History or Game of "Telephone." *American Folklore Society Newsletter* 19(2):3–4.

Brunvand, Jan Harold. 1981. *The Vanishing Hitchhiker: American Urban Legends and Their Meanings*. New York: W. W. Norton.

_____. 1984. *The Choking Doberman and Other "New" Urban Legends*. New York: W. W. Norton.

_____. 1986a. *The Study of American Folklore*. 3rd ed. New York: W. W. Norton.

_____. 1986b. *The Mexican Pet: More "New" Urban Legends and Some Old Favorites*. New York: W. W. Norton.

———. 1998. *The Study of American Folklore.* 4th ed. New York: W. W. Norton.
———. 2001. *The Encyclopedia of Urban Legends.* Santa Barbara, Calif.: ABC-CLIO.
Buchan, David. 1981. The Modern Legend. In *Language, Culture and Tradition*, ed. J. D. A. Widdowson and A. E. Green. Papers on Language and Folklore Presented at the Annual Conference of the British Sociological Association, April 1978. Pp. 1–15. Sheffield: The Centre for English Cultural Tradition and Language.
Bullen, Frank T. 1899. *The Cruise of the Cachalot: Round the World after Sperm Whales.* New York: D. Appleton.
Burne, Charlotte Sophia. 1914. *The Handbook of Folklore.* Rev. ed. London: Sidgwick and Jackson for the Folk-Lore Society.
Burne, Charlotte S., Antonio Machado y Alvarez, and E. Sidney Hartland. 1885. The Science of Folklore. *The Folk-Lore Journal* 3(2):97–120.
Burns, Thomas A. 1969. Folklore in the Mass Media: Television. *Folklore Forum* 2(4):90–106.
———. 1970. A Model for Textual Variation in Folksong. *Folklore Forum* 3(2):49–56. Reprinted in Oring 1989:245–253.
Burns, Thomas A., with Inger H. Burns. 1976. *Doing the Wash: An Expressive Culture and Personality Study of a Joke and Its Tellers.* Norwood, Pa.: Norwood.
Byrne, Pat. 1997. Booze, Ritual, and the Invention of Tradition: The Phenomenon of the Newfoundland Screech-In. In *Usable Pasts: Traditions and Group Expressions in North America*, ed. Tad Tuleja. Pp. 232–248. Logan: Utah State University Press.
Campion-Vincent, Véronique. 2005. *Organ Theft Legends.* Jackson: University Press of Mississippi.
Cancian, Francesca. 1960. The Functional Analysis of Change. *American Sociological Review* 25(6):818–827.
Carey, James W. 1986. The Dark Continent of American Journalism. In *Reading the News*, ed. Robert Karl Manoff and Michael Schudson. Pp. 146–196. New York: Pantheon.
Carpenter, Inta Gale, and Ricārdas Vidutis, eds. 1984. Floor Discussion. *Journal of Folklore Research* 21(2–3):156–163, 181–186, 205–210, 228–238, 249–256.
"Cat Greeting Kills Woman." 1988. *Santa Rosa (Calif.) Press Democrat*, 9 June, A4.
Caughey, John. 1986. Epilogue: On the Anthropology of America. In *Symbolizing America*, ed. Hervé Varenne. Pp. 229–250. Lincoln: University of Nebraska Press.
Chafets, Ze'ev. 1985. *Double Vision: How the Press Distorts America's View of the Middle East.* New York: William Morrow.
Chatterton, Edward K. 1930. *Whalers and Whaling.* London: P. Allan.
Church, Albert Cook. 1960. *Whale Ships and Whaling.* New York: W. W. Norton.

Clark, Robert T., Jr. 1955. *Herder: His Life and Thought.* Berkeley: University of California Press.
Clark, Ronald W. 1980. *Freud: The Man and the Cause.* New York: Random House.
Clements, William M. 1973. Unintentional Substitution in Folklore Transmission: A Devolutionary Instance. *New York Folklore Quarterly* 29(4):243–273.
_____. 1980. The Chain on the Tombstone. In *Indiana Folklore: A Reader,* ed. Linda Dégh. Pp. 259–264. Bloomington: Indiana University Press.
Clifford, James. 1986. On Ethnographic Allegory. In *Writing Culture: The Poetics and Politics of Ethnography,* ed. James Clifford and George E. Marcus. Pp. 98–121. Berkeley: University of California Press.
Clifford, James, and George E. Marcus, eds. 1986. *Writing Culture: The Poetics and Politics of Ethnography.* Berkeley: University of California Press.
Coben, Stanley. 1976. The Assault on Victorianism in the Twentieth Century. In *Victorian America,* ed. Daniel Walker Howe. Pp. 160–181. Philadelphia: University of Pennsylvania Press.
Cochrane, Timothy. 1987. The Concept of Ecotypes in American Folklore. *Journal of Folklore Research* 24(1):33–55.
Coffin, Tristram P. 1963. *The British Traditional Ballad in North America.* Rev. ed. Philadelphia: The American Folklore Society.
Coggeshall, John M. 1986. "One of Those Intangibles": The Manifestation of Ethnic Identity in Southwestern Illinois. *Journal of American Folklore* 99(392):177–207.
Cohen, Anne B. 1973. *Poor Pearl, Poor Girl: The Murdered-Girl Stereotype in Ballad and Newspaper.* Austin: University of Texas Press.
Colcord, Joanna C. 1938. *Songs of American Sailormen.* New York: W. W. Norton.
Cooperson, Michael. 2005. Probability, Plausibility, and "Spiritual Communication" in Classic Arabic Biography. In *On Fiction and Adab in Medieval Arabic Literature,* ed. Philip F. Kennedy. Pp. 69–81. Wiesbaden, Germany: Harrassowitz.
Correll, Timothy Corrigan. 2005. Believers, Sceptics, and Charlatans: Evidential Rhetoric, the Fairies, and Fairy Healers in Irish Oral Narrative and Belief. *Folklore* 116(1):1–18.
_____. 2008. "You Know the Needle-Boy, Right?" Variation in Rumors and Legends about Attacks with HIV-Infected Needles. *Western Folklore* 67(1):59–100.
Crapanzano, Vincent. 1977. The Life History in Anthropological Fieldwork. *Anthropology and Humanism Quarterly* 2(2–3):3–7.
_____. 1980. *Tuhami: Portrait of a Moroccan.* Chicago: University of Chicago Press.
Crowley, Daniel. 1966. *I Could Talk Old-Story Good: Creativity in Bahamian Folklore.* Berkeley: University of California Press.

Cuddon, J. A. 1976. *A Dictionary of Literary Terms.* Rev. ed. Garden City, N.Y.: Doubleday.
Dale, Rodney. 1978. *The Tumor in the Whale: A Collection of Modern Myths.* London: Duckworth.
Danielson, Larry. 1977. Introduction. *Western Folklore* 34(1):1–5.
———. 1979. Toward the Analysis of Vernacular Texts: The Supernatural Narrative in Oral and Popular Print Sources. *Journal of the Folklore Institute* 16(3):130–154.
Darnton, Robert. 1975. Writing News and Telling Stories. *Daedalus* 104(2):175–194.
Davies, Christie. 1990. *Ethnic Humor around the World: A Compartive Analysis.* Bloomington: Indiana University Press.
———. 2001. Jokes that Follow Mass-Mediated Disasters in a Global Electronic Age. In *Of Corpse: Death and Humor in Folklore and Popular Culture,* ed. Peter Narváez. Pp. 15–34. Logan: Utah State University Press.
Davis, Gerald L. 1992. "So Correct for the Photograph": "Fixing" the Ineffable, Ineluctable African American. In *Public Folklore,* ed. Robert Baron and Nicholas R. Spitzer. Pp. 105–118. Washington, D.C.: Smithsonian Institution Press.
Davis, Kenneth C. 1996. *Don't Know Much about the Civil War: Everything You Need to Know about America's Greatest Conflict but Never Learned.* New York: William Morrow.
Davis, Murray S. 1971. That's Interesting! Toward a Phenomenology of Sociology and a Sociology of Phenomenology. *Philosophy of Social Science* 1(2):309–344.
de Caro, Francis A. 1968. Finding a Lost Watch. *Indiana Folklore* 1(1):25–27.
———. 1972. Folklore as an "Historical Science": Anglo-American Viewpoint. Ph.D. dissertation, Department of Folklore, Indiana University.
de Gubernatis, Angelo. 1872. *Zoological Mythology; or, The Legends of Animals.* New York: Macmillan.
de Saussure, Ferdinand. 1966 [1909–1911]. *Course in General Linguistics.* New York: McGraw-Hill.
Dégh, Linda. 1972. Folk Narrative. In *Folklore and Folklife: An Introduction,* ed. Richard M. Dorson. Pp. 53–84. Chicago: University of Chicago Press.
———. 1975. *People in the Tobacco Belt: Four Lives.* Canadian Centre for Folk Culture Studies, Paper 13. Ottowa: National Museum of Canada.
———. 1984. Uses of Folklore as Expressions of Identity by Hungarians in the Old and New Country. *Journal of Folklore Research* 21(2–3):187–200.
———. 1991. What is a Legend after All? *Contemporary Legend* 1:11–38.
———. 1994. *American Folklore and the Mass Media.* Bloomington: Indiana University Press.

———. 1995. *Narratives in Society: A Performance-Centered Study of Narration.* Helsinki: Suomalainen Tiedeakatemia.
———. 1996. What is a Belief Legend? *Folklore* 107:33–46.
———. 2001. *Legend and Belief.* Bloomington: Indiana University Press.
Dégh, Linda, and Andrew Vázsonyi. 1974. Legend and Mass Media. In *The First LACUS Forum*, ed. Adam Makkai and Valerie Becker Makkai. Pp. 279–287. Columbia, S.C.: Hornbeam.
———. 1975. The Hypothesis of Multi-Conduit Transmission in Folklore. In *Folklore: Performance and Communication*, ed. Dan Ben-Amos and Kenneth S. Goldstein. Pp. 207–252. The Hague: Mouton.
———. 1976. Legend and Belief. In *Folklore Genres*, ed. Dan Ben-Amos. Pp. 93–123. Austin: University of Texas Press.
Denby, Priscilla. 1971. Folklore in the Mass Media. *Folklore Forum* 4(5):113–125.
Denver, John. 1970. *Take Me to Tomorrow.* RCA LSP-4278.
"Disneyland of Death." 1959. *Time,* 7 December, 107.
Dobler, Robert. 2009. Ghosts in the Machine: Mourning the MySpace Dead. In *Folklore and the Internet: Vernacular Expression in a Digital World*, ed. Trevor J. Blank. Pp. 175–193. Logan: Utah State University Press.
Dolby-Stahl, Sandra K. 1985. A Literary Folkloristic Methodology for the Study of Meaning in Personal Narrative. *Journal of Folklore Research* 22(1):45–69.
Dolgin, Janet L., David S. Kemnitzer, and David M. Schneider, eds. 1977. *Symbolic Anthropology: A Reader in the Study of Symbols and Meanings.* New York: Columbia University Press.
Dorson, Richard M. 1939. *Davy Crockett: American Comic Legend.* New York: Spiral Press for Rockland Editions.
———. 1945. Print and American Folktales. *California Folklore Quarterly* 4(3):207–215.
———. 1946. *Jonathan Draws the Long Bow.* Cambridge, Mass.: Harvard University Press.
———. 1952. *Bloodstoppers and Bearwalkers: Folk Traditions of the Upper Peninsula.* Cambridge: Harvard University Press.
———. 1955. The Eclipse of Solar Mythology. *Journal of American Folklore* 68(270):393–416. Reprinted in Dundes 1965:57–83.
———. 1959. A Theory for American Folklore. *Journal of American Folklore* 72(285):197–215.
———. 1961. Ethnohistory and Ethnic Folklore. *Ethnohistory* 8(1):12–30.
———. 1963. Current Folklore Theories. *Current Anthropology* 4(1):93–112.
———, ed. 1968a. *Peasant Customs and Savage Myths: Selections from the British Folklorists.* 2 vols. Chicago: University of Chicago Press.
———. 1968b. What is Folklore? *Folklore Forum* 1(4):37.

_____. 1969. A Theory for American Folklore Reviewed. *Journal of American Folklore* 82(325):226–244.
_____. 1971 *American Folklore and the Historian.* Chicago: University of Chicago Press.
_____. 1972. Introduction: Concepts of Folklore and Folklife Studies. In *Folklore and Folklife: An Introduction*, ed. Richard M. Dorson. Pp. 1–50. Chicago: University of Chicago Press.
_____. 1973. *America in Legend: Folklore from the Colonial Period to the Present.* New York: Pantheon.
_____. 1978a. American Folklore vs. Folklore in America. *Journal of the Folklore Institute* 15(2):97–111.
_____. 1978b. Editor's Comment: We All Need the Folk. *Journal of the Folklore Institute* 15(3):267–269.
_____. 1978c. Folklore in the Modern World. In *Folklore in the Modern World*, ed. Richard M. Dorson. Pp. 11–51. The Hague: Mouton.
Douglas, Ann. 1975. Heaven Our Home: Consolation Literature in the Northern United States, 1830–1880. In *Death in America*, ed. David E. Stannard. Pp. 49–68. Philadelphia: University of Pennsylvania Press.
du Sautoy, Marcus. 2008. *Symmetry: A Journey into the Patterns of Nature.* New York: Harper.
Dunbar, David, and Brad Reagan, eds. 2006. *Debunking 9/11 Myths: Why Conspiracy Theories Can't Stand Up to the Facts.* New York: Hearst.
Dundes, Alan. 1963. Structural Typology in North American Indian Folktales. *Southwestern Journal of Anthropology* 19(1):121–130.
_____, ed. 1965. *The Study of Folklore.* Englewood Cliffs, N.J.: Prentice-Hall.
_____. 1969. The Devolutionary Premise in Folklore Theory. *Journal of the Folklore Institute* 6(1):5–19.
_____. 1971. Folk Ideas as Units of World View. *Journal of American Folklore* 84(331):93–103.
_____. 1977. Who Are the Folk? In *Frontiers of Folklore*, ed. William R. Bascom. AAAS Selected Symposium Series 5. Pp. 17–35. Boulder, Colo.: Westview.
_____. 1980. *Interpreting Folklore.* Bloomington: Indiana University Press.
_____. 1983. Defining Identity through Folklore. In *Identity: Personal and Socio-Culutral: A Symposium*, ed. Anita Jacobson-Widding. Pp. 235–261. *Uppsala Studies in Cultural Anthropology 5.* Uppsala: Acta Universitatis Upsaliensis.
_____. 1984. *Life is Like a Chicken Coop Ladder: A Portrait of German Culture through Folklore.* New York: Columbia University Press.
_____. 1989. The Anthropologist and the Comparative Method in Folklore. In *Folklore Matters*, ed. Alan Dundes. Pp. 57–82. Knoxville: University of Tennessee Press.

———. 1997a. *Two Tales of Crow and Sparrow: A Freudian Folkloristic Essay on Caste and Untouchability*. Lanham, Md.: Rowman and Littlefield.
———. 1997b. *From Game to War and Other Psychoanalytic Essays on Folklore*. Lexington: University Press of Kentucky.
Dundes, Alan, and Alessandro Falassi. 1975. *La Terra in Piazza: An Interpretation of the Palio of Siena*. Berkeley: University of California Press.
Dundes, Alan, and Carl R. Pagter. 1975. *Work Hard and You Shall Be Rewarded: Urban Folklore From the Paperwork Empire*. Bloomington: Indiana University Press.
Dunlop, Donald. 1975. Popular Culture and Methodology. *Journal of Popular Culture* 9(2):375–383.
Durkheim, Émile. 1964 [1895]. *The Rules of Sociological Method*, trans. Sarah A. Solway and John H. Mueller. 8th ed. New York: The Free Press.
Dwyer, Kevin. 1977. On the Dialogic of Fieldwork. *Dialectical Anthropology* 2(2):143–151.
———. 1982. *Moroccan Dialogues: Anthropology in Question*. Baltimore: The Johns Hopkins University Press.
Eckstorm, Fannie H. and Phillips Barry. 1930. What is Tradition. *Bulletin of the Folk-Song Society of the Northeast* 1:2–3.
Eff, Elaine. 1990. To Keep Tradition Going: Conserving Baltimore Screen Painting. In *Folklife Annual 90*, ed. by James Hardin. Pp. 132–143, Washington D.C.: Library of Congress.
Ellis, Bill. 1982–83. Legend Tripping in Ohio: A Behavioral Survey. *Papers in Comparative Studies* 2:61–73.
———. 1987. Why are Verbatim Texts of Legends Necessary? *Perspectives on Contemporary Legend II*, ed. Gillian Bennett, Paul Smith, and J. D. A. Widdowson. Pp. 31–60. Sheffield: Sheffield Academic Press.
———. 1994. "The Hook" Reconsidered: Problems in Classifying Adolescent Horror Legends. *Folklore* 105:61–75.
———. 2001a. Haec in sua parochial accidesse dixit: The Rhetoric of 15th Century Contemporary Legends. *Contemporary Legend*, n.s., 4:74–92.
———. 2001b. *Aliens, Ghosts, and Cults: Legends We Live*. Mississippi: University Press of Mississippi.
Elon, Amos. 1975. *Herzl*. New York: Holt, Rinehart, and Winston.
Epstein, Edward J. 1981. The Selection of Reality. In *What's News: The Media in American Society*, ed. Elie Abel. Pp. 119–132. San Francisco: Institute for Contemporary Studies.
Erikson, Erik H. 1959. *Identity and the Life Cycle*. New York: International Universities Press.
———. 1963 [1950]. *Childhood and Society*. New York: W. W. Norton.
———. 1968. *Identity: Youth and Crisis*. New York: W. W. Norton.
Evans, Timothy H. 1988. Folklore as Utopia: English Medievalists and the Ideology of Revival. *Western Folklore* 47(4):245–268.

Ewing, Katherine P. 1990. The Illusion of Wholeness: Culture, Self, and the Experience of Inconsistency. *Ethos* 18(3):251–278.
Farmer, John S., and W. E. Henley, eds. 1970. *Slang and Its Analogues: Past and Present.* New York: Arno.
Feintuch, Burt. 1988. Introduction. In *The Conservation of Culture: Folklorists and the Public Sector*, ed. Burt Feintuch. Pp. 1–16. Lexington: University Press of Kentucky.
———, ed. 2003. *Eight Words for the Study of Expressive Culture.* Urbana: University of Illinois Press.
Fenichel, Otto. 1946. *The Psychoanalytic Theory of Neurosis.* London: Routledge and Kegan Paul.
Final Discussion. 1983. On the Analytical Value of the Concept of Tradition. In *Trends in Nordic Tradition Research*, ed. Lauri Honko and Pekka Laaksonen. Pp. 233–249. Helsinki: Suomalaisen Kirjallisuuden Seura.
Fine, Elizabeth C., and Jean Haskell Speer. 1992. Introduction. In *Performance, Culture, and Identity*, ed. Elizabeth C. Fine and Jean Haskell Speer. Pp. 1–22. Westport, Conn.: Praeger.
Fine, Gary Alan. 1979a. Small Groups and Culture Creation: The Idioculture of Little League Baseball Teams. *American Sociological Review* 44(5):733–745.
———. 1979b. Cokelore and Coke Law: Urban Belief Tales and the Problem of Multiple Origins. *Journal of American Folklore* 92(366):477–482.
———. 1992. *Manufacturing Tales: Sex and Money in Contemporary Legends.* Knoxville: University of Tennessee Press.
Fine, Gary Alan, and Patrica A. Turner. 2001. *Whispers on the Color Line: Rumor and Race in America.* Berkeley: University of California Press.
Finnegan, Ruth. 1991. Tradition, but What Tradition and for Whom? *Oral Tradition* 6(1):104–124.
Fiske, John. 1872. *Myths and Myth-Makers: Old Tales and Superstitions Interpreted by Comparative Mythology.* Boston: Houghton Mifflin.
Flegg, Graham, Cynthia Hay, and Barbara Moss. 1985. *Nicolas Chuquet, Renaissance Mathematician.* Dordrecht, Holland: D. Reidel.
Fletcher, Kathy. 1990. Where My Navel String is Buried: Folklore Memories of Home from the Employees of ETI. Unpublished manuscript.
Fogelson, Raymond D. 1982. Person, Self, and Identity: Some Anthropological Retrospects, Circumspects, and Prospects. In *Psychosocial Theories of the Self*, ed. Benjamin Lee. Pp. 67–109. New York: Plenum.
Foley, John Miles. 1988. *The Theory of Oral Composition: History and Methodology.* Bloomington: Indiana University Press.
Fox, William S. 1980. Folklore and Fakelore: Some Sociological Considerations. *Journal of the Folklore Institute* 17(2–3):244–261.
Frank, Geyla. 1979. Finding the Common Denominator: A Phenomenological Critique of the Life History Method. *Ethos* 7(1):68–94.

Frazer, James G. 1934 [1910]. *Totemism and Exogamy: A Treatise on Certain Early Forms of Superstition and Society.* London: Dawsons.

———. 1942 [1890]. *The Golden Bough: A Study of Religion and Magic.* Abr. ed. New York: Macmillan

Freeman, James M. 1979. *Untouchable: An Indian Life History.* Stanford: Stanford University Press.

Freilich, Morris, ed. 1983. *The Pleasure of Anthropology.* New York: New American Library.

French, Stanley. 1975. The Cemetery as Cultural Institution: The Establishment of Mount Auburn and the "Rural Cemetery Movement." In *Death in America,* ed. David E. Stannard. Pp. 69–91. Philadelphia: University of Pennsylvania Press.

Freud, Ernest L., ed. 1960. *The Letters of Sigmund Freud.* New York: Basic Books.

Freud, Sigmund. 1953–1974. *The Complete Psychological Works of Sigmund Freud,* ed. James Strachey. 24 vols. London: Hogarth Press and the Institute of Psycho-Analysis.

Friedman, Pearl. 1942. A Second Experiment on Interview Bias. *Sociometry* 5(4):378–381.

Fulton, DoVeanna S. 2004. Comic Views and Metaphysical Dilemmas: Shattering Cultural Images through Self-Definition and Representation by Black Comediennes. *Journal of American Folklore* 117(463):81–96.

Gabbert, Lisa. 2000. Religious Belief and Everyday Knowledge: A Functional Analysis of the Legend Dialectic. *Contemporary Legend,* n.s., 3:108–126.

Gailey, Alan. 1988. Tradition and Identity. In *The Uses of Tradition: Essays Presented to G. B. Thompson,* ed. Alan Gailey. Pp. 61–67. Ulster: Ulster Folk and Transport Museum.

———. 1989. The Nature of Tradition. *Folklore* 100(2):143–161.

Galanter, Marc. 2005. *Lowering the Bar: Lawyer Jokes and Legal Culture.* Madison: University of Wisconsin Press.

Galtung, John. 1967. After Camelot. In *The Rise and Fall of Project Camelot: Studies in the Relationship between Social Science and Practical Politics,* ed. Irving L. Horowitz, Pp. 281–312. Cambridge, Mass.: MIT Press.

Gans, Herbert J. 1980. *Deciding What's News: A Study of CBS News, NBC Nightly News, Newsweek, and Time.* New York: Vintage.

Geertz, Clifford. 1973. *The Interpretation of Cultures.* New York: Basic Books.

———. 1988. *Works and Lives: The Anthropologist as Author.* Stanford: Stanford University Press.

Georges, Robert A. 1971. The General Concept of Legend: Some Assumptions to be Reexamined and Reassessed. In *American Folk Legend: A Symposium,* ed. Wayland D. Hand. Pp. 1–19. Berkeley: University of California Press.

———. 1991. Erasing, Appropriating, Concealing, and Denying the Identity of the Folklorist. *Western Folklore* 50(1):3–12.

Georges, Robert A., and Alan Dundes. 1963. Toward a Structural Definition of the Riddle. *Journal of American Folklore* 76(300):111–118.

Georges, Robert A., and Michael Owen Jones. 1980. *People Studying People: The Human Element in Fieldwork.* Berkeley: University of California Press.

Gerould, Gordon Hall. 1923. The Making of Ballads. *Modern Philology* 21:15–28.

———. 1957 [1932]. *The Ballad of Tradition.* New York: Galaxy

Gillon, Edmund V., Jr. 1972. *Victorian Cemetery Art.* New York: Dover.

Ginzberg, Louis. 1968. *The Legends of the Jews.* 7 vols. Philadelphia: The Jewish Publication Society of America.

Glanz, Rudolf. 1986. The Wandering Jew in America. In *The Wandering Jew: Essays in the Interpretation of a Christian Legend*, ed. Galit Hasan-Rokem and Alan Dundes. Pp. 105–118. Bloomington: Indiana University Press.

Glassie, Henry. 1975. *Folk Housing in Middle Virginia: A Structural Analysis of Historic Artifacts.* Knoxville: University of Tennessee Press.

———. 1989. *The Spirit of Folk Art: The Girard Collection at the Museum of International Folk Art.* New York: Harry N. Abrams.

———. 1993a. Günümüzde Geleneksel Türk Sanatı [Turkish Traditional Art Today]. Istanbul: Pan Yayıncılık.

———. 1993b. *Turkish Traditional Art Today.* Bloomington: Indiana University Press.

———. 1995. Tradition. *Journal of American Folklore* 108(430):395–412.

———. 1996. Discussion. Annual Meeting of the American Folklore Society, Pittsburgh, Pennsylvania, 17 October.

Glazer, Mark. 1988. The Superglue Revenge: A Psychological Analysis. In *Monsters with Iron Teeth*, ed. Gillian Bennett and Paul Smith. Perspectives on Contemporary Legend III. Pp. 139–146. Sheffield: Sheffield Academic Press.

Gluckman, Max. 1963. *Order and Rebellion in Tribal Africa.* New York: Free Press.

Goldberg, Christine. 1984. The Historic-Geographic Method: Past and Future. *Journal of Folklore Research* 21(1):1–18.

Goldenweiser, Alexander A. 1910. Totemism: An Analytical Study. *Journal of American Folklore* 23(88):179–293.

Goldstein, Diane E. 2004. *Once Upon a Virus: AIDS Legends and Vernacular Risk Perception.* Logan: Utah State University Press.

Goldstein, Kenneth S. 1967. Experimental Folklore: Laboratory vs. Field. In *Folklore International: Essays in Traditional Literature, Belief and Custom in Honor of Wayland Debs Hand*, ed. D. K. Wilgus. Pp. 71–82. Hatboro, Pa.: Folklore Associates.

_____. 1971. Strategy in Counting-Out: An Ethnographic Folklore Field Study. In *The Study of Games*, ed. Elliott M. Avedon and Brian Sutton-Smith. Pp. 167–178. New York: John Wiley. Reprinted in Oring 1989:185–195.

Golovakha-Hicks, Inna. 2006. Demonology in Contemporary Ukraine: Folklore or "Postfolklore"? *Journal of Folklore Research* 43(3):219–240.

Gomme, G. Laurence. 1910. Heredity and Tradition. *Folklore* 21(3):385–386.

Goodale, Mark. 2006. Ethical Theory as Social Practice. *American Anthropologist* 108(1):25–37.

Gorman, Christine. 1988. On the Wings of Mythology. *Time*, 2 May, 67.

Granot, Yehoshua. 1969. Fouad's Rooster. In *Written in Battle*, ed. Mordechay Barkay. Pp. 197–210. Tel Aviv: Ledory.

Greenleaf, Elizabeth B. 1933. *Ballads and Sea Songs from Newfoundland*. Cambridge, Mass.: Harvard University Press.

Greenwood, Mary Ellen. 2004. Hunting for Meaning: How Characterization Reveals Standards for Behavior in Family Folklore. *Western Folklore* 63(1–2):79–100.

Grice, H. Paul. 1975. Logic and Conversation. In *Syntax and Semantics*, vol. 3 of *Speech Acts*, ed. Peter Cole and Jerry L. Morgan. Pp. 41–58. New York: Academic Press.

Grider, Sylvia. 1980. The Hatchet Man. In *Indiana Folklore: A Reader*, ed. Linda Dégh. Pp. 147–178. Bloomington: Indiana University Press.

Grieg, Gavin. 1963. *Folk-Song in Buchan and Folk-Song of the North-East*. Hatboro, Pa.: Folklore Associates.

Grimm, Jacob. 1966 [1835]. *Teutonic Mythology*, trans. James Steven Stallybrass. 4 vols. New York: Dover.

Grünbaum, Adolf. 1984. *The Foundations of Psychoanalysis: A Philosophical Critique*. Berkeley: University of California Press.

Gummere, Francis B. 1907. *The Popular Ballad*. Boston: Houghton Mifflin.

Guri, Hayyim. 1968. *Dapim Yerushalmi'im* [Jerusalemite Leaves]. Israel: Ha-Kibbutz Ha-Meuchad.

Gutowski, John A. 1972. The Art of Professional Wrestling: Folk Expression in Mass Culture. *Keystone Folklore Quarterly* 17(2):41–50.

_____. 1980. Traditions of the Devil's Hollows. In *Indiana Folklore: A Reader*, ed. Linda Dégh. Pp. 74–92. Bloomington: Indiana University Press.

Hall, Gary. 1980. The Big Tunnel. In *Indiana Folklore: A Reader*, ed. Linda Dégh. Pp. 225–257. Bloomington: Indiana University Press.

Hanauer, J. E. 1935. *Folk-Lore of the Holy Land*. New and enlarged ed. London: Sheldon.

Handler, Richard, and Jocelyn Linnekin. 1984. Tradition, Genuine or Spurious. *Journal of American Folklore* 97(385):273–290.

Harris, Neil. 1966. *The Artist in American Society.* New York: George Braziller.
Harvey, David. 1990. *The Condition of Postmodernity: An Enquiry into the Origins of Culture Change.* Cambridge, Mass.: Blackwell.
Hautala, Jouko. 1954. *Suomalainen kansanrunoudentutkimus* [Finnish Folklore Research]. Helsinki: Suomalaisen Kirjallisuuden Seura.
Hävernick, Walter. 1968. Tradition und Kontinuation. *Zeitschrift für Volkskunde* 64:22–24.
Hawes, Bess Lomax. 1992. Happy Birthday, Dear American Folklore Society: Reflections on the Work and Mission of the Folklorist. In *Public Folklore*, ed. Robert Baron and Nicholas R. Spitzer. Pp. 65–73. Washington D.C.: Smithsonian Institution Press.
Henry, William, III. 1984. Embroidering the Facts. *Time*, 2 July, 66.
Herodotus. 1942. *The Persian Wars*, trans. George Rawlinson. New York: Modern Library.
Herr, Michael. 1975. What's Your Age, Boy? *Esquire* 84 (November), 96–103.
Herstein, I. N., and I. Kaplansky. 1974. *Mathematical Matters.* New York: Harper and Row.
History of Forest Lawn. n.d. 3 parts. Part 1:http://www.youtube.com/watch? v=o2kwcThmYQA; Part 2: http://www.youtube.com/watch?v=vSzfW8–65LQ; Part 3: http://www.youtube.com/watch?v=oBXMPnM3H70.
Hobbs, Sandy. 1978. The Folktale as News. *Oral History* 6(11):74–86.
_____. 1987. The Social Psychology of a Good Story. In *Perspectives on Contemporary Legend II*, ed. Gillian Bennett, Paul Smith, and J. D. A. Widdowson. Pp. 133–148. Sheffield: Sheffield Academic Press.
_____. 1989. Enough to Constitute a Legend? In *The Questing Beast*, ed. Gillian Bennett and Paul Smith. Perspectives on Contemporary Legend IV. Pp. 55–75. Sheffield: Sheffield Academic Press.
Hobsbawm, Eric. 1984. Mass-Producing Traditions: Europe, 1870–1914. In *The Invention of Tradition*, ed. Eric Hobsbawm and Terence Ranger. Pp. 263–307. Cambridge: Cambridge University Press.
Hobsbawm, Eric, and Terence Ranger, eds. 1984. *The Invention of Tradition.* Cambridge: Cambridge University Press.
Hofer, Tamás. 1984. The Perception of *Tradition* in European Ethnology. *Journal of Folklore Research* 21(3–4):133–147.
Hohman, Elmo Paul. 1928. *The American Whaleman: A Study of Life and Labor in the Whaling Industry.* New York: Longmans Green.
Honko, Lauri. 1964. Memorates and the Study of Folk Beliefs. *Journal of the Folklore Institute* 1(1):5–19.
_____. 1983. Research Traditions in Tradition Research. In *Trends in Nordic Tradition Research*, ed. Lauri Honko and Pekka Laaksonen. Pp. 13–22. Helsinki: Suomalaisen Kirjallisuuden Seura.

Howard, Robert Glenn. 2005. A Theory of Vernacular Rhetoric: The Case of the "Sinner's Prayer" Online. *Folklore* 116(2):172–188.
Howe, Daniel Walker. 1976. Victorian Culture in America. In *Victorian America*, ed. Daniel Walker Howe. Pp. 3–28. Philadelphia: University of Pennsylvania Press.
_____, ed. 1976. *Victorian America.* Philadelphia: University of Pennsylvania Press.
Hughes, Helen MacGill. 1940. *News and the Human Interest Story.* Chicago: University of Chicago Press.
Huntington, Gale. 1964. *Songs the Whalemen Sang.* Barre, Mass.: Barre.
Hurwood, Bernhardt J., trans. 1968. *The Facetiae of Giovanni Francesco Poggio Bracciolini.* New York: Award Books.
Hyman, Stanley Edgar. 1957. The Child Ballad in America: Some Aesthetic Criteria. *Journal of American Folklore* 70(277):236–239.
Hymes, Dell. 1974. The Uses of Anthropology: Critical, Political, Personal. In *Reinventing Anthropology*, ed. Dell Hymes. Pp. 3–79. New York: Vintage.
_____. 1975. Folklore's Nature and the Sun's Myth. *Journal of American Folklore* 88(350):345–369.
Indvik, Julie, and Mary Anne Fitzpatrick. 1982. "If You Could Read My Mind Love": Understanding and Misunderstanding in the Marital Dyad. *Family Relations* 31(1):43–51.
Ivey, Saundra Keyes. 1977. Ascribed Ethnicity and the Ethnic Display Event: The Melungeons of Hancock County, Tennessee. *Western Folklore* 36(1):85–107.
Jabbour, Alan. 1989. On the Values of American Folklorists. *Journal of American Folklore* 102(405):292–298.
Jacobs, Joseph. 1893. The Folk. *Folklore* 4(2):233–238.
Jacobs, Melville. 1959a. *The Content and Style of an Oral Literature: Clackamas Chinook Myths and Tales.* Chicago: University of Chicago Press.
_____. 1959b. Folklore. In *The Anthropology of Franz Boas: Essays on the Centennial of His Birth*, ed. Walter Goldschmidt. Pp. 119–138. San Francisco: American Anthropological Association and Howard Chandler.
Jakóbczyk, F. 1973. On the Generalized Josephus Problem. *Glasgow Journal of Mathematics.* 14:168–173.
Jakobson, Roman and Petyr Bogatyrev. 1980 [1929]. Folklore as a Special Form of Creation. Trans. John M. O'Hara. *Folklore Forum* 13(1):3–21.
Jameson, Fredric. 1984. Postmodernism, or the Cultural Logic of Late Capitalism. *New Left Review* 146 (July–August), 53–92.
Jansen, William Hugh. 1979. The Surpriser Surprised: A Modern Legend. In *Readings in American Folklore*, ed. Jan Harold Brunvand. Pp. 61–90. New York: W. W. Norton.
Jastrow, Marcus. 1950. *A Dictionary of the Targum, the Talmud Babli and Yerushalmi, and the Midrashic Literature.* 2 vols. New York: Pardes.

Jay, Robert. 1974. Personal and Extrapersonal Vision in Anthropology. In *Reinventing Anthropology*, ed. Dell Hymes. Pp. 367–381. New York: Vintage.

Jennings, Gary. 1980. *Aztec*. New York: Avon.

Johnsen, Birgit Herzberg. 1989. Tradition, Milieu, and Cultural Values. In *Nordic Folklore*, ed. Reimund Kvideland and Henning K. Sehmsdorf. Pp. 150–162. Bloomington: Indiana University Press.

Johnson, John William. 1998. Tradition. In *Encyclopedia of Folklore and Literature*, ed. Mary Ellen Brown and Bruce A. Rosenberg. Pp. 658–660. Santa Barbara, Calif.: ABC-CLIO.

Jones, Ernest. 1964. *Essays in Applied Psycho-Analysis*. 2 vols. New York: International Universities.

Jones, Michael Owen. 1976. Alternatives to Local (Re-) Surveys of Incidental Depth Projects. *Western Folklore* 35(3):217–226.

_____. 1987. *Exploring Folk Art: Twenty Years of Thought on Craft, Work, and Aesthetics*. Ann Arbor, Mich.: UMI.

_____. 1989. *Craftsman of the Cumberlands: Tradition and Creativity*. Lexington: The University Press of Kentucky.

_____. 1991. Why Folklore and Organization(s)? *Western Folklore* 50(1):29–40.

_____. 2000. "Tradition" in Identity Discourses and an Individual's Symbolic Construction of Self. *Western Folklore* 59(2):115–140.

Josephus, Flavius. 1927. *The Jewish War, Books I-III*, trans. H. St. J. Thackery. The Loeb Classical Library. Cambridge: Harvard University Press.

_____. 1928. *The Jewish War, Books IV-VII*, trans. H. St. J. Thackery. The Loeb Classical Library. Cambridge: Harvard University Press.

_____. 1970. *The Jewish War*, trans. G. A. Williamson. New York: Penguin.

Jung, C. G. 1949. *Psychological Types*. London: Routledge and Kegan Paul.

Kakar, Sudhir. 1979. Preface. In *Identity and Adulthood*, ed. Sudhir Kakar. Pp. viii-xiii. Dehli: Oxford University Press.

Kalčik, Susan. 1975. "... like Ann's Gynecologist or the Time I was Almost Raped": Personal Narratives in Women's Rap Groups. *Journal of American Folklore* 88(347):3–11.

Kaplan, Abraham. 1964. *The Conduct of Inquiry*. San Francisco: Chandler.

Katriel, Tamar. 1986. *Talking Straight: Dugri in Israeli Sabra Culture*. Cambridge: Cambridge University Press.

Kerr, David. 1991. On Not Being a Folklorist: Field Methodology and the Reproduction of Underdevelopment. *Folklore* 102(1):48–61.

Keyes, Cheryl L. 2000. Empowering Self, Making Choices, Creating Spaces: Black Female Identity via Rap Music Performance. *Journal of American Folklore* 113(449):255–269.

Kirshenblatt-Gimblett, Barbara. 1982. The Cut that Binds: The Western Ashkenazic Torah Binder as Nexus between Circumcision and Torah.

In *Celebration: Studies in Festivity and Ritual*, ed. Victor Turner. Pp. 136–146. Washington DC: Smithsonian Institute Press.

———. 1983. The Future of Folklore Studies in America: The Urban Frontier. *Folklore Forum* 16(2):175–234.

———. 1988. Mistaken Dichotomies. *Journal of American Folklore* 101(400): 140–155.

———. 1989. Objects of Memory: Material Culture as Life Review. In *Folk Groups and Folklore Genres: A Reader*, ed. Elliott Oring. Pp. 278–285. Logan: Utah State University Press.

———. 1994. On Difference. *Journal of American Folklore* 107(424):233–238.

———. 1995. From the Paperwork Empire to the Paperless Office: Testing the Limits of the "Science of Tradition." In *Folklore Interpreted: Essays in Honor of Alan Dundes*, ed. Regina Bendix and Rosemary Levy Zumwalt. Pp. 69–92. New York: Garland.

———. 1996. Topic Drift: Negotiating the Gap between the Field and Our Name. *Journal of Folklore Research* 33(3):245–254.

———. 1998. Folklore's Crisis. *Journal of American Folklore* 111(441):281–327.

Klein, Barbro. 2000. The Moral Content of Tradition: Homecraft. Ethnology, and Swedish Life in the Twentieth Century. *Western Folklore* 59(2):171–195.

Klintberg, Bengt af. 1989. Legends Today: Tradition, Milieu, and Cultural Values. In *Nordic Folklore*, ed. Reimund Kvideland and Henning K. Sehmsdorf. Pp. 70–89. Bloomington: Indiana University Press.

Kluckhohn, Clyde. 1945. The Personal Document in Anthropological Science. In *The Use of Personal Documents in History, Anthropology, and Sociology*, ed. Louis Gottschalk, Clyde Kluckhohn, and Robert Angell. Social Science Bulletin 53. Pp. 79–177. New York: The Council.

Knapp, Mary, and Herbert Knapp. 1976. *One Potato, Two Potato: The Secret Education of American Children*. New York: W. W. Norton.

Knuth, Donald E. 1973. *The Art of Computer Programming, Vol. I: Fundamental Algorithms*. Reading, Mass.: Addison-Wesley.

Kodish, Debora. 1993. On Coming of Age in the Sixties. *Western Folklore* 52(2–4):193–207.

———. 1997. Outside Memory. Paper presented at the Annual Meeting of the American Folklore Society, October 29–November 2, Austin, Texas.

Koestler, Arthur. 1964. *The Act of Creation*. New York: Macmillan.

Köstlin, Konrad. 1997. The Passion for the Whole: Interpreted Modernity or Modernity as Interpretation. *Journal of American Folklore* 110(437):261–276.

Kotkin, Amy J., and Steven J. Zeitlin. 1983. In the Family Tradition. In *Handbook of American Folklore*, ed. Richard M. Dorson. Pp. 90–99. Bloomington: Indiana University Press.

Krohn Kaarle. 1971 [1926]. *Folklore Methodology: Formulated by Julius Krohn and Expanded by Nordic Researchers*, trans. Roger L. Welsh. Austin: University of Texas Press.
Kruckemeyer, Kate. 2002. "You Get Sawdust in Your Blood": "Local" Values and the Performance of Community in an Occupational Sport. *Journal of American Folklore* 115(457):301–331.
Kuhn, Thomas S. 1962. *The Structure of Scientific Revolutions*. Chicago: University of Chicago.
La Barre, Weston. 1958. The Influence of Freud on Anthropology. *American Imago* 15(3):275–328.
Labov, William, and Joshua Waletzky. 1967. Narrative Analysis: Oral Versions of Personal Experience. In *Essays on the Verbal and Visual Arts*, ed. June Helm. Proceedings of the 1966 Annual Spring Meeting of the American Ethnological Society. Pp. 12–44. Seattle: University of Washington Press.
Lang, Andrew. 1910. *Custom and Myth*. London: Longmans, Green.
———. 1970 [1905]. *The Secret of the Totem*. New York: AMS.
Langlois, Janet. 1978. Belle Gunness, the Lady Bluebeard: Community Legend as Metaphor. *Journal of the Folklore Institute* 15(2):147–160.
Langness, L. L., and Geyla Frank. 1981. *Lives: An Anthropological Approach to Biography*. Novato, Calif.: Chandler Sharp.
Laplance, J., and J.-B. Pontalis. 1973. *The Language of Psycho-Analysis*, trans. Donald Nicholson-Smith. New York: W. W. Norton.
Lau, Kimberly J. 2002. The Text which is Not One: Dialectics of Self and Culture in Experimental Autoethnography. *Journal of Folklore Research* 39(2–3):243–259.
Lawless, Elaine J. 1983. Brothers and Sisters: Pentecostals as a Religious Folk Group. *Western Folklore* 42(2):85–104.
———. 2001. *Women Escaping Violence: Empowerment through Narrative*. Columbia: University of Missouri Press.
Laws, G. Malcolm, Jr. 1957. *American Ballads from British Broadsides*. Philadelphia: The American Folklore Society.
———. 1964. *Native American Balladry*. Philadelphia: The American Folklore Society.
Leach, Edmund. 1976. *Culture and Communication*. Cambridge: Cambridge University Press.
Lear, Martha Weinmann. 1980. *Heartsounds*. New York: Simon and Schuster.
Lecocq, James Gary. 1980. The Ghost of the Doctor and a Vacant Fraternity House. In *Indiana Folklore: A Reader*, ed. Linda Dégh. Pp. 265–278. Bloomington: Indiana University Press.
Lehmann, Arthur C., and James E. Myers, eds. 1985. *Magic, Witchcraft, and Religion: An Anthropological Study of the Supernatural*. Palo Alto, Calif.: Mayfield.

"Leopard Kills Tot." 1988. *Santa Rosa (Calif.) Press Democrat*, 27 May, A7.
Lessa, William A., and Evon Z. Vogt, eds. 1979. *Reader in Comparative Religion: An Anthropological Approach*. 4th ed. New York: Harper and Row.
Lévi-Strauss, Claude. 1955. The Structural Study of Myth. *Journal of American Folklore* 68(270):428–444.
_____. 1963a. *Totemism*, trans. Rodney Needham. Boston: Beacon.
_____. 1963b. The Bear and the Barber. *The Journal of the Royal Anthropological Institute of Great Britain and Ireland* 93(1):1–11.
_____. 1966. *The Savage Mind*. Chicago: University of Chicago Press.
Levitt. Steven D., and Stephen J. Dubner. 2005. *Freakonomics: A Rogue Economist Explores the Hidden Side of Everything*. New York: William Morrow.
Lévy-Bruhl, Lucien. 1966 [1923]. *Primitive Mentality*. Boston: Beacon.
Lewis, Oscar. 1970. *Anthropological Essays*. New York: Random House.
Lewis, Sinclair. 1961 [1922]. *Babbit*. New York: New American Library.
"Lightning Hits Couple." 1988. *Santa Rosa (Calif.) Press Democrat*, 27 June, A6.
Limón, Jose E. 1983. Western Marxism and Folklore: A Critical Introduction. *Journal of American Folklore* 96(379):34–52.
Lindahl, Carl. 1986. Psychic Ambiguity at the Legend Core. *Journal of Folklore Research* 23(1):1–21.
_____. 2004. Afterword. *Journal of Folklore Research* 41(2–3):173–180.
Linton, Ralph. 1924. Totemism and the A.E.F. *American Anthropologist* 26(2):296–300.
_____. 1937. One Hundred Per-Cent American, *American Mercury* 40: 427–429.
Littleton, C. Scott. 1965. A Two-Dimensional Scheme for the Classification of Narratives. *Journal of American Folklore* 78(307):21–27.
Lloyd, A. L., and Ewan MacColl. 1956. *Thar She Blows: Whaling Ballads and Songs*. Riverside RLP 12–635.
Lomax, Alan. 1977. Appeal for Cultural Equity. *Journal of Communication* 27(2):125–138.
Lord, Albert. 1965. *The Singer of Tales*. New York: Atheneum.
Loved One, The. 1965. Directed by Tony Richardson. 122 min. MGM/UA. Videocassette.
Lynd, Helen Merrill. 1961. *On Shame and the Search for Identity*. New York: Science Editions.
Mac Fhraing, Rob Alasdair. 1948. Àireamh Muinntir Fhinn is Dhubhain, agus sgeul Iosephuis is an dà fhichead Iudhaic. *Proceedings of the Royal Irish Academy* 52 (Section A):87–93.
Maccoby, Eleanor, and N. Maccoby. 1954. The Interview: A Tool of Social Science. In *Handbook of Social Psychology*, ed. G. Lindzey. Pp. 449–487. Cambridge, Mass.: Addison-Wesley.
MacKenzie, W. Roy. 1928. *Ballads and Sea Songs from Nova Scotia*. Cambridge, Mass.: Harvard University Press.

Mackin, John H. 1969. *Classical Rhetoric for Modern Discourse*. New York: The Free Press.
Mandelbaum, David G. 1973. The Study of Life History: Gandhi. *Current Anthropology* 14(3):177–206.
Manning, Frank E. 1990. Victor Turner's Career and Publications. In *Victor Turner and the Construction of Cultural Criticism*, ed. Kathleen M. Ashley. Pp. 170–177. Bloomington: Indiana University Press
Marcus, George E., and Michael M. J. Fischer. 1986. *Anthropology as Cultural Critique: An Experimental Moment in the Human Sciences*. Chicago: University of Chicago Press.
Martin, Joanne, and Melanie E. Powers. 1983. Truth or Corporate Propaganda: The Value of a Good War Story. In *Organizational Symbolism*, ed. Louis R. Pondy, Peter J. Frost, Gareth Morgan, and Thomas C. Dandridge. Pp. 93–107. Greenwich, Conn.: JAI Press.
Masheter, Carol, and Linda M. Harris. 1986. From Divorce to Friendship: A Study of Dialectical Relationship Development. *Journal of Social and Personal Relationships* 3(2):177–189.
Mason, Otis T. 1891. The Natural History of Folklore. *Journal of American Folklore* 4(13):97–105.
Masson, Jeffrey Moussaieff, ed. 1985. *The Complete Letters of Sigmund Freud to Wilhelm Fliess, 1877–1904*, trans. Jeffrey Moussaieff Masson. Cambridge, Mass.: Belknap Press.
Mazo, Jeffrey Alan. 1996. A Good Saxon Compound. *Folklore* 107:107–108.
McCall, George J., Michal M. McCall, Norman K, Denzin, Gerald D. Suttles, and Suzanne B. Kurth. 1970. A Collaborative Overview of Social Relationships. In *Social Relationships*, ed. George McCall, Michal M. McCall, Norman K, Denzin, Gerald D. Suttles, and Suzanne B. Kurth. Pp. 171–182. Chicago: Aldine.
McDonald, Barry M. 1997. Tradition as a Personal Relationship. *Journal of American Folklore* 110(435):47–67.
McDowell, John Holmes. 2010. Coaxing the Corrido: Centering Song in Performance. *Journal of American Folklore* 123(488):127–149.
McIntyre, Lynn, Kim Raine, Heather Hobson, and Jutta B. Dayle. 2001. Origin Stories from Children's Feeding Programs in Atlantic Canada: Heart-Wrenching Tales or Contemporary Legends? *Contemporary Legend*, n.s., 4:108–125.
McKeon, Michael. 2004. Tacit Knowledge: Tradition and Its Aftermath. In *Questions of Tradition*, ed. Mark Salber Phillips and Gordon Schochet. Pp. 171–202. Toronto: University of Toronto Press.
McLuhan, Marshall. 1964. *Understanding Media*. New York: Signet.
McWilliams, Perry. 1978. The Alamo Story: From Fact to Fable. *Journal of the Folklore Institute* 15(3):221–233.

Mechling, Jay. 1989. "Banana Canon" and Other Folk Traditions between Human and Nonhuman Animals. *Western Folklore* 48(4):312–323.

———. 1991. Homo Narrans across the Disciplines. *Western Folklore* 50(1):41–51.

———. 2006. Solo Folklore. *Western Folklore* 65(4):435–464.

Meley, Patricia M. 1991. Adolescent Legend Trips as Teenage Cultural Response: A Study of Lore in Context. *Mid-America Folklore* 18(1):1–26.

Milligan, Linda. 1990. The "Truth" about the Bigfoot Legend. *Western Folklore* 49(1):83–98.

Mitchell, Roger E. 1979. The Press, Rumor, and Legend Formation. *Midwestern Journal of Language and Folklore* 5(1–2):5–61.

Montefiore, Alan. 1993. Structure of Personal Identity and Cultural Identity. In *Jewish Identity*, ed. David Theo Goldberg and Michael Krausz. Pp. 212–242. Philadelphia: Temple University Press.

Montell, William Lynwood. 1986. *Killings: Folk Justice in the Upper South*. Lexington: University Press of Kentucky.

"Mother, Daughter Die on Same Day." 1987. *Santa Rosa (Calif.) Press Democrat*, 19 September, Bl.

Müller, Max. 1871–1876. *Chips from a German Workshop*. 4 vols. New York: Scribner, Armstrong, and Co.

Mullen, Patrick B. 1972. Modern Legend and Rumor Theory. *Journal of the Folklore Institute* 9(2–3):95–109.

Munasinghe, Mohan. 2008. Addressing Climate Change and Sustainable Development Challenges Together: The Role of Statistics. UN Conference on Climate Change and Official Statistics. Oslo, Norway 14 April. http://unstats.un.org/unsd/climate_change/docs/presentations/1030a_Munsinghe_session1.pdf.

Myers-Moro, Pamela. 1989. Thai Music and Attitudes toward the Past. *Journal of American Folklore* 102(404):190–194.

Nadel, S. F. 1937. A Field Experiment in Racial Psychology. *British Journal of Psychology* 28(2):195–211.

Needham, Joseph, with Wang Lin. 1979. *Mathematics and the Sciences of Heaven and Earth*. Vol. 3 of *Science and Civilization in China*. Cambridge: Cambridge University Press.

Neulander, Judith S. 1998. Jewish Oral Traditions. In *Teaching Oral Traditions*, ed. John Miles Foley. Pp. 225–238. New York: Modern Language Association.

Newell, William Wells. 1963 [1883]. *Games and Songs of American Children*. New York: Dover.

Newman, Philip L. 1965. *Knowing the Gururumba*. New York: Holt, Rinehart, and Winston.

Nickerson, Bruce. 1974. Is There a Folk in the Factory? *Journal of American Folklore* 87(344):133–139.

Nicolaisen, W. F. H. 1987. The Linguistic Structure of Legends. *Perspectives on Contemporary Legend II*, ed. Gillian Bennett, Paul Smith, and J. D. A. Widdowson. Pp. 61–76. Sheffield: Sheffield Academic Press.

Norkunas, Martha. 2004. Narratives of Resistance and the Consequences of Resistance. *Journal of Folklore Research* 41(2–3):105–123.

Northall, G. F. 1892. *English Folk-Rhymes*. London: Kegan Paul, Trench, and Trübner.

Noyes, Dorothy. 2009. Tradition: Three Traditions. *Journal of Folklore Research* 46(3):233–268.

Odlyzko, Andrew, and Herbert S. Wild. 1991. Functional Iteration and the Josephus Problem. *Glasgow Mathematical Journal* 33:235–240.

OED. 1989. *Oxford English Dictionary*. 2nd ed. 20 vols. New York: Oxford University Press.

Olrik, Axel. 1965 [1909]. Epic Laws of Folk Narrative. In *The Study of Folklore*, ed. Alan Dundes. Pp. 129–141. Englewood Cliffs, N.J.: Prentice-Hall.

Opie, Peter. 1963. The Tentacles of Tradition. *Folklore* 74(4):507–526.

Opler, Morris Edward. 1945. Themes as Dynamic Forces in Culture. *American Journal of Sociology* 51(3):198–206.

Oring, Elliott. 1966. The Life History of Igor Slatz. Unpublished.

———.1968. Folk Games and Game Theory. *Folklore Forum* 1(2):16–23.

———. 1973. "Hey, You've Got No Character": Chizbat Humor and the Boundaries of Israeli Identity. *Journal of American Folklore* 86(342):358–366. Reprinted in this volume.

———. 1975. The Devolutionary Premise: A Definitional Delusion. *Western Folklore* 34(1):36–44. Reprinted in this volume.

———. 1978. Transmission and Degeneration. *Fabula* 19(3–4):193–210. Reprinted in this volume.

———. 1981. *Israeli Humor: The Content and Structure of the Chizbat of the Palmah*. Albany: State University of New York Press.

———. 1984. *The Jokes of Sigmund Freud: A Study in Humor and Jewish Identity*. Philadelphia: University of Pennsylvania Press.

———. 1986a. Folk Narratives. In *Folk Groups and Folklore Genres: An Introduction*, ed. Elliott Oring. Pp. 121–145. Logan: Utah State University Press.

———. 1986b. The Concepts of Folklore. In *Folk Groups and Folklore Genres: An Introduction*, ed. Elliott Oring. Pp. 1–22. Logan: Utah State University Press.

———. 1987. Jokes and the Discourse on Disaster. *Journal of American Folklore* 100(397):276–286.

———, ed. 1989. *Folk Groups and Folklore Genres: A Reader*. Logan: Utah State University Press.

———. 1990. Legend, Truth, and News. *Southern Folklore* 47(2):163–177. Reprinted in this volume.

———. 1992. *Jokes and Their Relations*. Lexington: University Press of Kentucky.

———. 1994. The Interests of Identity. *Journal of American Folklore* 107(424):242–247.

———. 1996a. Theorizing Trivia: A Thought Experiment. *Journal of Folklore Research* 33(3):241–244. Reprinted in this volume.

———. 1996b. Folklorizing Theory. *The Folklore Historian* 13:30–32.

———. 2003. *Engaging Humor*. Champaign: University of Illinois Press.

———. 2008. Legendry and the Rhetoric of Truth. *Journal of American Folklore* 121(480):127–166. Reprinted in this volume.

Ortner, Sherry B. 1984. Theory in Anthropology Since the Sixties. *Comparative Studies in Society and History* 26(1):126–166.

Ortutay, Gyula. 1959. Principle of Oral Transmission in Folk Culture. *Acta Ethnographica* 8:175–221.

Pandey, Swati. 2006. Katrina a Year Later: Hooked, Lied, and Snookered. *Los Angeles Times*, 20 August, home edition.

Park, Robert E. 1923. The Natural History of the Newspaper. *American Journal of Sociology* 29(3):273–289.

Pascal, Roy. 1960. *Design and Truth in Autobiography*. London: Routledge and Kegan Paul.

Paul, Robert A. 1989. Psychoanalytic Anthropology. *Annual Review of Anthropology* 18:177–202.

Pawlaczyk, George. 2005. Officials Debunk a Disturbing Katrina Legend. *Chattanooga Times Free Press*, November 13.

Payne, Jessica M. 2004. Critical Historiography of the Present: A Response to "Looking Back, Moving Forward" by Peggy Bulger. *Journal of American Folklore* 117(465):337–343.

Pelto, Pertti J., and Gretel H. Pelto. 1978. *Anthropological Research: The Structure of Inquiry*. 2nd ed. Cambridge: Cambridge University Press.

Pentikäinen, Juha. 1973 [1960]. Belief, Memorate, and Legend. *Folklore Forum* 6(4):217–241.

Peppard, Murray B. 1971. *Paths Through the Forest: A Biography of the Brothers Grimm*. New York: Holt, Rinehart and Winston.

Perlstein, Rick. 1997. Barry's Kids. *Lingua Franca* 7:25–26.

Peters, Nancy Kammen. 1988. Suburban/Rural Variations in the Content of Adolescent Ghost Legends. In *Monsters with Iron Teeth*, ed. Gillian Bennett and Paul Smith. Perspectives on Contemporary Legend III. Pp. 221–235. Sheffield: Sheffield Academic Press.

Phillips, Mark Salber. 2004. Introduction. In *Questions of Tradition*, ed. Mark Salber Phillips and Gordon Schochet. Pp. 3–29. Toronto: University of Toronto Press.

Phipps, Anne. 1980. The Runaway Patient: A Legend in Oral Circulation and the Media. *Indiana Folklore* 13(1–2):102–111.
Pictorial Forest Lawn. 1953. Glendale, Calif.: Forest Lawn Memorial Park.
Pimple, Kenneth. 1996. On (Not) Defining Folklore, or Theorizing . . . What? *The Folklore Historian* 13:18–24.
Pisarski, Sheryl. 1980. A Porter County Seer. In *Indiana Folklore: A Reader*, ed. Linda Dégh. Pp. 130–146. Bloomington: Indiana University Press.
Plummer, Ken. 1983. *Documents of Life: An Introduction to the Problems and Literature of a Humanistic Method*. London: George Allen and Unwin.
Poggie, John J., Jr., and Carl Gersuny. 1972. Risk and Ritual: An Interpretation of Fisherman's Folklore in a New England Community. *Journal of American Folklore* 85(335):66–72. Reprinted in Oring 1989:137–145.
Poulsen, Richard C. 1982. Hawks and Coyotes on Western Fences: The Symbolism of Slaughter. In *The Pure Experience of Order: Essays on the Symbolic in the Folk Material Culture of Western America*, ed. Richard C. Poulsen. Pp. 56–69. Albuquerque: University of New Mexico Press.
Pratt, May Louise. 1986. Fieldwork in Common Places. In *Writing Culture: The Poetics and Politics of Ethnography*, ed. James Clifford and George E. Marcus. Pp. 27–50. Berkeley: University of California Press.
Propp, Vladimir. 1968 [1928]. *The Morphology of the Folktale*. 2nd ed. Austin: University of Texas Press.
Proschan, Frank. 1992. Fieldwork and Social Work: Folklore as a Helping Profession. In *Public Folklore*, ed. Robert Baron and Nicholas R. Spitzer. Pp. 145–158. Washington D.C.: Smithsonian Institution Press.
Radcliffe-Brown, A. R. 1939. *Taboo*. Cambridge: Cambridge University Press.
———. 1952 [1929]. The Sociological Theory of Totemism. In *Structure and Function in Primitive Society* by A. R. Radcliffe-Brown. Pp. 117–132. New York: The Free Press.
Radin, Max. 1930–35. Tradition. In *Encyclopaedia of the Social Sciences*, ed. E. R. A. Seligman. 15 vols. New York: Macmillan.
Rank, Otto. 1952 [1909]. *The Myth of the Birth of the Hero: A Psychological Interpretation of Mythology*. New York: R. Bruner.
Ranke, Friedrich. 1925. Grundfragen der Volkssagenforschung. *Niederdeutsche Zeitschrift für Volkskunde* 3:1–20.
Ranke, Kurt, ed. 1966. *Folktales of Germany*. Chicago: University of Chicago Press.
———. 1973. Oral and Literary Continuity. *Folklore Forum* 6(3):127–138.
Raskin, Victor. 1985. *Semantic Mechanisms of Humor*. Dordrecht, Holland: Reidel.
Reuss, Richard. 1974. That Can't Be Alan Dundes: Alan Dundes is Taller than That! *Journal of American Folklore* 87(346):303–317.
Richards, I. M. 1991. The Josephus Problem. *Mathematical Spectrum* 24:97–104.

Riesman, David. 1950. *The Lonely Crowd: A Study of the American Character*. New Haven: Yale University Press.
Rieti, Barbara. 1991. "The Blast" in Newfoundland Fairy Tradition. In *The Good People: New Fairylore Essays*, ed. Peter Narváez. Pp. 284–297. Lexington: University Press of Kentucky.
Rihtman-Augustin, Dunja. 1978. Traditional Culture, Folklore, and Mass Culture in Contemporary Yugoslavia. In *Folklore in the Modern World*, ed. Richard M. Dorson. Pp. 163–172. The Hague: Mouton.
Robidoux, Michael A. 2002. Imagining a Canadian Identity through Sport: A Historical Interpretation of Lacrosse and Hockey. *Journal of American Folklore* 115(456):209–225.
Robinson, W. J. 1960. The Josephus Problem. *Mathematical Gazette* 44(347):47–52.
Rodriguez, Sylvia. 1998. Fiesta Time and Plaza Space: Resistance and Accommodation in a Tourist Town. *Journal of American Folklore* 111(439):39–56.
Romano, Carlin. 1986. The Grisly Truth about Bare Facts. In *Reading the News*, ed. Robert Karl Manoff and Michael Schudson. Pp. 38–78. New York: Pantheon.
Rosenblatt, Roger. 1984. Journalism and the Larger Truth. *Time*, 2 July, 88.
Royce, Anya Peterson. 1982. *Ethnic Identity: Strategies of Diversity*. Bloomington: Indiana University Press.
Rubin, Barbara, Robert Carlton, and Arnold Rubin. 1979. *L.A. in Installments: Forest Lawn*. Santa Monica, Calif.: Westside.
Rubin, David C. 1995. *Memory in Oral Traditions: The Cognitive Psychology of Epic, Ballads, and Counting-Out Rhymes*. New York: Oxford University Press.
Ruby, Jack, and Barbara Myerhoff. 1982. Introduction. In *Crack in the Mirror: Reflexive Perspectives in Anthropology*, ed. Jack Ruby. Pp. 1–35. Philadelphia: University of Pennsylvania Press.
Rupp, George. 1999. Facing the Global Future. *Columbia University President's Report 1998–99*. http://www.columbia.edu/cu/news/report/99/future/futureb.html.
Rushforth, Scott. 1992. The Legitimation of Beliefs in a Hunter-Gatherer Society: Bearlake Athapaskan Knowledge and Authority. *American Ethnologist* 19(3):483–500.
Russell, Ian. 1987. Stability and Change in a Sheffield Singing Tradition. *Folk Music Journal* 5(3):317–358.
"Safety Record Overturned." 1988. *Santa Rosa (Calif.) Press Democrat*, 5 June, A1.
Salamon, Hagar. 2001. Political Bumper Stickers in Contemporary Israel: Folklore as Emotional Battleground. *Journal of American Folklore* 114(453):277–308.

Sapir, Edward. 1930–35. Symbolism. In *Encyclopedia of the Social Sciences*, ed. E. R. A. Seligman. 15 vols. New York: Macmillan.

Schudson, Michael. 1978. *Discovering the News: A Social History of American Newspapers*. New York: Basic.

———. 1997. Paper Tigers: A Sociologist Follows Cultural Studies into the Wilderness. *Lingua Franca* 7(6): 49–56.

Schütze, Martin. 1920. The Fundamental Ideas in Herder's Thought. II. *Modern Philology* 18(6):57–70.

———. 1921. The Fundamental Ideas in Herder's Thought. III. *Modern Philology* 19(2):113–130.

———. 1922. The Fundamental Ideas in Herder's Thought. IV. *Modern Philology* 19(4):361–382.

———. 1923. The Fundamental Ideas in Herder's Thought. V. *Modern Philology* 21(2):113–132.

Schwartz, H. and Jerry Jacobs. 1979. *Qualitative Sociology: A Method to the Madness*. New York: The Free Press.

Seeger, Charles. 1966. The Folkness of the Non-Folk and the Non-Folkness of the Folk. In *Folklore and Society: Essays in Honor of Benj. A. Botkin*, ed. Bruce Jackson. Pp. 1–9. Hatboro, Pa.: Folklore Associates.

Seitel, Peter. 1980. *See So That We May See: Performances and Interpretations of Traditional Tales from Tanzania*. Bloomington: Indiana University Press.

Shaaber, M. A. 1966 [1929]. *Some Forerunners of the Newspaper in England*. New York: Octagon.

Sharp, Cecil. 1907. *English Folk-Song: Some Conclusions*. London: Simpkin.

Shaw, David. 1984. Recycling the News: Just Laziness or Plagiarism. *Los Angeles Times*, 6 July, 1, 22–23.

Shils, Edward. 1981. *Tradition*. Chicago: The University of Chicago Press.

Shuman, Amy. 1993. Dismantling Local Culture. *Western Folklore* 52(2–4):345–364.

———. 2005. *Other People's Stories: Entitlement and the Critique of Empathy*. Urbana: University of Illinois Press.

Sigal, Leon V. 1986. Sources Make the News. In *Reading the News*, ed. Robert Karl Manoff and Michael Schudson. Pp. 9–37. New York: Pantheon.

Simmel, Georg. 1950. *The Sociology of Georg Simmel*, ed. and trans. Kurt H. Wolf. London: The Free Press of Glencoe.

Simpson, Jacqueline. 1981. Rationalized Motifs in Urban Legends. *Folklore* 92(2):203–207.

Sims, Martha C., and Martine Stephens. 2005. *Living Folklore: An Introduction to the Study of People and Their Traditions*. Logan: Utah State University Press.

Sjöman, Marianne. 1992. Current Research in the Nordic and Baltic Countries. *NIF Newsletter* 4:13–23.

Slotkin, Edgar M. 1988. Legend Genre as a Function of Audience. In *Monsters with Iron Teeth*, ed. Gillian Bennett and Paul Smith. Perspectives on Contemporary Legend III. Pp. 89–111. Sheffield: Sheffield Academic Press.

Smith, Anthony. 1978. The Long Road to Objectivity and Back Again: The Kinds of Truth We Get in Journalism. In *Newspaper History from the Seventeenth Century to the Present Day*, ed. George Boyce, James Curran, and Pauline Wingate. Pp. 153–171. Beverly Hills: Sage.

———. 1979. *The Newspaper: An International History*. London: Thames and Herson.

Smith, David Eugene, and Yoshio Mikami. 1914. *A History of Japanese Mathematics*. Chicago: The Open Court.

———. 1917. On the Origin of Certain Typical Problems. *American Mathematical Monthly* 24(2):64–71.

Smith, Georgina. 1979. Aspects of Urban Legend as a Performance Genre. *Lore and Language* 2(10):41–44.

———. 1981. Urban Legend, Personal Experience Narrative, and Oral History. *ARV: Scandinavian Yearbook of Folklore* 37:167–173.

Smith, Moira. 1984. The Kernel Story: A New Conversational Genre. *Folklore Forum* 17(2):199–207.

Smith, Paul S. 1974. Tradition—A Perspective: Part I, Introduction. *Lore and Language* 2(1):15–17.

———. 1975. Tradition—A Perspective: Part II, Transmission. *Lore and Language* 2(3):5–14.

———. 1978. Tradition—A Perspective: Part III, Information, Perception and Performance. *Lore and Language* 2(8):1–10.

———. 1986. Tradition—A Perspective: Part IV, Variation on the Prospective Adopter's Access to Information. *Lore and Language* 5(1):3–38.

———. 1989. Contemporary Legend: A Legendary Genre? In *The Questing Beast*, ed. Gillian Bennett and Paul Smith. Perspectives on Contemporary Legend IV. Pp. 91–101. Sheffield: Sheffield Academic Press.

Smith, Robert J. 1989. Introduction: The Folk in American Folkloristics. In *The Folk: Identity, Landscapes, and Lores*, ed. Robert J. Smith and Jerry Stannard. University of Kansas Publications in Anthropology 17. Pp. 1–8. Lawrence: University of Kansas.

Sobek, Maria Herrera. 1988. The Devil in the Discotheque: A Semiotic Analysis of a Contemporary Legend. In *Monsters with Iron Teeth*, ed. Gillian Bennett and Paul Smith. Perspectives on Contemporary Legend III. Pp. 147–157. Sheffield: Sheffield Academic Press.

Spencer, Baldwin, and F. J. Gillen. 1899. *The Native Tribes of Central Australia*. London: Macmillan.

Spicer, Edward H. 1971. Persistent Identity Systems. *Science* 174(4011):795–800.

Spiro, Melford. 1969. Discussion. In *Forms of Symbolic Action*, ed. Robert F. Spencer. Proceedings of the 1969 Annual Spring Meeting of the American Ethnological Society. Pp. 208–214. Seattle: University of Washington Press.

St. Johns, Adela Rogers. 1959. *First Step Up Toward Heaven: Hubert Eaton and Forest Lawn.* Englewood Cliffs N.J.: Prentice-Hall.

Stackpole, Edouard A. 1958. *Scrimshaw at Mystic Seaport.* Mystic, Conn.: Marine Historical Association.

Stahl, Sandra Dolby. 1989. *Literary Folkloristics and the Personal Narrative.* Bloomington: Indiana University Press.

———. 1977. The Personal Narrative as Folklore. *Journal of the Folklore Institute* 14(1–2):9–30.

"Stalking the Wild Alligator." 1988. *Time*, 20 June, 31.

Stecker, Robert. 2000. Is It Reasonable to Attempt to Define Art? In *Theories of Art Today*, ed. Noël Carroll. Pp. 45–64. Madison: University of Wisconsin Press.

Steinschneider, Moritz. 1880. Abraham Ibn Ezra. *Supplement zu historische-literarische Abteilung für Mathematik und Physik* 25:59–128.

Stephens, Mitchell. 1988. *A History of News: From the Drum to the Satellite.* New York: Viking.

Stoll, David. 1999. *Rigoberta Menchú and the Story of All Poor Guatemalans.* Boulder, Colo.: Westview.

Strathern, Andrew. 1979. *Ongka: A Self-Account of a New Guinea Headman.* New York: St. Martin's.

"Supreme Court Voids Abenaki Land Claims." 1992. *New York Times*, 18 June, D23.

Suttles, Gerald D. 1970. Friendship as a Social Institution. In *Social Relationships*, ed. George McCall, Michal M. McCall, Norman K, Denzin, Gerald D. Suttles, and Suzanne B. Kurth. Pp. 95–135. Chicago: Aldine.

Sutton, Horace. 1958. Ever-Ever Land. *Saturday Review*, 5 April, 23–35.

Tait, Peter Guthrie. 1898–1900. *Scientific Papers.* 2 vols. Cambridge: Cambridge University Press.

Tangherlini, Timothy R. 1990. "It Happened Not Too Far From Here. . . .": A Survey of Legend Theory and Characterization. *Western Folklore* 49(4):371–390.

Tannen, Deborah. 1981. Talking New York: It's Not What You Say, It's the Way You Say It. *New York*, 30 March, 30–33.

———. 1990. *You Just Don't Understand: Women and Men in Conversation.* New York: William Morrow.

Tavarelli, Paola. 1987–88. Dyadic Traditions in Mixed Couples. *Folklore and Mythology Studies* 11–12:67–79.

Taylor, Charles. 1989. *Sources of the Self: The Making of Modern Identity.* Cambridge: Harvard University Press.

"Teddy Buckled, Driver Didn't." 1988. *Santa Rosa (Calif.) Press Democrat*, 4 March, B3.
Tedlock, Dennis. 1983. *The Spoken Word and the Work of Interpretation*. Philadelphia: University of Pennsylvania Press.
Thompson, Stith. 1953. Advances in Folklore Studies. In *Anthropology Today: An Encyclopedic Inventory*, ed. A. L. Kroeber. Pp. 587–596. Chicago: University of Chicago Press.
Thompson, Tok Freeland. 2003. "Ladies and Gentlemen, The North Road Pounders!": An Inquiry into Identity, Aesthetics, and New Authenticities in Rural Alaska. *Journal of Folklore Research* 40(3):273–288.
Thorat, S. K. 1979. Passage to Adulthood: Perceptions from Below. In *Identity and Adulthood*, ed. Sudhir Kakar. Pp. 65–81. Dehli: Oxford University Press.
Titon, Jeff Todd. 1980. The Life Story. *Journal of American Folklore*. 93(369):276–292.
Toelken, Barre. 1996. *The Dynamics of Folklore*. Rev ed. Logan: Utah State University Press.
———. 1998. The End of Folklore. *Western Folklore* 57(2–3):81–101.
———. 1998. The Yellowman Tapes. *Journal of American Folklore* 111(442): 381–391.
———. 2004. Beauty Behind Me; Before Me. *Journal of American Folklore* 117 (466):441–445.
"Town Awakens To a Polite Visitor." 1988. *Santa Rosa (Calif.) Press Democrat*, 17 May, A1, A8.
Turner, Frederick. 1990. "Hyperion to a Satyr": Criticism and Anti-structure in the Work of Victor Turner. In *Victor Turner and the Construction of Cultural Criticism*, ed. Kathleen M. Ashley. Pp. 147–162. Bloomington: Indiana University Press.
Turner, Patricia A. 1993. *I Heard It Through the Grapevine: Rumor in African-American Culture*. Berkeley: University of California Press.
Turner, Victor W. 1955. A Revival in the Study of African Ritual. *Rhodes-Livingtone Journal* 17:51–56.
———. 1962. *Chihamba, the White Spirit: A Ritual Drama of the Ndembu*. The Rhodes-Livingstone Papers No. 33. Manchester: Manchester University Press.
———. 1965. Some Current Trends in the Study of Ritual in Africa. *Anthropological Quarterly* 38(3):155–166.
———. 1966. The Syntax of Symbolism in an African Religion. *Philosophical Transactions of the Royal Society of London*. Series B, 251:295–303.
———. 1967. *The Forest of Symbol: Aspects of Ndembu Ritual*. Ithaca: Cornell University Press.
———. 1968. *The Drums of Affliction: A Study of Religious Process among the*

Ndembu of Zambia. Oxford: Clarendon Press and the International African Institute.

———. 1969a. Forms of Symbolic Action: Introduction. In *Forms of Symbolic Action*, ed. Robert F. Spencer. Proceedings of the 1969 Annual Spring Meeting of the American Ethnological Society. Pp. 3–25. Seattle: University of Washington Press.

———. 1969b. *The Ritual Process: Structure and Anti-Structure*. Chicago: Aldine.

———. 1969c. Symbolization and Patterning in the Circumcision Rites of Two Bantu-speaking Societies. In *Man in Africa*, ed. Mary Douglas and Phyllis M. Kaberry. Pp. 229–244. London: Tavistock.

———. 1973. Symbols in African Ritual. *Science* 179(4078):1100–1105.

———. 1975. *Revelation and Divination in Ndembu Ritual*. Ithaca: Cornell University Press.

———. 1976. African Ritual and Western Literature: Is a Comparative Symbology Possible? In *The Literature of Fact*, ed. Angus Fletcher. Pp. 45–81. New York: Columbia University Press.

———. 1978. Encounter with Freud: The Making of a Comparative Symbologist. In *The Making of Psychological Anthropology*, ed. George Spindler. Pp. 558–583. Berkeley: University of California Press.

Tylor, Edward Burnett. 1874 [1871] *Primitive Culture*. 2 vols. Boston: Estes and Lauriat.

Valk, Ülo. 2006. Demonic Possession and Real Estate: Ghosts in Contemporary Estonian Folklore. *Journal of Folklore Research* 43(1):31–51.

Vansina, Jan. 1965. *Oral Tradition: A Study in Historical Methodology*, trans. H. M. Wright. London: Routledge and Kegan Paul.

———. 1985. *Oral Tradition as History*. Madison: University of Wisconsin Press.

Varenne, Hervé, ed. 1986. *Symbolizing America*. Lincoln: University of Nebraska Press.

Victor, Jeffrey. 1990. Satanic Cult Rumors as Contemporary Legend. *Western Folklore* 49(1):51–81.

Voigt, Vilmos. 1983. Folklore Function in the Development of Creativity. *Ethnologia Europaea* 13(2):180–188.

von Sydow, Carl Wilhelm. 1948. *Selected Papers on Folklore*. Copenhagen: Rosenkilde and Bagger.

Walker, Thomas. 2008. Lore's Labors Lost: Archie Green and the Restoration of Worlds of Labor. *Journal of Folklore Research* 45(2):229–238.

Wallace, Edwin R., IV. 1983. *Freud and Anthropology: A History and Reappraisal*. New York: International Universities Press.

Ward, Donald, ed. 1981. *The German Legends of the Brothers Grimm*, trans. Donald Ward. 2 vols. Philadelphia: Institute for the Study of Human Issues.

Warren, Claude. 1959. *Modern News Reporting.* 3rd ed. New York: Harper and Row.

Watson, Lawrence C., and Maria-Barbara Watson-Franke. 1985. *Interpreting Life Histories: An Anthropological Inquiry.* New Brunswick, N.J.: Rutgers University Press.

Waugh, Evelyn. 1947. Death in Hollywood. *Life,* 29 September, 73–84.

_____. 1965 [1948]. *The Loved One.* New York: Dell.

Weiner, Annete B. 1995. Culture and Our Discontents. *American Anthropologist* 97(1):14–21.

Weisberger, Bernard A. 1961. *The American Newspaperman.* Chicago: University of Chicago Press.

White, Geoffrey M. 1989. Heartlands and Borderlands: Reflections on the First SPA Conference. *Ethos* 17(4):504–512.

White, Hayden. 1980. The Value of Narrativity in the Representation of Reality. *Critical Inquiry* 7(1):3–27.

White, Leslie A. 1949. *The Science of Culture: A Study of Man and Civilization.* New York: Grove Press.

_____. 1959. *The Evolution of Culture: The Development of Civilization to the Fall of Rome.* New York: McGraw-Hill.

Whittaker, Elvi. 1992. The Birth of the Anthropological Self and Its Career. *Ethos* 20(2):191–219.

Wilgus, D. K. 1959. *Anglo-American Folksong Scholarship Since 1898.* New Brunswick, N.J.: Rutgers University Press.

Wilson, Michael. 1997. *Performance and Practice: Oral Narrative Traditions among Teenagers in Britain and Ireland.* Aldershot, England: Ashgate.

_____. 1998. Legend and Life: "The Boyfriend's Death" and "The Mad Axeman." *Folklore* 109:89–95.

Wilson, William A. 1973. Herder, Folklore and Romantic Nationalism. *Journal of Popular Culture* 6(4):819–835. Reprinted in Oring 1989:21–37.

_____. 1975. "The Vanishing Hitchhiker" among the Mormons. *Indiana Folklore* 8(1–2): 79–97.

_____. 1976a. *Folklore and Nationalism in Modern Finland.* Bloomington: Indiana University Press.

_____. 1976b. The Evolutionary Premise in Folklore Theory and the "Finnish Method." *Western Folklore* 35(4):241–249.

_____. 1979. Folklore and History: Fact amid the Legends. In *Readings in American Folklore,* ed. Jan Harold Brunvand. Pp. 449–466. New York: W. W. Norton.

_____. 1982. On Being Human: The Folklore of Mormon Missionaries. *New York Folklore* 8(3–4):5–27.

_____. 1983. Mormon Folklore. In *Handbook of American Folklore,* ed. Richard M. Dorson. Pp. 155–161. Bloomington: Indiana University Press.

———. 1986. Documenting Folklore. In *Folk Groups and Folklore Genres: An Introduction*, ed. Elliott Oring. Pp. 225–254. Logan: Utah State University Press.

———. 1989. Richard M. Dorson as Romantic-Nationalist. *Journal of Folklore Research* 26(1):35–42.

———. 1991. Personal Narratives: The Family Novel. *Western Folklore* 50(2):127–149.

Wissler, Clark. 1926. *The Relation of Nature to Man in Aboriginal America*. New York: Oxford University Press.

Workman, Mark E. 1993. Tropes, Hopes, and Dopes. *Journal of American Folklore* 106(420):171–183.

Wright, Thomas. 1969 [1846]. *Essays on Subjects Connected With the Literature, Popular Superstitions and History of England in the Middle Ages*. 2 vols. New York: Burton Franklin.

Wyckoff, Donna L. 2000. "It Has All the Earmarks . . .": Spotting Contemporary Legends Early; Predicting Their Course. *Contemporary Legend*, n.s., 3:161–183.

Yassif, Eli. 1982. Review of *Israeli Humor: The Content and Structure of the Chizbat of the Palmah* by Elliott Oring [Hebrew]. *Kirjat Sefer* 57:141–147.

———. 1999. *The Hebrew Folktale: History, Genre, Meaning*. Bloomington: Indiana University Press.

Zeitlin, Steven, Amy J. Kotkin, and Holly Cutting Baker. 1982. *A Celebration of American Family Folklore*. New York: Pantheon.

Zinn, Howard. 1970. *The Politics of History*. Boston: Beacon Press.

Zweig, Ferdynand. 1969. *Israel: The Sword and the Harp*. London: Heinemann Educational.